add

TOWNSMEN
OR TRIBESMEN

CONSERVATISM AND THE
PROCESS OF URBANIZATION
IN A SOUTH AFRICAN CITY

PHILIP MAYER

WITH CONTRIBUTIONS BY
IONA MAYER

SECOND EDITION

CAPE TOWN
OXFORD UNIVERSITY PRESS
LONDON   NEW YORK   TORONTO
1971

Oxford University Press, Ely House, London W. 1

GLASGOW NEW YORK TORONTO MELBOURNE WELLINGTON
CAPE TOWN SALISBURY IBADAN NAIROBI DAR ES SALAAM LUSAKA ADDIS ABABA
BOMBAY CALCUTTA MADRAS KARACHI LAHORE DACCA
KUALA LUMPUR SINGAPORE HONG KONG TOKYO

Oxford University Press, Oxford House, Cape Town

First Published	1961
Second Impression	1962
Third Impression	1963
Fourth Impression	1965
Second Edition (paperback)	1971

The first edition of this book formed Volume Two of
*Xhosa in Town: Studies of the Bantu-speaking Population
of East London, Cape Province,* edited by Philip Mayer,
and was published on behalf of the Institute of
Social and Economic Research, Rhodes University,
by the Oxford University Press, Cape Town

❀ PRINTED IN THE REPUBLIC OF SOUTH AFRICA BY
THE RUSTICA PRESS, PTY., LTD., WYNBERG, CAPE

PREFACE TO THE SECOND EDITION

This edition includes a new chapter (chapter 19), based on research conducted during a return visit from September to November 1970. The chapter is concerned with the new situation facing the conservative 'resisters', and with the relations between the historical categories of Red and School Xhosa, as they appear today.

I am indebted to many people, some of them old acquaintances of ten years ago. Mr. Venter is still manager of Bantu Administration in East London, and Councillor A. Addleson, then Mayor of East London, is now Chairman of the East London Joint Location Advisory Board. Both put their great expertise at my disposal once again. The Manager of the new township of Mdantsane, Mr. E. B. Keeton, inevitably had to bear the brunt of my questioning and gave me generously of his time.

I am fortunate in having been able to secure the assistance of Mr. Enos Xotyeni, who also worked with me in the original field study. His enthusiasm and experience have made a major contribution.

I am grateful to Durham University for allowing me research leave for this and other research in the Eastern Cape, and to the Institute for Social and Economic Research, Rhodes University, which has made a much appreciated grant towards the cost of the fieldwork.

Grahamstown
December 1970

PHILIP MAYER

ACKNOWLEDGEMENTS

The following acknowledgements are gratefully made:

The National Council for Social Research (Department of Education, Arts and Science) financed the project, and made a further grant for publication. The Council left us complete freedom. Opinions expressed and conclusions reached in this volume are those of the author, and are not to be regarded as representing the views of the Council.

The Buffalo Catchment Association requested a comprehensive study of the catchment area of the Buffalo River; it thereby prompted the Institute of Social and Economic Research at Rhodes University to undertake the Border Regional Survey, which has provided the general framework for this and companion studies. In particular Mr. J. A. Chew (Secretary of the Association) and Mr. R. Ginsberg were a constant source of support and encouragement. On behalf of the Association Mr. Chew generously put office accommodation in East London at our disposal.

The co-operation of many administrators and officials has been essential for this kind of work. They gave it freely, and with much-appreciated courtesy. Special mention is due to the Chief Bantu Commissioner, King William's Town (Mr. J. A. C. van Heerden); the Location Manager, East London (Mr. P. Venter), and his staff; the Bantu Commissioner, East London (Mr. G. Pike); the Bantu Commissioner and Assistant Bantu Commissioner, King

William's Town (Mr. R. A. Bowen and Mr. D. B. Muir); and the Chairman of the Native Affairs Committee, East London Municipality (Mr. D. J. Sobey). The Bantu Commissioners of East London and King William's Town collected data for the map reproduced at the end of the book. Messrs. Venter and Sobey read and commented on the draft of Chapter 3.

The Vice-Chancellor and Council of Rhodes University granted me study leave during part of 1957.

The Board of Management of the Institute of Social and Economic Research at Rhodes University not only sponsored the work, but made a grant towards rural fieldwork. Mr. E. T. Sherwood (Secretary of the Institute until January 1959) gave valuable administrative assistance. Professor D. Hobart Houghton helped to see the volume through the press.

To the Chairman of the Border Regional Survey Committee (Professor D. Hobart Houghton) and to my fellow members, thanks are offered for prolonged co-operation and assistance.

Several colleagues gave generously of their time and patience. Dr. W. D. Hammond-Tooke and Dr. W. D. Terry of Rhodes University read the entire manuscript. Professor Max Marwick of the University of the Witwatersrand read and commented on parts of Chapters 1 and 18. Mr. L. Fourie of Rhodes University did likewise for the draft of Chapter 3. Mr. L. W. Lanham of Rhodes University gave advice on the orthography of Xhosa words.

Mr. Christopher Board, of the Department of Geography, University of Cambridge, drew the original end-map, which has been redrawn for this edition by the publishers.

The clerical staff of the Institute of Social and Economic Research, under Mrs. H. S. Mostert, were unfailingly helpful.

Mr. John D'Oliveira accompanied me to the East Bank Location on several occasions taking photographs, one of which is reproduced on the cover of this volume.

Innumerable Xhosa, both in town and in the country, helped to make this work possible by their willingness to supply the raw data. In some cases considerable demands were made on their time and their courtesy. To all those who co-operated in various ways—providing information or comments, case histories or reminiscences, facts, theories, observations, or subjects for photographs—sincere thanks are offered.

P.M.

Rhodes University, Grahamstown

CONTENTS

INTRODUCTION

Most of the Bantu-speaking workers in the modern cities of Southern or Central Africa have migrated into town, either temporarily or permanently; that is, they were born in rural areas where tribal traditions are still much in evidence The Union of South Africa has by far the oldest as well as the largest cities in the region, but is no exception to this rule. With full support from the South African Government, the system of recruiting most urban workers from the countryside, as migrants, still prevails.

This book is one of three co-ordinated studies recently made in a fair-sized South African town—East London, Cape Province.[1] East London, a White town with segregated non-White quarters ('Locations'), has been in existence for some 110 years. Today its locations hold a Bantu-speaking population of over 65,000, including a nucleus of born-and-bred townspeople. Despite their common involvement in the urban economy, there are many fields of behaviour in which the country-bred and town-bred Bantu[2] in East London tend to act differently. It has interested me to see how much more rapidly these differences are reduced by some categories of the country-bred than by others. In fact two types of response, a 'conservative' and a 'progressive' response, stand out in clear contrast. In this book I have documented the facts and have tried to find a sociological explanation. In doing so, I have endeavoured to attach an acceptable meaning to that perilous phrase, 'the process of urbanization'.

One of my aims has simply been to record. It seems fair to say that in South African cities today, despite the long history of co-existence by White and Black, one half knows little about how the other half lives. I have therefore made a point of including much detailed illustration of the lives and outlooks of the migrant workers.

The standpoint from which the material has been analysed needs more comment. Like other writers on African towns, I have necessarily been concerned with the interplay between 'urban' and 'tribal' phenomena, but in the local circumstances my definitions of these terms could not always be the same as theirs. Nobody would expect 'urbanization' to imply exactly the same in the East London context as in the indigenous towns of West Africa;[3] but there are significant differences even in relation to other 'White'-created towns, closer at hand. This is particularly clear if one compares the interesting urban studies recently made in the Rhodesian Copperbelt, and published since 'Townsmen or Tribesmen' was begun.

A Copperbelt mining town is a polyglot community where workers from many different tribal areas find themselves thrown together. Here Epstein,

---

[1] Of these, *The Black Man's Portion* by Dr. D. H. Reader gives the basic sociographic data relating to the locations as a whole. *The Second Generation*, by Dr. B. A. Pauw, will be concerned with some social institutions of Bantu born in East London. At the time of writing both volumes are still in preparation.

East London has been used before as a field for Bantu studies. Part III of Monica Hunter's memorable book on the Pondo people, *Reaction to Conquest*, gives an account of location society as it was in the 1930's. In the 1940's Dr. D. Bettison made a general sociographic survey ('A Socio-economic study of East London, Cape Province, with special reference to the non-European peoples'; unpublished M.A. thesis, Rhodes University, 1950). Expansion and industrialization have greatly changed the face of East London meanwhile.

[2] For the present-day connotation of the word 'Bantu' in the South African context cf. *Xhosa in Town*, vol. 1 (*The Black Man's Portion*), General Foreword.

[3] Cf. *The Sociological Review*, new series, vol. 7, July 1959, special number on 'Urbanism in West Africa', ed. K. Little.

Mitchell, and Gluckman have struck a phase of urban development in which the interplay between the workers' sectional (tribal) interests and their common (urban) interests is sociologically noteworthy. Hence a good deal of their discussion has turned on the theme which might be summarized as 'trade unions transcend tribes'.[4] It has demonstrated that in certain interactions the urban workers still attach prime importance to their respective tribal identities, but that industrial work involves them in new sets of relations, in which they eventually become aware of the irrelevance of tribal categories. It is at work, then, that they form 'typically urban associations',[5] notably trade unions. The analysis emphasizes the fact that a man in town can switch back and forth from 'urban' to 'tribal' behaviour according to the immediate situation. He may be content to follow 'tribal' patterns in his urban domestic life, yet deprecate a 'tribal' system of representation for dealing with the White management of the mines. The operative principle has been referred to as 'situational selection'.

The Copperbelt studies (in other words) illustrate the antithesis 'urban'–'tribal' in terms of situations, or sets of relations, rather than in terms of people. Whether one person might deserve to be called more 'urban' (or 'urbanized') than another, is not the question at issue.

In East London the salient sociological features are very different. Trade unions do not transcend tribes. There are no different tribes to be transcended, for almost all of this large labour force is drawn from the solidly Xhosa-speaking Native Reserves in the hinterland. Nor are there any trade unions to speak of. The Government does not recognize them; it discourages all associations in which the town-dwelling Bantu might seek to express opposition to White employers or authorities. Rather than form important new relations at work, the East London workers might be said merely to undergo common experiences there. If they are conscious of common interests they do not express these, except verbally.

On the other hand, in East London one's attention is drawn by certain social categories which have not so far been emphasized in the Copperbelt studies. Social opposition appears between those East Londoners who regard themselves, and are regarded, as 'townsmen', and those who are regarded as being 'in town but of the country'. Influx control and other administrative measures help to accentuate this division. Within the country-bred category, again, there is a still sharper opposition between the so-called 'Red' and 'School' categories, reflecting a bitter conflict over the desirability or undesirability of adopting 'White people's ways', which has split the Xhosa for several generations.

Townsman and countryman, Red and School, are the basic categories of social interaction within the East London locations. Given that these cleavages are contained by the one tribal group, but are not transcended by any massive urban associations, the focus of interest naturally shifts to the cleavages themselves. This means that it shifts away from the relations and situations of work to those of leisure, where people are at liberty to act out their different convictions.

[4] Epstein, A. L., *Politics in an Urban African Community*, Manchester University Press, 1958; Mitchell, J. C., *Tribalism and the Plural Society*, inaugural lecture given in the University College of Rhodesia and Nyasaland, O.U.P., 1960; Gluckman, M., 'Tribalism in modern British Central Africa', in *Cahiers d'études africaines*, Ecole pratique des hautes études, Sorbonne, 1960, p. 55 ff.
[5] Gluckman, op. cit., p. 58.

Hence there is a need to modify the concept of 'situational selection' which was used to good purpose in the Copperbelt. In East London, one can indeed take it that appropriate 'urban' behaviour will be selected in most wage-earning situations. But in the remaining situations—at leisure in the East London locations—each person is involved in a further process of selection, whose outcome cannot so easily be predicted *a priori*. To put it broadly, he can choose between Red, School, or 'townsmen's' patterns. The reference groups are distinct, but as the possibilities of transferring allegiance from one reference group to another are considerable, a man's choices have a particular significance: they show whether or not he intends to remain within his original social category. This question of choice as a determinant of mobility could not arise where the social categories (as in the Copperbelt) are ethnic, birth-determined ones.

Dr. Pauw's book on *The Second Generation* (the third volume of the present series) is devoted to the town-born Bantu in East London. These people can be characterized as fully 'urban', or 'urbanized'; their main social ties are all contained within the town, and the urban traditions are the only ones that count for them. Just as one needs to distinguish this category of 'fully urban' people in East London, so one needs to distinguish the process of change in relationship and behaviour patterns by which selected migrants (or their children) become destined as recruits to the category. This can fairly be termed a process of urbanization, and characterized as a form of social mobility. Its study requires that we concentrate on following up personal relations rather than on analysing social structures.[6]

Townsmen or Tribesmen is concerned with this process, and still more, perhaps, with resistance to the process. The emphasis on resistance, or conservatism, has been dictated by local circumstances too. If anything in this centenarian town has the fascination of the unexpected, it is not the ample evidence of 'urban' behaviour—whether observed in work or in leisure situations—but the doggedly 'tribal' behaviour of some people in some leisure situations. East London, a typical enough South African town in other respects, has special features which may encourage this. Being a border town by origin, and still almost surrounded by vast native reserves, it is a place where town and tribe can be said to remain at unusually close quarters. It happens, also, that the areas nearest East London are numerically dominated by 'Red' people, with their long experience in obstinate tribal conservatism. Another consideration is the prevalence of discouraging shanty-town conditions in East London, at a time when so many other shanty towns—including the Rooiyard of Dr. Ellen Hellman's well-known analysis[7]—have given place to municipal housing with far more amenities.

A word should be added about my use of the word 'migrant'. In this book 'migrant' is not meant to imply that a person's visits to town are merely seasonal or periodic. It means anyone living in town who also has, or recently had, a home in the country. Most East London migrants stay in town for years.

[6] Mitchell in an unpublished paper on 'The Study of African Urban Social Structure', delivered to the C.C.T.A. Conference on Housing and Urbanization, Nairobi, January 1959, makes a useful distinction between 'structural', 'egocentric' and 'categorical' relations. The present book deals with urbanization in terms of the latter two types.

[7] *Rooiyard:* A sociological survey of an urban native slum yard, Rhodes-Livingstone Papers, No. 13, 1948.

I have tried to make my material accessible to the general reader, by avoiding highly technical writing and what a distinguished colleague has called the 'grand language' of sociology. This applies even to the more theoretical sections (e.g. chapter 18 and parts of chapter 1). Even so, the 'practical' reader might prefer to skip those.

My wife did much to keep the work going, especially at times when teaching had first call on me. Her part in the book as a whole has been immeasurably greater than her contribution of one chapter and her collaboration in two others might seem to indicate. I am deeply grateful to her.

PART ONE

THE PROBLEM AND ITS SETTING

I

Labour Migrancy and the Process of Urbanization

'MEN OF TWO WORLDS'

There have been Xhosa in East London from its beginnings, for more than a hundred years. Today this city is one of two major urban centres in the eastern Cape Province, with over 43,000 White residents and nearly 70,000 others.[1] Almost all of the non-White residents are drawn from the Xhosa-speaking peoples—a Bantu group about three million strong at present, with its strongholds in the near-by Ciskeian and Transkeian Reserves.

Even if town life is nothing new to the Xhosa as a people, few of those in East London today are townsmen born and bred. This is due partly to new growth, partly to the local prevalence of migrant labour rather than permanently town-settled labour. In 1955 as many as 86 per cent of all adult Xhosa in East London were found to be of country origin.[2] They are 'men of two worlds'. Perhaps one should say 'of three worlds', for if the country home is one world East London itself comprises two others—the White town where the Xhosa works and the non-White town where he lives meanwhile.

The migrant's rural home of origin may be in a Native Reserve area, where Xhosa peasants till the soil as independent landholders; alternatively it may be in a farming area, where the land belongs to White farmers and the Xhosa families are accommodated on condition of labour rendered. In East London itself, the non-White town consists of 'The Locations' (Native locations), set apart by law and custom from the White residential and business areas. In the locations more than fifty thousand people jostle together, some in decent houses or cottages but most in shacks or hovels, and from here most of the able-bodied go forth every morning to do their day's wage-earning in White East London. The rest of the non-White population lives scattered about the White areas, in domestic servants' quarters on White employers' premises.

White East London, the migrants' third world, is a modern industrial and commercial centre, a considerable seaport and a holiday resort. Outside the business centre its residential suburbs are strung out for several miles along

[1] Cf. Reader: *The Black Man's Portion*, chapter 3.
[2] Ibid.

the hills, the river banks and the sandy coastline. In this White world the Black person is allotted and accepts certain roles, above all the role of employee. The main reason why country-born Xhosa come to East London in the first place is to work for or under White East Londoners—as factory hands, general labourers, railway and harbour workers, domestic servants, shops' messengers —and earn wages which will supplement the scanty living they make in the countryside, or perhaps provide their sole means of support.

The migrant is not only permitted but compelled to participate in the White-dominated world. Under present regulations, if he fails to get himself employment in the East London area the authorities can return him from there to the country. But the limits of participation are narrow and rigid. In the White world the Black man can hardly act but as the employee of a White employer or the subject of White authorities. In practically all fields of activity, except those concerned with employment, government and administration, the Black and White populations of East London must act separately, while in those excepted fields the Black and White actors must confront each other in opposed or complementary roles.

By contrast with the migrant's rural home East London seems a world on a much larger scale; but this contrast needs careful definition. White dominion is so old in South Africa that the Xhosa—even those who have never left their peasant homes—have for long been geared into a large-scale society of 'Western' type. Through several generations they have been the tax-paying subjects of a supra-tribal government located far away; have played their modest parts, as consumers and producers, in a complex economy; and have been provided with schools and missions linked into nation-wide systems. For the ordinary Xhosa this external system of 'wide-scale relations' (to borrow a term from the Wilsons[3]) has been superimposed on an internal system in which the tribal patterns and the small-scale values have been left largely undisturbed. Kinship, clanship, age-grouping, and other such criteria of ascribed status have kept their supreme significance within the local community. What happens when the Xhosa migrates to East London is, in the first place, that he becomes more actively engaged in the external, large-scale system, particularly in matters of employment, money dealings, and official regulations or administration. But to say this does not explain what adjustments he has to make meanwhile in the internal, small-scale system.

This book deals with migrant life in East London, but not primarily with the migrants' adjustments to the White world as such: i.e. not mainly with race relations, work situations, or the contrasts between tribal and White people's expectations. The 'two worlds' with which we shall be concerned are those of rural Xhosa and urban Xhosa society, with only indirect reference to the third or White world. This does not mean that the theme of 'Westernization' will fail to appear. In South Africa today, many so-called White ways and values are learnt by Black people mainly from Black people. Within the East London locations many Black teachers, preachers, business men, and others actively transmit 'Westernization'; the neighbours, friends, workmates, and other informal agents of community pressure remain entirely Black. Seeing that Black and White interact in so few fields, the reference group of the rural Xhosa who becomes urbanized, or who wants to become urbanized, can only be an urbanized Black group; the destiny of the one who becomes 'civilized'

[3] Wilson, G. & M.: *The Analysis of Social Change*, 1945.

may be to join a Black *élite*, but not to move significantly closer to any White people.

The limited scope of the present book is to discuss some behaviour patterns of country-born Xhosa migrants in East London, with special reference to the question whether these migrants seem to be undergoing 'urbanization'. The discussion is focused on categories of persons who move between country and town and on the changes (or absence of changes) in their behaviour patterns, rather than on a total urban system absorbing (or failing to absorb) these new persons into its structure. The study of absorption—of which the theoretical basis has been lately expounded by Eisenstadt[4]—requires not only a working knowledge of the absorbing society but a clear abstract model for representing its structure; in the case of East London it might be premature to claim the latter. In any case the town is not necessarily the permanent receiving end for these Xhosa.

THE XHOSA-SPEAKING PEOPLE AND THE RED-SCHOOL DIVISION

East London is unlike some other South African towns of comparable size and importance in not being a meeting-ground for different tribal groups. In 1955 Reader found that 96 per cent of the location population were Bantu (the other 4 per cent being Coloureds); Xhosa-speakers accounted for over 90 per cent. Xhosa proper made up 56 per cent of the total, and Mfengu (also Xhosa-speaking) 34 per cent; some other Xhosa-speaking groups—Bhaca, Mpondo, Mpondomise—also figured among the remainder.

For practical purposes the three million Xhosa-speakers whose mother country is in the Ciskei and Transkei—the Xhosa proper, Mfengu, Thembu, Mpondo, Mpondomise, Bhaca, Bomvana—can be regarded as one group divided into tribes or sub-tribes. Besides speaking the same language and having similar cultures they are united by their history of neighbourhood and by ties of intermarriage. The Mfengu, whose ancestors were assimilated as refugees from Natal in the early nineteenth century, are set a little apart from Xhosa proper by their remembered 'foreign' origin. Under provocation individual Xhosa may sneer at Mfengu 'dependence' or 'liking to curry favour'; the Mfengu may accuse the Xhosa of 'arrogance' or 'out-of-date pride'. But as a whole the common loyalties easily outweigh the distinct loyalties. In normal situations the difference does not count, and a person only discovers whether another is Xhosa or Mfengu when he has heard what his clan-name is.[5] 'Xhosa' will be used in this book as a shorthand term for 'Xhosa-speaking', embracing Mfengu.

Thus tribal categories cannot here be observed as 'significant categories of interaction', as was done in Mitchell's analysis of the Copperbelt for example.[6] Far more important, both in East London and in its rural hinterland, is a different categorization altogether. For several generations the whole Xhosa-speaking population of the Ciskei and Transkei has been divided between two opposed cultural camps—between 'Red' people and 'School' people. One of the original objects of the present study was to see whether the two types of Xhosa responded as differently to the challenge of town as they do to the task of living in the countryside. It was soon found that, at any rate,

[4] Eisenstadt, S. M.: *The Absorption of Immigrants*, London, 1954.
[5] The historical background of Xhosa-Mfengu relations is referred to in chapter 2.
[6] Mitchell, J. C.: *The Kalela Dance*.

it would be impossible to gain any insight into 'urbanization' in East London without constant reference to the Red–School differentiation.

The people known as *abantu ababomvu*, 'Red people', or less politely as *amaqaba*, 'smeared ones' (from the smearing of their clothes and bodies with red ochre), are the traditionalist Xhosa, the conservatives who still stand by the indigenous way of life, including the pagan Xhosa religion. 'Red' Xhosa are not just a few picturesque survivals: on the contrary, they are a flourishing half of the Xhosa people today, and are particularly strong in the areas nearest to East London. The antithetical type, *abantu basesikolweni*, 'School people', are products of the mission and the school, holding up Christianity, literacy and other Western ways as ideals. 'School' people—it must be added—are not just town people or people under town influence. The town Xhosa do in a broad sense belong within the 'School' category, but theirs is a separate branch of School culture with a flavour all its own. The primary division into Red and School lies within the countryside itself, where two folk cultures (to use the term in Redfield's sense) are carried on simultaneously. Red Xhosa rustics and School Xhosa rustics, both attached to their own distinctive ways of life, are both faced with the need to make adjustments in town. In this book 'School' will be used to mean the rural School folk culture: the townspeople will be specified as such.

The distinctiveness of the rural School culture relates to the considerable time-depth of its traditions. It is more than a century and a quarter since White missionaries, administrators and traders got to work in the Xhosa countryside. As an area of actual White settlement this ranks among the oldest in sub-Saharan Africa, White and Black having both claimed it as home since the 1820's. The School Xhosa may have four or five generations of School ancestors behind him, and the town where he goes for a job, or the farm where he works for a White master, may have been within their social horizon as it is within his own. In East London and other east Cape towns, along with the concrete office blocks and modern houses, early Victorian buildings are part of the familiar scene. In effect the Red Xhosa are those who have been looking askance at White people and their ways in every successive generation since what would be identified in England as the time of George IV; the School Xhosa are those who have looked and have accepted.

THE MEANING OF URBANIZATION

Being concerned with the urbanization of migrants this study is concerned with what might be called a form of social mobility—movement of individuals between rural and urban Xhosa society. Xhosa in East London are people who have moved, or whose forebears have moved, from country into town: but we are entitled to call urbanized only those who have moved in some profounder sense than the mere physical change of abode.[7] This profounder sense is what one would like to identify.

This discussion begins, therefore, from the well-established starting-point that urbanization must be something different from stabilization as such.[8] Stabilization—as the word is used by some sociologists and anthropologists—

---

[7] Various attempts to define 'urbanization' in the African context are discussed in *Social Implications of Industrialisation and Urbanisation in Africa South of the Sahara*. Cf. especially M. McCulloch, p. 212 ff.; J. C. Mitchell, pp. 696 and 704; E. Hellmann, p. 730 ff.

[8] Cf. Mitchell, J. C.: 'Urbanisation, Detribalisation and Stabilisation in Southern Africa', p. 693 ff. in *Social Implications of Industrialisation and Urbanisation in Africa South of the Sahara*.

is a concept of the length of stay in town, related to other relevant factors such as the person's age and how much time he has spent outside the town. It is a concept of something that can be measured in figures, though the selection and calculation of the figures may be beset with difficulties. For present purposes we need not be concerned with the statistical refinements that are needed to make the concept of stabilization an accurate working tool. In any case stabilization will always be a quantitative concept, while the thing which concerns us here is a qualitative concept. The condition of urbanization, properly so called, refers not just to the length but to the quality of the life that is lived in town. When the implied quality is present, admittedly, the individual will show a preference for remaining 'stabilized' in town, but the converse is not equally true—an individual who stays long in town will not necessarily show the genuine urbanized quality. He may be actually planning a return to the country; he may dislike town life, and consider himself an outsider. In a place like East London, where so many residents start as subsistence peasants trying to supplement rural incomes, this is no mere academic possibility.

It seems desirable to get beyond a catalogue of those superficial urban features which are inevitably imposed on *all* residents in the East London locations, however temporary their stay, or however little urbanized they may feel at heart. To start with, it is common to practically all the Xhosa in East London—from the born townsman to the rawest rustic new-comer—to be involved in town jobs, which mean satisfying the requirements of White employers through the length of the working day. All of them have to buy food and shelter. All have to conform to a minimum standard of town-style dress. All are debarred for the present from rustic or 'tribal' activities such as tending livestock or building mud huts. But, as Fortes has remarked, many adaptive patterns, proper to certain situations in town, can 'drop off like an old coat' if or when the person returns to the country.[9] Moreover, even in town they can be combined with ways of acting and thinking (in other situations) which are not 'urban' at all.

One way of sorting out the fully or genuinely urbanized Xhosa in East London from the others might be to see where people have their main roots, or can be said to be at home. By the country-rooted is meant those migrants who are in the location but not of it. They are staying in town but regard themselves, and can be regarded, as having their real homes or roots in the country. By the town-rooted is meant the core of East Londoners whose homes and roots are there and there only. Children who are born and grow up in East London are naturally town-rooted, but this is not the only way to qualify. Country-born people can become town-rooted too, by deciding to stay on permanently and become incorporated in the town community. They are then immigrants rather than migrants.

When a rural Xhosa first comes into East London the question of mobility might be expressed by asking whether he will ever become identifiable as an immigrant in this sense. Field-work showed that for a high proportion of the Xhosa who come to East London the answer is 'no', but the reasons for the 'no' have to be considered. It is not necessarily because their stay in town has been or will be a short one. On the contrary: often they are remaining country-

---

[9] Fortes, M.: 'Culture Contact as a Dynamic Process', in *Methods of Study of Culture Contact in Africa*, p. 87.

rooted through long years of almost continuous residence in town. Many keep this up through a lifetime. After a whole working life spent in East London one man will pack up and go 'home' to his 'own place', though another will stay on, feeling that by now town itself is 'home'. To isolate the factors that make for these different patterns would be to learn something about the process called urbanization.

Distinguishing between town-rooted and country-rooted people, however, cannot be the whole of the matter. It is a structural distinction; it says little about culture and values, little about the 'way of life' and attitudes. In the literature on Africa, perhaps, urbanization (or detribalization) has sometimes tended to serve as a blanket term obscuring the fact that two distinct modes of change may be involved, according to the distinction between 'structure' and 'culture' as conceived of in classical anthropology. On the one hand one can think of change in the individual's *social universe*; on the other hand, of change in his *patterns of behaviour* or values. In speaking of a process of urbanization (or of detribalization) it would be well to make clear which mode we are mainly thinking of, or whether we restrict the term to processes in which both modes are combined.

In defining the urbanized person as the town-rooted person we would be focusing solely on the structural aspect—on the question of social ties formed and maintained; of incorporation within a town community; or of roles played in town and roles elsewhere abandoned or rejected. We would be saying that a person deserves to be called urbanized if and when he appears to have a 'home' in town. On the other hand it would be possible, and perhaps quite as justifiable, to focus on cultural aspects instead—to assess a person's urbanization in terms of his 'way of life', his institutionalized activities, and especially his values and attitudes. The truly urbanized person, in this definition, would be one who is fully confirmed in 'urban' modes of behaviour—private life included—and (above all) in valuing these positively. The question of values is important, for in many situations people might conform outwardly, but still remain inwardly determined to revert to pre-urban patterns when opportunity arises.

Thus for purposes of field-work the question behind 'How do the migrants act?' might have been 'What evidence do we find for their becoming tied to the urban community by basic social ties?'; or it might have been 'What evidence do we find for their adopting typically urban behaviour patterns, attitudes and values?' In practice it seemed desirable to work with both concepts, but to keep them separate in principle and application.

The Xhosa themselves imply some such distinction between structural and cultural processes. In Xhosa the word *ukutshipha* means to abscond from home (i.e. the country home) and 'vanish' in town. *Itshipha*, the absconder, is an extreme case of the town-rooted or structurally urbanized person. He is the one who leaves his parents, wife or children in the country without news or knowledge of him. He has cut himself off from the home community; he is lost almost as completely as by death. He is the opposite of the men who keep up home ties—*amagoduka*, the 'home-visitors'. *Itshipha* is a derogatory term, thought to be derived from the English 'cheap' (indicating that one is too easily taken up by new things). A second derogatory word, *irumsha*, indicates a turncoat in the 'cultural' sense. *Ukurumsha* is to adopt 'town ways' in preference to one's own tribal or rustic Xhosa ways. In its narrowest sense it means to speak a language not one's own, but above all to speak English—in rustic eyes the sign of the townsman as against the countryman.

To call a man *irumsha* does not imply that he is severing ties with his family or community at home, or even that he is becoming town-rooted; it merely refers to his personal habits. To call him *itshipha* on the other hand does not say anything about his habits; it merely indicates the breaking of social ties. The 'turncoat' may still come home to roost in the rural community; while the 'absconder' may still, for all one knows, be as far as ever from acquiring the veneer of truly urban culture.

One can in fact find Xhosa in East London who seem to have become urbanized in one sense but not in the other. Some have become town-rooted but do not at all value the diacritic institutions of the real townspeople. They mean to stay in Rome but will not do as the Romans do: instead they attach themselves to their own particular cultural minority, and recreate as far as possible the moral and cultural atmosphere of their old (pre-urban) homes. And on the other hand there are people who become strongly attached to cultural patterns learnt in town but still feel rooted to their homes in the country. Their spiritual home may be with the really-urban townspeople, while their actual home remains in the country.

In the first place, then, neither mode of urbanization—becoming town-rooted or becoming urban-cultured—can be said to go automatically with stabilization; but in the second place, neither mode need necessarily keep pace with the other. It is only where both have been achieved by the same individual, perhaps, that one should speak of 'urbanization' in an unqualified way.

FIELDS OF BEHAVIOUR FOR INVESTIGATION

Whether one is interested in structural or in cultural transfer of allegiance, it is not on the basis of wage-earning activities that one could hope to identify urbanized and non-urbanized Xhosa in East London. Not only are almost all Xhosa there compelled to hold jobs in the White-dominated economy, but they are almost all confined to the same range of jobs—to unskilled or semi-skilled work—where proficiency in 'civilization' is irrelevant. This is very largely a matter of laws and conventions which are beyond their power to alter. Although a small range of white-collar and professional occupations is open to them in addition, the proportion of people in these even among the town-born Xhosa remains exceedingly small. Leaving aside the nature of the job, participation in workers' organizations would also not provide any generally applicable index. Trade unions for Native workers are not recognized in South African law today (though Coloureds and Asiatics, as well as Whites, have recognized unions); in East London the voluntary non-recognized 'trade unions' sometimes organized by or among Xhosa workers have little scope. It is nearly thirty years since this town saw its last Native trade-union movement on a big scale—Kadalie's I.C.U., which for some time, when Kadalie himself lived in the location, had a considerable following there.

The field of politics, in the modern sense, is another which seemed unlikely to repay investigation for our purposes. Local government is a matter in which exceedingly few East London Xhosa now participate or show much interest, despite the fact that once upon a time this town was a pioneer in setting up its Location Advisory Board. (As an illustration it may be mentioned that the poll in local elections, during most of the 1950's, averaged between 1 per cent and 2 per cent of those entitled to vote.) The once-active Vigilance Association had practically ceased to exist during the time of this investigation. As for politics on the wider scale, the local branches of the African National Congress and of its Youth League had also lost impetus. The general turning-point seems to have been the suppression of the 1952 riots, the most serious explosion to have occurred yet in the East London locations.

It is true that the uniform factors of being employed, and being under political domination, are far-reaching ones, but they do not affect all fields of migrant life equally. As Epstein says,[10] there remain parts of the total field of social relations in town which can be considered as largely 'sealed off'. Watson has demonstrated the similar point that 'a man can participate in two different spheres of social relations and keep them distinct and separate'.[11] In the case of an East London migrant the employer or foreman may implant certain habits in the matter of factory work, and the authorities may secure conformity to certain regulations, but neither of these need have much influence on—for example—the migrant's attitude towards his country home and friends, or his mode of worship, or his mode of recreation, or his magical beliefs and practices, or his spending habits (subject to financial limitations) and 'style of life'. The present investigation has been concentrated largely on these sealed-off fields. It is here in the free spheres of personal life and leisure—particularly the domestic, kinship, recreational and religious fields—that one has the best opportunities for contrasting the ideal types of rustic and urban Xhosa, and deciding how far an individual is undergoing urbanization as a result of his sojourn in East London.

(a) Criteria for town-rootedness

In considering the structural urbanization of individuals (the change from being effectively country-rooted to being effectively town-rooted) it was not found practicable to think in terms of their taking up new positions in a new structure. The difficulty arises from the great difference in kind between the structure of the East London location 'community' and that of any Xhosa rural community. In the rural community we can discern structure in the classic sense—an inclusive system of interlocking or logically complementary roles.[12] A person seems to 'fit in' in one or other of the ways prescribed by the structure. In East London on the other hand the 'structure' which confronts us seems an immense tangle of criss-crossing interrelations involving many diverse and not logically co-ordinated roles and categories. We can see, for instance, an opposition between town-rooted and country-rooted people there; opposition of Transkeians and Ciskeians; opposition of upper, middle, and lower 'classes'; of different occupational groups; of different religious categories; of different associations; but we cannot see any overriding principles which articulate all these into a coherent whole. They remain on different planes; often one feels as if confronted by a social conglomeration rather than a 'structure'. Accordingly, the image of a new-comer finding himself a definite niche in an over-all social structure, or assuming a part in an organic system of roles—a helpful image if we were concerned with persons moving from one

---

[10] Epstein, A. L.: *Politics in an Urban African Community*, p. 233.
[11] Watson, W.: *Tribal Cohesion in a Money Economy*, p. 6.
[12] Cf. Nadel, S. F.: *The Theory of Social Structure*.

'integrated' community into another—did not seem to help here; that is, not for practical purposes, even if it could be worked out in the theoretical field.

An alternative is to think of rootedness as something to be apprehended from the *migrant's own* point of view. That is the viewpoint adopted here: the work has been concerned mostly with the migrant's own network of relations, to use the term as do Barnes and others.[13] The network is the total of ego's inter-personal relations with other individuals. In any particular network the individuals concerned do not constitute a group, in the sociological sence: they form something which—like a kindred—can only be defined with ego as the central point of reference.

By definition every migrant—unless he becomes *itshipha*—has his network partly in the country and partly in town. The question is how it seems to be distributed, and particularly the distribution of the individuals who seem to be of most importance to ego personally. A country-rooted migrant continues to lay the main emphasis on people in the country and on his relatedness to them, even if he can only keep up these relations *in absentia*. A migrant who becomes town-rooted mainly emphasizes people and relations in town. An *itshipha* no longer accepts or recognizes the old country-located part of his network at all.

The immediate dependants—wives and children—can normally be considered to fall automatically in the category of most important or most emphasized individuals (except in the case of the *itshipha* who may cast them off with the rest of his rural connexions). In the ordinary way a man who keeps his wife and children in the country while he himself stays in town is giving a prima facie indication of country-rootedness. A town-rooted man would have his wife in town and rear his children there; if circumstances prevent a migrant from doing this they also prevent him from becoming thoroughly town-rooted. Migrants who regularly visit the country and continue in full interaction with kin, neighbours or other associates there, and those who claim to have their 'best' friends or lovers there, are also indicating country-rootedness.

Interests of property also needed to be considered. Acquiring a house property in town is not invariably a sign of genuine town-rootedness, since these properties—as many migrants have discovered—can be exploited for cash profit even in the owner's absence, and eventually turned into cash again. On the other hand, acquiring or keeping up a property in the country can properly be considered a sign of country-rootedness. A Xhosa rural homestead can hardly ever be thought of as an 'investment' in this sense. Its only meaning is as a home for oneself or one's dependants.

Besides objective criteria—location of kin and other connected persons, regularity of country-visiting, location of property—account was also taken of subjective content, what might be called the psychological orientation. Orientation was gauged by answers to such questions as 'where is your real home?', 'where would you live now if you were free to choose?', 'where do you intend to retire when you can leave off working?' Such questions and answers would not be a sufficient test of rootedness without the objective criteria as well, since they might reflect an orientation that was merely sentimental, or even a fictitious one put on for the investigator's benefit.

By such criteria, many individuals in town were found to be either clearly town-rooted or clearly country-rooted. However, others were found to be

[13] Cf. Barnes, J. A.: 'Class and Committees in a Norwegian Island Parish', *Human Relations*, vol. 7, No. 1, p. 43; and Bott, Elizabeth: *Family and Social Network*, especially pp. 58–9.

doubly rooted, laying stress on their ties in both country and town. In most cases this reflected their sense of insecurity in town. They would like to root themselves there but dared not cut loose from the country altogether. An account of these 'conditionally urbanized' people will be found in the chapters on School peasant migrants.

(b) Criteria for cultural urbanization

In the fields with which we are mainly concerned—of domestic, kinship, and leisure life—certain institutions can be considered ideally part of urban as against rural Xhosa culture. In town for example there are recreational opportunities which even the most civilized of School Xhosa cannot experience in the country: cinemas, dance-halls (for jiving and ballroom dancing), cafés, beauty contests, daily newspapers. Many migrants avail themselves of these, but many others continue to entertain themselves on typically rustic patterns instead: that is, even when in town they hold 'traditional' beer-drinks or dance and sing in rustic Xhosa style.

Again, there are different norms for family and kinship attitudes. It is probably not true to say that the townsman can be distinguished from the countryman by his lack of interest in the wider kin. Second- or third-generation East Londoners may have widely ramifying kin relations there. But there is a different feeling between the generations and the sexes, reflected in different patterns of family life, especially as regards the relations of a woman to her husband and to her parents-in-law. By and large, both of the rural Xhosa cultures—School as well as Red—are distinctly more patriarchal in tone than that of the townspeople.

As to dress and style of life, superficially every Xhosa in town has to make himself appear more urban than he might appear in the country. Even a 'blanket-wearing' Red man knows well that he must 'dress for town'. But still there are degrees. The real East Londoner can often detect people who are of the country by details such as the fit of the jacket or the length of the skirt, the arrangement of the woman's doek (turban) or the ear-rings and bracelets. Further, one might mention a difference of manner and expression, which is far easier to feel than to describe. The really urban person tends to be quicker, to be 'smarter', to look at you in a different way. Xhosa from the country have their distinct impressions of the townsman—his smiles, his smartness, his superficial politeness, which may mean anything or nothing. Those who come to identify themselves as townspeople pick up some of these mannerisms.

We have to remember, of course, not to confuse an opposition of institutions with an opposition of persons. Some Xhosa in East London (especially the town-born) are adept in the town institutions only; some—especially among Red and humbler School migrants—never learn to participate in many of the urban institutions, so that they can be considered as adept in the rustic culture only. But other migrants are found to be adept in both cultures, or sufficiently so that one must regard them as having been culturally 'urbanized' without having been correspondingly 'detribalized'. It is a matter of being able to adjust to different situations and contexts. When a man acquires this ability— one may say—he can come and go freely between rustic and urban circles, always retaining the other set of patterns in a latent state. He can act in an urban fashion among urbanized friends in town, but fall back into country ways without apparent effort when he revisits the country or retires there.

This 'double-cultured' type of person—like the other type who remains rustic even when in town—will not become a preacher of town ways when he is back in the country; he is not likely to be despised there as *irumsha*.

The testing of values was desirable to indicate how far various urban patterns have been internalized by an individual and how far they are simply being conformed to as something imposed by external pressures. In the course of a limited anthropological study, it was possible to select only a few pointers to values and to record direct verbal statements. In this way an effort was made to cover certain basic themes: religious and supernatural beliefs; views on the proper relations between the generations and the sexes, and on seniority and 'respect'; attitudes towards 'tribal customs'; aspirations for one's own and one's children's future; evaluation of town and country ways, and of town and country people.

(c) The diachronic aspect

Even if we could devise completely satisfactory ways of identifying town-rootedness and urban culture, or their absence, there would remain the problem of dynamics. The word 'urbanization' can be taken to indicate a state, but equally or more interesting is its alternative sense as a process. The field study, restricted in time, had to try to uncover the gradual shift, the change in emphasis, whereby a person over a longer period may shift his roots and/or his culture. In other words there was the problem of adapting synchronic methods to diachronic problems.

Only a search into the life-history can show whether a given person is becoming relatively more town-rooted or less town-rooted than he was before. Nor is it helpful to make generalized assumptions or go by rule of thumb. For example, it is natural to assume that if any change does take place over a long period in town, it must be a change *towards* greater town-rootedness; but this proved to be wrong. Many peasant migrants become more strongly country-rooted as they approach middle age or old age, than they were during their younger years: the bias has shifted first towards town, and then away again.

Uprooting and re-rooting may be dramatized by some particular act such as allowing the land rights in the country to be taken over by someone else or bringing the wife and children into town. A shift in culture—in habits and values—is not so easily dramatized. Some informants felt there had been one decisive moment, e.g. the moment when they had first consciously tried to dress like real townspeople, or had joined a certain church congregation in town. But more often no special event could be cited, only an awareness of gradually having changed.

Though much thought was given to this problem of dynamics in the present study, no claim is made to have dealt with it by any methods more exalted than those of common sense. It was made an object to investigate life-histories, besides aspirations for the future; and not only to draw out factual particulars of the respondent's past but also to make him evaluate his present state as compared with past states, e.g. to compare his own idea of 'home', his own cultural ideas now, with the ideas he had when he first came to town.

THE AGENTS OF CHANGE

It seems sometimes to be suggested that the mere fact of living in a town, of being constantly exposed to its atmosphere, will more or less automatically tend to make a person urbanized. This would involve some unusual assumptions. In normal contexts the metaphor of 'cultural atmosphere' is not meant to convey that individuals learn conformity as they breathe, without being taught. On the contrary, anthropologists have drawn attention to the 'socialization'— in a transitive sense—of children, as a task falling upon particular persons, related to ego in particular ways. Thus in a rural Xhosa community we would look for the main agents of socialization to the parents, siblings and other kin, near-seniors, age-mates, teachers, clergy. Some of these wield specific disciplinary sanctions, others do not; but the teaching of the socio-cultural lessons requires face-to-face contact even if it is by means of example or precept rather than formal discipline. This is particularly true, of course, in a preliterate society.

When anyone enters a new social milieu he needs, as it were, to be socialized over again. This applies to the country-bred Xhosa who comes into East London as a migrant. Even in the free or sealed-off fields of life, he finds an environment so different that the learnt rules on which he could rely for purposes of life in the country can no longer be sufficient or always appropriate. Rather than take it that he will breathe in the requisite new rules from the 'atmosphere' or pick them up from the pavements, we still have to think of face-to-face influencing.

Part of the network being in the country, it may be that part of the resocialization for town emanates from there. In fact we shall see how a youth may learn from parents and others in the country, before he ever sets foot in town, several rules about 'how one ought to' behave there; and as long as relations are kept up with the home people their influence cannot be discounted. But the influence of other associates who surround him when he is actually in town may be critical too. Will they re-echo the expectations of his people in the country, or will they expect quite different behaviour from him? When he is among them, will he find it natural to go on visiting home regularly, and to remain faithful to his old cultural values; or will he feel them exerting moral pressure towards *ukurumsha*, or towards town-rootedness, perhaps even *ukutshipha*?

There is therefore another question to be considered about the network besides that of its distribution. It is the question what 'kind of people' (speaking in terms of cultural standards and values) make up that part of the network which is located in town. For our purposes the critically important people are those with whom ego's relations are domestic, friendly or sociable; those with whom he finds himself having to live, eat, sleep, drink, worship or amuse himself while he stays in town. It is through them, presumably, that he may be induced to change rustic habits for urbanized ones, in the senses we have defined.

In the country, only persons of rather homogeneous culture are available as ego's domestic and sociable partners, but in East London the variety is considerably greater. There seems to be nothing to prevent the migrant from finding himself in relation there with people whose expectations are very different from those of his rustic circle—with town-born people, with those of different religious and educational background, and so on. On the other hand, since country-rooted migrants both Red and School make up much of the East London population, it is also possible that he may find himself among people 'of his own kind', similar to his people in the country, and in such a case his resocialization for town purposes could presumably be undergone with much less damage to his old habits and norms.

FORMATION OF TIES IN TOWN

We shall therefore have to consider how the town-located part of a migrant's network comes to be formed, and particularly how he meets the most intimate of his associates there.

To begin with, there will be an obvious contrast between the formation of his country-located network and that of his town-located network, as a whole. Within the Xhosa rural setting, the composition of every individual's network seems to be largely or almost entirely foreordained and predictable. This is a general feature of the 'integrated' or 'clearly structured' type of community. The general pattern of each person's network will follow directly from the structure; it can be roughly inferred by anyone who knows the structure.

In the Xhosa rural community, ego must necessarily have person-to-person relations with his own kindred, his neighbours, and his local age-mates. These are ascribed relations; he accepts, he does not engineer them. It is also true that as long as he remains there he cannot contract out of them. Such ascribed relations account for most if not all of a Xhosa's rural network.

Not only is the general *pattern* of such a network ordained by the social structure (i.e. the fact that everyone must have relations with his kindred, neighbours, local age-mates, etc.), but the *identity of the individuals* composing it seems very little capable of variation. That only one collection of individuals can be identified as ego's kindred goes without saying, but the principle is almost equally true for his neighbours or his local age-mates. There being little mobility within or between these peasant communities, it is not usual for a man to replace one set of them by another. Thus for practical purposes it seems fair to say that in Xhosa peasant conditions the individuals once ascribed to ego as members of his network are mostly likely to remain within it, until removed by death.

Variable factors, such as accident and personal choice—variable in the sense that they and their effects cannot be inferred from knowledge of the social structure—therefore seem to be left with little to do for the *composition* of the network, within the rural community. All they do there is to influence the *tone* or emotional content of each of the relations in the network. The 'success' of the relation, in terms of personal harmony or feeling, remains to be achieved, while the relation as such is ascribed.

When a migrant moves away from such a home setting these features of his original network are not materially altered. All that happens is that the ability to influence the success of the ascribed relations takes on a new aspect. The migrant now has the choice of keeping them up to a greater or a lesser degree. But at the same time the migrant must face the necessity of acquiring a new section of network at the place he moves to. If he were moving into another 'small-scale' or 'integrated' type of community, he might—as has already been suggested—step into a niche that carries, by implication, its own complement of ready-made or structurally ascribed network relations. But in a place like East London, with its lack of over-all unitary structure and its shifting population, network composition cannot be prophesied. It seems to be mainly dependent on variable factors.

In the East London locations not even the general pattern of a migrant's network is structurally predetermined. For many migrants (let us say) the town-located section of the network will largely be made up by fellow-employees, fellow-lodgers, and a landlord; but these relations are not necessarily entailed by the urban social structure. Other migrants have no fellow-lodgers or individual landlords—they live in municipal houses; or no fellow-employees —they set up in business independently. The town-located networks of different migrants may thus be constructed on noticeably different patterns. In town, moreover, within the network pattern which applies for any particular individual, the actual personnel are variable and are not ordained as permanencies. Suppose that ego's network does include landlord, fellow-lodgers, and fellow-employees: the identity of the individuals who play these parts in relation to him can be changed wholesale time and again, whenever he changes his job or his lodgings. The same applies to people encountered in other town settings: at church, in the shebeen, at the local shop. Any of these, who are regularly encountered and become known by name and personality, can be considered to enter into the network; but the availability of *other* shebeens, *other* churches and shops, is part of the very nature of town life, so that in contrast to the limited options of the country, ego has several or many alternative sets of personnel available to play similar parts for him.

In many town-located relations a migrant's personal freedom of choice is strictly limited, not indeed by structural ascription, but by factors equally beyond his control. Many of his associates in town are thrust upon him by chance; he cannot know whom he will have to encounter at a particular place of work, or in a particular lodging. He may choose his lodging-house but he cannot choose his neighbours. However, when we come to the kind of relations with which we are specially concerned—those of a domestic, friendly or sociable order—for the first time we see the factor of personal *choice* in full operation. Here in fact lies a great novelty of town, compared with the country. Now as never before the migrant chooses all the individuals who will be in *closest* personal relation to himself. If chance gives him his workmates, choice decides with which of them (if any) he will spend the lunch-break eating and chatting, or the evenings visiting and drinking. If chance ordains the neighbours and the fellow-lodgers, choice is responsible for the room-mates, who form the true domestic circle.

We shall see, for instance, how much variety is possible when a migrant selects his domestic circle in town. No single pattern is obligatory: he may decide to live with a brother, or an age-mate, or a group of several age-mates, or a male friend or friends related in neither way, or a concubine, or his wife (with or without the children), or he may form a one-man domestic unit on his own. This makes a sharp contrast to the structural predetermination at home, where he would automatically be ascribed to a domestic circle consisting of his close kin. Again, we shall see that in town, where population is dense and people move about a good deal, the mere physical fact of living near together does not compel individuals to enter into sociable or friendly relations. In the country on the other hand, social structure demands that one exchanges hospitality with neighbours. In town people drink with companions of their own choosing in a setting of their own choosing; in the country etiquette lays down who shall drink with whom.

Thus the closest personal relations in town are most especially the creation of the migrant himself. He constructs this part of his network by his own acts of choice. In this it differs from the country-located part of his network, and also from the remainder of the town-located part, both of which—though for different reasons—appear to him as data, fixed by factors beyond his control.

If these personal associates in town—as we have argued—provide the most important cultural pressures towards or against urbanization, then the principal agency of the migrant's urbanization is one which he himself calls into being. He is the architect of the intimate social environment which will help to mould him into an urbanized man or a resister as the case may be. This is a further reason why it would be useless to try to assess the urbanization of the migrants on mechanical grounds of stabilization in town.

CHOICE IN REGARD TO INSTITUTIONS

In considering the migrant's personal relations in town—it may be said—we are considering something within the sphere which Firth has identified as social organization.[14] Organization versus structure, choice versus ascription, is the keynote of the contrast between the town-located and the country-located sections of the migrant's network. In the course of investigation it emerged that the Red migrants on the one hand and the School migrants on the other tend to employ markedly different forms of organization, with correspondingly different effects on their prospects of urbanization.

The contrast between structure (in the rural setting) and organization (in the East London setting) can be observed not only in regard to relations, but also in regard to institutions and habits.

For the Xhosa migrant, childhood socialization in the country has been the task of learning a unitary culture. There are two cultural possibilities—Red and School—but, having opted for one of these (or having had it chosen by his parents) the individual finds most of his institutional patterns ascribed to him accordingly. Throughout life, given his particular status, e.g. as youth, mature man or old man, he will know how to dress, how to worship, how to regard school education. Habits in any of these fields are related to habits in others; one does not 'dress Red' and sit for matriculation, or attend Red dances and become a confirmed church member.[15] By contrast, the resocialization which has to be undergone in town can wear no such straightforward aspect. The migrant does not drop into a predetermined complex of cultural patterns or institutions, in which each single factor seems to be logically entailed by the others. He does not do this any more than he drops straight into a structural niche with a complement of logically entailed network relations. Instead, he is confronted by an institutional diversity which imposes on him the constant need to pick and choose. He must build up his own synthesis of habits and institutions from a wide available variety, just as he must build up his own network of relations.

It is not only a question of there being Red migrants, School migrants and town-born people all available in town as possible cultural mentors with different norms. It is also a question of the greater diversity within the town culture itself.

Particularly in the free or personal spheres which we regard as critical for urbanization, the institutions encountered in East London are in themselves

---

[14] Firth, R.: *Elements of Social Organisation*; 'Some Principles of Social Organisation', in *J. of the R. Anthropologic. Inst.*, vol. 85, parts I & II, pp. 1-18.
[15] See chapter 2.

far more diversified than the institutions encountered in a Xhosa rural community. That is to say, several *alternative* answers are often provided (within the town culture itself) to a single cultural question. Consider the institutions of recreation or amusement open to Xhosa in town. They include such alternatives as rugby, tennis, horseracing, cricket, golf, gambling, ballroom dancing, jiving, shebeen drinking, private drinking, bioscope, concerts and 'shows'. These are available as alternatives. No single one of them is regarded as basic or compulsory to everyone; nor is any one of them entailed on any person by reason of his particular place in the social structure. In the rural community on the other hand, institutions of recreation appear much less diversified, and the individual is given little choice as to his participation. There is the *intlombe* for each age-grade of young people; stick-fights for male youths; beer-drinks for maturer people. The local School culture provides the only alternatives available: but these are not practicable alternatives from an *individual's* point of view, since Red people have usually to abstain from School amusements and vice versa.[16] It is also difficult to contract out of the institutions ascribed to one on the basis of one's social position in the rural community; a Red young person who keeps out of the *intlombe* of his age-mates, or a mature Red man who keeps out of beer-drinks, is not acting in an approved manner.

Another field of greater institutional diversification in town is that of religion; at any rate the multiplicity of denominations and sects there contrasts strongly with the religious homogeneity of the Red (pagan) rural community, and even the School rural community will not have so many religious varieties available locally.

Religion, like recreation, serves to illustrate the well-known principle of associations playing a greater part in urban than in peasant life; but the variety of town life does not depend only on that. The whole style of life seems far more open to choice; the wide range of consumer goods available is reflected in the various alternative conventions of house-furnishing, dress, eating and so on. People have their different socially patterned ideas about the style and number of material possessions that is necessary.

It is because of this *intrinsic* diversity in town institutions—because diversity itself is institutionalized there, one might almost say—that we get the picture of some sort of class structure, as against the more nearly classless society of the rural community. The various class patterns of which one becomes aware in town are different syntheses or combinations built up out of the available alternative institutions. Thus 'better-class' people in the East London locations are inclined to select ballroom dancing and a careful style of dress in preference to jiving and a flashy style, and so forth, although the attributions are never quite rigid.

If living in town seems to call for more choosing between alternative institutions than living in the country, the migrant is, in practice, more squarely confronted with the opportunity (or the burden) of choice than the town-born person is, simply because he *is* a migrant—a new-comer, making his way in on his own, starting with a clean sheet. The town-born person is surrounded by kin, friends or seniors who have been responsible for his socialization since his birth and who have directed his choices by some kind of moral right. Through his inertia or through their moral pressure, he may have come to take a certain pattern of life more or less for granted. The migrant has left the moral pressure and the certainty behind him in the country.

[16] See chapter 2.

It is the migrant, for example, who has the widest actual liberty of choice in kinship and domestic habits—who can make up his mind to live with his wife in town, or apart from her; to keep his children with him or send them to the country; to live alone, or with other men; to select between the alternatives of *ukushweshwa* concubinage, 'visiting', and casual liaisons.[17] It is the migrant who has the choice of visiting his closest kin weekly or monthly or never. It is the migrant, compelled in any case to leave aside his rustic clothes, who chooses to model his appearance on the standards of this or that class or set. He chooses whether to go to church or not, whether to gamble or drink or use the recreational facilities. Town public opinion—if there is such a thing—does not impose on the migrant any particular set of choices. As far as that is concerned, he could build up his own synthesis at pleasure. He would be limited only by the inherent incompatibility between certain pairs of institutions: e.g. between public drinking and certain forms of Christian religion. Town, as such, does not confront him with an organized moral community, but only with various reference groups, which cannot actually wield sanctions.

THE ASPIRING AND THE SATISFIED

If the study of urbanization in East London has largely been concerned with migrants' choices it has necessarily touched on their aspirations too. Three rural Xhosa come into the location at the same time, in similar economic circumstances. One is hoping to learn 'civilized ways' and to strike roots in town. The second is only hoping to get back to his country life as fast as finances will allow. The third has conflicting aspirations, or ones which are not clear yet. But it is according to their aspirations that each must make his different choices: whether to go about with new friends or stick to old ones; whether to go home every month, or only at Christmas; whether to try a dance at the Peacock Hall this evening, or sit in his room drinking kaffir-beer with the boys from home; whether to turn a willing or a deaf ear to the street-corner revivalist talking about Christ's salvation; whether to take a woman of the town or a country-born woman as temporary sexual partner; whether to bring the wife into town, where to keep the children, what sort of clothes to wear, how to use the money that is left after paying for food and rent. These and a myriad other choices, smaller or greater, fit together to produce a picture of urbanization on the one hand, of resistance to urbanization on the other.

And what lies behind the aspirations that lie behind the choices? There must be assumed to be interplay of many factors; of all the factors which—in their total effect—cause the person to be either satisfied, or dissatisfied, with the life he was leading before he came to town. Some of these will be factors of personal temperament, hardly to be reached by sociological techniques. Some will have more objective content, such as the presence or absence of property rights in the country, the good or bad relations with kin at home; but even these will depend for their force upon the way in which the individual himself evaluates them. One man decides to stay in town for good because the homestead in the country seems too poor to feed extra mouths; another with just as poor a home, but determined to get back, scrapes and saves out of his town wages so that after thirty years in East London he can at last afford to be a peasant again.

In thinking of Xhosa migrants in East London as individuals with greater or

[17] Cf. chapter 16.

lesser propensities to become urbanized, one needs a pair of concepts which (for want of better names) may be called the aspiring and the satisfied. Here as elsewhere it seems useful to remember that there can be two kinds of referent, one cultural, the other structural. A man may be aspiring or satisfied either with regard to his social status or with regard to his culture, or both.

A migrant could be considered status-aspiring if, for example, he was a farm servant bitterly dissatisfied with the status of farm servant as such, and feeling that the best road of escape was to become a townsman. Women from the country often turned out to be status-aspiring, e.g. women who found the position of widow in the in-laws' homestead, or of unmarried mother still at the parental home, oppressive and humiliating, and preferred the relative independence of earning a living in town. Red peasants (men), as against the farm servants, were rarely found to be status-aspiring in a comparable sense. Though they might be ambitious to improve their lot by earning money—money to stock a kraal, to furnish bridewealth for a marriage, to support an old parent, to put by for old age—they were generally content with the status of peasant as such.

For the Xhosa, the argument of status is most apt to revolve around considerations of independence and personal dignity. The need to take orders from the White town employer, plus all the threatening incidents of location life—demands for permits, raids by the police, curfew and other restrictions—rub in the fact that the White man is master. In the peasant countryside the subordination of Black to White is far less obvious and can even be ignored. In the reserve (so runs the Xhosa idea) a man can be his own master, can live his own life, without depending on the willingness of some White man to pay him for his labour. In this way the high value set on independence and dignity leads many peasants to cling on to their country homes, and so to remain country-rooted indefinitely. But it may have the opposite effect on those who at home felt under-privileged or oppressed. This applies above all to the farm servants. Some farm servants want to stay in town for the same reason that the peasant wants to leave it, namely, to escape from a 'master'. The dependence on a master, in the farms, is directer and more inescapable than anything experienced in town.[18]

None of these forms of status aspiration or ambition, however, necessarily correlates with *cultural* aspiration. The embittered farm servant, the dissatisfied woman, the peasant trying to earn money for his homestead or his marriage, may be perfectly well satisfied with the institutions of their original *culture* as such. The point is specially clear with the farm servants. On the farm, these people are apt to be the most conservative of Red Xhosa, profoundly tradition-bound and unwilling to recognize any superiority in non-Red ways or ideas. It is the argument of status and only of status that brings them to consider settling permanently in town. A Red farm servant often seems to be pulled in opposite directions by considerations of status and of culture. He would like to become a townsman for status reasons but not for cultural reasons. He is willing to become town-rooted, he does not want to be urban-cultured.

The factor of cultural aspiration (or its absence) has an important bearing on the choices that people make when they get to town and are faced by the socio-economic ladder of location society—a ladder which has no real counterpart in the relatively undifferentiated rural community. The culture-aspiring

18 Cf. Chapter 10.

person may feel a desire to climb; the culture-satisfied person may stay contentedly at the bottom, to which his rustic habits and attitudes initially consign him. Usually, though not always, the culture-aspiring person turns out to be one of School—not Red—background.

Culture-aspiring people naturally find more scope in town than in the country, and may come with the deliberate intention of enjoying the opportunities for 'civilization' that will confront them there. But this will not always mean a break with the country home. Status considerations may pull the person back to the country. A peasant migrant may make conscious use of his time in town to become personally more sophisticated, or better-educated—to change, perhaps from a Red into a School man, or from a humble School to a civilized School man—and at the end of it all he may go back to the country, because only there can he count on a living and independence in old age.

CONCLUSION

The industrial and commercial expansion of East London has been particularly marked during and after the Second World War.[19] It has depended on a growing supply of Xhosa workers from the Ciskei and Transkei. Coming newly into town, these have had to rub shoulders with real townsmen, of several generations' standing, to whom rural Xhosa life is not even a memory. Even if he is not Red but School, the migrant must be aware of profound cultural differences between the townsman and himself, and of the opposition of sentiments and interests which exists between rustics and cockneys anywhere. The one has grown up in peasant Africa, the other in the slums of a modern industrial city.

Because the labour is migrant, and because current policy aims at keeping it so, this increasing social traffic has to be thought of as a two-way traffic. On the one hand, rural society has stood to be affected in that increasing numbers of its people have been spending parts of their lives in town. Town—it might be said—has become the third and most recent threat to traditional Xhosa ways (the first two threats having long been constituted by Church and School). The expansion of town carries the possibility of growing numbers of Xhosa learning to prefer the urban sort of life (even if not being able to live it permanently); of their going home and spreading its gospel through the countryside. On the other hand, the society of town itself must have been affected through these infusions of rustics, who now outnumber the town-born people there by about six to one.

It may be said that the answers to both questions—i.e. the effects of migration on rural society and on urban society respectively—are largely bound up in the question of how migrants behave in town, and whom they associate with. What kind of new social equipment the migrant carries home to the country, what kind of gospel he spreads there, will depend largely on the way he has lived in town and the relations he has formed there; on the manner in which he has been fitted into or on to the urban social structure for the period of his stay.[20]

[19] Cf. Houghton, D. H. (Ed.): *Economic Development in a Plural Society*.
[20] Of course the over-all effect of migration on the rural society also depends on the particular structure of that society, as has been shown especially by Schapera, I. (*Migrant Labour and Tribal Life*); Fortes, M. (*Culture Contact as a Dynamic Process*); Watson, W. (*Tribal Cohesion in a Money Economy*), and Gluckman, M. (Foreword to Watson's book).

2

The Rural Background: Red and School Xhosa

That two dramatically different sets of institutions exist within the Xhosa countryside is not hard to see. One becomes aware of it before a word has been spoken, through the glaring contrasts in dress and personal appearance. There are women—the Red women—who go about like a commercial photographer's dream of picturesque Africa, their arms and shoulders bare, their brightly ochred skirts swinging, their beads, brass ornaments and fanciful head-dresses adding still more colour. And there are others—the School women—who go in cotton print dresses of sober shades, with neat black head-dresses and heavy black shawls, looking as proper as mid-Victorian or as sombre as Moslem wives. To see a dance for Red youth and a 'concert' for School youth, a sacrifice in one homestead and a prayer-meeting in the next, or even a Red and a School family meal, is to realize that these belong to two different worlds, in spite of the language and the peasant background being one. The Red–School division, which has been partly documented for the Mpondo,[1] for some Transkeian peoples,[2] and also among the Zulu,[3] must here be discussed as a general feature of the Xhosa countryside from which nearly all East London migrants come.[4]

The Xhosa think of this division as bisecting their entire population. No figures are available for the over-all proportion of Red to School people among them, but it has been possible to make a special census of the peasant population of two parts of the Ciskei in 1958–9—the East London and King William's Town districts—thanks to the generous co-operation of the Bantu Commissioners concerned. Every headman in these districts was asked to state the numbers of Red and of School homesteads in his own location. The total results showed that the East London district peasants are 85 per cent Red (4,176 Red and 763 School homesteads), while those of King William's Town district are 45 per cent Red (5,145 Red and 6,320 School homesteads). The enumeration did not take account of the twenty or thirty thousand Xhosa

---

[1] Hunter, M.: *Reaction to Conquest*, e.g. pp. 6, 351, 377, 554.
[2] Hammond-Tooke, W. D., refers to it repeatedly in his ethnographic surveys of Transkeian and Ciskeian Districts, published as Ethnological Publications of the Department of Native Affairs, Union of South Africa: *The Tribes of Mount Frere District*, pp. 22, 23, referring to Bhaca; *The Tribes of Willowvale District*, 1956, pp. 59, 60, referring to Gcaleka; *The Tribes of Umtata District*, 1957, p. 54, referring to Thembu; *The Tribes of King William's Town District*, 1958, p. 58; cf. also his 'General Ethnographic Survey of the amaBhaca' (unpublished Ph.D. thesis), 1952, pp. 109–11.
[3] Vilakazi, A.: 'A Reserve from Within', article in *African Studies*, vol. 16, No. 2, 1957, pp. 93–101.
[4] I hope to publish separately a fuller account of my own findings on Ciskeian reserves.

farm servants living on White-owned land in the two districts; these are known to be predominantly Red.

Xhosa themselves, when asked to explain the Red–School opposition, do so in terms of cultural differentia: Red people do things this way while School people do them that way. 'The difference between a Red man and myself', said a young School countryman, 'is that I wear clothes like White people's, as expensive as I can afford, while he is satisfied with old clothes and lets his wife go about in a Red dress. After washing I smear vaseline on my face: he uses red ochre to look nice. He is illiterate whereas I can read and write. I want to educate my children, but he just wants to circumcise his boys so that he should have a daughter-in-law. A Red man attends sacrifices but I attend church. I pray for my sins when I am sick. He knows nothing about sins, and approaches a diviner for his illnesses. I was baptized, he was sacrificed for. I must not use any words that are obscene, but he uses any type of words, even in the presence of his elders, without fear of rebuke.'

Values, as well as institutions, differ profoundly. Exposed for several generations to mission and School influences, School Xhosa have internalized their own distinct ideas of what constitutes a good man or woman, or a successful life; what makes for shame or for honour; how children should be reared; how leisure should be enjoyed; how money should be earned and spent; what makes a home comfortable or a girl attractive; what words can be uttered in polite conversation. But to say that there are the two sets of cultural patterns, including two sets of values, does not show the full quality of the Red–School division. Before describing more fully the cultural differences—many of which are highly relevant to possible urbanization—something must be said about the structural aspect. This is at least equally important for understanding what happens when Red and School Xhosa are transplanted to East London.

Though in many country places Red and School peasants live side by side— occasionally even sharing the same homesteads—they have relatively few common fields of activity. United as they are in a common political structure, and intertwined by bonds of clanship, kinship, and neighbourhood, they carry on separate associational lives. They also manage to infuse into their relations a great deal of the spirit of in-group versus out-group. There are parts of Xhosa country where the Red-School 'problem' hardly arises, in a practical sense, because a whole rural location is either solidly Red or solidly School.[5] There are other places where a mixed location is subdivided geographically, the Red people congregated at one end and the School at the other. But where the population is really intermixed, Red homesteads alternating with School homesteads, the cleavage is kept up by a kind of self-imposed aloofness. The ideal is to have good neighbourly relations, to be on good terms, without associating much on a voluntary level. The housewives may do small neighbourly services for each other, the families may attend each other's celebrations of a birth, a wedding or a death—celebrations that will take Christian forms on one side, pagan forms on the other. But the children grow up separately, and conscious of the separation. On weekdays the School child goes to school; the Red child goes out herding, or helps with household tasks, or just roams around. On Sundays the School women go to church, while the Red house-

---

[5] For this reason it is not reflected in the *Keiskammahoek Rural Survey* of 1952 (cf. especially vol. III, *Social Structure*, by Wilson, Kaplan, Maki and Walton). The Keiskammahoek area is almost solidly School.

wives busy themselves at beer-drinks. At week-ends the Red youth of the neighbourhood are gathered together for the traditional entertainments called *intlombe* or *mtshotsho*; the Red girl after ochreing her face and arranging her beads will spend the whole night there singing and clapping, and her boy-friend dancing. But the School girl having put on a clean blouse and skirt sets out for the 'meeting' of the Church youth. While the School boys play football, the Red boys play at stick-fighting.

A sense of opposition is accepted as a normal part of the social atmosphere. The child learns from infancy a largely unflattering stereotype of the other group and its ways, and mutual teasing starts early. The Red child, in particular, may get used to hearing himself taunted. 'I used to be very shy of going about with School boys at my home in Mtyolo, even though I liked them, because they used to laugh at us for going naked, and call us "smeared ones", or "heathens" or "ochred ones".' Over and above this, a child learns that not-mixing is a moral issue. The neighbours may be decent people whom one must treat with politeness, but it is 'not good' to play too much with 'those rough Reds' or 'those half-White School children', as the case may be. The School parents are perhaps the most uniformly insistent: 'My parents used to forbid us to mix with the Red children of our own age at Tsomo as they said these would teach us wrong things which were against Christianity and education.' 'When I asked mother why she was so particular that I must not mix with Red boys, nor ever attend the boys' *imitshotsho*, she said that I could not be both School and Red, the two didn't go together.' But there are many diehard Red parents who are just as particular: 'My parents and many other Red parents at Kentani used to warn us not to play with School children because they would tell us about White people's things which might interest us too much, and make us *amatshipha* [absconders] when we grew up.'

The balance of relations is partly determined by the proportion of each kind of people in the local community. For example, in a location that is mainly Red it often comes about that the School boys may be tempted to attend the *imitshotsho*, or if pressure from their elders prevents this they may still 'play sticks' against Red boys, allowing the prestige ranking of boys to be measured by this standard. Conversely, where there is a large School majority the Red young people may be tempted to the School 'tea-meetings' and 'concerts'. However, that it is wrong to mix too much remains a moral principle throughout adult life. All the churches, in varying degrees, preach against participation in Red sacrifices and Red drinks and entertainments. (Some allow members to go to sacrifices as spectators, but they must not partake of the sacrificial meat.) 'In church we used to be told not to attend the Red sacrifices, *intlombe*, initiation dances, and so on, as they were said to be damnable. So we got scared of them.' 'A School man must not participate in any pagan performances which are condemned by the holy Scriptures.' 'Ancestor sacrifices are condemned as abominations before God in the books Genesis and Deuteronomy.'

At least one institution which both sections consider fundamental—namely male circumcision and initiation, around the age of 20—is nearly always carried out separately by each. In all-Red or all-School locations, the circumciser comes to operate on all the local candidates at once, or on smaller local groups. But in mixed locations he finishes one kind before starting the other. If a boy happens to be the only candidate of his own kind in the neighbourhood he will go a long way to join up with others, rather than be circumcised together with neighbours' boys of the opposite camp. There are separate seclusion huts, separate (and somewhat different) coming-out ceremonies.

The kinship and clan structure is formally common to Red and School alike. It is not uncommon for an individual to be able to count certain people of the 'other' kind among his kin or affines. But these interpersonal links leave the distinction between the two fundamental social categories unaffected. Above all, intermarriage is rare. (This significant fact has also been observed for the Mpondo, Bhaca and Thembu.[6]) 'Mixed' household groups can be met with occasionally, but they normally result from the conversion of one spouse (generally the wife) *after* marriage, or perhaps from the conversion of an adult son or daughter. It may be added that the tone of Red and of School family relations is apt to differ in practice, although in principle most School rural people still abide by the traditional patriarchal ideals of the Xhosa.

Politically, Red and School Xhosa are not differentiated. They are subject to the same overriding White authorities, and acknowledge the same tribal chiefs, appointed and paid by the Government. They attend the *inkundla* (locational meeting, under the headman) together. One might almost liken it to a federal structure, the two sections being united for over-all political purposes, divided for specific internal purposes.

In the eyes of the Xhosa themselves Red and School are essential and mutually exclusive reference groups. Everyone has to be assigned either to one or to the other. In field-work the question 'Are you Red or School?' never failed to draw an answer that was categorically clear. Any doubts referred to the individual's own allegiance (which might be changing) but not to the categories themselves: 'I am School now though I used to be Red'; 'I am Red but would like to become School'. Each reference group has its own ideal self-image stated in terms of cultural practice, and it is this ideal type that Xhosa informants sketch when they are asked to explain what it actually means to be Red or School. Each formula in terms of 'Red people do it this way, School people do it that way' has become more than a simple statement of fact: it has become a kind of manifesto of group spirit.

The four fields in which differences are considered critical are those of dress and externals, religion, education and 'manners'. In all these fields Xhosa tend to see a dichotomy, though in terms of actual behaviour the observer might often trace a continuum. The religious cleavage is stated as a Christian–pagan contrast, for example, but this idealizes what is practically a continuum, through the 'pagan–Christians' and the 'Christian–pagans'; through some Xhosa who do belong to churches but still sacrifice in the Xhosa manner; through some who never become full church members but attend services with some regularity; and so forth. It is the same with the schooling/no-schooling contrast: along this axis, between the illiterate who is the Red ideal type and the graduate who embodies the highest aspirations of School people, there lies all the range of those who have passed through more or fewer years of schooling, primary or secondary. Even in dress, there is a kind of continuum from the ochred blanket to the well-fitting lounge suit as normal week-day

---

[6] Hunter: *Reaction to Conquest*, pp. 351 and 357, states that (among the Pondo) 'School people and pagans tend to marry within their own groups'. Hammond-Tooke speaks of the Red and School categories among the Bhaca as being 'endogamous' ('General Ethnographic Survey of the amaBhaca', unpublished thesis, p. 110). He has made the same observation among the Thembu of Umtata district (verbal communication).

attire; that is, one can regard as intermediate the wearing of ear-rings and bead decorations together with jackets and trousers. But though one can trace these lines of continuity they do nothing to obscure the sharp cleavage between Red and School as reference groups. The two basic groups are able, as it were, to contain deviants or deviations to a considerable degree. *Just* a few years at school, *just* one smart jacket, are not conceived as making a Red man School, any more than *just* going to an occasional sacrifice makes a School man Red. By leaning towards one or two practices associated with the out-group, a man does not change his fundamental allegiance, but simply declares himself rather less correct within his own group. A real change of allegiance must be signified by change 'all along the line'.

There are, indeed, Xhosa words for people in transitional states. The existence of these terms, and the fact that they are nearly all opprobrious, does not belie but rather supports the assertion that only two reference groups are recognized as basic. School people can be heard to refer scornfully to *amagoba dyasi*, 'those who bend their coats', i.e. who turn up their too-long sleeves, or *amadopholo*, 'those who bind' their trousers at the ankles, implying a wish to dress in Western style but a painful ignorance of how it should be done. Or they will speak of *ombolo mbini*, a 'two-sided' person, or *ilulwane*, a 'bat' (which in the Xhosa way of thinking is 'both a mouse and a bird'). Both School and Red Xhosa will use the word *iguquka*, 'one who changes', to denote a new convert to Christianity as against a 'real' established School person. But none of these terms for people in transition will be applied by any individual to *himself*. They all carry the derogatory implication that one is trying to become recognized as School but has not achieved this, or not yet.

In the country it is difficult (though not impossible) to move from the Red to the School section without joining a church. But in town, as will be seen in a later chapter, a Red migrant may well detach himself from the Red people without attaching himself to School Christians. Changes in dress and manners, combined with neglect of typically Red institutions (such as sacrificing), may be enough to do the trick. In town, accordingly, a good deal is heard about the 'half-Reds' who—according to rustic standards—are 'neither one thing nor the other' and 'lack moral standards' of any sort, either Christian or pagan. They are thought of as a typically urban phenomenon.[7] If the 'half-Red' should ever return to the country for any length of time or settle there permanently, he will have to adapt himself again to the basic rural dichotomy, by allying himself with either the Red or the School section and modifying his habits accordingly.

SOME CULTURAL DIFFERENTIALS

(*a*) *Dress and externals*

Before the arrival of the White man the Xhosa had already brought the symbolic idiom of dress to a fine art. Many social distinctions besides that of sex—notably gradations of seniority and marital status—were formally reflected in outward insignia. When the missionaries imposed on their converts the necessity of dressing decently (by then White standards) the range of 'uniforms' was virtually doubled. Each section, the Red and the School, has had since then its own parallel but different ways of indicating status by dress. But the

[7] For similar phenomena among the Zulu cf. Vilakazi, A.: *A Reserve from Within*. See also chapter 11 below.

contrast which strikes the eye first and most forcibly is the over-all contrast between Red dress as a whole and School dress as a whole. Red dress in the country gives the clear effect of 'Native costume'; rural School dress varies from a drab kind of Victorian fashion to a passable version of current White styles. The general colour-scheme of a Red community—ochred figures moving on a background of green veld and blue sky—is something not easily to be forgotten; the School community looks completely different. The idea of announcing what one is through one's appearance has a strong hold on both sections.

Most Xhosa terms used to denote Red people are concerned with their distinctive appearance. The one referring to the ochre colouring—'Red people' (*abantu ababomvu*)—is the one which they themselves prefer. There are others more condescending or derogatory: 'smeared ones' (*amaqaba*), because they smear red or white clay on themselves; 'ochred ones' (*oonombola*); 'woolly ones' (*amavosi*), because they do not cut their hair short; 'those with blankets over their shoulders' (*amatyatha ngubo*), because the traditional man's dress is fastened like a toga; 'those who go naked' (*iintsukaze*), because of their unconcern about bodily exposure; 'those who wear a penis sheath' (*amagqishela*).

Today the rural Xhosa, generally speaking, needs to be able to dress himself or herself in three different manners: for every day, for best, and for going to town. The Red and School people meet these needs differently according to their (respectively) negative and positive evaluations of 'White people's things'. Among Red Xhosa, traditional Xhosa dress—or what is regarded as such—constitutes women's everyday wear, and is the best dress for both sexes. The Western-style dress necessary for going to town is not highly valued and is often diluted by the addition of some 'Xhosa' ornaments. For School people, on the other hand, the value of 'best' is carried by the most respectable or smartest Western-style clothes, while 'Xhosa' dress and ornaments are deliberately avoided altogether.

The Red women's dress is highly elaborated, being different for senior girls, junior girls, newly married wives, junior wives, senior wives; even pregnant and nursing mothers wear their special insignia. Swinging skirts cut out of 'Kaffir-cloth' are coloured brick-red, either by store-bought packet dyes or by rubbing with natural ochre: their length helps to indicate the wearer's age-status. An extra covering round the hips is often a striped hand towel, but the nursing mother wears a special 'apron'. A mature woman's head is always covered by a doek (Afrikaans, 'cloth')—a piece of material twisted up as a turban. Some ways of fixing doeks indicate the wearer's status or life-stage while others are fanciful patterns made up at will. Young girls need wear no doeks; they can also go with bare breasts.

Round a woman's neck may be an amulet or charm, perhaps made out of a cow's tail-hairs (the *ubulunga*), or a necklace specially for nursing mothers. If she has a suckling child her face will usually be marked with white clay. 'Best' dress is indicated by more abundant decoration of the skirt with black braid or pearl buttons. There are other items merely decorative that can be added at pleasure—rows of brass coils on the forearm, strings of coloured beads round the neck, wrist or ankle, cosmetic yellow or red colouring around the eyes, and scarifications on the stomach.

This catalogue serves to show that practically all the material elements of the 'Xhosa' dress today are store-bought: cloth, braid, towelling, beads, buttons, bangles, packet dyes. Some women have their skirts made up at a store by sewing-machine. The only element that has survived from the traditional past is the over-all design—a design originally carried out in skins and ochre and cowries. Yet the dress keeps the appearance and all the symbolic value of a 'tribal' costume.

Red women's 'dress for visiting town in', if they possess any, is normally kept locked away in a box; it is a cotton dress something like the daily dress of conservative School women. Still, even in this temporary attire the Red woman will visibly betray her Redness to a discerning eye. Her doek will be twisted in some characteristically Red way, or her bangles, beads or amulets will show out through the cotton.

The Red man also possesses some rough kind of European-style dress, which he wears at home in the country for everyday purposes, reserving his ochred 'Xhosa' clothes for best. He is normally seen in long trousers, a shirt, and some sort of jacket, usually ragged or patched. But he declares his redness by the detail: ear-rings, or bangles, or a traditional kind of tobacco-bag, or a woollen cap. To go to town he may invest in a 'proper' suit or jacket, without necessarily discarding these Red details. It is true that there are individual cases of Red men who take much pride in their 'town clothes'. Some Red migrants have been seen setting out from Tshabo, to catch the train back to work, looking like perfect urban gentlemen in neat lounge suits, one or two carrying leather attaché cases. But generally speaking the Red man regards urban-style dress as a working dress first and foremost. For him it has none of the social or emotional meaning of the real 'best' dress, which is a red-ochred blanket fastened over one shoulder, and a great amount of beadwork worn round the neck and ankles. That was how these same urban-looking migrants had turned out for the *intlombe*, during their week-end at home.

Since the man's best (i.e. 'traditional') dress appears only on special occasions, small Red details of the everyday dress are interpreted as national badges, like the red skirts of the womenfolk. A migrant interviewed in East London said that 'there was no need' for him to look exactly like a School man even when in town. 'I could easily if I wanted to, but I don't. I prefer to dress like a proper Red man.' He pointed out his woollen hat, ear-rings, leg-rings, bracelets, and tobacco pouch ('which my sweetheart made for me at home'). 'I do not want it to be doubted by anybody that I am Red.' Another said more simply: 'The reason why I do not dress neatly in the School way, is that I do not want to look like what I am not.'

If the Red Xhosa have managed to combine White-derived elements into a 'native' dress, the School Xhosa have combined them into a dress which is obviously of White-inspired type but (among the more conservative) obviously a 'folk' costume too. As in other parts of Africa the women's dress has been frozen in styles current among local Whites many years before. Conservative School women still wear the long skirts, long sleeves and high necks recommended by missionaries to a bygone generation. The material they prefer is what is known as German print—a cheap cotton with a dark-blue or dark-grey background. The sale of such prints by the yard is a major business of traders in these parts of the Cape. The School woman always wears a doek, which in her case is traditionally black; the fantastic shapes beloved by Red women are avoided. A large black alpaca shawl with a fringe—typical Victorian finery—is common for 'best'.

However, the influence of town is beginning to be seen more and more, and there are many districts where the younger School women break the uniformity of colours and silhouettes. As against the red-ochre uniformity on the one hand, and the German-print uniformity on the other, there may be ventures into anything that exists within current White fashion itself. Tighter clothes and more exposure of legs and arms may go with this 'modern' style, but the head-covering is still essential. Those who want to go one better than the old-fashioned black doek use a coloured doek.

As for men, the essential difference from the Red everyday dress is a negative one—the absence of the typically Red ornaments. A School man never has a traditional 'Red blanket' dress of his own, though it is not unknown to borrow one in order to attend a family sacrifice. His own best dress, for Sundays and special social occasions, is a lounge suit, shirt, tie, and socks and shoes.

A Red homestead, at least from inside, is as easy to identify on sight as Red people. However well-to-do the Red person may be, his hut is practically always a round one and contains little or no Western-style furniture. People sleep on the floor, and on rush mats, each wrapped in his or her blanket. There will rarely be a table or proper chairs: Red people squat on the floor to eat, or sit low on logs or simple home-made stools.

Many School people have given up the traditionally round hut in favour of the 'White people's style'—rectangular, with a division into two or more rooms. The School home is furnished as fully as means allow. Even the poorest will have an iron bed with a cheap mattress, or a rough table and a couple of straight-backed chairs, or an old dresser whereon crockery and glasses are set out in rows. Those who can afford it will go much further, with (sometimes) a real dining-room or bedroom suite, household linen and an abundance of decorated china. Sewing-machines are often to be seen.

(b) Schooling

It would be inaccurate nowadays to identify the Red people as 'illiterate' and the School people as 'school educated'. There is a growing number of Red people who can read and write, and an only slowly diminishing number of School people who are illiterate, or nearly so.[8]

But though some Red children are given the same amount of schooling as some School children the basic attitude towards it is different. It is by intention that most Red parents keep their children's schooling—if any—strictly limited. They undertake it, often enough, only as a sort of concession to these modern times in which it has proved useful or even necessary to have one literate individual around the home. Complete illiterates (it is also thought in most Red families) will be handicapped in the search for desirable jobs in town. These considerations have slightly softened what used to be an unyielding opposition to school education in any form, based on the feeling that school is a White institution inappropriate to a 'real Xhosa'. 'My father was very much against education. All educated people (he said) are half Xhosa and half

[8] Reader's one-in-ten survey of the East London Bantu population (who are mainly of country origin) indicates that only 1 per cent of Red males there claimed to have any secondary education as against about 13 per cent of non-Red males. The percentages of illiteracy were not recorded. About 20 per cent of Red males appear to have reached Stds. III–VI, as against about 60 per cent of non-Red males. (In this survey Reader's informants are not categorized as Red or School, but religious affiliations are shown. 'Ancestor Belief' and 'No Religion' may be taken to represent the Red population, and the various Christian denominations to represent the School plus urban population.)

White.' 'My father felt that education changes the African's way of thinking, and makes him think like a White man.'

The one child who in many Red families is selected to get a little schooling is prevented from staying on at school long enough to get 'spoilt'. The recollections of a number of female and male informants illustrate the motivations of Red parents in sending their children to school: 'My father sent me to school, but when I was doing Standard I he took me out of school again, saying I had had enough education. High education, said my father, had spoilt many a Xhosa child. The School girls, he said, hardly ever got married. He ordered me to strip off my school dress and put on my Red dress again. My brother and sister have never attended school and I simply joined them again in Red life.' 'All that my father wanted was that I should be able to read and write a Xhosa letter. One of the reasons that caused him to send me to school was that when he received a letter from anywhere he had to take it to some educated man to read for him. He disliked this, because the contents might be strictly private family matters.' 'It was my late father's desire to educate one of his children. The choice fell on me. I was considered the most suitable for education because I was said to have a quiet nature. I was obedient to my father and he was sure that education would not spoil me.' 'I attended school in the White kind of clothes, which my father bought for me in town. When I was doing Standard II my father took me away from school to work at home, and I became a Red boy once more.' 'It was on my mother's suggestion that I attended school in my Red costume, to show that I was still Red, that I had not abandoned our way of life.' (This is a rare bold gesture: nearly always, the pressure of the teacher or of the other children ensures that any child who attends school does so in 'proper' dress.)

But children who never go to school at all are still easily the largest category in the Red group. And most of those who go, having simply done their couple of years in primary school, are able to return to the Red way of life without much heart-searching. There remain just a few who carry on as far as the end of primary schooling (Standard V or VI). A 'highly educated' Red person (e.g. matriculant or university student) would be a contradiction in terms.

Some of these schooled Red people, especially among the few who have completed Standard V or VI, become inclined—as we shall see later—to break away from the Red way of life when once they come to town to work. Yet there are others who manage to remain good Reds in spite of their education: especially women who after being schooled have married Red husbands. The extent to which schooling actually threatens the Red way of life remains problematic. The more intelligent Red men in the country are devoting much thought to this very question. I remember, for instance, one occasion when I raised the subject with a group of councillors in the house of the Chief of the amaNdlambe. One Red elder, who so far had remained almost silent, suddenly rose to his feet and (trembling with emotion) declaimed: 'Listen to my words. Give school education to all our children, and there will be no Red people left in one generation.' With this he left the meeting. Yet there are many senior Red men who think otherwise: 'A man does not belong to the School people simply because he has been to school. He is still Red if he attends the dances, sacrifices, initiations, and other things which are for Red people.' Some Reds who have been to town feel that to be uneducated is to be 'blind': 'We shall only be able to fight against the oppressive laws of the White men through education.' But they are careful to add that they wish to remain 'real Xhosa'.

On the whole, it is clear, Red people are more welcoming to the school than to the church. A few Red men in the country now serve on the local school boards. Some parents take care to make the distinction between church and school quite clear to their children, especially in places where the schools have been closely connected with the local missions.

By contrast, the characteristic attitude of School people towards education is 'the higher the better'. Prestige is involved. Though many children of School families fail to get any schooling at all, or get very little, their parents usually seem apologetic and volunteer special explanations.

One reason why School people value schooling, no doubt, is that it may pave the way to better earnings. School people have a high regard for white-collar jobs, even if these mean staying semi-permanently in town. But the teacher, the clerk, the nurse, after all, are only the lucky few. Most School people can command jobs little or no better than those open to illiterates. They 'make nothing' out of their education in a material sense. In the last resort the appeal of school education to School people is, it seems, about as symbolic as is the appeal of illiteracy to Red people. The School people value education principally as a diacritic sign, a part of a way of life. They send their children to school because that is the done thing, because not sending them 'is a pity' or suggests that one is 'not civilized'. The more ambitious think that all children, girls as well as boys, ought to go on to high school 'if possible'.

(c) Christianity

A Xhosa asked about the basic differences between Red and School people will often put the acceptance or rejection of Christianity first of all: 'A Red person does not pray as I do.' 'I attend Church, I serve God, a Red person serves the ancestors.' This emphasis is natural since the acceptance of missionary teaching was what identified and separated off the School section at the beginning. But the sense in which School people are 'Christians' and Red people 'pagans', nowadays, needs defining.

As far as the Red section is concerned, it would be correct to say that the pagan Xhosa religion—the ancestor cult and all that goes with it—is still centrally important. In many a Red rural district the domestic ritual cycle is as intact, probably, as in any other part of Africa today. Sacrifice and divination are part of everyday life. Migrants go to much trouble and expense to get home for an important sacrifice, especially to 'bring home the father'. Diviners consulted by the sick and the worried are not slow to diagnose an offending of the spirits. Secure at the domestic level, the Xhosa ancestor cult has successfully survived the collapse of the political structure and the transformation of Xhosa tribal chiefs into mostly Christian employees of the Native Affairs Department.

A fair number of Red people, however, also dabble in superficial Christianity. The child who is selected to attend school, to become the reader in the family, sometimes goes to church at the same time, 'because father thought church was part of the school work'. When occasion arises at the house of a Christian neighbour, well-disposed Red people may be found happily taking part in hymn singing or even prayer. Red women (usually widows) who have reached middle age, sometimes start going to church. 'At this age we are no longer attracted by things which the church forbids.' Red people in trouble are some-times pleased to be prayed for by Christian neighbours at the same time as they are treated by diviners or herbalists. Christian prayers are often invited as a contribution to pagan funerals.

A Red person could not, however, become a church *member*, or be baptized, without crossing the line to the School section. Occasional attendance at, or even participation in, one or more Christian rites is one thing, but conversion is another. Converts to Christianity are called in Xhosa *amagqoboka*, 'people having a hole', which Red Xhosa explain in a derogatory sense—the converts were the quislings who originally 'opened a hole' in the Xhosa nation and let in the white-skinned enemy. Christians explaining the same word prefer to say that the 'hole' is where the heart has been pierced by the word of Christ.

Though all full Church members are School people, not all School people are full church members. But School people feel one ought to 'belong to' a church in some sense at least. In the country (though not necessarily in town), any School person when questioned can name 'his' church. It may be one of the many mission churches under White control, or it may be an independent or semi-independent Bantu church. Some attend church from genuinely religious motives; others frankly say that they go there 'as a place to while away the time and for seeing nice girls'. A person may attend 'his' church regularly, rarely, or never, but he will not easily drop the nominal affiliation. Many say that 'a man may not attend the church himself but he will encourage his wife and children to attend'. There is in fact a large surplus of women over men in the *active* membership of nearly all the churches. Church provides outlets—in organization, in entertainment, in emotional releases—which, it seems, Xhosa women enjoy all the more because of their subordinate position in the patriarchal Xhosa social structure.

But these Christians, including the full church members, are often also partly committed to the ancestor cult. Some admit it openly, others try to conceal it. 'I am a Christian who believes in God', said a Presbyterian from Tsomo, 'and I also have a belief that our ancestors look after us. But I believe God is the Almighty; while Red people believe in the ancestors most of all.' Though Christians are not supposed to attend or participate in pagan sacrifices, many of them do so. A considerable proportion, even of full church members, actually conduct sacrifices at their own homes. The statement, 'A Red person sacrifices to his ancestors but I do not', must be taken as the official standard rather than the literal truth.

RED, SCHOOL AND THE WHITE MAN

In short, the fields of behaviour where the differentiation is considered specially critical are the fields in which one section has been struggling to acquire Western cultural habits while the other has been struggling to keep them out. In Xhosa accounts the question of likeness or unlikeness to the White man is often mentioned as the touchstone. 'I am not one of those Xhosa who try to ape the White man; I only want to appear what I am, a real Xhosa.' And on the other side, 'What makes me different from Red people is that as a School man I have a taste for White people's things, such as nice clothes, and beds and tables'. The one is proud of his taste, and the other of his distaste.

The White people, the bearers of the new culture, were also the destroyers of Xhosa political independence in a series of fierce wars; today they are the entrenched dominant caste who (as Xhosa see it) 'keep the African down'. Hence the Red Xhosa see the School Xhosa as 'collaborators', and themselves as nationalist resisters. In the light of nineteenth-century political history and continued Black–White opposition, one is tempted to call the whole cultural issue a translation of an unresolved political conflict. This point will be further illustrated in the next chapter. For the Red people—as Gluckman says of the Zulu—opposition to the White group tends to go with a heightened resistance to White ways and appreciation of 'tribal' ones.[9]

As is well known, White men first appeared to the Xhosa in their two oddly assorted capacities—those of missionary and of conqueror—at the same time. The missionaries did not wait to come in until after soldiers and politicians had finished the work of conquest. They sometimes practically led the way, or worked *pari passu*. In fact the politicians and the missionaries were not always two separable categories here.

The memoirs of William Shaw, one of the earliest and most respected of east Cape missionaries, can be used for illustration. Shaw for instance records that after the war of 1819 the Colonial Government 'resolved to commence a Mission in the country of the Gaika [section of the Xhosa], on its own account, and to constitute the Missionaries at the same time its agents or representatives, making them the channel of all communications to and from the chief Gaika'.[10] The station thus set up, at Chumie, 'was a species of combined political and religious Mission . . . under the immediate instructions and control of Government'.[11] The principle of 'combined political and religious missions' was one which Shaw disliked, but he had to acknowledge that at many periods during the Kaffir Wars missionary effort paid handsome political dividends. He claimed as an achievement that 'Those who have embraced the Christian religion under the instruction of our Missionaries have almost without an exception proved *true and loyal* [Shaw's italics] to the British Government in times of war and rebellion'. Referring to the war of 1834–5, Shaw claims that 'the great influence which the Mission at this period exercised over Pato's tribe, kept them from joining their country-men in that war'.[12] There is a similar reference for the war of 1846–7.[13]

Another witness, Charles Brownlee, in a farewell to Christian followers, congratulated them on the fact that 'during the war of 1850 to 1853, one thousand five hundred of your converts, who refused to take any part in the war, fled with you to King William's Town. They were of great service to Government and to private individuals in many ways.'[14]

The Xhosa, it may be recalled, kept up warlike resistance for a whole century. They harassed soldiers and settlers until the ending of the 9th Kaffir War in 1877. And those whom the British found 'true and loyal' were by definition, from the Xhosa point of view, untrue and disloyal. The tendency to equate converts with traitors was therefore inevitable.

The Mfengu became the type of 'traitor' *par excellence*. Having fled from the Zulu wars in Natal, and being forced to accept a somewhat subordinate status in return for Xhosa protection, they gladly turned to the British as possible

[9] Gluckman, M.: *Analysis of a Social Situation in Zululand.*
[10] Shaw, William: *Story of My Mission*, p. 321.
[11] Ibid., p. 325.
[12] Ibid., p. 393.
[13] Ibid., p. 295 f.
[14] Brownlee, Charles: *Reminiscences of Kaffir Life and History*, p. 77.

deliverers, and proved easy material for the missionaries. In 1835, at the height of the 6th Kaffir War (for example), Mfengu Christians deliberately placed themselves under the protection of the British Government. 'The exodus of the Fingoes from the house of Kaffrarian [i.e. Xhosa] Bondage commenced under the immediate command of Colonel Somerset, on the 9th of May, 1835', writes Shaw. 'They moved along with the [British] troops; and the natives connected with the Mission stations of Butterworth, Clarkebury, and Morley, under their respective Missionaries, travelled with the Column.'[15]

Both the Mfengu and the converted Xhosa won rewards from the British at the expense of the Red Xhosa nationalists. According to the far-reaching peace terms imposed by Cathcart after the 1850–1 war, the Gaika (Ngqika) section of the Xhosa had to evacuate their lands in the Amatola mountains 'which had been their favourite residence for several generations ever since their forefathers arrived in that part of Southern Africa'. The evacuated country was partly filled up with Mfengu and partly with missionized Xhosa— groups under Kama, Sewane, and Pato 'which were to a considerable extent under the influence of the Missionaries and . . . in various ways had assisted the British forces'.[16]

The majority of Mfengu are School people of long standing. To this day the Xhosa will, if provoked, sneer at the Mfengu as traitors, while White people find Mfengu 'easier to get on with'. The reproach which attaches to the Mfengu in the eyes of Red Xhosa is only an extreme form of that which attaches to School people generally—that behind every one there lurks a White man. 'In my opinion the trouble with the School people is that they do not know what they are. They are sometimes Xhosa and sometimes White men. Yet they will never be White men.' 'The School people are like bats who are neither birds nor animals: they are neither Bantu nor White in their customs.' 'We Red people are as we were meant to be by Mdali, the Creator.' 'We Red people are suspicious of educated people because they are betrayers of their people, they betray other Natives to gain advantage from the White men.'[17]

The School section of the Xhosa recognize a common framework embracing themselves and White people. Caste barriers may divide, but the common aspiration towards 'civilization' unites. But Red people, in their tribal way, cannot recognize such a framework. They neither feel themselves to be members of one society together with the White man, nor recognize a common cultural goal. The Red Xhosa, accordingly, do not in any significant sense 'look up to' White people. They merely look across at them as over a gulf.

To the Red Xhosa the White people remain first and foremost a foreign 'tribe' who have fought and beaten the Xhosa; the principal political grievance is that they have continued to exploit their victory in a 'cruel' manner, per- petuating their own domination by force. 'The White men were rightly des- cribed by our forefathers as "helpers and killers" (iintsuza-mbulala). When they first came they pretended to be friendly. Our forefathers gave them amasi and meat. They gave our forefathers brandy and taught them to drink tea and coffee . . . with what result? They made themselves owners of the land by force. They came as harmless friends, but later when they had grown strong

---

[15] Shaw: *Story of my Mission*, p. 529.
[16] Ibid., p. 177.
[17] This runs parallel to Gluckman's observation in Zululand: 'this affiliation of the Christian Zulu to both colour-groups creates a certain tension between them and pagan Zulu, which is only partly resolved by the ties between them.' *Analysis of a Social Situation in Zululand*, p. 21.

enough they showed what they really were.' 'It is quite obvious that their intention is to keep us down and rule us for ever. They hate any man who preaches unity to us. Why were African leaders arrested [in the Treason case, 1957]? Because White men want Africans to live like children.' 'They are very cunning in that they do not allow us to keep any dangerous weapons. We are no better than women because of their denying us firearms.'

The happy past to which the Red person looks back is the period before the Kaffir Wars, when there were no White men; the dream he would entertain for his future is that of getting away from the White men again—away into Xhosa independence and dignity. Meanwhile no inconsistent cultural aspirations complicate the straightforward political opposition. 'There is nothing I like about them or their way of life. There can never be any peace between a Xhosa and *Umlungu* [the White man].' 'I do not like *Umlungu* because he does not like me, witness all the oppression we see.' 'If a man for no reason at all takes up a hostile attitude toward myself, then I cannot like him and I cannot see any good in him. He is my enemy.'

Thus the Red attitude towards White civilization, as such, remains detached if not hostile; above all there is no impulse to learn or imitate. It would not be worth the trading of one's independence. 'I have nothing in particular against the White way of life. As a different race from us their way of life ought to be different too. It is their bad attitude towards us that I don't like. I don't care how they live, if they don't offend others.' 'There is nothing that strikes me favourably about the White way of life. I am quite satisfied with the Xhosa way.'

While lip service is sometimes paid by Red people to the value of education, this is not for its own sake, not because it is thought to enable one to live a 'better' life, nor because such a life ranks higher in the prestige scale, but simply because the life of educated people as seen from a distance appears to be physically easier. 'Education is a good thing brought by White men. I have never been to school myself, but I know of boys who went through school and college, and who are now teachers, earning very good pay for very little work. I too would like that easy kind of life.'

The attitudes of School people hold a strong element of ambivalence and are naturally much more complex. The School person for whom the word 'civilization' sums up something desirable, and fit to be enjoyed by Black and White alike, cannot simply dismiss the White man with the formula 'I like nothing about him'. Instead of two distinct and hostile societies facing each other over a history of open war, the School person rather thinks in terms of a common society whose Black members are unjustly suppressed and prevented from rising to their proper level. When he complains of 'being kept down' he does not mean, like the Red man, that he would like to escape right away from the White people, but—on the contrary—that he would like to get closer to them. The 'cruelty' of White people is shown precisely in that they prevent a Xhosa from sharing in the fruits of their civilization. This aspect (as the next chapter will show) becomes particularly important to the School Xhosa when he migrates to town: for town is identified as 'the place of White people' and the home of 'civilization'.

In the situation of conquest and domination each section feels that its own reaction has been the 'right' one on principle. The fact that the School section has humbled itself before the White man still seems to the Red people to be the unforgivable mistake—the almost criminal mistake—which no civilized advantage can ever outweigh. The 'never-the-twain-shall-meet' attitude of Red Xhosa towards White people is as uncompromising as that of many White South Africans towards Natives. They are as dogmatic about the fundamental opposition and the folly of attempted compromise. But the School people can reply that not they, but the Reds, are the real 'betrayers of the nation'. 'Reds do nothing for the advance of the African people. They have no programme for the future.' 'They are not helping us educated people in struggling for freedom by action.' 'What is the use of sticking to old and useless ways of tradition which have no longer any meaning?' 'Their conservatism is only obstinacy. They will not advance any good reasons for not becoming educated.' 'They are simply too lazy to think and too lazy to be responsible men.'

The co-existence of two factions in a tribe—traditionalists on the one hand, mission or school products on the other—is of course nothing unusual in Africa, but in most places it seems to be thought that time and opportunity are the main factors controlling the spread of Westernization; that the question is not whether, but how soon, the tribal culture and identity will be submerged. In the case of the Xhosa, time and opportunity have been more lavishly available than almost anywhere else in Africa. There are no 'untouched' Xhosa. The schools and the missions, the converted brethren and neighbours, the near-by White settlements, towns and seaports, as well as the White administrators, have been there for five generations. With all this, however, instead of School ways progressively ousting Red ways, it looks almost as if the Red–School cleavage has crystallized for the present, and has been accepted by Xhosa on both sides as an enduring social feature.

The factor mainly responsible for this situation is the extraordinarily strong positive conservatism of the Red people. Time, which should have been on the School side, has failed, in so far as the will to resist the 'new' ways has become the standard of Red morality.

Research has not yet had much to say about the historical 'splitting of the Xhosa nation' in its sociological aspects. It is clear that by the second generation after the arrival of the missionaries—i.e. by the last third of the nineteenth century—a large proportion of Xhosa had already joined the School camp, but how this affected Xhosa society can only be surmised. Even the relation between the siting of early missions and the present geographical distribution of School people is far from simple. In some places where there is an old-established mission centre, e.g. Peelton or Mount Coke, a strong School community can be found nowadays. But in others, e.g. St. Matthews, solid Red areas are close at hand. In Tshabo—an old-established though minor station—Red homesteads begin almost next door to the Mission Church.

The nearness of town does not seem to erode Red communities either. The reserves nearest to East London are all predominantly Red (see map at end of the book). The National Road running from East London to Port Elizabeth passes through some of the most conservative Red areas. High-tension wires carrying electricity to White people's homes and factories run above the heads of peasants, ochre-clad, daubed with clay, making their way to an ancestor-sacrifice or a dancing party. At least in the Ciskei, School ways do not seem to have made much further headway in this generation.

Until recently there have been no pressing land-tenure reasons why anyone should have to stay in a Red community if he would rather move to a neighbourhood of converts. Nor is the continued existence of the Reds simply a reflection of exclusiveness on the School side. It would not be a hard task for any Red person to carry out the simple changes that would place him in the School camp. To join a church, to attend a primary school or send his children to school, to adopt a more European-looking dress as his normal dress, and to rearrange his home similarly, needs no great financial effort. More important, becoming School clearly does not mean joining an *élite* either moral, religious, or intellectual, since the School Xhosa today are not an exclusive 'Christian community' in the sense of a group of church devotees insisting on difficult Christian standards. The Red group does not automatically get the reversion of backsliders who for failure to conform to Christian precepts are expelled from their churches. Such people will either join another church (which, owing to the multiplicity of competing sects, is never difficult) or simply remain 'School people who do not belong to a church'.

In any case, the danger of expulsion from one's church seems less acute for Xhosa Christians than for Christians in some other parts of Africa where the churches are younger and perhaps more ambitious. The elsewhere familiar figure of the backslider, finally and decisively cast out for relapsing into polygamy, or drink, is comparatively rare in the major churches here. The temptation to polygamy is negligible; few Xhosa today, even among the Reds, have more than one wife. Extra-marital relations constitute a greater enemy of Christian sex morality: but in this respect, as also in regard to drink, the average Xhosa Christian takes care to conceal his sins from church authorities. Thus discretion has become an important notion for School Xhosa.

Far from being the accommodating residual group—the refuge of defeated Christians—the Red Xhosa are in fact rather an exclusive group themselves. It may require more of a moral effort to remain Red, nowadays, than to become School. It requires a conscious determination to resist a great many pressures and influences—the proselytizing church eager for new Christians, the school board eager for more pupils, the lure of (possibly) higher wages, and the ubiquitous appeal of 'White people's things' displayed in the country trading store or the shops in town. The idea of backsliding would seem to fit the lapsed Red as well as, if not better than, the lapsed Christian. The convert to a church, the willing school-goer, and the 'dressed-up person', can be seen from the Red viewpoint—backsliders falling away from the ways of the ancestors.

MUTUAL CRITICISMS AND THEIR BASIS

One of the pressures which Red Xhosa have to resist is a rather sneering attitude towards their 'uncivilized pagan ways'. School people, on whom the ideals conveyed by the word 'civilized' have taken hold, are not afraid of saying that Reds are gross and uncouth as well as that they are 'holding back the nation' by their senseless clinging to 'out-of-date things'.

Red people, in some respects, are sensitive to these criticisms. They freely admit that School people are much 'smarter'. They may have to ask School neighbours to write and read letters for them. They are ready to respect a high position attained through education and will receive a teacher (for example) with more deference than is due to his age. Some Red people said that in a really well-equipped School home they not only feel awkward; they feel humble. They are sensitive to the ridicule implied in nicknames like 'smeared ones' and 'woolly ones'. Red people may call themselves *amaqaba*, but they hate to hear School people doing the same.

School people are openly and loudly critical about the 'dirty habits' of Red people. Their lack of 'shame' (i.e. of concern about bodily exposure) is always reproved. 'The nakedness of Red people is intolerable.' 'They are shameless about exposing every part of their bodies publicly.' 'The nakedness of Red men at *umdudo* [pagan marriage ceremony] is a thing I hate. The bride-groom wears nothing but a small skin on the back.' 'They like to go naked in the presence of children. That shows you what kind of thoughts they have.' 'When Red people are awakened from sleep by someone, they leave their blankets down on the mat and open the door naked.' This characteristically different attitude to nakedness gives the School people one of their hostile nicknames for the Reds (*iintsukaze*).

Lack of shame about excreta is also censured. 'Reds are careless about their children's faeces, encouraging dogs to clear it up.' Dirty and unhygienic habits have become a stereotyped reproach (not entirely justified). 'A Red woman will be spitting even while another person is eating.' 'You can see the mothers searching for lice on the children's heads.' 'They have no respect for cleanliness. You will see them taking a dirty child to a doctor.' 'School men would not care to fall in love with Red women, because they are very dirty and hardly ever wash their bodies after sleeping with men.' 'The Reds do wash their bodies but they do not wash their clothes as often as we do.' It must be admitted that clothes-washing is more of a business for the Red women, since they wear no underclothes (in the modern sense) under their heavy ochred outer garments.

Another complaint is that Red people embarrass School people by their 'careless talk', 'their filthy language'. 'Red children are not taught to avoid gross expressions.' 'I hear Red men and women constantly using shocking language in public. They will freely exchange in the open air words of a most obscene nature.' 'Judged by Christian standards their language is very bad.' What this boils down to is that the School people have a higher standard of verbal prudery, particularly in regard to sex and excreta. Some charitable School people are ready to explain that the 'bad language' of the Red section is only their manner of calling a spade a spade. 'The Reds just say freely what-ever they think.' 'When they use that sort of language it is not really meant to be obscene.' 'They talk in that rough way because they are raw people, they have no conscience about it.' But however this may be, mixing with Red people offers constant threats to the School sense of shame.[18]

The way in which the Red Xhosa have held their own, in face of proselytizing White people and critical School brethren, amply demonstrates the strength of their inward moral pressure towards conservatism. But it reflects something else too—a doubt as to how much could really be gained by turning School. Generally speaking, Red people do not think the School way of life is really profitable in a worldly sense. Nor do they see any other unequivocal attractions in it. The Red person—in the country—is still able to feel that he has the best of things himself.

[18] The lack of *verbal* prudery, among Reds, must not be confused with general sexual permissiveness. On the contrary it goes hand in hand with a firm demand for sexual restraint (except in permitted situations). The contrast is sometimes ironic, as in a Red man's complaint that town-style dancing is 'immodest': 'If a man and woman stand together all night, what is to prevent them getting sexually excited? Why invite temptation? When you stay close to a woman like that, your penis gets very stiff. It seems to know that the vagina is near.'

To begin with economics, the School peasant's advantages, such as they are, fail to impress the Red peasant. For although School families may be in a position to earn more cash (as wages), they will also spend more. A high level of spending does not count as economic success in the eyes of Red peasants. What impresses them is a high level of saving and investment in 'worth-while things'. Here the School section falls down. The Xhosa as a whole are a poor peasantry but it is the School people who are kept the poorer—in the sense of capital—by the call to spend money on dress and other 'frills'. What Brownlee wrote nearly a century ago is as true in substance today as it was then: 'To the missionaries mainly we owe the great revenue now derived from the native trade. . . . The Red kaffir by a continuous service of six years, and receiving ten shillings a month or a cow in the year, would at the end of that time be a wealthy man, possessed of twenty head of cattle; whereas the Christian, who would require the whole of that amount for the purchase of clothing for himself and his family, would at the end of the same period be no better off than when he entered service.'[19]

School people hardly deny that it is the Red family who often stand the better chance of achieving economic success, peasant-style; the thriving flocks and herds, and the hoard of banknotes. 'Red people', said School informants, 'are rich, they have lots of money hidden away.' 'They have money, because they stick to very simple clothing, and do not spend so much on dress as we do.' Red Xhosa themselves are even more eloquent about this, because it is one of the points that seem to offer hope for the future of their way of life. 'The School people are always hungry for money because they waste it for little things, copied from the White man; the School people just cannot keep money.' 'I know that many School people, when they go to town, become shy of coming home to the country again. They have no money to buy stock, which is the sign of a good man. They have wasted their money on clothes, furniture and good food.' 'The School people have nice homes built in the White people's way, but if anyone wants to go to borrow money from the rich people in Nxaruni, he would not find it among the School people, but he would easily get it among the Reds.' 'The other day I was cheated by a School man. When I challenged him he only said to me, "You have had a good lesson. You amaqaba have lots of money. You people don't use your money. You just keep it in the box till it rots." I kept quiet, I only said, "The School people only think in terms of money and cheating".' 'I know from experience that the School people are paupers. They waste their money. What is this thing hanging from their necks—the tie—what is it for, really?'

The only counter-argument heard from School people is that 'Reds themselves are wasting lots of money in unnecessary sacrifices, and ceremonies which are based on superstition, instead of investing for the future of their children'.

Just as both sections agree about the rather better success of Reds in the peasant economy, so both agree about their better success in managing the primary kinship relations. The School section both pities itself and is pitied for a breakdown of family morality. In the Red section the patria potestas still flourishes. In the School section, due perhaps to Christian influences, there are signs of a war between the patriarchal aspirations of the men on the one hand and the independent tendencies of their wives, sons and daughters on the other.

[19] Brownlee, Charles: Reminiscences of Kaffir Life and History, p. 373.

School women and children have, as it were, not been emancipated, but have got out of hand. The negative results are that it is more often the School parent whose daughters have illegitimate children, or whose sons abscond.

Red people express pride in their own 'sense of relationship' and 'sense of respect'; conversely they take a poor view of School family standards, especially censuring the lack of respect for seniors. 'We Red people keep a very close relationship and contact with our relatives. You need only compare a sacrifice, and all the relatives attending it, with a Christian wedding, where you find just the close friends of the kraal.' (This is not necessarily true.) 'We can see that the School people do not respect their elders, they do not look after their parents well, and do not obey them.' 'I heard of a young School girl who was pregnant and was scolded by her father and mother. She answered back all the time they were speaking. In the end she said to her mother, "I can't understand why you are so excited, just because I have taken after you. You got married because my father had made you pregnant. Maybe my boy friend will marry me too." A Red girl would never dare to answer her parents back when she had done such a shameful thing.' 'School young wives [abatshakazi] have no respect for the parents-in-law. They do not stay under them. They call them "dilapidated old things". With us Red people, the newly married hardly answer back to their parents-in-law, and they hardly ever build their own homesteads soon after marriage.' 'Recently a much-respected School man sent away his stepmother without a penny, after the burial of his father. A person who has been a wife to your father you must respect as a mother. Red people would not have the heart to just send her away.' 'A rich School man passed away in East London not long ago. Only a week after his burial his sons were in court about their father's estate. Our Red custom is that the eldest son takes custody, and that for at least one year the bereaved people must stay without touching anything that belonged to the deceased. Not to observe this is very shameful.'

Almost any School informant would be just as ready to acknowledge that Red families are better at managing their women and children, and in the kinship field generally. They envy this greater success without, apparently, knowing how to set about copying it. 'Those Reds have a strong sense of relationship.' 'Red women have a great respect for their menfolk.' 'The Red husbands never forget to send something [i.e. meat] to their wives during sacrifices.' 'They have respect for their families and people of their clan.' 'The senior group of young people, among the Reds, have great respect for their parents.' 'They are better than us at holding their children. I think it must be because they have a better way of training their children, as compared with us School people, particularly where girls are concerned.'

A sore point for School people is the apparently much higher proportion of School girls who have illegitimate babies. Among School people in the Keiskammahoek area, some years ago, nearly half the mothers were found to have borne one or more illegitimate children.[20] Whereas School Xhosa are so accustomed to these births that they will usually be ready to enumerate their own or their daughters' or sisters' illegitimate children in a quite matter-of-fact way, Red people regard a young girl's pregnancy as a calamity, and will put up an impenetrable smokescreen rather than divulge to an outsider the history of a child of dubious parentage. For this reason among others no comparative

[20] Wilson, Kaplan, Maki and Walton: *Keiskammahoek Rural Survey*, vol. III, *Social Structure*, p. 99.

figures are adduced here, but all field-work impressions supported the general Xhosa view. There must indeed be solid foundation for it. In these small rural face-to-face communities, where everyone knows everyone's business, illegitimate pregnancies could not occur on a large scale among Red young girls without general awareness of the fact.

It must be emphasized that this refers to *girls*. Many unmarried mothers are also found among Reds, and are openly acknowledged, but they are mostly not girl mothers: they belong to the distinct category of *amankazana*.[21] The real offence, in Red eyes, is for a *young marriageable* girl to become pregnant, and the Red–School difference on which both sides insist is in the sexual morality and behaviour of these girls. It is related to the fact that the traditional Xhosa technique of *ukumetsha* (external intercourse) is still practised by young people on the Red side but has been mostly abandoned on the School side.[22]

Red Xhosa distrust the sexual morality of both School girls and School youths. 'The School girls do not seem to be careful about pregnancy. I have heard them say that a certain girl (unmarried) must be barren because she had never had a baby. They seem to make a show of pregnancy. I would be afraid of being made pregnant by a young man who has not been given my father's consent to have me as his wife.' 'School people's love affairs are kept private and this encourages their women to have many lovers.' 'School boys have intercourse with girls who have had babies, whereas we believe that a girl who has had a baby will have a bad effect on a boy.' And School people have a correspondingly high opinion of the sexual morality of Red 'children' as compared with their own. 'They are strong-charactered in sexual matters.' 'Red children do not have so many pregnancies when they are under their parents.' 'Red young people are open with their love affairs.' 'The love affairs of a Red boy are known even by his mother. But I [a School man], before I was 20, was even afraid to let my sisters know.'

The tendency to secrecy which characterizes School love affairs is seen by both sections as one of the distinguishing features of the whole School culture. Next to sexual matters it applies specially to drinking and smoking. The Red man prides himself that he is able to enjoy his pleasures openly while the School man can only taste them secretly. Secrecy augurs deceitfulness: 'The School people are a very wrong lot, because they do things secretly under the cloak of religion.' 'School people are crooks and liars.' 'School people are liars who twist the language.' 'School people are very cunning, and very treacherous.'

The School man, as a rule, himself appreciates the Red 'openness': 'Red people are not secret about things. They drink openly, they smoke openly, while we Christians smuggle these things in and pretend to be good.' 'Reds don't drink secretly and pretend to be non-drinkers merely to please people.' 'The Reds are kind and they are open. If there is anything they don't understand they ask plainly.' 'Red people are true. They never bluff to suit the occasion.' 'The Reds are straightforward people. If they quarrel with one they say it out then and there.'

Thrift and prosperity, respect for seniors, authority of parents, chastity of girls, openness and honesty—these, then, are points where the Red Xhosa's own good opinion of themselves is reinforced by the concurrence of the School section. Conversely the spendthrift, the defeated father, the sexually incontinent

[21] See chapter 15.
[22] See chapter 16.

girl or youth, and the hypocrite, are all stereotypes which the School section sadly recognize as their own. In each case there is, perhaps, enough objective reality behind the stereotype to make plausible the Red Xhosa's lack of enthusiasm for being 'converted'. Of course the School way of life has its own positive qualities, its wider horizons, its windows on to a richer civilization. It brings greater issues into view. These the Red people fail to appreciate. They see little except that it has become poorer in some solid family virtues, while also losing many of the joyful potentialities of the Red way.

CONCLUSION

One word might be used to sum up the basic distinction between the Red and School Xhosa today, namely the word 'tribal'. These two categories of Xhosa are not equally 'tribal', in whichever sense we interpret the word.

As Mitchell has argued, 'tribalism' can be an important category of inter-action between groups or persons within a wider system, without necessarily implying the survival of a 'tribal structure' inside any one group itself.[23] Both Watson and Epstein, again, have stressed that the African today can behave in many situations primarily as a tribesman and yet be simultaneously involved in other sets of relations which cut right across tribal lines.[24] These two arguments have something in common in that they both stress a distinction between what might roughly be called a narrower and wider, or an internal and external, system of relations. Mitchell's paper, however, is largely con-cerned with fields of behaviour where tribal categories play a notable part in the wider system; while Epstein is concerned partly with these, but largely with situations where tribalism no longer counts in the wider system.

In this study we have to consider the Red and School Xhosa in a context where the use of tribes as categories in the wider system cannot be observed in terms of real social interactions. We have been considering Red and School Xhosa—that is—in their own countryside, where they live close to or among each other, but largely sealed off from actual contact with non-Xhosa tribes;[25] and we shall go on to consider them in East London where the same applies. Nevertheless, some basis exists for adjudging the Red Xhosa to be more 'tribally' minded, even in terms of a wider system, than the School Xhosa are. This basis can be found in the distinctive Red and School attitudes towards 'foreign ways'.

For the Red Xhosa, the identity of the tribe in contraposition to other tribes is largely a matter of two things: a distinctive history and a distinctive, exclusive way of life. They are conscious of a common past (largely expressed in terms of descent from common ancestors) but also of a common present duty to maintain the distinctive way of life which history and the ancestors have sanctioned for them and them alone. In their eyes the Red way of life, handed down from the ancestors, is proper for the tribe, the whole tribe and none but the tribe. The tribe has had (they might say) the misfortune of being conquered and politically dominated by foreigners (i.e. White people), but as long as it preserves its distinctive way of life it preserves its own soul. This preservation is threatened whenever Xhosa people take over elements from the cultures of

[23] Mitchell, J. C.: *The Kalela Dance*, p. 30.
[24] Epstein, A. L.: *Politics in an Urban African Community*, p. 232. Watson, V.: *Tribal Cohesion in a Money Economy*, p. 6.
[25] By non-Xhosa is meant, of course, not belonging to the Xhosa-speaking group of tribes, as defined on p. 3.

foreign peoples, including, of course, the White people. Thus the 'tribalism' of the Red Xhosa takes the form of opposing any blurring of intertribal boundaries on the cultural level; any participation in the institutions of non-Xhosa, or sharing of common institutions with them. This opposition is moral in that it is referred to the ancestors. There results the ideal of exact coincidence between the bounds of group, culture and history, which may be called essentially 'tribal'.

The very institutions which distinguish School from Red Xhosa are those of a supra-tribal or supra-national tendency. School education, church and civilized habits are shared or meant to be shared, in principle, by any ethnic group which it is possible to encounter in the hotch-potch of South Africa; they even stretch into the world beyond. Basically, this is just why the Red Xhosa do not like them and abstain from co-operating with School people in their context. Red people 'do not want to get mixed up' in things that tend to obscure the distinction between a 'real Xhosa' and a foreigner. School people are, in some respects, quite glad to do so. For instance, the ordinary School Xhosa would be quite happy to admit that as between a highly educated member of his own 'tribe' and a highly educated Swazi, a good deal must exist in common. The higher a man rises on the School ladder of education and 'civilization', the more he must find himself like other educated and civilized people, of whatever ethnic group. Behind the immediate Xhosa reference group, therefore, there lies for School people a more comprehensive reference group embracing 'civilized Africans' or even 'all civilized South Africans'. A Red Xhosa on the other hand not only realizes that he has much less in common with people of other tribes; he is glad to have it so.

Of course, the difference must not be overstressed to the extent of suggesting that School people have no particular 'Xhosa loyalties'. For many purposes, no doubt, the School person if plunged into a multi-tribal setting would still regard tribal categories as fundamentally important. But there is still a real contrast with the Red person who remains permanently and for *all* purposes bound to his own (Red) people, in the sense that only among them can he find and practise a way of life which he believes to be morally right for himself. The School Xhosa has got outside these limitations in so far as he could theoretically conceive of the possibility of living a morally right kind of life among non-Xhosa.

3

'The Place of White Men': The East London Setting

THE XHOSA AND THE TOWNS

The Xhosa do not generally use the current English or Afrikaans names of the towns known to them, but speak of Johannesburg as *Erawutini*, King William's Town as *Iqonce*, and so on. Their name for East London (which, like some other of the 'vernacular' names, probably has an Afrikaans root) is *Emonti* (cf. *mond*, river mouth). People in the hinterland often refer to it as just 'town': *edolophini* (from Afrikaans *dorp*) is most commonly used by Red people, and *tawuni* (from English 'town') by the more educated.

Although *Emonti* is a familiar feature well within the Xhosa social horizon, and although more than half its population are Xhosa, country people speak of it as of an alien land. Whether regretfully or not, they imply that it cannot belong to them nor they to it: 'Town is not for us.' 'Town is not a place of the Xhosa. The homes of Xhosa are in the country.' Towns as such are, as it were, the territory of a foreign tribe—the White people. To go there is to submit to being 'under the White man' or at least 'at the place of White men', *Emlungwini*. Sometimes a Xhosa who wants to contrast the national dignity of his own people with the 'dependence' of the Coloureds will point out that 'the *Amalawu* [Coloureds] are not a nation since the only homes they have are in the towns of the White people'. The town life is the insecure life.[1]

When country-towns first began to form in the eastern Cape soon after the start of White settlement, the Xhosa can have felt little in common with them. The Xhosa had no village tradition themselves, their own pattern being one of dispersed homesteads. Needless to say, the strangeness of town in rustic eyes has been immensely increased since then by the advances of technology. But the main reasons today for looking on the towns as 'places of the White man' are administrative and political. Official policy has long been tending to take the line that the towns are integral parts of White South Africa while the proper homeland of the Bantu is in the reserves. That there exists a large town-settled Bantu population, with no present 'home' elsewhere, cannot be overlooked; but current policy aims at keeping these people on a permanently different administrative footing from White citizens. Even the town-born have no such entrenched rights in town as their fellow-Bantu have in the reserves. In the words of the Secretary of the Department of Bantu Administration and Development, Dr. W. W. M. Eiselen, 'the magnitude of the movement into the cities during the last few decades has created [an] erroneous impression,

[1] For a similar feeling of insecurity in town among a Northern Rhodesian people (in spite of the different legal and administrative framework) cf. Watson, W.: *Tribal Cohesion in a Money Economy*, p. 8.

and there was, under the previous government, a tendency to accept this redistribution of the Bantu population as both inevitable and permanent. The present government [however] has . . . [reaffirmed] that the Bantu have no claim to permanency in the European areas, that they are in these areas as workers, and can therefore own no real estate and can claim no political rights outside the Bantu reserves.' 'All the Bantu have their permanent homes in the Reserves.'[2]

A feature which East London shares with other South African towns, unlike some of those elsewhere in Africa, is that the respective numbers of White and non-White population are not very unequal. The 1951 census gave the White population as 43,400 and the Bantu as 39,700. Reader's investigation in 1955 indicated that the then true figure for the Bantu was considerably larger, probably in the region of 66,000.[3] Like most modern towns in Africa and all those in South Africa, East London follows the segregated pattern of 'colonial' towns (as defined by Balandier)[4] with a sharp division between the White and non-White quarters ('town' and 'Native location'). The pattern of residential segregation is strongly backed by current official policy (e.g. the Group Areas Act of 1950), but it goes back far into the past: in fact to the beginning of East London's history a hundred years ago. From the start (as Reader has described) the Xhosa labour force was segregated outside the bounds of the town proper, and was subjected to intensive controls, as befitted members of a tribe still intermittently at war with the White settlers.[5]

East London's one main and two other (much smaller) Native locations, administered by or on behalf of the Municipality, exist for the purpose of dormitories, enabling a Xhosa labour force to be kept available for White employers while remaining otherwise out of sight of White homes and social centres. One can think of two linked unequal towns, the White town owning and controlling the Black one, which it has called into being largely for its own convenience. Except for the narrowly limited relations of employment and administration—which are intrinsically unequal, and foster a sense of opposed rather than common interests—each half lives mainly in and for itself.

Since segregation drastically limits the effectiveness of East London as a milieu for culture contact in the ordinary (White–Black) sense, perhaps its operations should be briefly recalled here. The City Council is an all-White body in which location people have no direct representation or voice. National political parties, with a few numerically insignificant exceptions, are not open to both races; voting rights are not shared. The slender parliamentary representation of South Africa's Bantu population, by means of four White members, is now being abolished. The recognized trade unions exclude the Bantu, and although it is not illegal for Bantu to form so-called unions of their own, these have no official standing, recognition or powers. (Native workers are catered for instead by labour boards appointed by the Minister of Labour.) Politics apart, in East London there are practically no common associations, or none which in effect serve to bring Black and White citizens together. Location people and White people are expected to worship in separate churches. Numbers of Xhosa belong to 'Independent' churches which have no White

[2] 'Harmonious Multi-Community Development', article in *Optima*, March 1959.
[3] Reader, D. H: *The Black Man's Portion*, chapter 3.
[4] Article in *Social Implications of Industrialisation and Urbanisation in Africa South of the Sahara*, Unesco, 1956, pp. 497–8.
[5] Reader, D. H., op. cit., chapter 2.

connexions. Schools for the two races are quite separate, and fall under different Government departments; Xhosa schools have almost entirely Xhosa staffs. Interpersonal bonds cannot easily develop. As intermarriage is ruled out by law and custom, the Black and White sections are never linked by any recognized bonds of kinship; and as sociable mixing is customarily discouraged with almost equal emphasis, friendships remain practically out of the question too. The average Xhosa's knowledge of English and/or Afrikaans—the usual media of communication between Black and White—remains superficial, while few White East Londoners know Xhosa even of the 'kitchen-kaffir' brand. Even the casual contacts are diminished by segregatory rules, many with a legal backing. Cafés, hotels and places of amusement are strictly segregated. One field which does remain open for casual interaction is that of commerce: there is no colour bar to prevent the Xhosa from spending money in a White shop in town, nor (for that matter) hiring the services of a White professional man.

It follows that situations in which the whole East London population (White and non-White) can be said to act or respond in common are exceptionally rare. Those events which do appear to evoke some common response, e.g. horse races and football matches, involve only trivial interests. Common symbols are few and far between. There is a profound absence of communication. Most of this could, no doubt, be said with nearly as much truth of many modern towns in Africa, but so far South Africa remains the part of the continent where the segregation principle has the strongest tradition.

It is true that many Black faces can be seen within the confines of the White town. This could not be otherwise, for most White enterprises have Black employees and most White households Black servants. About 15,000 domestic servants 'live in' in the White areas, being provided with separate rooms in the backyards of their employers' houses. About 22,000 more Black people are at work in White areas during the day, but housed in the location at night. (Both figures are Reader's calculations for 1955.) There is also a flow of casual shoppers or sightseers into the White business areas. Still, even for a living-in domestic servant, the location community is and must remain the context of personal ties (kinship, marriage, friendship), and of participation in associations; life in these senses is lived at week-ends or after working hours. The purposes for which the Xhosa enters the White town are formal and instrumental. Curfew laws emphasize his exclusion: no location resident is allowed in White parts of town between 11 p.m. and 5 a.m. without a special pass.

Moreover, while Black faces are common enough in town, the appearance of a White face in the locations is so uncommon as to draw stares. It is not only that casual visits are officially discouraged—at present no White person may enter the location without an official permit—but that occasion and inclination are lacking. The average White East Londoner may spend a lifetime in the city of his birth without ever setting foot in its locations; nor (probably) will he even wish to, for the locations repel by their poverty and squalor, and unnerve by their dense concentration of 'the other' race.

THE LOCATIONS

The East London locations are by no means pleasant places. There is an acute ecological contrast between location and town—a contrast seen almost daily by the Xhosa going out to work, though rarely or never by the White resident. Overcrowding and bad housing are the basic problems at present. In 1955, according to Reader's calculations, the locations altogether held 51,340 Bantu, of whom 44,610 lived in the East Bank Location (officially known as 'Duncan Village') at a density of 141 to the acre; 5,660 in the West Bank Location at 166·5 to the acre; and 1,070 in the Cambridge Location at 85·6 to the acre. These densities should be compared with the average of 12 persons per acre calculated for the White residential parts of town.[6]

Only about a fifth[7] of location people were living in municipal houses, where minimum standards are enforced. The other four-fifths dwelt in shanty-town conditions. East London is unusual in the degree to which municipal building has lagged behind need; from 1928 to 1940, for example, none was undertaken at all. For the most part the Xhosa here, without sufficient skill or capital, were left for years to run up their own housing and also to provide for most of the new arrivals from the country, including the flood of migrants who streamed in during the wartime and post-war expansion. A few private houses are comparable with municipal houses in terms of decent construction. The rest are mainly wretched shacks and shanties, and they are bursting at the seams. In 1955 the 2,089 private houses in the East and West Bank Locations held an average of nearly 20 persons per house.[8]

While it is generally admitted that East London's locations are handicapped by a bad inheritance of municipal indecision, inaction and neglect, great changes are now being planned. The Municipality has recently announced an ambitious scheme for an entirely new location (or 'satellite town'), ultimately capable of accommodating 100,000 or 125,000 people as tenants in 25,000 municipal houses. It is to be built some little way from the White town (as is now favoured in South Africa) in the vacant area between Umdanzani and Fort Jackson, 15 miles out. As the new location grows the existing locations are to be pulled down gradually. However, the new location still exists only on paper, and meanwhile the present ones will have to continue in existence for an indefinite time. The official tendency is to count on another thirty years at least; the Council itself is to start on the building of 1,000 new houses there, with thirty-year leases.

Meanwhile the existing municipal and privately owned housing sections look very different from each other. On the one hand are straight rows of uniform cottages—in the case of the Duncan Village brick-built, and each standing in its own little garden; and on the other, a chaos of wood-and-iron structures (i.e. of corrugated iron sheets on a beam framework), jostling at irregular intervals and angles. For many years the people of East Bank Location have given unofficial names to different parts of the private housing area, some of which express their sentiments directly or ironically. Thus one slummy area to the east of the Ngcambanga stream is sardonically christened 'New Brighton', after the big municipal housing district in Port Elizabeth; another is Tulandivile ('Keep quiet, I have understood!'). On the other side of the stream, besides Maxambeni ('sugar pockets', supposed to have been concealed there when stolen), is Gomorra, the 'place of sin'. In the shanty areas generally, the original demarcation of plots—there are no fences—has been obscured by the proliferation of shacks, sheds and outbuildings behind and between the main

[6] Reader, D. H., op. cit., chapter 3.
[7] Reader, D. H., op. cit., chapter 7: Population histograms (ignoring the 'persons away').
[8] Ibid. The figures have been adjusted to discount the 'persons away'. By including these Reader arrives at a figure of 49,600 persons in private housing, or 24 per house.

houses. Most of the buildings are shabby and many are decrepit. The wood-and-iron construction is both cheap and easy, and adequate to the mild climate, but without proper painting there is nothing to conceal its ugliness. In its total effect the main East London location is a slum with a rural overtone as its only redeeming feature. Fowls peck around the unpaved streets; streams run in wet weather. People are often outside in the sun. The bush and green hills are not far away.

In accordance with general South African policy no location people enjoy freehold rights. The land belongs to the Municipality; in the case of a privately owned house 15s. a month must be paid for a site permit. Some occupiers of municipal houses have been able to buy their houses, but not the sites. The authorities have always retained the right to alter the boundaries of the location or have it removed from one site to another. Several such moves have occurred in the past. With the announcement of the scheme for the new location, the sense of insecurity, always more or less chronic in the old locations, has been heightened, and it is beginning to be said that nobody wants to build decently there now, or to spend money on improvements. (The Native Affairs Committee of the Municipality has recommended that in future, if location people apply for permission to build shops or rebuild houses in materials other than wood-and-iron, they shall bear the responsibility of removing the improvements at their own cost, should the lease be terminated or the location pulled down.)

In general the being without freehold rights is quoted by the people as a major reason for feeling unsafe in town, or not really at home there. 'In town there is no security because we have no homes of our own. The whole life here is on lease.' 'We have no real property here. That is why town is a place for White people.'

A Xhosa wishing to buy a wood-and-iron property in the location may need £100, £200 or more. This is considered a worth-while investment, for by letting or subletting the owner can hope to make several pounds a month, at the rate of something like £1 per room. Migrants normally turn to wood-and-iron houses in search of their lodgings, for occupiers of municipal houses are mostly forbidden to sublet. Reader found that 1,760 private house sites had registered lodgers, as against 390 municipal houses.[9] (There is also a large population of unregistered and therefore illegal lodgers, not allowed for in these figures.) For many years accommodation has been at a premium, and it is safe to say that every location wood-and-iron house, in whatever condition it may be, is let as a profit-making concern, if not rackrented. Practically every room must serve as combined eating, sleeping, cooking, and living-quarters for a household group, so that one thinks in terms of persons per room rather than per house—still less of rooms per household.[10] Private landlords have tended to build on more and more rooms, either as lean-tos or separately, on purpose for letting. This practice is now officially forbidden, but properties of eight, ten or more rooms have already become common. Usually the additions are progressively worse built and worse cared for. While the main house may continue to present quite a decent façade, therefore, it is only by going into the yard behind that one can get an idea of the actual squalor. Some added-on 'rooms' are no more than dark, crazy, leaking little sheds.

9 Ibid.
10 Ibid.

The interiors of the houses vary more than the exteriors. One dingy wood-and-iron structure, inside, may be furnished and arranged with bourgeois comfort and sufficiency, while another will present a real slum interior. But since most location people are poor the general standard is poor likewise, and the migrant is doing well if his chosen lodging is no worse than shabby and sparsely equipped. He is likely to find the room largely filled by an iron bed (one altogether, not one for each occupant), which may have on it a cheap mattress and blanket, or perhaps only some old sacks; the other important feature is a 'kitchen corner', usually comprising a table on which stand a pail and dipper for water, a small primus stove, and a few cheap metal or crockery utensils. Sometimes the walls are papered with newspaper or magazine pages. Water supply consists of an occasional tap along the street from which the household requirements are collected in paraffin tins or buckets. While municipal houses have their own lavatories, the whole wood-and-iron housing area of the East Bank depends on communal latrine blocks (36 blocks, comprising 361 W.C. pans, or about one W.C. per hundred head of population in 1958). Early-morning queues of people waiting to relieve themselves are a daily sight in the location. Some residents prefer the simpler method of throwing their slops out of the house.

Inside, the usual method of lighting is a small paraffin lamp; outside, street lights are few and far between, and the terrors of the night—in the form of thugs and tsotsis—can be very real. The visible contrast at night might be interpreted symbolically, the White town being picked out in the bright lights of a modern city while the location area is visible only as a faint murky glow.

Except for the main thoroughfares the location streets, being unpaved, tend to become morasses in wet weather and dust-bowls in drought. Inside, on the whole, lodgings are kept fairly decently. Fleas, bugs, and rats may be much in evidence, but visible dirt is not common. Rural Xhosa lay great emphasis on cleanliness indoors and it may be that by carrying the same values over into their urban life they save the location many an epidemic. Nevertheless the incidence of disease is high and the death-rate among infants and children extremely high by Western standards. Infant mortality is estimated by Reader at about 375 per 1,000 live births.[11]

Few Xhosa are satisfied with the living conditions they encounter in East London. A hundred and seventy-five, including migrants and others,[12] were asked (among other questions) to say what they 'like about life in town' and what they 'dislike about life in town'. Few would give more than one positive answer under the first head, and often enough this one answer was 'money'. 'The only thing I like here is the money.' 'We are only here for money, otherwise we would rather stay in the country.' Under the second heading, on the other hand, complaints in abundance would pour forth, sometimes prefaced by the remark 'I hate everything in town', or 'I dislike the whole life here'. Many referred to the physical conditions, the shortage of accommodation, 'crowding together', 'queuing at the lavatories', 'filth in the streets', 'no proper homes'.

[11] Reader, D. H., op. cit., chapter 3.
[12] These 175 respondents included Red, School and farm migrants and also townspeople. Both sexes and all ages were represented. Other questions put to them included: 'In which way would you not like to become like a White person?'; and 'What further characteristics of the White people would you wish to acquire?' Most of the remarks quoted here and throughout the present chapter are taken from their responses. The remainder are spontaneous remarks which were recorded in various contexts during field-work.

Secondly there were complaints about the social atmosphere, though these were balanced by appreciative comments from a number of people; this is an aspect which will be discussed in a later chapter. But there was another and very frequent type of complaint whose sources must be analysed here— the complaint of being 'too much under the White man' and 'oppressed by the White man's bad laws'. The migrant spoke of being 'kept down', 'exploited' and 'treated without respect' by White men. In other words he complained of the operations of the political, economic, and social colour bars as found in town: they affect him differently from colour bars in the country. Town gives the average Xhosa his first intense experience of Black–White relations on the group or political level.

BLACK AND WHITE: THE EXPERIENCE OF SUBORDINATION

In the reserves White people occur as isolated figures with whom the Xhosa has (mainly) commercial dealings on an interpersonal basis. The White storekeeper, a well-known figure in almost every rural locality, supplies the local Xhosa with consumer goods and buys up their cash-crops. (The phrase 'we deal at the same store' is sometimes used by Xhosa to express the fact of living in one country area.) In some parts there are White farmers near by, with whom livestock can be traded. To the Xhosa peasantry around them the only real significance of these various White individuals, apart from trading, is that they may act as links with the outside world in emergency: may be asked to drive an injured Xhosa to the nearest hospital, or telephone an urgent message to some relative working in town. White people are much more important, of course, in the life of the farm servant, being the 'Masters' on whom everything depends, but this relation is still a personal, patriarchal one. Neither the peasant nor the farm servant meets White people *en masse*; nor has either much experience of White authorities in everyday life.

Coming to town the Xhosa not only finds White people in a far greater numerical concentration than he has experienced before, but is kept much more sharply aware of legal and social differences between 'them' and 'us'. He is meeting them on 'their' ground instead of his own, and not for a minute can he doubt where the political and economic mastery lies. The twin cities of East London may confront each other across a chasm, but even in the locations where White people are so little in evidence physically, life is dominated by their unseen presence. There is much regimenting of the Xhosa and little or no legitimate outlet for objection. When voicing their sense of being 'under the White man' in town, the Xhosa often added a comment that the White man 'deliberately' arranges things to 'keep us down', out of 'cruelty' or 'jealousy'. 'We are oppressed by bad laws in town. It is very wrong, in our Xhosa way of thinking, to ill-treat people who are under your rule or "in your kraal", for we Xhosa are governed by conscience, and we believe that such ill-treatment invites bad luck. But White people are not governed by any conscience.' 'It is clear from the laws they make for us that they want to keep us down for ever and that they take advantage of our weak position.' 'Generally, you can see from their laws that they are very anti-Black. Many of them would be very pleased if slavery could be revived.' 'If one reads about things done to Native employees it seems clear that the White people want to oppress us to extinction.' It will be shown that influx control and other urban regulations are regularly fitted into this concept.

To set these ideas in their context one must consider the economic, social and administrative systems as experienced in town. To start with economics: the pay and conditions of the Xhosa worker are, as a rule, determined by the White employer single-handed. As was said, there is no collective bargaining for Bantu workers in South Africa; the present official machinery of labour boards is not 'representative' of them in the trade-union sense. Almost always the workers are competing for jobs, not the employers for labour. The level of wages remains low. Few employers in East London would deny that higher wages for the Xhosa are desirable on welfare grounds (though they would emphasize that major increases cannot be justified on direct economic grounds because of the low productivity of the labour). In general the Xhosa have little or no access to 'better' or higher-paid types of job in East London—not only because they lack the skills, but because of legal or conventional barriers reserving these occupations for the White, Asiatic, or Coloured groups. A few Xhosa who have obtained the necessary qualifications are employed as teachers, clerks, or nurses, but not necessarily (or usually) at the same salaries as White people earn in similar capacities. For the jobs which are offered to the Xhosa in industry and commerce, the median wage for males (according to Reader's calculation) was 58s. per week in 1955.[13] Houghton's calculation is that 64 per cent of incomes (in a sample of 1,349 male Xhosa in East London in 1955–6) fell between 45s. and 60s. weekly.[14] At current prices the ordinary Xhosa in East London lives, as has usually been the case, in inescapable poverty.

Years ago East London witnessed a struggle of Bantu workers for higher wages, organized by Clements Kadalie and his Industrial and Commercial Workers Union (I.C.U.). Orders for a general strike were given in 1930, and were effective in that 86 per cent of the workers are said to have come out. But Kadalie was arrested and eventually called it off. There was no gain in wages on the whole and a number of strikers lost their jobs. Kadalie's prestige diminished as a result and did not recover during the ensuing years of general economic depression.[15] Trade unionism has never again played an important part among Bantu workers there. Today, even what might be called the worker's last freedom—the freedom to walk out if one is dissatisfied—has been rendered largely academic for the migrants. Influx control regulations (which will be discussed below) tend to tie them to their jobs.

It is impossible for the Xhosa to remain unaware of the much higher standard of living on the other side of the colour line. Houghton calculates that in East London the incomes of White males 'are approximately five times those of urban Native males'.[16] In the popular stereotype held by the Xhosa it is not unlikely that the differences appear even greater than they are. Bitter comments are often heard. 'We have the same needs as other sections of the population, and have to buy at the same prices. It is very unjust that their pay is so much higher.' 'A White man with Standard 6 gets the same as a Native graduate.' 'In case of injury the Native worker will be compensated with a few pounds, but a White man for the same injury gets hundreds. Why is this?'

[13] Reader, D. H., op. cit., chapter 4.

[14] In Houghton, D. H. (Ed.): *Economic Development in a Plural Society*, chapter 8.

[15] For an account of the 1930 strike see Hunter, M.: *Reaction to Conquest*, p. 568 ff.; for Kadalie's organization and its activities in 1932, ibid., p. 463. Kadalie and his movement are discussed at length in Roux, E.: *Time Longer than Rope*, chapters XV and XVI.

[16] *Economic Development in a Plural Society*, chapter 8.

Many remarks about low wages were couched in terms of deliberate exploitation. 'Natives are underpaid by White men on purpose so that they may be kept low in status and not become rich like White men.' 'A White man is so jealous and selfish, he does not want his Native employees to prosper.' 'White men want something for nothing.' 'Where money is concerned they have no conscience at all, and no consideration for the financial needs of dependent people.' 'White men are pleased to suck the blood of other people when young and kick them off when old and unable to work. If you break your health in his employment he has finished with you.'

In migrants' eyes town is 'the place for money', and money is liked; but it is also 'the place where money is everything', and this aspect is disliked, principally because it means a strong sense of dependence upon the White people who pay the wages. The fictional or highly optimistic notion that 'in the country one can live without money' retains a great deal of emotional power as a symbol of independence. 'There is no security here as there is in the country where you can carry on without money.' In the country the farm servant is pitied or despised for being 'always at the White man's beck and call': in town this becomes the common lot. Older Xhosa men in particular seemed to find something inherently repugnant in being 'ordered and bullied' to do 'another man's work'. 'I prefer country life, for there you work for no man, you are your own master.' 'If not for the money I would never come here to be ruled by the White man.' Farm servants, used to the 'indignities' of employment, sometimes expressed appreciation of town for the very reason that 'You are finished with the boss after working hours'. 'It is not like the farm where the boss or missus may call on you any time of day or night to do anything for them.' Some of these economic attitudes are further discussed in chapter 8.

Outside the economic field, the incidents of the social colour bar become daily experience for men who, in the country, had had little occasion to meet them. 'White people do not want us to stay with them in town. Why? Have we got an offensive smell? What about our womenfolk who do their domestic work?' 'Their children will call an old Native man "boy", will spit on Natives walking on pavements in town and sometimes throw stones at them.' 'One is not keen to go and worship in a White church for one can be kicked out like a dog.' Common incidents of town life breed deep resentment: 'White people humiliate a Native father in the presence of his family. A father has to take to his heels on the approach of the police, if his lodger's permit has not been renewed: "Run, *tata*, run!" his children shout.' 'A young White foreman will clap a much older Native on the face with his open hand or kick him on the buttocks.' 'I hate the foolish names the White people give us. A White employer will call you "boy" making no difference between father and son. Or he will call you "Jim" though that is not your real name.'

In Xhosa eyes White people present a solid front, united at least on the policy of 'keeping the Native down'. 'They are all united against the Africans.' 'It is futile to report a White man to White officials because they will not believe you.' 'In a dispute the magistrate will decide by the colour of skin, not the evidence. "Mr. X cannot tell a lie", the official will say in judging a case between him and a Native.' 'They are united and do not want Natives to know their secrets.' 'If you annoy a White farmer in Komgha, another White person in East London who hears about it feels annoyed too, for they are all united.' 'In the presence of Xhosa the White men do not say to each other "you Boer", "you English", or "you are German" and "you are Jewish".'

It ought to be added that pleasant relations at an individual level are not ruled out. Just as a White employer may complain about 'the Natives' in the abstract but speak warmly of a particular Native employee, so a Xhosa may fulminate against 'White people's cruelty' or 'arrogance' in general but praise a given employer or foreman as being kind and understanding. At work a kind of camaraderie sometimes develops; the foreman cracks a joke with his 'boys', the housewife receives confidences from her 'girl'. However, personal appreciation, where it does occur, has to be contained within the limits of the formal master-servant relation. It cannot spread or deepen into any other kind of relation. Its practical significance for our purposes is merely in showing that the political consciousness has not reached the out-and-out militant stage, when it would be difficult or impossible to admit having any positive feelings towards anyone in the opposite camp.

The stereotype of White men as oppressors is only partially offset by a stereotype of their humanity to helpless people—the sick, the aged, the destitute, young children. 'It is good about the White people that they have built a place where old men and women are cared for; some of our own old people in the reserves are left in horrible conditions.' 'Last year I saw a long queue of our old people and cripples receiving Christmas gifts at the Peacock Hall. I praise the White man for this.' 'In cases of illness they forget the colour bar. The White trader will telephone for the ambulance or carry the patient to hospital in his own car. This I admire and I wish our people could copy this spirit of help first and pay afterwards.' 'They are sympathetic to an old widow like me.'

But even more important than the economic or social aspects of being 'under the White man' in town are the political and administrative aspects. A detailed account of location administration would be out of place in this book, but it seems necessary to outline two matters in which the contrast with Xhosa rural life is particularly striking: namely the distribution of authority and the content or incidence of regulation.

(a) The distribution of authority

Though the Xhosa are under White rule everywhere, in the reserves the White authorities—the 'Office' with the Native Commissioner and his staff, and the South African Police—seem not only literally but figuratively miles away. White authority is mostly mediated to the peasant Xhosa through interposed Xhosa authorities, notably the location headmen. A rural location also has its *inkundla*, an open moot under the chairmanship of the headman, where every adult male is entitled to speak his opinion. It is true that Xhosa even in the country complain that their chiefs, headmen, or *inkundla* are effectively hamstrung by the White authorities in the background; that 'the White people do not want us to have a final say in anything', that 'they rule us in our own country', and that 'even a chief may be punished by White men like an ordinary person'. But in town, with the at least temporary failure of representative institutions there, the domination is felt to be much more direct, and much more oppressive.

The urban locations are administered from the location office where a location manager is in charge. This senior White official is appointed and paid by the East London Municipality (which, as has been said, is an all-White body, elected by the White ratepayers only). A committee of the Municipal Council deals with location matters and reports on them to the Council. The location manager is instructed partly by the Council and partly by the central Government (the Union's Department of Bantu Administration and Development). It is not in being White-controlled that the urban administration differs from that of the rural reserve, but in coming far closer to the Xhosa personally. Everyone in the East London locations is bound to know 'the office' (*offisi*, or *Loyiti*, the latter name derived from that of Lloyds Building). Most, especially if they are migrants, need to have fairly frequent dealings with it. Together with the South African Police, the Municipal Police, and the Magistrate's Court, 'the office' constitutes in Xhosa eyes the seat of all effective power in East London. There the White man or his agent appears to seal a Black man's fate by nothing more than a rubber stamp or a slip of paper.

In principle the East London locations also have their system of Black representatives comprising advisory board, vigilance association and (more recently) ward headman. But such powers as these have are merely consultative, and (moreover) were not being effectively exercised at the time of this investigation.

East London established its Location Advisory Board in 1921, and was thus one of the first South African towns to do so. One of its leading Board members, Mr. R. H. Godlo, was prominent for many years in the National Congress of Advisory Boards. The Board was designed to consist of a nominated White chairman and secretary and nine non-White members (three of these being Council nominees and six elected), and to co-operate with the White authorities in a purely consultative capacity. There was a long-standing feeling in the locations that it ought to be given more real power (as Hunter mentions in 1932).[17] Nevertheless it provided scope for democratic processes, in which the migrants too could participate, if not in large numbers then at least with spirit. The public were allowed to attend its monthly meetings at the Peacock Hall, and every year there were the elections of the six members, at which anyone with a lodger's permit was entitled to vote. These elections were often fought in a lively manner. Conservative candidates, candidates representing I.C.U. policies, and those representing the African National Congress or its Youth League, made their bids for the voters' favour at various times.

The body which actually played a greater part in location political life was the (non-statutory) Vigilance Association, called in Xhosa *Iliso Lomzi*, 'the eye of the community'. A migrant with a lodger's permit could join, and vote for the executive committee. The Association held regular meetings at the Peacock Hall—which used to be crowded out by hundreds of participants—and was generally recognized as representing 'the people's views'. As one informant put it, it used to function 'exactly like an *inkundla* in the country, with the difference that not only men could attend, but the old and young of both sexes'. The Vigilance Association worked in loose conjunction with the Advisory Board, in that the six elected Board members used to report back to the Association, and receive a sort of mandate from it to put the people's views at the next Board meeting.

Shortly after the war both these institutions went into a phase of dramatic decline, from which they have not recovered. In about 1947 a new and rather

---

17 Hunter, M.: *Reaction to Conquest*, p. 469.

radical local branch of the A.N.C., together with the A.N.C. Youth League began to divert the attention of politically minded location people from the 'futile palavers with the Municipality' which, it could be claimed, never seemed to bring about any real improvement of conditions. By 1952 public support of the Vigilance Association had declined to the point where some observers described it as dead.

After the 1952 riots[18] the A.N.C. and the Youth League suffered the paralysis affecting the location's political institutions generally, but the Youth League had recovered enough by 1955 to be able to turn its attention to the local political bodies, which it now quickly 'conquered'. (For a long time the leading spirits in both of them had been older and rather conservative location residents.) What made this clean sweep possible was not public unanimity so much as public apathy. East London is well known in A.N.C. circles as a place where the movement has been relatively weak. The unopposed stand of six A.N.C. supporters at the Advisory Board election of 1955 could have been an opportunity for a big gesture of public support, but the total poll was only 287 — 1 or 2 per cent of the electorate. The Board as such, too, had lost its interest for most location people. 'Years ago a Board member could speak his mind without fear, but nowadays you are not safe in speaking against any motion that has been proposed by the authorities.' (Compare the comment made by a White member of the local administration, that the elected members 'have not the guts to stand up and say something or demand something'.) As for the Vigilance Association, reckoned practically dead already, the new leadership hastened the process of disintegration. Older and influential men withdrew from the Association complaining that the new men were far too inexperienced. Accusations against 'these youngsters, elected only by youngsters' were violent and often grotesque. 'Each of them has rendered pregnant no fewer than three girls. Who can accept such men as leaders and representatives of the people?'

In 1957 the administration introduced a revised constitution for the Advisory Board, in terms of which elections are now triennial instead of annual, and voting rights are confined to householders (i.e. registered tenants of municipal houses or registered occupiers of sites in the shack area). This means that most migrants have lost the vote. They are no longer directly represented vis-à-vis the White authorities.

The new constitution has also introduced a system of headmen. Instead of the location voters being on one common roll there is a new division into six constituencies (wards), and each ward representative elected to the Board is *ex officio* designated headman of his ward. In this capacity he has a local committee of ten 'elders' to assist him, elected by ward people at a meeting under his chairmanship. The headmen are not necessarily close to the *migrant* population. In fact the whole scheme (it was hoped) would bring the 'solid' or conservative element of town-rooted people more to the fore in local government.

It is still too early to judge how the new system will work, even judged as a representative organ for the town-settled people. The poll of the new (restricted) electorate in 1957 was still very low in percentage terms. This might be an index of the effectiveness of the national A.N.C. policy of boycotting local elections, dating from 1957. Or it might only reflect a continued popular lack of interest. But among the migrants, at any rate, it seems to be widely felt that

[18] These are briefly described in Reader, op. cit., chapter 2.

the new Board-members-cum-headmen do not really 'represent the people'. A popular version is that they are six 'position-seekers' who profited by the A.N.C. boycott of elections to get themselves in unopposed. The location public, meanwhile, are no longer admitted to the monthly meetings of the Advisory Board.

In this way the headman system has started under a considerable handicap. The hearing of petty cases is one of the functions assigned to them under the new arrangement (jurisdiction in all more serious matters remaining with the magistrate's court), but 'one never sees anyone taking his difficulties to these headmen, because they are not favoured by the people'. As for their not representing the people's voice, 'Each ward takes a different line of its own on certain matters, there being no mother-body, as the Vigilance Association used to be'. 'Headmen and committees never come together to hear our voice.' Above all the headmen are suspected of being on the 'wrong' side: 'They have to repeat to the officers of the administration everything that we say to them. This shows that they are not for the people but for the White men.' 'We take it that they are White puppets.'

Lacking confidence in the effectiveness of the official 'intercalary'[19] authorities, the migrants in town are tempted to turn to others who act the part unofficially or even illegally. In the seats of White power—the location office, the police station, and the magistrate's court—a number of Xhosa are employed in subsidiary capacities, as clerks, constables and so forth. Because of their nearness to the source of power, these are regarded by many location people as key figures. Most migrants appear to be firmly convinced that the good will of the man who actually wields the rubber stamp is vital: that he either makes the decision himself, or has the power to 'speak for' the applicant to some all-important White man behind the scenes. Consistently with this belief, it seems reasonable to offer bribes to Native clerks and constables. If one can trust a mass of admittedly one-sided evidence, bribery or attempted bribery of these people is an everyday commonplace. One does not hear (on the other hand) of bribing Advisory Board members: it would not seem to be worth while.

Clerks and constables, in their private lives, are ordinary location Xhosa, whose relatively high incomes and good jobs entitle them to respect; but as their work is to do the bidding of their White masters they tend to be regarded with a certain reserve. 'Clerks and policemen are the slaves of the White man.' But in mitigation it may be allowed that they 'cannot help it'. 'We don't like the way the police chase us for passes. They are state servants. But then, they are working to support their families.' 'I realize that what they do is only the way they have to earn their bread and butter.' 'After all, they are human beings.'

More sophisticated Xhosa blame the clerks and constables, not indeed for accepting bribes, but for accepting them on false pretences, i.e. in situations where the favourable outcome of an application is certain on routine grounds. 'Before issuing a duplicate of a lost poll tax receipt, the clerk shakes his head and looks very grave. "This is a bad case," he says, "very bad; I will see what I can do"; he adds something about not being "ungrateful". The man in trouble, poor fellow, does not know that issuing duplicates is part of the clerk's work anyway, so he is overjoyed. "Let us go outside to pass water", he whispers, and when they are outside he slips the clerk five shillings.'

19 For this usage cf. Mitchell, J. C.: *The Kalela Dance*, p. 16.

(b) The incidence of regulation

In an urban as compared with a rural setting, public health and safety naturally call for extra measures of control; these affect the Xhosa in East London like anyone else. But in addition there are special measures aimed directly at non-Whites in South African towns, and particularly at migrants. The more naïve types of Xhosa migrant informants, including nearly all the Reds, admitted to feeling bewildered by so many rules and regulations. 'In town we are arrested for many things which we do not know.' 'Nobody knows all the small laws. One only gets to know of them when someone is arrested and fined.'

Whether because of Black–White opposition, or because of incomplete adjustment to urban living, they appeared unable to appreciate the reasonable or practical aspects of almost any urban regulation. To take one example: in town no livestock may be kept, slaughtering may be done only at the municipal abattoir, and the retailing of meat or milk requires a special licence. The hygienic intentions of these rules were ignored. Migrants more commonly cited them as instances of 'oppression': 'the White people are interfering with our customs'. Fresh home-killed meat is indeed a staple of ritual, ceremony, and hospitality among rural Xhosa, while 'the milk of one's own cows' figures prominently in the peasant ideal of self-sufficiency. Accordingly, in town many Xhosa lay themselves open to punishment by illegally introducing livestock and slaughtering them (often in most insanitary conditions), or by peddling the milk of a few cows which they graze without permission near the municipal boundaries.

Again, in the country the peasant feels free to augment his income by what means he pleases, but in town any independent occupation such as that of petty trader or artificer requires a special licence. Few migrants believed either that the licensing system serves a useful purpose or that it is administered fairly. 'White people are very jealous and will not allow us to run any businesses without their consent.' 'White people, not wishing us to be independent of them, will do all in their power to embarrass or inconvenience our businesses. For six years I have been running a taxi: twice my vehicle has been declared "not roadworthy" by the traffic police and put off the road. Numerous items were pointed out to me as having to be repaired. . . . I had to spend £35 the first time and £23 the second. There were other cars on the road much worse than mine. Indian-owned and Coloured-owned taxis rarely suffer this unwarranted interference. It is because the White police, especially the Boers, hate seeing a "kaffir" drive a motor-car.' To judge from field-work it seems that the majority of the location's petty traders, hawkers, and craftsmen, the sellers of vegetables or fatcakes, firewood or secondhand clothing, as well as the cobblers and carpenters, are in fact unlicensed. Either they are unable to afford the fee or to comply with the necessary standards, or they are too ignorant to know how to get a licence, or too careless to bother. Like their more necessarily illegal brethren, the peddlers of liquor or drugs or of home-killed meat, they are obliged to work in secrecy and to keep a constant look-out for the police.

While Xhosa themselves complain about drunkenness being rife in the East London locations, they also take the liquor controls as a serious grievance. As 'kaffir beer' plays a great part in ceremonial and sociable life (of Red people particularly), a man in the country is used to having beer brewed by his wife, or buying, if necessary, from someone else who brews at home for sale (*mbara*, 'bar'). In East London home-brewing requires a permit, which will be issued only for a limited quantity; in any case many migrants are in town without women to brew for them. There was no public or municipal beer-hall at the time of the investigation, and home-brewing *for sale* was strictly forbidden. In effect large numbers of women home-brewers were meeting the demand, concealing supplies in their shacks or backyards. It is the supplier who bears the brunt: the possibility of detection and fine is regarded as an inevitable business risk. Fatalism does not preclude resentment. 'Why should the White traders at North End sell us sprouted kaffir-corn when the police will arrest us for brewing beer from it? This is very unfair and very cruel.' 'White people are very jealous in that they do not let us sell beer. If it is true—as I hear—that the City Council means to put up a beer-hall itself, this confirms my opinion of their selfishness.' 'Why forbid us to sell beer to our own people?' Side by side with the illegal beer trade goes on an abundant traffic in spirits (which are entirely forbidden by law to Natives, except those who hold certificates of exemption, based on educational qualifications). There is a regular market in these spirits in the country too, for *ibhoteli*, 'the bottle' (of brandy), has its honoured place by now in almost every major ceremonial of the Xhosa; but in town both the demand and the risk of detection are greater. In some School circles in town, spirits are almost as important for sociability as kaffir-beer to the Reds.

But of all the regulations that press on the Xhosa in 'the White man's place', none presses so hard as influx control, and the system of official registration which goes with it. Country people are not unused to official papers: poll-tax receipts have long been necessary in the reserves and farms, and more recently reference books (for which every Native is officially photographed and fingerprinted). But in town, mainly owing to influx control, both the official papers and the importance attached to them multiply so greatly that life itself seems to depend on having the correct passes, permits, endorsements, and certificates. Because the aim of influx control is to prevent an undue movement of population from the rural Native areas to the towns, it obviously deserves special consideration in a study of urbanization.

INFLUX CONTROL AND MIGRANT LIFE

Influx control as such is nothing new in South Africa, or in East London, where it was applied during the depression of the 1930's. From the national point of view it represents an attempt to grapple with an urgent socio-economic problem. The poverty of the rural reserves is constantly driving their inhabitants to look for work in town, but the towns cannot necessarily provide work for all those who may want it, let alone housing and other services. The danger envisaged is that of large pools of unemployment forming in the towns, with the almost automatic consequence of an increase in crime and general misery. The towns have their own nuclear populations of settled Xhosa, who, it may well be argued, ought to have first claim on jobs, since unlike the migrants they have nothing behind them in the country. The problem is seen as that of regulating the flow of migrants so that there shall always just be enough workers for the local economy; and also of forcing employers to absorb the local unemployed before hiring workers from farther afield.

At present influx control may be called one of the principal obstacles for any Xhosa who might wish to make his *permanent* home in East London. As is well known, in terms of the Natives (Urban Areas) Act of 1945, a Native who has been born in a town and lived in it all his life is entitled to be regarded as a 'permanent resident'. A migrant can achieve this status only by meeting stringent conditions, i.e. showing proof of ten years' *continuous* employment with one employer in the town, or fifteen continuous years with different employers. Even the so-called 'permanent' resident may forfeit his permanent status and be expelled from town, e.g. if he becomes habitually unemployed, or is convicted of an offence, or absents himself from town for long periods. But the Native who is not a permanent resident needs special permits to enter or remain in town at all. (Teachers, ministers, and a few other special categories are exempt from this requirement; in East London their numbers are negligible.) These temporary permits are given or withheld at the discretion of the authorities. Being unemployed normally involves their withdrawal or non-renewal.

Only a minority of the Xhosa migrants to East London have achieved or can achieve the relative security of 'permanent residents' there. In 1957 a senior official estimated that his office dealt with roughly equal numbers of 'exempt' males (i.e. the permanent residents, plus those in the special occupational categories) and 'non-exempt' (i.e. those requiring permits). But it must be taken into account, first, that the exempt category included all the town-born males (as distinct from migrants); and secondly, that numbers of migrants avoided passing through the office altogether, and lived 'underground' in the location without either exemption or permits.

To the ordinary migrant it is a question of getting not one but a series of permits. First the Bantu commissioner's office at home, and the District Labour Bureau and Municipal Labour Bureau in town, must all be satisfied that labour conditions justify his entry. Then he is given a work-seeker's permit, valid for fourteen days. Then, if he finds a job within the fourteen days, and has his service contract or certificate of registration filed at the office, his reference book will be stamped with the coveted endorsement: 'Permitted to remain within the proclaimed area of East London while employed by. . . .' But then he still requires an official lodger's permit (issued only to those with service contracts in force). And even then the lodger's permit must be renewed every month. (Literally thousands of men queue up at the office each month for this purpose.) The system, of course, puts jobs at a premium. Every migrant knows that if he does not want to be 'endorsed out of town', i.e. have his reference book stamped 'forbidden to re-enter the proclaimed area of East London until . . .', he is practically obliged to take the first job that offers within his fourteen days, and to stick to it afterwards. From his point of view employers and authorities are in unholy alliance. The demand for labour fluctuates seasonally, as well as from year to year; any recession results in the screw automatically being tightened. A man who falls unemployed, and gets himself 'endorsed out of town' for a period, also sees the prospect of ultimate exemption receding from his view; he has broken the continuity necessary for qualifying as a permanent resident.

Influx control also divides families. The 'exempt' or 'permanent' residents have one great advantage in that their wives and children require no additional permits to stay in town with them. The non-exempt have to apply for special endorsements for this purpose, which are becoming harder to obtain. Since 1957, indeed, a wife has little hope of joining her (non-exempt) migrant husband in East London except as a worker in her own right, or on a temporary visitor's

permit valid for seventy-two hours. If the number of Native births in town
has continued to rise nevertheless, one reason doubtless is that *working* women
have been let in fairly freely. Only in 1958 was the reference-book system
extended to females, and even now it applies only to those wanting to stay in
the location—not to the domestic servants with quarters in town.

A third effect of influx control, clearly, is to prevent migrants from coming
and going between town and country, work and home, as they would mostly
like to do. If a migrant has not kept his job he will not have kept the permits
he needs when he wants to re-enter town. Home-visiting, therefore, is only
safe within the limits of off-duty week-ends and public holidays, or the employer's
agreed leave of absence.

To illustrate the thorough-going nature of influx control it may be mentioned
that in one year (1956) 80 per cent of all Transkeian migrants whose service
contracts ran out (for any reason) were endorsed out of East London. In the
following year, according to the location manager, altogether 5,700 women
were sent out. Official raids are staged to catch offenders. Two or three policemen (only one of whom is White, in most cases) set out in the early hours of the
morning to raid houses and inspect the permits of the occupants. Permits
may also be demanded from people found in the street. Anyone whose permits
are not in order joins 'the queue' which, swollen by successive additions,
follows the police on their house-to-house tour, and ends up at the police
station hours later. (Lately a van is being used to ferry them.) What happens
next depends on the seriousness of the technical offence. One man may get off
with paying £3 admission of guilt, another may be prosecuted and perhaps
endorsed out of town.

On the other hand, perhaps it should be stressed that the questions of going
and coming, becoming urbanized or not becoming urbanized, still remain
partly open for the migrant's own choice. The vast and impersonal administrative machine, harnessed to economic and political forces beyond the
migrant's control, does not grind out all the answers for him automatically.
It merely sets the limits: it increases the difficulty of getting in or staying in,
particularly for some classes and at some times, but an individual's fate at any
given time depends on a number of basically unpredictable factors: on trends
in the labour market, on the discretion of the administering authorities, on
how many applicants with higher priority happen to apply for jobs at the same
time as himself; also, on the chance that the official net may fail to catch him
if he does contravene regulations.

It can well be imagined that the local authorities, despite valiant efforts,
cannot enforce all the regulations all the time on a population of this size.
Contravenors go to ground in the locations, where nobody informs on them,
since nobody is in sympathy with influx control. Some make a living by illegal
enterprise, such as unlicensed hawking or brewing; some live with and on
their friends; some, as Reader has described, take themselves off to the bushes
on the outskirts of the location, where they can be considered safe from arrest.
Both sides feel that the sanctions are not fully effective. Some location people
say that influx control does not so much keep migrants out as raise money
from them by way of fines. The location manager himself reported in 1957
that 'early morning raids . . . are not effective. . . . It has been established
that prosecutions for entering the locations unlawfully have no deterrent
effect.'

THE MIGRANT'S VIEW OF INFLUX CONTROL

By now all Xhosa migrants, even the rawest rustics, can say something about 'this new law'. (Though based on an act of 1945, influx control, in East London, has been strictly applied only since 1952.) The name of section 10 of the 1945 Act ('sex-ten' to the illiterate) has become almost a byword. 'I had heard of sex-ten before I ever came to town. My age-mates taught me about it.' What any migrant can grasp is that 'town is full' and 'it is hard to get in'—ideas made easier to assimilate, no doubt, by the sight of the gross physical over-crowding in the location and the queues at the office.

Influx control favours certain types of workers at the expense of others—the town-born and the steady employee at the expense of the country-born and the job-changer. In Xhosa eyes this selection lacks any acceptable moral basis. According to their stereotypes, preferring town-born people to rustic people is preferring a 'smart', 'slick' type at the expense of a 'simple and honest', 'hardworking' type. And though they can respect the feat of holding down one job for ten years, they realize all too well that being out of work must not necessarily mean a man is a poorer workman or a worse character than his neighbour. It was only a very occasional informant who could be heard mildly praising section 10 for its encouragement of the 'best' workers. 'This law is specially meant for loafers, to prevent them from changing jobs every few months. I myself have worked steadily for the South African Railways and Harbours for over seventeen years.'

Migrants often suggested that influx control had been devised for the special convenience of the employers. 'It takes away from us the little freedom we had in the choice of job. Nowadays you are liable to be chased out of town if you don't stick to your job, so you have just got to stick to it, even if it is a bad one and underpaid.' That 'we are being married [tshatiswa] to our employers' is a popular cliché. 'Our White foreman has explained to us that "if you men run away from this job, you must know that you will not get new permits to seek work in East London".' Some migrants spoke of 'the law that compels a man to remain in his job for at least ten years'.

But many also imputed political motives of a more sinister kind. In the first place influx control was seen as another of the White devices 'to keep the amaXhosa down'. 'It is a bad law which applies only to Africans.' 'The White people oppress us in that they forbid us Transkeians to come and go. We do not come for pleasure but because of financial need.' 'I hate the cruelty of White people, and their bad treatment of Natives in towns.' 'They make these laws specially for us. Do they carry passes themselves?' 'I hate their way of oppressing us by these passes, permits and regulations.' Secondly and more specifically, influx control was interpreted as a deliberate punishment for the East London riots of 1952 (which more or less coincided with the beginning of its stricter enforcement). The authorities emphatically deny that there is any truth at all in this 'revenge' interpretation, especially as influx control is a national not a local policy, and is geared to economic trends in the first place. Nevertheless the idea still keeps its hold on Xhosa minds. 'Before the riots of 1952, workseekers from any place could go to the Office and easily obtain the document entitled "Permit to seek work", and a man was also free to refuse a job he did not like. . . . This regulation (section 10) was put into operation as an outcome of the riots, as an attempt to check on potential criminals.'

The recognition that 'East London is full' does not take the migrant as far as realizing that Xhosa workers themselves would be the worst sufferers if chronic unemployment and overcongestion were allowed to increase (which, in present circumstances, might well be the first effect of lifting influx control). The strongest impression, not unnaturally, is of the acute hardships which the regulations are bound to cause in very many individual cases. The feeling is bitter and is bitterly expressed. 'Section 10 is a thorn in the flesh of every man.' 'Influx control is an iniquitous thing.' 'It has made this town a very bad place.' 'I hate the police raids and I feel life is not safe.' 'The permits make life very uncertain.' 'I loathe these regulations.' Everyone knows someone who has been arrested and fined, or expelled, or prevented from bringing in his wife; everyone knows from his personal experience the irritation of being divided from relatives. 'The authorities forbid us to visit our own families.' 'We cannot even accommodate our own relatives and visitors freely when we stay in town, though we could prove beyond doubt that they are innocent people.' 'Even your wife is not free to come to you.' The denial of lodgers' permits to those who cannot find jobs is seen as adding insult to injury: the Xhosa cannot see why they should be forbidden to house and care for the unemployed themselves, if they wish. 'Since my husband died at Mncotsho I have had to come to town, but for health reasons I could not find work. . . . I share rooms with my younger brother. But the Office would only give me a temporary visitor's permit and I was told it would not be renewed. So for nearly two years now I have been dodging the police, leaving my brother's room early in the morning to go and hide in the bushes round the location. I am not the only one. There are many women doing the same. Why should African women be treated like this?'

Thus location people who would definitely back up the police in attempts to deal with 'real' criminality entirely withhold moral support when it comes to technical offences connected with permits and passes. 'In town our people are treated as criminals for little things, such as failing to produce a pass.' 'I hate one thing in town and that is the raids. The police have no respect for anybody when raiding, they enter the room in a very rude manner.' 'Round the corner is a policeman who will arrest you just for not having all the papers.' 'You go to jail here for nothing at all.' It is a point of honour to give warning when the pass raids are seen approaching.

To some extent, undoubtedly, the already formidable difficulties of migrants under influx control are exaggerated by their lack of skill in coping with the regulations. A population which is largely illiterate or semi-literate does not take kindly to the written formalities or the routine of the official mill. In 1956 not many migrants questioned on the subject were found to show an accurate knowledge of, or interest in, the technical details and procedures. While most people clearly understood the difference between illegal and legal residents (for instance), much less was made of the difference within the legal category— between the 'permanent' status conferred by exemption and the 'temporary' status conferred by permits. On the whole one did not find migrants carefully and purposefully working towards exemption. It is likely that not a few missed their chances through ignorance or inexperience, through failing to preserve documentary evidence of employment, failing to report to the Office when going home for a visit, or leaving a job just short of the critical ten-year period. A man 'in grave difficulties over my permit' had had eight and a half years' continuous employment in one job. He had been home to Kentani 'for personal reasons', for several months, and on his return to town was 'surprised' to hear that there would be no permit for him. 'They said I had stayed away too long, and had not notified the Office beforehand. They also said that if only I had had my job ten years instead of eight and a half, everything would have been all right.' Similarly, there were still many informants who seemed to have only a vague awareness of the restrictions on bringing in one's wife. 'I am told that nowadays it is getting harder to have your wife to stay with you, but I do not know why this is.'

With small knowledge and less skill, then, the migrants have been fighting a battle of permits largely in the dark. Apart from luck, they have put their trust mainly in 'influence' and bribery, directed at the Native clerk or constable. 'When I returned to East London I found there was great difficulty in getting new permits. They wanted to turn me away. In the end I had to give £2 to a certain Native constable. I knew that he had influence.' 'I am only here in town today because I bribed my way through.'

A slight economic recession in 1958 provided a new object lesson in the implications of influx control, its full harshness having hitherto been disguised by years of economic expansion. The law, it seems, is now becoming more widely understood. But however well the migrant may now realize the importance of qualifying for exemption he is no more able than before to make sure of achieving this at will. Since ten or fifteen years' complete continuity of employment is something that nobody can possibly guarantee by his own effort alone, the reliance on luck, influence and bribery seems likely to continue.

'WHITE MEN'S WAYS'

One more aspect remains to be considered of Xhosa migrants' experience at 'the place of White people': namely the view they obtain there of White civilization as such, and how they evaluate it. Coming to town might conceivably modify the views held in the country, and set 'Xhosa ways' and 'White ways' in a new perspective. Mitchell and Epstein[20] have shown how in a Rhodesian urban community the sense of a fundamental Black–White cleavage does not preclude the highest value being set on 'civilized' attainments derived from White models. Such attitudes must be relevant to 'urbanization'.

Because of the tremendous social barriers in town, some Xhosa migrants expressed a sense of utter inscrutability: 'I can only look at the White people here, I know nothing about the way they are living.' 'I have never talked to White people properly; I am unable to say that I know their ideas.' But more often the migrant was ready to express decided opinions about the White way of life in town, and it proved very easy to collect a large volume of material.

It has already been said (Chapter 2) that the basic attitudes of Red and School Xhosa towards White civilization are radically different; in fact, that the very definition of Red and School turns on the former having rejected and the latter having accepted 'things of the White man' as aspirations of their own. It seems that basically the Red attitude remains the same in town as in the country. Red migrants may have to 'dress for town' and conform to the White man's working habits there, but the Red commendation of aloofness persists; abstinence from 'White people's things' remains a virtue. Several of the following chapters will bear this out. When questioned in town about their views of White life and their desire to imitate it, Red migrants answered in

[20] Mitchell, J. C., and Epstein, A. L.: 'Occupational Prestige and Social Status among Urban Africans in Northern Rhodesia', *Africa*, vol. 29, January 1958.

the same general terms as Red peasants in the country: 'I like nothing about
the White man, being quite satisfied with what I am myself.' 'All I can say is
that the White man is free from all these pass laws and enjoys all the privileges.
Otherwise there is no good quality in him which I would be eager to acquire.'

Red Xhosa, like others, are struck by the material 'success' of White East
Londoners, expressed in their so much higher standard of living, but although
many said they 'would like to copy this easy way of life' this was little more than
a vague expression of envy. There was no apparent eagerness to master the
urban technology oneself. Cleverness and its products can be allowed to remain
part of that other, alien world. 'White people are very clever; look at the
motor-cars they have invented [informant is a taxi-driver], look at the flying
machines and the firearms. How did they make a bullet? How did they make
it go at that speed? . . . I still cannot understand what keeps an aeroplane in
the sky. . . . All these things are admirable about the White man. To my mind
they are *umlingo*, magic work. . . . Even the writing of a letter is something very
wonderful to me. A man takes a pen and paper, he moves his hand across,
making marks, yet all those funny-shaped marks represent a message which
will be sent to a man who perhaps may be at *Erawutini* [Johannesburg].
It may be very simple to you, yet it is *umlingo* to me.' 'The White doctors kill
you to remove something from inside your body and then bring you back
to life. I do admire this.'

Red migrants' experience of town often brings them up against the White
man's tendency to ignore personal considerations in functionally specific
contexts. They object to this, which may be called one of the fundamentals of
urban civilization. 'A White man goes by law and it does not matter how
bad or cruel the law may be. We Africans shut our eyes in some cases and pass
by as if nothing had happened.' 'When you are ill, the dishes, cups and saucers
that you use cannot be used by other people. Why? What about the feelings
of the patient? The School people are copying this shameful White way.
The White people are responsible for all this unkindness to relatives.' 'When a
White male is ill he is nursed by a female, who will even wash his body. . . .
This I do not like. . . . The only woman who should nurse a man is his wife,
she is well acquainted with his private parts.' 'Among White people a young
man because of his education will be made boss over much older men and these
must obey him. This should not be.'

Seen from the Red point of view the minutiae of the 'civilized' urban way
of life have no glamour, but are merely absurd or distasteful. Imitation would
be not an upward movement but only an outward one—a dissociation from
one's own people, a probably vain and certainly stupid attempt to cast oneself
on to the wrong side of the gulf. 'The White way of life is the stiff sort of life.
They eat very little and slowly, they take a long time to finish drinking a cup of
tea. His hair must always be well combed. This way of life in my opinion is
unnatural.' 'The White way of dancing I do not like, where a man and a woman
stand together holding one another all night.' 'White people have a white
skin and their women therefore use white powdery stuff on their faces, to
look perfectly white I suppose. . . . Some African girls, black as they are, have
copied this style, and very foolish they look. Have you ever seen a black cat
after it has rolled in a heap of wood ash? It is neither black nor white and it
looks very ugly.'

It would not be right to give the impression that the Red view of the White urban way of life is entirely negative. For instance, the Red migrant—as well as other types of Xhosa—could often be heard to admire the moral success of the White people in managing to conduct decent family lives in town. It was a Red informant who said: 'There is only one thing I really like about the White man and that is his decent home life—father, mother and children staying peacefully together in their house. Everything is provided for, everyone is looked after.' Another emphasized that 'their young children are never neglected, whereas among us in the location you can see a lot of dirty children neglected by their mothers, children not properly dressed, with running noses, sitting in the middle of the streets, and crying till they can cry no more'. Pictures of White domestic life are easily obtained in town, at first or second hand, through the peephole of domestic service. The verdict is unexpectedly flattering, not least among the Red people. There was praise for the White father as a 'man who works hard for his children's future' and 'thinks of his family before himself'; the children were praised too for 'being under control', 'heeding their parents and not running away', 'discretion in not revealing family matters to others'; the White wives, it was commonly said, 'are always faithful to their husbands', and quarrels between spouses 'are never heard'. The daughters are continent: 'you never come across a White girl who has a baby before marriage.' Widows were described as 'being under protection', they 'need not fear being accused of witchcraft'. The inheritance of a dead father 'is shared out peacefully', for the guardians 'do not rob the young sons' and an eldest brother 'will not seize the portions of the others'. However, it is important to remember the background of these appreciative comments. What they mirror are in fact the major anxieties of the migrants about their *own* people's lapses from 'proper Xhosa' standards in the environment of town. Wifely faithfulness, filial obedience or continence of daughters are admired not as something specific to the White tradition but as 'normal' human ideals. Repelled by the well-known but still tragic incidents of family life in the urban locations—children out of control, marriage breakdowns, illegitimacy, irresponsibility of fathers—the Red Xhosa looks across to the White town, where, apparently, the 'other' group still manage these things far better, just as the Xhosa themselves did 'in olden days'. 'In former times our girls, also, never had illegitimate babies.'

Moreover, that White townspeople manage to preserve normal family harmony and stability where Xhosa often fail, is regarded as part of their good luck in enjoying a so much higher standard of living. 'If we had money we could live happily with our families too.' 'You don't find White children running away from their parents like Native children—I think because the White child can get everything he wants at home.' Beyond this fairly simple equation the Red admiration of White family life in town gives way to mistrust. Red informants saw contrasts to themselves (for example) in the less subordinate role of the wife in the White household and family, and the less regard paid to wider kin. Here the Red man (and sometimes the School man too) would speak out clearly for the patriarchal and personalistic values of his own society. 'Among White people the woman rules, the husband must obey. What is this? I do not like it.' 'White people only look after their own families. It is not like a Native kraal where you will find many children of different ages; some are the man's own children, some are his late brother's boys, and some the illegitimate children of his sister. This is an excellent Native way.' 'White people ignore their poorer relatives. This is bad. Children of the same stalk must love and respect each other as we Africans do.' Many Red migrants also criticized what they regarded as the immodest sexual habits of White townspeople ('Kissing a woman in broad daylight and in the presence of many eyes') and their lack of hospitality ('They only visit by invitations').

For Red migrants in East London, it is practically impossible that the local White population should serve as an *élite*. For one group to be regarded as an *élite* by another there must be both conjunction and disjunction. Disjunction is necessary in so far as the *élite* group must be recognized as something separate and different from one's own. Where one can identify oneself with a standard-setting group it is no longer definable as an *élite*, but only as a reference group. A certain exclusiveness (as Nadel has pointed out) is one of the attributes of an *élite* properly so called.[21] But there must also be a sense of conjunction, of some common frame of reference. The differences which mark off the *élite* become meaningful only in relation to the unspoken assumption of certain shared over-all aims or values. In the absence of this latter condition there can be no desire to imitate. A group which is regarded first and foremost as an enemy, or as utterly different and foreign, cannot be credited with embodying one's own highest values. Such factors, present in the relation of Red to White, make a mockery of the term *élite* in this context.

Town seems to have much more effect on School than on Red migrants in arousing new interests in White ways. A School migrant would claim that, having had some 'civilized tastes' already, he found town a place for acquiring more. Besides the 'love of money' or 'lust for money' (often mentioned), School migrants would cite their own 'liking for decent housing and surroundings', 'taste for Western diet and health rules', 'interest in travel', 'political inclinations', 'interest in public life including the legislative sphere'. There were frequent complaints that White people have aroused such appetites but withheld the means of satisfying them. 'While I have the appetite for White people's food I don't have the money to buy it. This leads to worry and frustration.' Imitability and the desire to imitate are both acknowledged, thus meeting one important condition for the definition of an *élite*.

Occasionally—but only very occasionally—one would find a School migrant whose expressed attitude to White people was entirely favourable, an Uncle Tom compound of admiration and gratitude: 'There is nothing I dislike about the White people. In all difficulties we go to them. When we have no food they give it to us on credit.' These rare individuals were mostly women of the simpler kind. In the far commoner case, the School person complained of being socially held back while culturally drawn on. 'White men enjoy greater privileges than Natives, according to the laws of the state. I should also like to enjoy those privileges.' 'To them all avenues are open, which are closed to us by the innumerable restrictions. We are pinned down by financial and political barriers.' 'I am worried by the discriminatory laws and bills passed and discussed by the Government. I am unhappy about the present political situation in this country.' 'Here the laws erect barriers for us on every hand. There are laws that forbid us to send our children to the schools we might prefer: laws that confine us to places which we do not like, and which perhaps are detrimental to our health: laws which prevent us from prospering like

21 Nadel, S. F.: 'The Concept of Social Status', *International Social Science Bulletin*, vol. VIII, p. 413, 1956.

other nations, e.g. in trade and commerce: laws that control our choice of residence.'

The better-educated School migrant, accordingly, expressed his political desires in such terms as 'political franchise', 'political freedom', 'freedom of speech and movement', 'being able to go about without red tape'. Given equal opportunity, the Xhosa would (he held) rival the White people in town at their own economic and cultural game: 'If we were given a chance there would be Black geniuses in all the spheres of life.' 'The White people want to dominate us for ever, that is why they are so unfair to us. Bhengu[22] has had a chance to show that even Black people have genius. Given a chance we would prosper both spiritually and commercially.' 'Nobody can ever tell me that a white cow has more intelligence than a black one. We are mentally and intellectually the same. The difference is in our opportunities.' 'We Xhosa are not employed in the better posts, under the false pretence that we are incompetent. . . . We lack opportunities. We have been prevented from prosperity.'

As to Christianity, School informants while implying admiration of its ideals would often say that these are less practised by White than by Black men. In this respect the White section cannot be said to appear in the light of an *élite*. 'I don't think that White people are true Christians today. They have many Christian ideals but they don't put them into practice. Look at the restrictions they impose on non-Whites.' 'The richest White men don't think at all about God, they attend no Church.' 'I do not think White men accept the word of God as we do, for if a Native is saved he loves everybody—a religious Native sympathizes with anyone in trouble.' In expressing hopes for a closer equality between Black and White, and a more genuine sharing of the benefits of civilization, the more religious-minded School migrants looked to Christianity to bring this about: 'One day religious White men, who have been saved, will come forward and treat Native peoples as human beings.' 'Religion states plainly that all human beings are the children of God and are the same and equal before him. Religion and salvation by faith will make White men see that economic possibilities must be the same for all. We shall have the same wages and we will respect each other.' 'South Africa ought to be a country of great interest where one gets a variety of nations with different talents living peacefully together. It is a bad country only because Satan is still ruling it, and God has just left him to satisfy himself, as he did with Job, a very good servant of his.' Other School migrants expressed the same sort of hope in non-religious terms. 'White men will come to their senses . . . and will recognize us as citizens of this country. In Ghana this has already happened. . . . The South African White people will release us . . . these hopes will certainly come true before thirty or forty years are up.' 'Ghana has paved the way.' 'Many White people who hate the Natives will leave, and we shall stay with those who have love for us. Our living together will be very harmonious.'

But meanwhile—to come down to details—the School migrant's desire to imitate the White man's ways (as he sees them) is by no means indiscriminate. In commenting on White kinship habits, many a School migrant informant fell little short of his Red counterpart in his obvious preference for a more patriarchal and personalistic system. In this respect at least he seemed poles apart from the ideal type of townsman. Thus the White man's 'independence' from his wider kin was censured by many School as well as Red migrants;

[22] Cf. chapter 12.

so were the 'not observing the rule of seniority', the 'immodesty' and the 'not showing respect to one's father and family'. On the other hand, there were also School migrants who appraised the same facts in the opposite way: 'A White man is independent and not a slave of his relatives. This is good. He loves his wife and children but has not got time for anybody who comes along and claims to be related.' 'After their wedding the White young couple start their own home. A very good thing this; the young woman becomes independent and learns to stand on her own feet.' 'It is good about the White man that he will obey anyone in authority. In rugby or cricket a doctor or lawyer will take orders from an ordinary man, if the latter has been elected to authority, unlike Xhosa who will always stand on their dignity.'

Together with the question how far White people serve as an *élite*, one has to ask how far the *élite* within the Black population itself is comprised by those Black people who absorb the greatest measure of White civilization. Red and School answers to this question could hardly be the same. The difference was confirmed by a small investigation which was undertaken into the prestige rating of categories of people in the East London locations. Open-ended questions designed to elicit ideas of prestige and ranking were put to forty migrants—twenty Red and twenty School. The migrants were asked 'which people in the locations' they thought (*a*) deserved most respect; (*b*) were the best, and (*c*) were the most important. Reasons were to be stated in each case.

The School respondents, on the whole, accorded prestige on grounds of civilized attainments. The question about 'respected' people drew from them the answer 'ministers of religion' (cited by religious-minded informants and those of humble background); 'doctors and lawyers' (cited especially by the more educated); 'successful business men', 'teachers', 'nurses'. Some simply answered 'those people with the highest education'.

The Red respondents appeared to think in quite different categories. They produced answers of two main kinds. The one kind cited 'those who are able to speak for us with the White man'; or, as one put it, 'those who make a bridge connecting the uneducated type of Native with the White people'. 'Teachers are important for they teach us the language of the White man.' 'Good educated people are the best in town: they help us when we get into any difficulties about passes or permits.' The second kind of answer cited 'those who can help us', not so much in relation to the White man specifically, but in terms of location life altogether. The 'doctors' and the 'business men' figured in this list, but not on the same grounds as alleged by School informants. The Red informants cited the doctor 'because he is kind to us when we are ill', or the business man 'because he gives us food on credit when we have no money'. Another characteristically Red reason for 'respecting' the business man was 'because he is nobody's servant and has money of his own'.

Taking this investigation to confirm what also became apparent on general grounds, it might be said that the Red migrants are little concerned with internal prestige ranking within the location society as such. The only internal ranking system which they feel concerns them personally is located somewhere else—in the rural home community. They are ready to accord prestige to those achievements of Xhosa in town which would earn it in the rural setting also, but not to 'civilized' attainments as such. Forced as they are into a new intensity of relations with the White administrator and employer, and feeling (as they do) singularly ill-equipped to meet these White men on White men's ground, they are more concerned with 'representation' or 'leadership' qualities which can be useful in this context. They are therefore inclined to award the palm to those fellow-Xhosa who fill 'intercalary' positions of an unofficial sort.

4

Tribesmen and Townsmen in the East London Locations

MIGRANTS AND IMMIGRANTS

As field-work was to show, the fact that some Xhosa in East London are town-rooted while others are country-rooted constitutes a social division of major importance there. It does not (of course) coincide with the categorization into the town-born 14 per cent and the country-born 86 per cent; country-born people may be anything from peasants temporarily visiting town to immigrants now fully town-rooted. Nor does it coincide with the official distinction between 'permanent residents' (qualified for exemption from permits) and temporary permit-holders. Those qualified for exemption by long employment may be town-rooted immigrants, but may also be country-rooted migrants all of whose week-ends and leave periods are spent 'at home'.

Short-term migrant workers are not found to be an important category in East London. It is well known locally that the Xhosa youth with a few months to spend away from home, for minor earning or for adventure, normally goes farther afield to one of the larger cities or mining centres. East London is the place where people go for long spells, for serious regular earning. Outside the small town-born minority, the 'typical' Xhosa found in East London is someone with considerable experience of both town and country. This is well illustrated by Reader's unpublished data on stabilization. Stabilization here carries the sense recommended by Mitchell, i.e. it refers to the number of years an individual has spent in town since the age of 15, compared with the years he has lived altogether since that age.[1] Reader, however, does not convert the data for the individual into a percentage index of stabilization, but uses them to allot the individual to one of four categories: (1) Fully stabilized (having spent as many years in an urban area since the age of 15 as present age would allow, or up to four years fewer); (2) Stabilized minus five (having spent in an urban area, since the age of 15, five to nine years fewer than present age would allow); (3) stabilized minus ten (ten to fourteen years fewer than present age would allow); (4) Stabilized minus fifteen (fifteen fewer years, or over fifteen). On this basis, an overwhelming majority of the men between 30 and 50 years old are found to fall into the middle categories, stabilized —5 or stabilized —10, indicating that they have many years of town *and also* of country experience.*

There is evidence, then, that the East London Xhosa are not predominantly a rapidly shifting population of peasant new-comers on brief visits, any more than they are predominantly a settled town-rooted population. The great majority are obviously men 'of two worlds' either in the sense of long-standing migrancy or of having immigrated. The stabilization data cannot distinguish between these senses because they cannot show *how* the division of time between

[1] Mitchell, J. C.: Urbanisation, Detribalisation and Stabilisation in Southern Africa', in *Social Implications of Industrialisation and Urbanisation in Africa* (UNESCO), p. 705 ff.

town and country has been arranged. A man of 45 claiming ten adult years in the country might have come to town at the age of 25 and remained there continuously ever since; or he might have come at 15 but have since returned to the country for a year at a stretch on ten separate occasions. The first interpretation looks like immigration, the second like long-standing migrancy. In the special circumstances of East London, however, such interpretations are complicated by an additional factor. Even a complete continuity of 'residence in town', for however long a period, is no proof that a man is not actually 'migrating'. The country homes of many Xhosa are so near that they can continue going home regularly at the end of the month or week, as well as on their annual holidays, while 'residing' in town. A few can even bicycle to their farm homes and back on a free afternoon.

It appears probable on all grounds that East London's country-born 86 per cent of population comprises many more migrants than immigrants. This probability receives strong support from data on wage remittances and on the residence of workers' families. Fourie and Lumsden, investigating male Native labour in 1955, found that 80 per cent of their whole East London sample sent remittances away.[2] As to marital status they found 45 per cent of the labour to be married men whose wives lived out of town—nearly double the figure for married men living with their wives in town (24 per cent). (The remaining 30 per cent, being unmarried or widowed, did not furnish data on location of families.[3]) That 'home-visitors' and men with wives away predominate over men with wives in town is also shown by Reader. His sample of 263 men attending for registration yielded only 56 (21 per cent) who lived with their wives in East London, as against a total of 138 (52 per cent) who went 'home' for weekly, fortnightly or monthly visits; the remaining 69 (27 per cent) also claimed to go 'home' but at less frequent periods.[4] Finally, it may be mentioned that the population pyramid shows a sharp decline in numbers of men in the higher age-groups, probably associated with a tendency for many of those over 55 or so to 'retire' to the country.

THE RED PROPORTION

There is reason to believe that at present between a half and a third of the *whole* male adult working population of East London (i.e. including town-born and other permanent residents) is Red. Reader applied questionnaires to a sample of men attending for registration at the East London mobile registration offices between August and October 1955, when compulsory registration of males was put into force. Except in so far as the few clerical and professional workers were excluded, this sample—he considers—could be regarded as representing 'the true East London labour force'.[5] He found the responses 'unexpectedly frank'.[6] Questions and responses included some which are relevant to the Red–School categorization:

Question: 'Do you like to wear a "blanket" rather than
European clothes?'   Yes: 192
                                                                    No: 160
Question: 'What church do you belong to?'

Various churches (combined total) 101
'No church' 98

[2] Houghton (Ed.): *Economic Development in a Plural Society*, chapter 7.
[3] Ibid., table 144.
[4] Reader: *The Black Man's Portion*, chapter 4.
[5] Ibid.
[6] Reader, op. cit. (Appendix on Method).

While these figures would indicate a Red proportion of just on a half, the responses under 'religion' in Reader's previous general survey (one in ten of location population, by house plots) had suggested a little under a third:

Males claiming to adhere to Christian churches: 71%
Males claiming 'Ancestor Religion' or No Religion (to be interpreted as 'No church'): 29%[7]

Remembering that not a few Red people have had superficial dealings with some church at some stage, and that they might be tempted to cash in on the fact so as to impress the White investigator (while no non-Red person, on the other hand, would be tempted to feign paganism), it seems clear that the figures for religion are much more likely to understress the Red element than to magnify it. Reader's survey does not provide any definitive figure for the Red population as such, as he did not start working with the Red–School categorization until a late stage in his field-work.[8]

Under present influx control regulations (it seems) many outgoing School migrants are due to be replaced by incoming Red migrants. With the object of protecting locally born workers against excessive competition, influx control gives priority to work-seekers from the nearest rural areas—in this case the East London magisterial district. This district is more solidly Red than the other areas hitherto supplying East London with labour on a large scale: namely the King William's Town district and the Transkei. Chapter 2 showed that 85 per cent of its peasant (i.e. reserve plus Trust Land) population is Red, compared with only 45 per cent in the King William's Town district (the farm servant population being mainly Red in both cases). No comparative figures are available for the Transkei, but it is well known that in the past Transkeian districts have been East London's main reservoir for a rather humble country-bound type of School migrant. A progressive 'Reddening' of the East London locations therefore seems almost inevitable.

Another implication of the official priority given to East London district workers is that the week-ending or commuting pattern of life—the kind of migrancy that can be concealed by stabilization data—will become relatively still commoner. The men with homes near by can remain most actively engaged in country life while appearing to become most 'stabilized' in town. Under influx control they have the best of both worlds in so far as they may even qualify for 'permanent' (exempt) status in town while regularly visiting the country. The men from the Transkei, on the other hand, have always been faced with a more drastic choice—either to bring the dependants into town or to be parted from them during employment. Influx control makes their choice much harder. To bring in the dependants, it will now become necessary to achieve 'permanent' resident status in town; but to achieve this status, it will be necessary first to endure ten or fifteen years of virtual separation, so as to present the necessary unbroken record of employment.

SEPARATENESS OF CATEGORIES IN TOWN

Given the distinctness of the Red and School categories in the countryside, theoretically it would be possible for East London to serve as a 'melting pot'. Even if the ties of individuals with their rural homes were not cut, their behaviour *while in town* might be expected to assimilate, resulting in an over-all

[7] From unpublished tables.
[8] Reader: *The Black Man's Portion* (Appendix on Method).

common culture and common structure for the locations generally, obliterating the differences between Red and School migrants there, and also some of those between the migrants and the townsmen. Common language and ethnic tradition would seem to make this relatively easy. Alternatively—to use a distinction of Stewart's[9]—town could act as a 'transmuting pot' where the Red and School migrants would all begin to model themselves on their fellow Xhosa, the 'real townspeople'.

The urban locations, and especially the wood-and-iron housing sections, are residentially mixed, in the sense that it would be impossible for Red and School to keep physically separate either from each other or from real townspeople. People of all categories have to live cheek by jowl, without even the strip of veld that in a 'mixed' rural location would divide off one homestead from another. Overcrowding intensifies this. Men often have to lodge three or four in a single room; adults jostle in the streets at the morning and evening rush hours, while children tumble together in the yards. And the town, unlike the country, does not allow for full dramatization of the cultural divisions in visual terms. Here are no ochred skirts, pearl-button decorations or 'Red blankets': every migrant is wearing his or her 'dress for going to town'.

However, the melting-pot process seems to have been effective only in a very limited sense, for three categories—townspeople, Red migrants and School migrants—are still clearly distinguishable in the locations, and very many of those concerned are keen to maintain their distinctiveness. The migrants, to a great extent, evidently prefer their original reference groups and stick to them. Of course, individuals do cross over, but—just as in the country—this can happen without the concept of the fundamental categories being obscured. Nor does it happen at such an overwhelming rate that any one group melts away. It is easier for School than for Red migrants to cross the line into the 'urban' group, and also more tempting, but there remains a solid core of School rustics, emphasizing their own standards which are neither those of the Red nor of the urban people. Still more do the Red rustics remain a category apart.

This failure of the 'melting pot' to amalgamate its contents is, of course, partly a function of something that has been referred to already—the absence or ineffectiveness of representative political institutions for Xhosa in East London today, and also the low level of trade union activity there. Taken as a whole the East London Xhosa can be said to have some common and some separate fields of interest. The main common fields are those of wage-earning, local government (in town) and national politics. In these fields they have failed to develop—or rather to perpetuate—common institutions and activities which could transcend the cleavages. The I.C.U., the A.N.C. and the Vigilance Association all offered possibilities, but with their successive decline there seems to be little left at the moment. It is in relation to the White man that all Xhosa in town find themselves in the same boat; in so far as the economic and political opposition to the White man is not expressed effectively, they cannot be articulate about their common interests.

In other fields, meanwhile, separateness between the different 'kinds' of Xhosa in town continues almost naturally. Its continuation is made possible by the habits of social abstinence which have been learnt within the peculiar cleft structure of the Xhosa countryside.

The Red migrant, who was used to staying out of School activities in the

[9] Stewart, George R.: *American Ways of Life*, pp. 23, 28.

country, finds it so much the easier to stay out of School plus urban people's activities in East London. The School migrant, who was reared to a distrust of 'low' company in the country, applies this principle in town, in relation both to the Red and to some of the urban people he meets there. Some of the ways of keeping separate will be documented in later chapters. Between them they show that certain fields of migrants' behaviour can sometimes be effectively 'sealed off' even from the influences of other town-dwelling Xhosa, let alone from the influences of White people.

MIGRANTS' STEREOTYPES: THE 'IMMORALITY' OF TOWNSPEOPLE: THE TSOTSI

The first major opposition, between townspeople as a whole and country people as a whole, becomes reflected in action on occasion. (One such occasion, when townsmen and countrymen were ranged against each other in militant array, will be described at the end of this chapter.) Some migrant informants expressed the sense of disjunction by suggesting that town Xhosa have lost their loyalty to the Xhosa people and its traditions, symbolized in the chiefs. 'People who have been born in town despise the native laws and are already absconders. The tsotsis are uncontrollable even by White men. They will not be easily controlled by chiefs. For they are already spoilt by knowledge of White men's law.' 'The town people live like Hottentots and white people and Indians who value only money and their own private good. The only good thing about the new Bantu Authorities idea [that chiefs shall have representatives or ambassadors in towns] is that now the townspeople will be made to participate in their own people's affairs.' 'At present even when our chiefs visit town they are very little cared for by these town people.'

While this kind of comment came mainly from Red men and from elderly, conservative School men, a more universal theme was the 'immorality' or 'wickedness' of the townspeople. They enjoy an extremely bad reputation all through the surrounding countryside. Hunter's observation that country Xhosa regard East London as a 'bad' place[10] is as true now as it was in 1932. (The reference is to the alleged immorality of town Xhosa themselves, quite apart from any 'oppression' by the White people.) The negative view inculcated in the country will be referred to again in chapter 5. It helps to produce the effect that the 'real' townspeople, far from acting as a general standard-setting group for all migrants, are very likely to be regarded in the exactly opposite way, as a negative example.

Xhosa who are in East London only temporarily, e.g. as domestic servants accompanying their employers on holiday, would often rather stay in the comparative safety of the White areas than venture into the locations, unless they have relatives or friends there 'to take care' of them. 'East London is a place where no African can trust another.' Within the locations, migrants' complaints about the 'immoral' atmosphere were as loud as those about the physical conditions or the subjection to White people. 'There is too much fighting and killing one another.' 'If someone is attacked in the street, who dares to intervene and stop the fight?' 'People here do not seem to attach much value to human life. There is too much drunkenness followed by fighting with knives. Young men and even women stab one another.' 'It is a common thing to come across a dead human body by the roadside.' 'Young men and women start drinking very early in life, as it is not difficult to get brandy.

[10] Hunter, M.: *Reaction to Conquest*, p. 433.

Even girls drink. Young children are sent to buy beer or brandy at the shebeens. There is also too much dagga smoking. These things increase day by day.' 'There are too many illegitimate children, who become reckless and irresponsible when they grow up because they never have any proper parental care.' 'You can do nothing here about the bad influence on your children.' 'If you have a daughter big enough for the bull, the next thing you notice is that she is pregnant.' 'Young men in town do not readily admit responsibility for making your daughter pregnant.' 'Abortion and infanticide are common in town.' 'In town most married women have lovers.' 'Diseases which are rare on the farm are common here in town; I mean syphilis and the other venereal disease.' 'There is so much thieving here, you cannot go to town leaving your room unlocked.' 'There is nothing astonishing about any criminal here. The only comment one will hear is, "He is aiming very high".'

In discussion migrants would not deny that country-bred people can also misbehave in town, but they would tend to attribute this to corruption by the real townspeople. Behind the 'wicked' Xhosa townsman again stands another villain. To the question why immorality should be so much rifer in town, a common answer was that it is all 'the fault of the White man'. 'Long ago a bottle of brandy was cheap and everybody was allowed to buy it. When the White people noticed that our people were quite used to it, they closed the channels of supply for us, so that we should crave for it. This resulted in illicit sale and black-marketing of liquor. They knew that we could thus be called criminals. They also wanted to increase their revenue from fines. Who then is to blame for the drunkenness here? White people are to blame. They mock us for our lack of control, and boast that they brought in religion. But they do not seem to be much good themselves at cutting out nice things forbidden by religion.' 'When White people introduced migrant labour they allowed our girls to stay in their yards as domestic servants as well as our young men. They gave them rooms and freedom to do anything they liked in those rooms at night. They taught them this useless idea of children being independent beyond a certain age. They broke them away from the control of their parents, and allowed their servants to cohabit in their yards. The cases of pregnancy were dealt with by the White magistrate instead of the *Inkundla*. The sentences being light, the young men never suffered any consequences for their doings. This encouraged carelessness. The women too seem to suffer little nowadays. They make a living out of their pregnancies, because the White man has instructed the payment of support to these girls. If the money were paid to their parents instead, the girls might have better control over themselves. I blame the White people because they have failed to make any strict rules to control this evil, as they so well know how to do in the case of other less important things. They like the state of affairs, and encourage it, so that we shall be poor and supply them with cheap labour. They just laugh at our folly, whereas they could easily pass a good law and suppress the evil.'

The girl who gets spoilt is one favourite symbol for the immorality of East London townspeople. Another, even more frequent, is the tsotsi. Tsotsi-ism always crops up sooner or later when country-born people talk about their impressions of town. It is the feature of town life that has come through most clearly to their consciousness, and has been absorbed into their own folklore. The tsotsi idea has become, even in the countryside, a kind of myth with a power rivalling that of the witch myth, and with definite parallels: for both tsotsi and witch embody the same basic concept—the reversal of 'ordinary decent' human values. Like the witch, the tsotsi is both terribly dangerous and terribly unpredictable, so that nobody knows who the next innocent victim may be.

One of the main features of 'tsotsi mythology' as heard from migrant informants is the 'boundless' nature of the tsotsi's criminality. He knows no inhibitions, no scruples, no remorse. He will do anything to anyone. There are plenty of ordinary criminals who rob because they are poor, or even occasionally assault harmless people on an impulse. But an ordinary criminal, 'physically strong and a fast runner, if given a fright while in the act of stealing, will turn his thoughts to escaping. He says to himself, "My feet!" He is afraid, because he knows he is doing wrong.' The genuine tsotsi (migrants said) is different, because he is 'a criminal with a black heart'. 'He has never learnt the difference between right and wrong.' He is absolutely ruthless. He does not hesitate to use his knife, and to aim where it kills. 'He knows where to strike; you are a dead man if you resist him.' He is just as merciless to women. 'If a tsotsi wants a woman, he will take anyone he fancies. Coming up with her in a deserted street, he just points at her and, without a word, signals that she is to follow him. The poor girl, knowing that she is in danger of her life, will follow the tsotsi to his room.'

The tsotsi as described by migrants robs, cheats and steals mercilessly, not caring if his victim is ruined. He chooses the last day of the month to lie in wait at the railway station, knowing that on this day there will be domestic servants setting out for home with all their wages on them. He looks out for innocent new-comers from the country and cheats them of the money they intend to live on while looking for a job. Because of his 'black heart' he is impervious to ordinary human appeals. 'A woman's screams for help mean nothing to him.' 'He lacks the feeling of a human being: taking a life is as easy to him as blowing one's nose.' 'The tsotsis have no conscience and no shame. They will steal the clothes off their own mother's back.'

In depicting a criminal who knows no mercy or conscience, who 'lacks the feelings of a human being', and who uses a concealed weapon (the knife), this mythology clearly enough resembles the familiar one of the witch. In some respects the tsotsi has become to the migrant town-dwellers what the witch has been to the rural community—the image of evil incarnate, the universal enemy, all the more to be feared because hidden in a veil of darkness. 'They are children of night.' 'They are humble during the day, and vicious in the dark.'

In classical witchcraft situations—among the Xhosa as elsewhere—the witch and the victim stand in a definite relationship in which are engendered hatred, envy or resentment. Appropriately enough to the 'impersonal' urban surroundings on the other hand, this new incarnation of evil remains a complete stranger to his victim. The source of evil in town is anonymous.

That there are good grounds to doubt the existence of witches, but none to doubt that of tsotsis, may seem obvious to a man of more urbanized background. 'If I am walking at night in the location', said a town-born man, 'I am more likely to meet a tsotsi than a witch. We see the tsotsis, we see how they waste human life, and nobody doubts their existence, whereas I have not yet met anybody who has actually seen a witch in person.' Few migrants can console themselves similarly with the non-existence of witches. But even to them the tsotsi may seem more frightful than the witch, to whom they have become accustomed. They feel more helpless against him. 'We have diviners and herbalists to counteract the evil work of witches, but we see no way to stop the work of tsotsis, which goes on every night.' Other country-rooted people still find the witch the more frightening of the two, even in town, precisely because of her more mystical nature. 'A tsotsi might be arrested for a murder, but you can never get a witch arrested for making you ill, because Europeans do not believe in witchcraft.' 'Provided you are not too much afraid, you might fight a tsotsi back and beat him, for he does not use any magic after all. But a vicious attack by witchcraft can render the strongest man helpless, as I have seen many times.' Some migrants are known to have left home and taken their families to town through fear of witches, but some are known to have sent their families out of town back to the country through fear of tsotsis.

Traditionally, in many African societies, witchcraft and the evil heart that goes with it are partly blamed on the witch's mother. They are 'learnt from the mother' or 'inherited from the mother'. Somewhat similarly, when tsotsis grow up apparently lacking in the moral faculty, many Xhosa migrants blame the mothers. Tsotsis are said to be children of unmarried mothers; of loose women. 'The youths who become tsotsis are those who are reared by mothers and grandmothers only.' The argument is that in the absence of a male head of the family (the natural implanter of morality by traditional Xhosa standards) nobody has taught them the elementary lessons of right and wrong. These 'children of the stomach'—so the argument runs—have been their mothers' darlings, not rebuked or beaten enough. If an older boy or a man was ready to punish the child for being naughty, the mother far from being grateful would rush out to defend her son and pick a quarrel in his presence: 'He is my very own child; I bore him in pain, but you think he is a piece of dirt that you can trample on as you like!'

The townspeople, to whom the tsotsi problem is often not only one of fear, but also one of domestic sorrow at sons who go to the bad, offered more complex and realistic theories than the migrants. They would speak in terms of working mothers, overcrowding, lack of work opportunity for juveniles, the influence of the bioscope and so on. Later it will be seen how the rival concepts and theories of tsotsi-ism provided an issue on which the rival factions of town and country people in East London came to blows recently.

TOWNSMEN'S STEREOTYPES: THE 'NAÏVETÉ' OF MIGRANTS

In return, the urban Xhosa's attitude to the countrymen and their ways tends to be one of condescension often verging on contempt. 'The town way' (*isidolophu*) is contrasted with 'the "home" way' (*isikhaya*), the latter implying something 'homely', uncouth and old-fashioned, though not necessarily bad in itself. 'Dom' (Afrikaans 'stupid') is also used of country people and ways. Without denying that country people may be morally 'better', urban Xhosa would emphasize their intellectual and cultural shortcomings.

Emaxhoseni, 'land of the Xhosa', and *esekhantri*, 'the country' are both used in the sense of 'primitive backwoods'. Hence *abantu basekhantri*, 'country people', is a derogatory term intended to suggest naïve migrants trying to imitate town sophistication. 'People from *emaxhoseni*', with similar implications, is used especially of Transkeians; so is *amaGcaleka*. Properly speaking Gcaleka country is that part of the Transkei which lies between the Kei and Bashee rivers, (today including the six districts of Willowvale, Idutywa, Kentani, Butterworth, Ngqamakwe, and Tsomo). All Xhosa-speaking people of this region, whether

Xhosa proper or Mfengu, may be referred to as *Gcaleka* (name of the predomi-nant Xhosa tribe there). Today the Gcaleka still have their own paramount chieftainship, separately from the Ngqika Xhosa. They are well known for their 'tribal pride' in their Gcaleka chiefs; together with this pride goes a particularly strong attachment to the country home. The Red–School division runs through Gcaleka country as through the rest of Xhosa country, but tends to be less obvious to the outsider *in town*, because of the common countrybound attitude. Even the School Gcaleka are exposed to much ridicule from the real townspeople for their rustic appearance and lack of smartness. 'The Gcaleka wear long baggy jackets, and their shoes don't match.' 'They are keen on fancy clothes, but with no idea of real smartness, and will follow fashions that we real townspeople have long given up.' But their most ridiculous feature, to a townsman, is their naïve rustic attitude to the 'wonders' of town, their lack of *savoir-faire*. 'Look at a Gcaleka walking in town: his body is stiff, the corner of his eye is on his own shadow, or the "mirror" [shop-window] in Oxford Street. The Gcaleka is *irawu* [from English "raw"], town amazes him, and he does not understand its ways.' 'Shake hands with the Gcaleka and have a friendly chat. He starts off by telling you about the wonderful things he has met with in town, as if you had never seen such things for yourself. And then he suddenly goes off on another subject: "How much did you pay for the suit you are wearing?" "You know, I have just the same tie as you are wearing today, but I keep it for Sundays." ' Together with the naïveté is said to go an undue submissiveness to White people. 'At the Vigilance Association meetings they would say nothing, for fear of repercussions. They are sort of neutral, as if it doesn't matter what happens. They say that town is exclusively a place for White men, and why should one be cheeky in another man's place?'

As field-work was not mainly concentrated on urban Xhosa, their stereotypes of migrants are not reported as fully as are the migrants' stereotypes of them; but some of the implications will become clearer when we come to consider the difficulties often encountered by those migrants who would like to live down their rustic backgrounds and find a permanent footing in 'urban' society.[11]

INTER-RELATIONS BETWEEN THE RED, SCHOOL AND URBAN SECTIONS

The Red and the School migrants relate to the real townspeople in different ways. Because School and urban people have in common a larger number of basic institutions than Red and urban people have (church, school, and other 'Western' forms), it is much easier for the School than for the Red migrant to find a particular standard-setting group to except from his general condemna-tion of the urban population. Selectively he may look up to the professional people, say, or the sophisticated well-to-do, or the zealous Christians. These do not set standards for a Red migrant: they remain alien from his world.

The School migrant is fully conscious of the 'class' ranking in town. In School as in urban circles the concept of *udidi*—'kind', quality or rank—plays an important part. Traditionally the word was applied to chiefs and other eminent men, and also to cattle of outstanding quality: today, in town, it is a measure of the comparative status of individuals in terms of education, occu-pation and living standards—the more civilized the better. When School migrants say that 'people of the same *udidi* ought to keep together', or that

[11] Cf. especially chapters 11 and 12.

'only those of the same *udidi* ought to marry', these are the kind of criteria they mean. 'Some of the nurses seem to want to marry uneducated men, instead of those of their own *udidi*. This will surely lead to trouble.' 'You cannot expect a teacher to enjoy drinking in a place where he finds all sorts of rough people, who are not of his *udidi* at all.'

In this kind of ranking the Red migrants must clearly find a place at the bottom, uneducated and 'uncivilized' as they are. However, the Red people themselves see the matter in a rather different light. They are not nearly so much concerned with their ranking in this scale as with another kind of prestige altogether—the kind for which they are used to measuring men at home in the rural community. By the tests which Red men consider relevant, many School migrants who pride themselves on a superior showing in town will have failed lamentably in the end: that is, they will have failed to accumulate savings, make their homesteads prosper or provide for the continuation of the family's good name in the country. The Red migrant is not unmindful of degrees of *udidi* among other people but considers them inapplicable to *himself*: he sees himself as standing outside this essentially non-Red system. Thus while the School and urban location-dwellers use a unitary ranking system in which they place Red people lower than themselves, the Red location-dwellers interpret the urban scene in a pluralistic way. Here as in the country they see two parallel ranking systems, one applying to their own and the other to the non-Red half of society.

In the rural community there are a few positions belonging to the common over-all structure which are accorded high ranking in both sections (the chief, headman, teacher, agricultural instructor, etc.). Otherwise the Red peasant when at home can afford to reject or ignore the School mode of ranking, including the significance attached by local School peasants to one's progress up the educational ladder. At home, as has been explained, School peasants' condescending or contemptuous attitudes to the 'uncivilized' Red man need not hurt, because the Red section is aware of having fairly solid advantages on its own side, by its own standards. In town, illiteracy and lack of civilized skill are more distinct disadvantages. But after all, this applies only in certain fields. A Red man may find he cannot aspire to the best-paid jobs available in town, but he can do equally well or better in an ordinary job,[12] and can find as many satisfactions in private and domestic life. In the context of authority and regulation the Red migrant does acknowledge the inferiority of his own equipment. 'One needs education to fight the laws of the White man in town.' 'It is an advantage to understand the language of those who rule us.' Thus the illiterates may feel more dependent upon 'the educated' than ever they were at home when they used to carry their letters to School neighbours to read. Their readiness to accord prestige to 'the educated' on these grounds has been mentioned in the previous chapter. 'The educated see where we cannot see.' But this conditional admission that educated people have special uses for town purposes does not shake the Red man's faith in the adequacy of his own Red culture for home purposes.

Even in town the palm for ultimate moral 'goodness' is not infrequently awarded to his own, Red section. 'The best people in town are the grown-up men with homesteads and responsibilities in the country.' 'The best people in town are the Red uneducated people. These will rally round when you are in

[12] Cf. chapter 8.

distress.' It was widely implied that by no means all educated people can be honest, and that the wily, unscrupulous lettered man will take advantage of the dependence of the illiterate Red man in town so as to cheat him of his money. In this way 'education' becomes a further symbol of cleavage between Red and non-Red. 'The educated people are everywhere in the high posts, e.g. in the Native Affairs Department, and if we go there for our affairs or in our difficulties they squeeze money out of us, because we are not as clever as they are.' 'The School people are employed in all the offices and charge the *uswazi* [gift or bribe] for every little thing they do for one. I cannot think of a place where we Reds want a lot of *uswazi* every time we oblige somebody.' Cautionary tales are told: 'He was an educated man, he met me at the station when I was new to town. He said he would help me to get a permit, but that it would cost money. I gave him £2—all the money I had. He went off and I never saw him again.'

It can be said that because of the institutions they share, and the common value for *udidi*, the urban and the School migrant sections of East London society appear as two who are in alignment together against the third, Red section; but that in other aspects it is the Red and the School migrants who seem to be aligned together, as countrymen, against the urban people. This is less straightforward than the bipartite division of the countryside. In later chapters the question of individual movement between the three categories will have to be considered, and the significance of the fact that in town one may cease to be Red without becoming at all involved in church adherence. Here it must only be said that the official moralities of the Red and School migrant sections inculcate different attitudes towards urbanization. School country people do not necessarily disapprove of their fellows 'becoming townspeople' and ceasing to be interested in the country, provided that this is done without undue loss of respectability. If it means a step upwards in the scale of *udidi* it may even be applauded. Red migrants, on the other hand, prefer country-rootedness on principle and only excuse a Red man for 'becoming a townsman' if he is thought to have been driven to it by real *force majeure*.

RED–SCHOOL ALOOFNESS IN TOWN

In East London, thrown close together as they are, School and Red migrants maintain many of the habits of mutual aloofness they have learnt in the country. Merely living as neighbours can be taken in one's stride. Basically, it offers no greater problems than existed at home. In exactly the country way, Red and School neighbours in town aim at keeping on good terms without associating much or becoming intimate. 'Here in East London', said a Red informant, 'School people occupy the rooms on either side of my own. It has been like this for the last five years. I talk to them and we can share a joke all right, but they are not my close friends. My close friends are Red people and my concubine is a Red woman.' Often enough the living close to the 'other' kind of people, becomes a grievance in itself, reinforcing the negative attitudes and the moral impulse to keep apart. On the School side, the expressions of this feeling reflect what one is tempted to call a class-conscious preoccupation with manners and minor conventions. 'At week-ends I cannot get any sleep, because our Red neighbours are singing and shouting. They are too noisy and too dirty.' 'Because this is an urban location, people with different ways of thinking have to be packed close together. A minister's family may be next to a Red blanket family. The children play together in the street, teaching each other what they have learnt at home. But we avoid mixing with these Red neighbours of ours, because they are careless about such things as language, style of life, love affairs, divulging secrets, ways of talking about other people.' 'Unfortunately in the residential places people are not grouped together according to the kind of people they are.' 'We School people always try to drive our children to the lavatories here, but I have never seen a single Red person doing this. The Red people just put them out of the door when they want to relieve themselves. This is not only because there are very few lavatories; it is also due to the carelessness of the Red parents and their lack of shame.' 'Their small children are afraid of lavatories.' Bad language is a frequent complaint. One School man who had taken up with a 'very beautiful' Red girl in town says that this soon cured him of all desire to associate with Reds. One night the girl came and started an argument outside his door. 'It was the middle of the night. I had another sweetheart with me. I asked who was knocking. The voice of my Red girl friend answered, shouting loudly, "Open the door, you pig! You are wasting time mounting that other woman of yours. Who do you think is mounting me?" (She used the verb *zeka* which is used for the mating of animals, not human beings.) She was shouting at the top of her voice. My neighbours looked very glum about this the next day, and I was quite shy of them myself.'

In town the Red exclusiveness stiffens up too. It produces an avoidance pattern with an even stronger moral basis. There is less insistence on 'class' criteria but more on basic personal ethics. 'School' and 'town' may be disparaged together: 'My uncles with whom I stayed first when I came to town warned me not to be friendly with School or town young men. They said these would teach me stealing, dice play, using a knife for fighting, seducing girls and denying paternity, and not caring to go home for week-ends. I have therefore kept to Red friends.' 'There are too many things that I hate in the way the girls here behave. School girls are staying in the next yard but I fear to mix with them lest I should learn all their evil tactics, which are contrary to the ways a Red girl behaves either in the country or in town.'

Who lives in the next room, in town, is something one cannot help. Who lives in the same room is quite another matter. Because of housing shortage and poverty, the man who can occupy a room by himself is in the minority. The question is whom to share with. The choice of room-mate is one of the most significant acts of association that a migrant undertakes in the course of his career in East London.[13] It is found that migrants sharing a room are almost always of one kind: all Red, or all School. In the rarely reported case of an exception the experiment ends in friction and a parting of the ways. Different habits, different values, make life at close quarters too much of a strain.

'In that room Reds were in the majority; we contributed money equally for our meals. The Red people were against our buying expensive food. They wanted samp and beans and sour porridge. They would not let us have meat more than once a week. When we School fellows wanted to go to concerts and dances at night, we were criticized by the Reds for wasting money. They hated to see one reading a book, and would disturb one on purpose. They said that reading a book or a paper was learning lies, and learning the knowledge of how to oppress them and rob them of their money. Mention of attending a bioscope

13 See next chapter.

was hated so much that if one did so they would never trust one again. They said the bioscope was the main reason for the theft among School people.

'They had a rule that a man who slept out was fined the sum of £1 or one bottle of brandy.[14] My School friend and I, who did not drink, never got anything out of it. They told us that we were not prevented from drinking, and that if we didn't like it the solution was to drink with them. They would not hear of using the fines for buying meat two or three times a week instead. They didn't think it was any waste to buy brandy.

'They didn't like seeing us smartly dressed, and said we were going to become absconders. If one had his hair cut he would become a centre of laughter, everyone belittling him and calling him *irumsha*. At night, before sleeping, the conversation was always about concubines, livestock, crops, or sacrifices. On Saturday night it was impossible to do anything because the Reds were nicely drunk. They would clap and dance till midnight. The room was kept carelessly and there were many bugs and fleas. We were reluctant to tell our School friends where we were staying, to keep them from visiting us. The Reds were always receiving visits from their own friends from various parts of the location. The older Red men kept the moneys for the youngsters of their home place, and carefully checked them from time to time. They were very strict about the youngsters not keeping their own money. But they did not like to see a School person keeping a youngster's money, even if he was a relative. They would advise the youngster—behind his back—that one must be careful because School people are crooks with money.'

Apart from neighbourly contact, the other main way in which Red and School people get thrown together in town is at work. Here again, the aim is to remain on good terms but not to grow intimate. The camaraderie of the work situation rarely blossoms into a Red–School friendship that involves visiting each other at home out of working hours. When questioned about their workmates, Red men could easily give the addresses where some other Red workmates lodged, and School men to those of some School workmates, but very few knew the address of workmates of the 'other' type.

Even the freemasonry of work and the common interest against employer or foreman do not always prevail over the latent Red–School opposition. When a work situation involves acute rivalry, or puts a premium on being in the boss's good books, it is not unlikely that Red and School will line up against each other. 'When I was employed at X's department store, School employees were being discharged in numbers all the time. Afterwards it was found out that two Red chaps, who were employed at the store-room, made reports to the manager about the School people, alleging that they stole sugar and other food to sell in the location. These Reds were aiming at getting the positions which School people already held.' 'At work the Red people are quite a nuisance, for they like to suck up to employers. They do that by sneaking on others. This is a thing which School people don't usually do at all.' As it happens, exactly the same accusation was made by Reds against their School colleagues: 'If one is employed with a School person one must be on the look-out always, otherwise one may get the sack one day. The School people like to tell tales about us to the White people so as to win their confidence. They always do things in secret.'

[14] See next chapter.

Outside work there are few activities that bring Red and School people into contact. (The A.N.C. Youth League in its hey-day some years ago was an exception.) Their recreational, religious, and sociable activities are separated almost automatically: because the institutional forms are different, the actors are also different. The School man knows that Red people entertain themselves in town by beer-drinks and *intlombe* parties, as near to the rural pattern as they can get. Just as in the country, School people keep away from the beer-drink, the *intlombe*, and the sacrifices of the Reds, while Red people shun the 'concerts', church socials, and church services of the School people. 'They have different interests', was a common formula. 'I have not made friends with any School people here in town because they have different interests to talk about, e.g. dances, concerts, sports, whereas I know nothing about these. I would only feel embarrassed among them, and they would feel just as embarrassed to have me there.'

Two institutions which are common to both migrant sections in town are savings groups and burial societies. *Umgalelo* (a simple savings group of a few friends) and *itimiti* (which combines this function with alcoholic sociability) go under the same names and forms in both sections. But they are parallel, not joint. The Red idea that 'you can't trust School people with money' comes into play. Red migrants run their own groups—without the book-keeping secretary who is usually found in a School group.

The burial unions consist mainly of country-rooted men who want to ensure that even if they die in town they can be properly buried, which means buried at home in the country. In some cases the burial union in East London is linked with a parallel organization in the home locations, and certain unions specially provide for the expense of moving the corpse 'home' for burial. (As one secretary commented, the lists of burial societies 'reveal beyond any doubt those people who have no more intention of returning home, i.e. these default with their subscriptions'.) Pagans prefer country funerals because the traditional Xhosa place for burial is near the homestead; Christians so that relatives should be able to tend the grave. Just as at home Red and School men attend the *inkundla* together for purposes which concern the entire location, so in town they may join together for the purpose of repatriating the dead. 'This is the only organization where pagans work hand in hand with Christians', a member remarked. But the usual qualification followed: 'You know that these Red fellows are very reluctant to do anything together with us School people. They regard us as rogues who want to rob them of their money. There are some Red chaps who could not be persuaded to come in and join because of this idea.'

THE MIGRANT-TOWNSMEN OPPOSITION IN ACTION: RIOTS OF 1952 AND 1958

Twice during this decade mass violence has shown up the depth of these social cleavages in the locations. The first occasion, in 1952, began with an uprising of black against white, but ended with the black front divided against itself—gangsters and hooligans pushing on the attack, ordinary citizens repudiating them, and migrants fleeing back to the country. On the second occasion, in 1958, the violence began with citizens ranged against gangsters but ended with migrants ranged against townspeople. The 1952 outbreak, because of its inter-racial aspect, attracted wide attention in and out of South Africa, and was by far the worse of the two disturbances; but that of 1958 will receive more space here, both because I was able to make observations at first hand and because of its special relevance to the theme of this chapter.

The riots of 1952 (to sum them up briefly) arose out of what was originally a non-violent protest movement against pass laws and similar restrictions, organized by the African National Congress on a country-wide basis. Africans were to demonstrate by deliberately breaking regulations and allowing themselves to be arrested and jailed. At the beginning of November 1952, a few months after the local start of the defiance campaign, the East London authorities forbade all public meetings in the locations. This ban was defied by a meeting on Sunday 9 November. In breaking up the meeting police used fire-arms, and several Xhosa (numbers unknown) were accidentally killed or wounded. Violence now broke out. Gangs of youthful Xhosa deliberately murdered two White people, one being a woman doctor, Sister Aidan of the Dominican Order, well known for her good services in the location. She was waylaid and killed in a brutal manner when on the way to help those wounded by the police: her body was burnt and mutilated after death. Xhosa gangs also began to roam the streets attacking mission and other buildings, several of which were burnt down or badly damaged. At this stage the authorities acted firmly, and order was restored within a few days. A number of Xhosa were subsequently put on trial for murder, arson and other offences in connexion with the riots. Five Xhosa were hanged and several of the political leaders were deported.

The main interest of these gruesome events, from the point of view of the present chapter, is the light they throw on moral divisions within location society itself. At the beginning of the original non-violent defiance campaign the locations may be said to have presented a more or less united front, in spite of some tactical disagreements between the local branches of the A.N.C. (less radical) and the A.N.C. Youth Movement (more radical). People let themselves be caught and jailed for deliberate breach of regulations at the rate of several hundred a month, probably about 1,500 in all. In a population of approximately 66,000 this figure is not overwhelming, but since it is beyond doubt that people of all ages, types and classes in the locations have consistently been irritated by the pass laws, those who did not care to participate openly can be supposed to have felt a degree of identification. There is no record of serious criticism, except from those who felt that the demonstration did not go far enough. After the murders of the two White people, on the other hand, the united front was broken. When questioned some six years later, most Xhosa in East London strongly repudiated both the murders and the arson. 'The people who did those things were only the tsotsis. They always like to do what is mad and evil. At that time they had their great chance.' Reader's evidence[15] indicates that even at the time the exploits of the gangs seemed to satisfy none but the gangs themselves. The general mood of the locations in the interval between the outbreak of the violence and its final crushing was one of dejection, with most people staying quietly indoors. Significantly, there were no signs of elation at the 'lesson' served out to the White foes, nor of satisfaction for the 'avenging' of the innocent Xhosa accidentally killed by police bullets. Above all, where there had been only 1,500 ready martyrs for the defiance campaign, there were now thousands more doubters whose first thought was to escape to a country refuge 'till the troubles in town should be over'. It is

---

[15] Op. cit., chapter 2.

estimated that some 5,000 Xhosa streamed out of East London in the weeks immediately after 9 November.

It is easy to say that the exodus of the 5,000 was motivated by a very proper fear of White reprisals. In face of the firm action of the authorities nobody can have doubted for long that the White people would keep the upper hand. But internal division made its important contribution too. It accounts for the notable fact that the murder of Sister Aidan served to sap resistance rather than inflame it. The murder did this because it caused the original issue—that of Black versus White—to be suddenly blurred by the internal issue between ordinary Black citizens and Black 'gangsters'. This murder fitted the category of what location people regard as tsotsi crime, as distinct from 'ordinary' crime. The defencelessness of the victim, the absence of provocation, the ugly act of mutilating the body, added up to something 'bare of all human feeling' in typical tsotsi style. The actors themselves well fitted the tsotsi stereotype: they were a gang of juveniles (including a few girls), and almost all of them (it was afterwards ascertained during legal proceedings) were products of fatherless homes.

The tsotsi and the White man have this in common (sociologically speaking), that ordinary location people can regard them both as common enemies: but the tsotsi is the more sinister in that—like the witch—he is an enemy within the gates. The rapid collapse of the riots shows that, generally speaking, the anti-White feeling of the ordinary Xhosa in East London—not having reached the untrammelled stage proper to an all-out struggle—could not command a wider moral support than the feeling against tsotsis. To many migrants, for whom urban tsotsi-ism contrasts with the 'goodness' of the country, the whole episode simply illustrated the nightmare quality of life in town, as such, where 'nothing is safe' and 'people behave like animals'. The exodus can be taken to reflect the migrants' chronic disgust with town no less than their immediate dread of punishment.

The much slighter disturbances which occurred in 1958 grew out of attempted reprisals by location citizens against the criminal gangs who burden their lives with fear and danger. There was to be a clean-up which would teach a necessary lesson to the young robbers, the pickpockets (abakunthuzi, lit. 'those who rub against one'), the dice boys, the wielders of knife and dagger, the perpetrators of rape and murder. Most of the criminal and semi-criminal gangs are made up of boys and youths, and most of these are amakwenkwe (boys) in the technical Xhosa sense, i.e. have not yet been initiated. The counter-movement was organized mainly by the mature men, fathers of families and solid characters. Originally, therefore, this was a kind of inter-generation struggle.

Tsotsi activities are always expected to increase towards Christmas, when there are extra opportunities to rob people of their wages or spending money. Towards the end of November 1958 location people were talking about the murder of a widow's son, and the murderer's alleged boast that this was neither his first nor his last victim. There was, as usual, a feeling that the police are quite incapable of dealing with the tsotsi menace. Bills began to be stuck up by tsotsis in location streets carrying the arrogant warning that people must not be out of doors after 9 p.m. if they wished to be safe from attack. This intensified anger as well as fear. 'The tsotsis are trying to make their own curfew and pass laws, and enforce these on their seniors.'

On Thursday 27 November a young man returning from a beer drink at dusk was set on in a street in the Amalinda Ward of Duncan Village—one of the most respectable parts of the location—by a gang of youths. Men from near-by houses ran out to the rescue, carrying their sticks. Most of the attackers escaped into the bush in Ngcabanga near by, but one was caught. This slight incident turned out to be the genesis of the 'clean-up' movement. The avenging men—who included a member of the Headman's Committee of Amalinda Ward—gave the youth a good hiding and took him to the police station. Here, it is said, he was given another beating by the police and locked up for the night: but in addition the men claimed that the police had thanked them for their manly action and given them permission to beat up any young hooligans they might find on the streets.

Meanwhile the gang reassembled, and their leader, according to report, called for terrible vengeance against the men who had taken their comrade to the police. Brandishing hatchets and knives they shouted that 'blood would be spilt that night'. The wife of one of the threatened men organized an escort party to see them home from the police station. It was discussion between the escorts and the original party which produced the idea of a public meeting to consider concerted action against young hooligans in general. The prime mover and organizer was the member of the Headman's Committee of Amalinda Ward, mentioned before. He is a country-born man in his 50's, who has made good money selling milk and snuff and has become a respected local figure, not least for his readiness to help people financially. He is a powerful speaker. His Red sympathies are conspicuous; he wears his hair long and smokes a Xhosa pipe.

After two unsuccessful attempts a well-attended meeting was achieved on Sunday morning (30 November). The large crowd included both Red and less-educated School people, though 'highly educated people' (it was widely remarked) showed no interest in this meeting and took no active part in subsequent events.

When the meeting had heard accounts of the Thursday evening's incident, and praise for the Amalinda men, someone proposed that men all over the the location should now take it on themselves to beat any members of youthful gangs whom they might meet in the streets. This was enthusiastically received. There were loud acclamations and shouts of 'that is the way to stop them!' A middle-aged townsman who insisted that the men could not take the law into their own hands, because they might beat the wrong boys, was received with groans and cries of 'Suka! suka!' (Get away!). The consensus was 'Maka betwe'—'they must be beaten'. It is significant that at the meeting the talk was of beating boys, not of beating tsotsis, criminals or gangsters. It is also significant that the man who spoke up about the need to exempt innocent boys was a townsman. A real cleavage was about to open between the town-bred and the country-bred on this point. Meanwhile word ran round the location that 'the men have declared war on the boys'.

It is important to consider the relation between the generation categories on the one hand and the town–country categories on the other. Few country-born youths go to work in East London before being initiated, and few migrant men are able, under present regulations, to bring their young sons to live in town with them. Thus the large majority of the amakwenkwe in town are necessarily either sons of townspeople, or, if they have country roots, sons of migrant (husbandless) mothers. In the category of mature men, on the other hand, the country-born element predominates. These facts created a possibility that any general conflict between men and boys might shape itself as a conflict between a migrant and a town faction. The possibility need not have been realized if the migrant men and the town-born men had really, as they at first imagined, felt common cause against the town boys. But in fact, although everyone (except the gangsters) resents gangsterism, the moral premises were quite different on the two sides. Two different concepts of discipline and morality, two different patterns of inter-generation relations, were implicitly involved.

To a rustic Xhosa—whether a Red or a traditionally minded Schoolman—boys as such are an essentially irresponsible and mischievous category. One reproaches a man when one says, 'He has acted like a boy'. All boys by nature require perpetual disciplining if they are not to fall into evil ways. It is not seen as a question of parental correction alone. A boy 'is a dog' and should be corrected by any responsible-minded senior when occasion arises. The natural mode of correction is physical chastisement. Even an *umfana* (young man) may be beaten on occasion; how much more a mere boy. And whereas an *umfana* would be wronged if he were beaten on any grounds except proven guilt, the mere boy has no intrinsic dignity to lose. An occasional beating can be a good 'lesson'. In town surroundings a boy has all the more scope to learn wickedness, and it is for his own good that he should receive preventative 'lessons' in good time. Moreover, among Reds especially, the boys of any neighbourhood are felt to have a kind of collective moral responsibility for one another, so that one need not be too fastidious about punishing only the active offenders. Through the organized life of the rural age-sets, run on a strictly local basis, 'the boys of X' maintain their corporate identity vis-à-vis, say, 'the men of X' or 'the boys of Y', and a lapse by any individual member 'gives a bad name to' the whole set. If the set want to keep a good name they must make it their own business to enforce proper standards on all their members by internal pressure.

In the eyes of the average country-born Xhosa, it is precisely the absence of this pervasive 'communal' discipline in town that turns the town boy into something much worse than a dog, namely a tsotsi. In the eyes of Xhosa townsmen on the other hand, many of the rural ideas of discipline appear 'old-fashioned' and 'out of place'. There may be admiration for the greater success of the rural and especially the Red father in controlling his children, but the supreme virtues of beating as a mode of discipline are not admitted. The stick is an essentially rural weapon. Town parents, also, are less ready to share with other adults the right of disciplining their own children. 'In town every man goes his own way.' The idea that 'every man is a kind of policeman' is claimed by country Xhosa as specifically their own.

When the chasing and beating of boys began all over the location on Sunday 30 November, the greatest gusto was noticed not in the respectable parts where the idea had started, but in 'bad' shack areas like Mekeni, Gomorra, and Tulandivile, where (*inter alia*) there is a higher proportion of Red men. Though there was no formal organization, the men went about in groups this day, and on subsequent week-days they likewise returned from work in groups. No man dared show himself out of doors without carrying a stick. Even teachers and other educated men, who held aloof, found that they had better carry sticks; every man carried his stick to and from work; delivery 'boys' (actually men) were seen with sticks fixed to their bicycles. Here the real function of the sticks was as insignia to distinguish men from boys. With the same idea, word went round that no men should wear berets. The *amakrwala* (youths in transitional stage after initiation) were in a delicate position. At first many helped the boys, but later when the clashes became more serious most joined the men.

For the first day or two the men's principal targets were still the actual tsotsis and delinquent boys. Large crowds watched as they went through the streets looking for boys of bad reputation. At first the boys' gangs tried retaliatory assaults on men walking alone through the bushes, but soon the emphasis turned to escape. Some known tsotsis went to the White town to lie low; others took to the bushes, where they were supplied with food by their brothers and girl friends. Stories of daring escapes went round. A group of men, it was said, went out to get a notorious gang leader known as 'Boy': they were disappointed to find nobody in his room but an attractive young woman in a black evening-dress and high heeled shoes, who—they realized only after 'she' had escaped from them—was Boy himself in disguise.

On Monday 1 December, the second day of beatings, ten youths were treated at the Frere Hospital for lacerations inflicted by sticks; on Tuesday, more than twenty. But nobody was killed. The country-born men claimed that they knew how to use their sticks 'to teach a lesson' without inflicting death; and townsmen, who had feared 'massacres', had to admit their admiration of this skill.

As the tsotsi type of youths escaped or became harder to find, the men took to assaulting other types. Their war-cry as they raided bushes, buses and houses was *sifuna amakwenkwe* ('we want the boys'). This could be rationalized by saying that catching all boys would help towards catching the actual tsotsis. 'We have to question boys generally about the whereabouts of the hooligans. If they refuse to tell we must beat them too.' 'We beat them so they will tell the hooligans to change their methods.' But it soon became clear that the net was widening indiscriminately. Obviously innocent boys, 'even those who were quietly working in town to support their widowed mothers', and some senior schoolboys, were beaten on their way home. The country-born boys (few in number in any case) also took fright. Inquiries at some factories confirmed that a number had requested to be given leave from work 'to go back to the country until things settle down'.

Eventually the men's leaders no longer denied or concealed the fact that they were after all boys as boys. 'All of the boys here need a warning. It is not only the sons of prostitutes who turn hooligans. For instance gambling has money in it, and might easily attract even a good type of boy, if he has not had a warning lesson.' 'When uncircumcised boys are rude and irresponsible, and have no respect for their elders, beating is our traditional way of training them.' It was argued that they—the migrant men—were now the only force in town capable of applying the necessary correction. 'The police can do nothing.' 'The parents are powerless in town.' 'In the country boys are held in check by men generally, and not only by their parents.' 'We men have had to act here because the Xhosa people in town are "spoilt".' The migrant men also insisted that they were impartial. 'We do not spare our own uncircumcised brothers, who are liable to be misled by the hooligans in town. Look what happened when we beat Malungisa [a country-born boy who had attacked a man and his wife with a knife]. His own father's brother's son praised us men, saying that he is a rotter with no respect for anyone, and that this was the right medicine for him.'

But whatever the isolated cases, it could hardly be denied that the migrant men were the least likely to have their own sons suffer, seeing that few of them had sons of this age in town. The townsmen and also the migrant women, who did have sons, began to express resentment. 'This is a foolish approach because it will soon lead to conflicts between men themselves; if a man assaults my son I will sue that man legally.' 'This is an action by men who have nothing to lose because their own sons are away in the country.' 'These country people have a very foolish way of thinking that a stick can settle matters.' As the beatings went on day by day the tension grew, and it came to be more and more clearly realized that what principally threatened was a split between migrant men on the one hand and townsmen on the other. 'We town-born people believe that the country-born only want to assault our sons and brothers, while the country people accuse us of protecting the tsotsis, and of only being willing to chase a country-born boy.' There was talk of an imminent 'faction fight' between the town and country sections. As one townsman put it, 'Whoever first had the idea of a sort of communal punishment of evil-doers should not have let it take this form of beating, because beating leads to retaliation and hatred. Town-born people do not see eye to eye in these matters with country-born people. Now the result is that they feel they really hate each other.'

Some migrants showed anger at the townspeople's second thoughts. 'The hooligans are starting to raise their heads again because they know that their parents and brothers are taking their side.' An article which appeared in the *Daily Dispatch* (East London's English newspaper) on Tuesday 2 December was said—not altogether without reason—to have expressed White approval for the men's activities. Many men who had been holding back out of fear of the administration now joined in. The growth of the movement gave irresponsible elements their chance, and excesses became more frequent. If drivers in the location did not stop their cars to be searched for boys their windows might be broken by sticks. Some men went from house to house searching for boys in any possible hiding-place, under beds or in cupboards: boys found hiding were dragged out and beaten in the presence of their screaming mothers. Occasionally —it was said—men entered women's houses pretending to search for boys, but really on the look-out for anything they could steal. The story of Boy's escape in female disguise served as a pretext for molesting young women. To prove that they were not boys (uncircumcised), young men were sometimes forced to expose their penis, even in the presence of women. One of the stories which went around the location in great detail was of a young-looking married man who was beaten unconscious and saved from further injury only by his wife exhibiting his circumcised state as he lay. These Rabelaisian incidents outraged all respectable feelings, but the men's party had its excuse: 'there is no time for *hlonipha* [respect] now, we are fighting.'

The administration had held back so far, except for considerably strengthening the police force in the location, but it now sent a traffic police car fitted with a loudspeaker to tour the location streets. From it Mr. Mashologu, a Bantu Baptist minister—a respected figure and also a nominated Advisory Board member—appealed to the men to surrender their sticks temporarily at the police station. The loudspeaker car was preceded by a municipal staff car and followed by a vanload of municipal police. The loudspeaker also invited the people to attend an open meeting of all residents at Mekeni. The meeting was held, and addressed by Colonel Landman, District Commandant of the South African Police. At his suggestion the meeting agreed to send a deputation of six men to discuss with their authorities the means of restoring order in the location; this deputation, however, was never sent.

The authorities had some anxious moments. When a squad of police went to the rescue of a boy who had been pulled out of a house, the crowd would not stand clear, until eventually the White inspector fired a shot into the air. But on the whole the intervention came at a psychological moment, when even the more ardent supporters of the movement had had their fill of action, and were beginning to feel somewhat bewildered by the forces they had unleashed. It was felt that intervention of the White man, by enabling every Xhosa to retire from battle with a good grace, had probably averted worse clashes between townspeople and migrants.

The comments of location people looking back on these events a few weeks later revealed the wide differences between the various cultures and outlooks. An educated man, for instance, voiced the common prejudice of his type against Red migrants: 'It was bound to go wrong. *Amaqaba* can never do anything successfully.' A townsman distinguished between 'the purpose of the action, which deserves praise' and 'the wrong methods adopted'. Red informants, however, almost to a man stood solidly behind 'their' enterprise: 'The action was most admirable. It was the only way to stop the evils these boys do. And now for some time there have been no groups of boys playing dice in the streets at night; no more whistling at night as the boys signal to others across the valley; no more screams for help by women. There is quietness at last in the location at night, and life is safer, because of the use of the stick.' 'As long as responsible men are not allowed power, the evil will continue. The police themselves are completely powerless to control things.' One admitted that there had been some excesses on 'his' side: 'When African men join together for a good cause, there are always a few who come in without sincere purpose.' But anothers regretted only that the action had been stopped half-way: 'We had resolved to patrol the streets by night, particularly at lonely spots where these boys are known to waylay women and men working night shifts. This was definitely a good idea. As things are, the boys will be up to their evil deeds again in no time.'

The events of 1958 compare with the riots in 1952 in one respect: in bringing out moral dissensions within the location itself, they drove the Black-White opposition temporarily into the background. In 1958 as in 1952, most of the location was basically relieved to have been 'saved' by White intervention from further violence and bloodshed.

In the last analysis all the different arguments used during and after the commotion can be viewed as rationalizations proper to the different social situations of the parties. The migrants in their rage against the knife-wielding dice-playing 'boys' were expressing their pent-up feeling about the rottenness and misery of location life in general. They threw their passions into a witchhunt. Like other witch-hunts, this one was intended both to purge the community of a sinister evil, and to reaffirm publicly the 'better' moral standards of which the hunters believed themselves to be the bearers. The townsmen on the other hand, much as they also loathe and fear tsotsi crime, stood too close to the tsotsi himself (in terms of personal ties and responsibility) to emulate this single-minded fury. They understood too well the compulsion of the many forces which may drive their sons on to the streets and into crime; and they lacked the automatic belief in the superiority of 'real Xhosa' (i.e. traditional and rural) standards.[16]

*NOTE ON STABILIZATION

The figures given here refer to the inmates of shack housing, where four-fifths of all location people live.

TABLE 1

Percentages of men in shack housing found to fall into each category of stabilization (three age-groups)

	Men aged 20–29	Men aged 30–39	Men aged 40–49
Fully stabilized	50%	10%	7%
Stabilized —5	43%	65%	31%
Stabilized —10	8%	20%	54%
Stabilized —15	(not applicable)	5%	9%
	100%	100%	100%

Two-thirds of all the men in their thirties, then, are stabilized —5. Taking the full range of possibilities which this implies (i.e. from a man of just 30 with a maximum of nine years in the country, to one already 39 with the minimum of five), each of these men must have spent from five to nine adult years in the country, *but also* anything from six to nineteen adult years in town. Turning to the men in their 40's, it is seen that more than a half are stabilized —10, so that they must have spent from ten to fourteen adult years in the country, but also anything from eleven to twenty-four adult years in town. The only other considerable categories in these age-groups are the stabilized —10 men in their 30's (from one to fourteen adult years in town, combined with ten to fourteen in the country); and the stabilized —5 men in their 40's (from sixteen to twenty-nine adult years in town, combined with from five to nine in the country).

The possibilities in the age-group 20–29 are more restricted, and here too the town-born element is stronger, for 'Bantu birth in this city' (to quote Reader) 'virtually only commenced in the generation following the First World War'. Both these facts help to account for the fact that the fully stabilized proportion reaches as much as a half. But it is possible, of course, that some of these 'fully stabilized' young men have spent a few adult years in the country—from one to four years, not enough to put them into the next category of stabilization. The other large category in this age-group—the 43 per cent who are stabilized —5—have combined from five to nine years of rural life with anything up to nine years of town life.

[16] Since this was written, further attempts have been made (late in 1959) both in East London and in Port Elizabeth to organize self-help by location citizens against the tsotsi menace. The matter has been discussed more deliberately and location authorities have co-operated.

PART TWO

RESISTING URBANIZATION

5

The Incapsulation of Red Migrants

1. HOME TIES AND DOMESTIC LIFE

This and the next two chapters will deal with some distinctive features of Red migrant life in East London. The main organizational principles are such as to incapsulate a man within an all-Red conservative circle. They appear to him in the form of two basic commandments: to keep up an unbroken nexus with the rural home, and to abstain from unnecessary contact with non-Reds or participation in non-Red kinds of activity. In that such incapsulation has become part of their normal plan for living, Red peasants (it is suggested) resist urbanization more effectively than any other category of Xhosa in East London. Whether a man's residence in town extends to six months, five years or a quarter of a century, observance of these rules can keep him country-rooted and culturally Red to the end of his stay.

Incapsulation is conservatism in action, and peasants are a byword for conservatism, but much in this pattern is specifically Red: the migrant remains incapsulated not just because he is a peasant, but because he is a Red peasant. Comparison with the School peasant migrants (chapters 13 and 14) will make this clear. The negative aspect of incapsulation in particular—the staying out, or staying aloof—comes most naturally to Red people, whose existence as such has always depended on proud conscious abstinence from things accepted by their non-Red neighbours. If the Red peasant distinguishes himself from the School peasant in the country by limiting his needs, his desires and his participation in regard to 'things of the White man', he distinguishes himself in East London by a similar limitation in regard to 'things of town'. However, incapsulation demands more than negative effort: it also requires feats of positive social organization by which the Red migrants can keep up active relations among themselves during their stay in town, while at the same time maintaining their nexus with the country home unbroken.

GOING TO WORK

A Xhosa peasant family's subsistence from agriculture in the reserves is usually poor and always precarious. These reserves, as a whole, are overcrowded, overstocked and increasingly threatened by erosion. Here, where the growing population tries to win its food from the dwindling soil, with drought as an occasional calamity or a semi-perpetual handicap, wage-earning has become accepted as a regular second front in the battle for economic survival and security.[1] Few peasant families can hope to make enough money from their own surplus produce. The money is needed for daily things like coffee, sugar, paraffin, and clothing, but it is needed for bigger things too: particularly for the annual taxes, and for the bad droughts when staple foods have to be bought in. There are few adult Red peasant men who have never gone to work outside their rural homes, apart from the invalid and the incompetent, the favoured eldest sons of well-to-do homesteads, or the younger members of large families, whose elder brothers have been able to earn sufficiently without their help.

Wage-earning, then, is a normal part of Red peasant life: and wage-earning has become practically synonymous with going to town. The White-owned farms have their largely separate labour reservoir (which is in effect a dispossessed class of landless men). The peasant may not object to doing seasonal casual labour on a farm, but he pities farm labourers and would think it a calamity if he or his son had to join them permanently. There are villages and small towns where a few Xhosa find work, but in the main the choice for wage-earning lies between the large cities and the mines. There are the distant great centres of Cape Town and Johannesburg, and the Rand mines, which run recruiting agencies in the peasant country-side. Nearer home there is Port Elizabeth; and nearest of all, East London.

As going to town is one of the regular expectations of the Xhosa boy a certain positive moral value is found to attach to it. Sons of peasants 'ought to' go to town. Among Red people, however, this moral value is simply a derivative of traditional kinship obligations and does not imply appreciation of town life as such. Towns, including East London, are evaluated as 'bad'; leaving home, and working under White masters, are also 'bad'; nothing less than the ultimate positive value of helping the kin and building up the homestead can outweigh these negatives.

Three main 'reasons for' going to town were alleged, each associated with a different stage of life: (1) Senior boys (approaching initiation) and *ikrwala* (youths in the transition stage just after initiation) go away to work for short periods to show their manliness and to earn some money for their personal use. This practice is called *ukutshintsha*, 'changing', and is supposed to enable a young man to 'change his clothes'. (A new set of clothes is used after initiation.) *Ukutshintsha* contributes nothing directly to the economics of the homestead and is not supposed to be prolonged. A spell of six months to a year is usual. (2) Young men (*abafana*) usually need to make money in earnest if they are to achieve the ideal of 'having their own homestead'. Only one son will inherit the parental homestead: the rest must provide for the expenses of building, equipping and stocking a new one. Marriage payments are another major item. Nowadays all men except the sons of rich fathers have to buy some or all of their bridewealth cattle themselves. (3) Mature men often have to go on earning because they have heavy family responsibilities or because they feel the homestead is not yet sufficiently 'built up'. There may be not only young children but aged parents to keep, or other dependants such as a brother's

[1] On the economic necessity for Xhosa peasants to seek work in the towns cf. Hobart Houghton, D., and Walton, E. M.: *The Economy of a Native Reserve*; *Keiskammahoek Rural Survey*, vol. II. Compare also I. Schapera's *Migrant Labour and Tribal Life*.

orphans or sister's illegitimate children. There may be something expensive that needs buying—a cultivator, a plough, some sheep or oxen.

Excluding *ukutshintsha* cases, the following were typical answers given by Red men in East London to the question 'Why have you come to town?' 'I wanted money for *lobola* [bridewealth].' 'My mother was urging me to get married, as I am the eldest son.' 'My father was ill; we had to pay for medicine. I did not want his cattle or sheep to be sold for this purpose.' 'There has been drought at home and food is short. I have to help my aged father.' 'When my father died I became responsible for a large family. This needs money.' 'I have my late father's younger brother's widow and children to support.'

Behind all such particular reasons lies the general reason: young men go to town because that is the done thing for young men: 'All *abafana* have to earn.' It belongs to the role of the young and youngish man, just as stick-fighting and love-making belong to the role of the boys, or ritual and judicial wisdom to the role of the old man. Here and there, somebody would say that, for him, earning was not a matter of financial urgency, but seemed right and prudent: 'My father says, and I agree, that by working in town you are protecting your cattle at home, which otherwise might have to be sold one day for this or that crisis.' 'My father has a large homestead, with cattle and sheep, and when he dies I shall inherit. I am not yet married: I look to him to get me a wife and pay *lobola* for me. My father is very strict with me. He forced me to come to town. I must work under *umlungu* [the White man] who will have no mercy on me. My father says that before he gets too old he wants to see for himself that I am able to endure hardship.'

The burden of wage-earning, which falls primarily on the young, has to be carried on by the older men in families where there is no competent son. Normally the Red peasant will look forward to 'retiring' from town when he has sons old enough to take his place there, if not before.

THE NEGATIVE PICTURE OF EAST LONDON

While the Red peasant accepts earning in East London as a regular way to discharge kinship duties, his preconceptions of this town are overwhelmingly unfavourable, even more so than of others. Distant places like Cape Town, Johannesburg, and the Rand, are spoken of as unpleasant but adventurous; they used to be places where most youths preferred to go for the 'adventure' of *ukutshintsha*. East London is not even adventurous. It has nothing in its favour but being the town nearest to home.

Red boys, of course, have ample opportunity to build up a mental picture of East London through contacts with people who have lived there. The nearer country places are full of 'week-enders' (who work in town and come home for Saturdays and Sundays); the more distant have their 'month-enders' and retired migrants. The boy can see the elderly and the sick returning 'to die at home', as the saying is. He can see the dozens of illegitimate children being reared by maternal kin in rural homes, most of whom are the result of their mothers' sojourn in East London. He learns that a girl who has been to work in East London is not regarded by his parents as a suitable sweetheart or wife; 'it is a place where even the best girls get spoilt'. He hears what dreadful things are done by tsotsis in town, causing even brave men to go in fear. Meanwhile he does not hear or see anything positive to offset these negative pre-impressions. The behaviour of the week-enders and month-enders, as well as of the retired migrants, implicitly confirms that country life tastes pleasanter than town life. No sooner do these people get home than they slip out of urban habits and clothes, and revert to being Red: and nobody, seeing them, can doubt that they are glad to do so. It is taken for granted that the intervals spent at home are the pleasantest part of migrant life and that the migrant is always tempted to overstay his leave.

Rarely can one find a Red man in the country ready to boast about East London or glorify his experiences there. Some are admired for having saved enough money to buy a house in town, but such a man does not usually claim to enjoy living in his town house. It is an investment: he is proud of it because of the money return, the rents, which will mainly go to 'build up the home-stead' in the country. Aside from such modest financial successes there is no folk-lore of the making-good type, as there is a folk-lore of fallen women and dangerous men.

East London has indeed an attraction for malcontents and deviants. It offers an escape. The threat of 'running away to town' is taken up nowadays by recalcitrant sons and daughters, or by discontented wives. 'We are too afraid of losing them', Red parents sometimes say, to excuse themselves for softness with their children (stern parental discipline being recommended by orthodox Xhosa tradition); 'we are too afraid that if we punish them hard, they will run away to town'. Escape is made possible by the wage economy of town, upsetting the force of the traditional arrangement whereby all effective control of this world's goods was vested in the senior males. In town a young man may be able to earn more than his father could. Even a woman can become self-supporting there. There are no practical measures by which a parent can forcibly prevent his offspring from running to town or—worse still—'melting away' there. If the spontaneous aversion engendered by the lurid pictures of town life should prove inadequate, there is only one reinforcement: moral feeling. And in Red peasant circles, accordingly, much is done to develop the internal moral sanctions. Filial piety, fear of the ancestors, love of home, are all invoked to rub in the lesson that town is 'bad' and absconding an ultimate sin.

Everyone in the Red countryside knows that a son who 'melts away' (*nyibilika*) in town is one of the worst misfortunes that can befall a peasant family. When someone 'melts away', or in other words becomes an absconder (*itshipha*), his family may consult a diviner. Sometimes the diviner explains it as a punishment sent by the ancestors, sometimes as an effect of witchcraft. Occasionally a returned migrant related how the ancestors forced him to come back to the country when he was on the point of becoming *itshipha* himself. A Tshabo man said that thanks to coming home he 'recovered completely' from a mysterious illness which had afflicted him in Pretoria. 'I was suffering from headaches there, and my whole body was painful. A diviner told me that I did not need any medicine to cure me, but that my ancestors wanted me to return home. Since I followed this advice I have had no more trouble.' A young Butterworth man in East London became insane for the same reason. The diviner said that the patient had been in East London too long, that the ancestors were not pleased, and he must go home, and kill a beast to appease the spirits. This was done and he recovered.[2]

The lessons that town is bad, forsaking home is bad, and changing one's

[2] Cf. also chapter 9.

ways is bad, form part of the moral teaching that is hammered into Red Xhosa youths at the time of initiation. It is an opportune time, for the age of initiation (about 20–22) is close to the age when the wage-earning life normally begins in earnest. Social manhood carries (*inter alia*) the obligation of helping to support one's family: a boy *may* work, a young man *ought* to work. Xhosa initiates have to listen to homilies, delivered at the 'coming-out' ceremonies, which are great formal occasions. Enveloped in white blankets they sit by themselves in front of the cattle-kraal. Facing them are the distinguished speakers; behind them is gathered the entire local population. All these homilies rub in the same lessons—the supreme value that ought to be attached to the parents, the ancestors, the carrying on of the homestead. 'Having one's own homestead' is held up as the proper ambition for every initiate 'now that he is a man'. Towns and town life, by implication, are things of no real value; it is not in East London that a Red man can fulfil his proper destiny.

The stock phrase 'there is nothing I like here except the money', or 'I am only here for the money', occurred with almost monotonous regularity in Red migrants' comments on town.[3] This dislike of town may well be the plain truth, but it is also the moral expectation; it is what a good Red peasant 'ought' to feel.

THE MORAL NEXUS BETWEEN EAST LONDON AND THE COUNTRY

(a) Home visiting

What helps to make East London seem less exciting than other towns is, of course, its relatively small distance from the country home. This is social as well as geographical. East London, the most accessible of the large centres, also is the one where the successive generations of Red peasant migrants have built up their own kind of communities-in-exile, with emphasis on 'remembering' the country homes and values.

At the country end, Red families can feel that their offspring will be relatively 'safe there, not quite out of control nor quite impossible to trace. At the other end, in East London itself, the majority of the exiled Reds are willing to carry a continued moral responsibility for their own 'home people'. The special flavour of the incapsulated Red life in East London is due to the fact that it is viewed as a sort of continuation and extension of the home community life. The triumph of incapsulation is that through its institutions the home agents of morality have been enabled to extend their grasp over distance and over time, from the rural homestead into the heart of the East London slums. The long arms of the parents, the long arms of the ancestors, are constantly pulling the Red migrant back out of reach of the 'perils' of urbanization.

One can discuss the mechanisms which serve to maintain incapsulation under two heads. The first is the insistence on actual contact with home by means of regular visiting. The second is the insistence on the solidarity of the 'people of one home place', the *amakhaya*, during their stay in town. These two practices interconnect—the *amakhaya* in town reinforce one another's resolve to keep on visiting home. But besides, in proportion as the one practice becomes difficult the other can come to the fore. Those Red men who cannot often visit their homes will throw themselves all the more eagerly into the corporate life of *amakhaya* in East London, with its imitations of the Red activities of home.

Red peasant families expect their migrant members to visit the rural home without fail 'as often as they are able'. Whenever a Red migrant has time off or leave from work he is supposed to make his way home, whether by bus or train or 'taxi', by bicycle or on foot, and to stay at home until he is due back at work. To stay over in East London would be considered a sign of incipient *tshipha*. Thus all incapsulated Red people in East London belong to the category which is distinguished in Xhosa as *amagoduka*, 'home-visitors'.

Most jobs in East London leave Saturday afternoons and Sundays free. There are occasional long week-ends through the year, occasioned by the various public holidays. Annual leave of two weeks a year is statutory in some occupations and usual in others. Many workers like to take it at Christmas 'when everyone goes home'. These are the formal limits of home-visiting. The practical limits are related to distance from home, because of the time needed for travelling and secondly the expense. Data collected by Reader confirm what migrants individually suggest—that the distance from home correlates inversely with the frequency of home-visiting. His sample of 207 married men who kept in touch with their homes[4] showed that the men with homes in East London districts were nearly all week-enders, while those with homes in the next nearest districts (remainder of Ciskei) mostly went home weekly, fortnightly or monthly; only the Transkei men were mostly forced by distance to visit home less than once a month.

| | Place of Domicile | | | | |
Goes home	East London district	Remainder of Ciskei	Transkei	Elsewhere	Total
Less than once a month	2	9	55	3	69
Fortnightly to monthly	5	29	13	1	48
Weekly or more often	46	34	6	4	90

Nearness to home, in terms of miles, does not mean that the visiting is done without effort or sacrifice. Red workers from Tshabo, for instance, are only 25 miles from their home and are nearly all 'week-enders', but it costs each man 4s. 6d. return rail fare each time, and there may be several hours' walking involved. The high outlay, amounting to perhaps a twelfth of a labourer's weekly earnings, is not regarded by Red people as a 'waste of money'.

Where the home is 'too far away', the fares 'too expensive', the migrant is expected to confine himself to one week-end at home a fortnight or one a month. If wages are paid monthly the week-end after the pay day is the natural time. There remain the workers, especially from the Transkei, who cannot get home oftener than once a year. For a considerable part of his life, perhaps, the face-to-face contacts of such a migrant with the place he calls 'home' are all compressed into the annual two weeks at Christmas time. This, as was said, is the situation where contacts between the home-people in town assume extra importance.

Why the insistence on spending free time at home? It is not primarily a question of economics—neither of providing extra labour at home, nor of saving money in town; the room-rent in town still has to be paid anyway. The kind of activity that a migrant takes part in at his country home, and the

[4] *The Black Man's Portion*, chapter 3.

kind of relation he keeps up there, depends partly on the individual and on the frequency of visiting. Some migrants were found to use part of their week-ends for odd jobs around the homestead—e.g. repairing fences—and some to take their annual leave at the ploughing season on purpose so that they could help with this 'man's work'. But on the whole they do not work under pressure while they are at home. The family of a man away in town are resigned to making good the loss of his services by calling on some other person—a kinsman or a neighbour. Economically speaking he is felt to be doing his bit for the homestead by earning. Generally, home-visiting was associated with pleasures. Even those who have the most time at home—the week-enders—were found to spend a great part of it in recreation. The rhythm of the whole Xhosa country-side has become geared to the Christian calendar, so that even in all-Red, all-pagan neighbourhoods Sunday is taken as a day for recreation, just as Christmas everywhere is a time for festivities. The *intlombe* and *umtshotsho* (all-night dancing and singing sessions), which are the standard Red amusements for young and youngish people, always take place through Saturday nights and Sunday mornings. Thus the week-ender gets home in time to take part, having changed his town clothes for Red dress and beads. The rest of his time at home is likely to be spent—as he expresses it—'going around seeing people', or 'sitting at home talking to people', or attending beer-drinks. The spells at home are holidays, whose special significance lies in the opportunity they give for renewing social relations with people at home. The man who fails to visit home is doing wrong precisely in that he indicates his lack of interest in those social ties.

Migrants are naturally kept informed of important family happenings, such as a death or a marriage or a major sacrifice, which ideally require their presence. A verbal message by friends who are travelling, or a letter written and deciphered if necessary by some literate neighbour, will inform the migrant that he must come home 'if he can'. Migrants also take leave and go home for important discussions: a consultation with the headman about the allotment of a homestead site, a discussion of boundaries with a neighbour, a family conference about somebody's marriage cattle or somebody else's pending lawsuit. All such participation helps to reinforce the sense that the migrant's personality is still integrally part of the home structure, that his roles there are still essential and still being discharged, although he is non-resident.

(b) Discharging kinship roles in absentia

It is basic to the Red ethic that the roles at home must never be repudiated. At first the migrant is probably earning money for his parents' sake, later for his own wife and dependants: all along (as was said) the morality of kinship is what sanctions the stay in town. The migrant's first problem—we might say —is how best to carry on discharging his kinship roles *in absentia*. Formidable as the task might seem, a Red man can go on being a fairly satisfactory member of his home circle in terms of weekly, monthly or even yearly visits. There are patterns of 'proper' kinship behaviour for absentee sons, husbands, and fathers.

A migrant son is being a good son as long as he sends money home regularly and visits whenever he can. If the father says he needs the money more than he needs the son's presence, that is an unarguable reason for staying longer in town. However, there is always, in the background, the idea of having to go back 'some day'. On the death of the father all sons must come home for a sacrifice. The heir—if not the others—ought then to stay at home permanently. In Red peasants, accordingly, filial piety may strongly revive the urge to go home after it has been comparatively dormant for many years. Some old Red fathers visit their sons in town to reassure themselves that they are not going to 'melt away' at the critical time.

Filial submission is made much of by Red Xhosa. The authoritarian aspects of the parent–child relationship are played up while (on the whole) the intimate aspects tend to be played down. The greater measure of success in keeping children obedient has been mentioned as one basis for the Red feeling of superiority over School people. The Red section emphasize not only the degree of filial submission but its duration. Even young adult sons and daughters may have to go on submitting to the parental thrashings which figure so largely in Red educational theory and practice; and even after marriage the Red Xhosa man is expected to regard himself as definitely 'under' his parents. A not uncommon unit of residence here is the three-generation extended family in which the middle-generation individuals remain permanently junior. Among Red Xhosa such a homestead group appears as a unified pyramid with the grandfather at the apex, rather than (as in some other systems) an aggregation of nuclear-family cells.[5] The 'young' couple or couples have little separate domestic life. The Red Xhosa's emphasis on continued filial subordination after marriage was brought out when informants were asked to say which they thought were the closest kinship ties a man can have at various stages in life. Among Red respondents, almost without exception, it was stated that a man's closest ties are with his parents 'always'—even after maturity, even after marriage. It is only among School people that the wife has begun to rival the parents as a man's 'closest' relative.

These attitudes are mentioned here because they continue to manifest themselves when a Red man migrates to town. For instance, it is taken for granted that for a long time to come he will regard his earnings not as his own property but as his father's, or as the property of the homestead. Even young married men said that to spend all their own earnings would be wrong. The father must receive substantial and regular remittances. If he chooses to put part of the money away as a nest-egg for the son who earned it, that is his own affair: he is under no obligation to do so.

To stay in town when recalled by the father, or to withhold money for one's personal gratification, would be filial disrespect and *ipso facto* disrespect to the ancestors. These considerations amount to grave sanctions against 'urbanization' in any sense. The general acknowledgement that the ancestors 'wish us to go on living in the real Xhosa way' is reinforced by the practical fact that the father demands all one's available spare time and money for the homestead.

If the role of son is bound up with the rural homestead so is the role of husband. Red young men have always been expected to regard their wives as wives 'of the kraal'. The particular form of the husband-wife relation, among Red peasants, is such that a husband who goes away to town is not necessarily conscious of a great deprivation of marital rights.

When they first go to town, the Red young men are mostly bachelors. It would, of course, be a serious weakness in the defences of Red conservatism if they made a practice of marrying town girls or girls met in town. But this does not happen. Marriage, in Red society, has to be prearranged between two

[5] Cf. chapter 17 for a discussion of the rearing of children by grandparents.

families. The prearrangements are not consistent with picking one's own wife in town. Even the younger informants supported the idea of arranged marriage, which means marriage arranged by the senior kin. A boy or youth expects to have free choice of his premarital sweethearts, but that is another matter; marrying a sweetheart is not the ideal. 'I know that my parents can choose a good wife for me', or 'I am content that my parents should decide', is a stereotyped Red utterance. It is therefore even possible for a Red migrant to become betrothed in the traditional way to a country girl while he himself is away in town. Betrothal could take place without his being consulted at all. In extreme cases he may even be married *in absentia*. The girl is *thwala*'d on his behalf (i.e. 'abducted' for the purpose of marriage, with her parents' connivance) and he finds her in the kraal, a ready-made wife, when he comes to visit at home.[6]

In whatever way she is married nobody will be allowed to forget that the *umtshakazi* (new wife) is a 'bride to the *umzi*' (homestead) first and foremost. The husband does not call her 'my wife' but 'the wife of my home' (*umfazi wakowethu*). He has no exclusive rights over her, other than the sexual right. There is, at this stage, much more stress on her duties as a daughter-in-law than as a wife. She works for and owes obedience to her husband's parents or senior kin. Her main concern (if she wants the marriage to last, as Red girls almost always do) is to make herself acceptable to the family as a whole, in which for the time being she is the most junior and humble member.

Far from setting a value on conjugal closeness, Red Xhosa etiquette actually forbids a young husband to be too intimate with his own wife. He must not appear to be monopolizing her. He should not speak to her too often, and whatever his feeling for her may be, he should conceal it under a mantle of 'respect'. Labour migration apart, younger Red couples show a marked degree of the 'role separateness' which has been observed to go with 'closed' networks in small-scale communities.[7] Husband and wife, having each their separate circles and separate activities, are the less dependent on each other emotionally.

Once the wife has borne a child a new kind of separation ensues. Traditionally there is a total prohibition of sexual intercourse during the whole lactation period. It is still widely observed by Red women in the country. The child is usually suckled for at least two years, during which time the wife is expected to remain chaste, though the husband may visit other women for sexual purposes. The Red Xhosa system is more extreme than many other Bantu systems in that intercourse as such—not merely conception—is said to be taboo. The nursing mother is not supposed to 'sleep under one blanket' with her husband. Even *coitus interruptus* (which many Red women anyway claimed to be ignorant of, when questioned in the country)[8] would, it is thought, be sufficient to affect her blood and thereby her milk, and dreadful tell-tale symptoms in the baby would give away her shameful behaviour. To disregard the taboo is to act 'like witches'. Senior relatives and migrant husbands alike help to maintain the hold which these ideas still have on Red country wives. The time for ending the suckling period, and thus the taboo on intercourse, is decided not by the couple themselves but by senior kinswomen. The person who gives permission for the 2-year-old to be weaned, and thus permission to

[6] The growing importance of *ukuthwala* marriages is discussed in Wilson M.: *Social Structure* (*Keiskammahoek Rural Survey*), p. 84. See also chapter 16, below.

[7] Bott, Elizabeth: *Family and Social Network*.

[8] Cf. footnote 2 in chapter 16.

conceive another child, is usually the husband's mother. (Xhosa approve of children being well spaced out; too much closeness in the siblings' ages is despised as a sign of the parents' weakness and incontinence.)

It can readily be seen how these features of traditional Xhosa marriage play into the hands of the labour migrancy system. They make it easier for a Red man to go on regarding himself as a satisfactory husband *in absentia*. They also make it harder for him to become town-rooted by moving wife or children to town.

Since his wife is not primarily 'his' wife, in an exclusive sense, the Red husband does not consider that he has any right to take her with him when he goes back to town. Leaving the wife at the family homestead has certain obvious economic advantages, but over and above this, the patriarchal values demand that such women remain under the *direct* control of the seniors at home. Thus while the School man may regard the wife's residence as a question for personal decision, the Red man does not see that there can be anything to decide. In his eyes the wife's place is in the family home. If he cannot go home to visit her as often as is considered desirable, she may visit him in town instead, but not for so long that he would appear to be removing her.

What applies to the wife applies all the more strongly to the children. Children, like wives, would be economic burdens in town: in the country they must herd livestock and help in other ways. Children, like wives, might easily 'get spoilt' and get out of hand in town; in the country, their senior kin keep them in order. A wife may visit her husband in town but she will not bring the bigger children with her. It is not regarded as a fit place for a child.[9]

As far as kinship goes, then, the Red peasant migrant typically remains country-rooted. Neither parents, wife nor children can rightly be transferred to the urban setting.

AMAKHAYA IN TOWN

The next question is the organization of the Red migrants inside East London itself.

All Red people in East London, that is, all who acknowledge themselves as Red, may be said to constitute a moral community there. The behaviour required by Red standards is diffusely sanctioned by the concern for what 'people here'—meaning Red people—would think; it matters much less what the School and town people may think by their own standards.

More specifically, however, each group of Red *amakhaya* (people 'of one home') forms a community on its own. This, which is really an extension of the community at home, constitutes by far the most effective vehicle of opinion and guardian of morality. The sanctions wielded by *amakhaya* do not stop short at diffused ones. The *amakhaya* groups, on occasion, act corporately, giving help, exercising restraint or imposing punishments on their own members.

'Home-people', *amakhaya*, is a term applied primarily to people from one's own rural location. A rural location (administrative unit, under a headman) constitutes a community with a corporate feeling: the boundaries are often based on old sub-chieftainship divisions. Naturally, rural locations have ties with the locations nearest to them, both positive (such as the ties resulting from marriages) and negative (such as the practice of stick-fights between their

[9] Cf. chapter 17.

respective gangs of boys). The definition of home-people in town may be stretched to include, if necessary, people from these near-by locations.

Theoretically, the School migrants from one's home place might be expected to count as *amakhaya*, but in fact the formal organization and the informal importance of the home-people in town are almost exclusively Red phenomena. Undoubtedly the importance attached to home-people in town is one of the main reasons why Red migrants resist urbanization more effectively than School migrants do; and it must be asked how a body of Red *amakhaya* there can manage to form itself into an organized community, in spite of the formidable obstacles. These obstacles include the inevitable physical scattering of home-people in town; the distance from the common home which was their original bond; their situation as members of a subordinated people, whose ultimate means of enforcing conformity can only be moral suasion and self-discipline; and, above all, the exposure all the time to the suggestive influences of rival non-Red ways of acting and thinking, which abound everywhere in town.

DOMESTIC LIFE

The domestic life of Red migrants in town can be taken as the starting-point. Owing to the acute shortage of accommodation there, even the tenant of a single room (*ibhoda*, 'boarder') can have his pick of would-be sub-tenants, just as the owner of a house can have his pick of would-be room-tenants. The house occupants jointly share the water-tap and communal latrine with others in the same street, but the separate rooms of one house do not share facilities within it: there is no common kitchen for example. Each shack room being a combined kitchen, living-room, and bedroom, for the man or men who occupy it, 'domestic relations' are those which involve staying in one room together, not staying in one house.

The Xhosa word for homestead (*umzi*) is used for a town house also, but in spite of the verbal equation of the owner of the house with the 'head of the homestead', the role is fundamentally different. An English term is applied to the tenants who rent the rooms (*ibhoda*, 'boarder').[10] Houseowner and tenants are not like 'people of one homestead', a group with a common loyalty. They need only try 'to be on good terms', and avoid major quarrels. Living in the same *room* is quite another matter. Besides being a domestic unit a group of room-mates must be regarded as a voluntary association. There is a financial element in the sense that sub-tenants contribute their shares of the rent, but the relation is not conceived of first and foremost as a commercial one. Red men say they choose to share rooms because they are 'good friends', because they 'like each other', because they 'know they will be happy together'. A man's room-mates, usually temporary, sometimes permanent, reflect his and their personal choice of companion, while his house-mates reflect only the decisions of his landlord, and his neighbours in the next-door shack must be accepted as an act of God.

Anything which breeds distrust or antagonism incompatible with a close personal relation, works against sharing a room. Nobody thinks it makes sense for Xhosa and Fingo young men to live together, nor for Red and School. Emergency does occasionally join such strange bedfellows, but they will quickly part.

[10] For the tenant of a municipal house (who is not immediately dependent on an individual landlord) the Xhosa word *umqesha* is used.

In the domestic life of the average Red migrant two broad phases can be distinguished. In the first phase, while the man is young, sharing a room with another man or men (first as sub-tenant, then as host) is a matter of preference. It can re-create something of the 'all-boys-together' atmosphere which *abafana* (young men) enjoy in the country. The second phase starts when the migrant grows older and begins to develop the outlook of an *indoda* (mature man). He now sets a higher value on peace and privacy, and although it costs more to keep on his room alone, he prefers to stay there by himself, or with a woman, or possibly with one steady male companion.

With Red people, the main determinant in all choices of room and room-mate is the desire to stay close to the home-people. In the first phase satisfaction is gained from 'living with' one's *amakhaya*, in the second phase 'living near' them. Each group of room-mates therefore constitutes a little cell of *amakhaya*. From these cells, as we shall see, neighbourhood clusters are formed, and also kinds of associative grouping which provide the framework for the organized life of Red migrants in town.

THE ROOM-SHARING PHASE

As Reader has described in detail, the migrant new-comer has to find somebody in town to 'take care of him', that is, receive, house, and feed him. He cannot pay until he gets a job and some money; he must find someone who feels sufficient sense of moral obligation to help him for nothing. This means finding either a kinsman or a man from home.

That a new-comer will go straight to his elder brother or ortho-cousin, if he has one in town, is self-evident by Red kinship standards. The younger brother regards the elder as his permanent guardian in town. Brothers are exceptions to the rule that a new-comer will go off within a few months to find a room of his own. They stay on together indefinitely unless or until some special reason arises for separation. In other cases, kinship *alone* is not usually the basis for staying together. Coming from the same rural community counts for more. A kinsman who is not an agnate, and so does not come from the same home place, will sometimes act as host (e.g. a mother's brother's son), but such arrangements rarely or never become permanent, and are said to be less congenial than staying with an unrelated man from home. When an agnatic kinsman is chosen, on the other hand, he is likely to be at the same time a man from home (lineage members usually live fairly close to each other in the country). The non-agnatic kinsman is bound to the new-comer only by the single tie of kinship, the agnate by the multiplex bonds of community as well.

In one sample of thirty-three Red men of various ages, twenty had turned to *amakhaya* when they came to town; ten had had brothers to put them up; and the remaining three had gone to non-agnatic kin. This supports Reader's findings that migrant new-comers as a whole 'are more likely to stay with non-relatives than with relatives when they first come to town', and that 'in five cases out of six these non-relatives are either age-mates or other neighbours from the same or adjacent locations in the rural place of origin'.[11] 'Age-mates' (*iintanga*) is a somewhat elastic term, but nearly always figures in the relation in one sense or another: out of the twenty Red migrants in the sample who had lodged with *amakhaya* at first, eighteen described themselves a *iintanga* to their hosts. The corporate organization of young men in the country

[11] *The Black Man's Portion*, chapter 8.

(which will be described later) makes it almost certain that the closest friendships there are formed with one's *iintanga*.

But men who were asked to explain their choice of their initial host often gave a long string of 'reasons', over and above the fact of being *amakhaya* and age-mates. The fathers, brothers, and neighbours at home might all be somehow involved in the relation, as well as the two young men themselves. 'This age-mate of mine was of the same *isiduko* [clan name], and our parents were friendly at home, and regarded each other almost as relatives.' 'His father is a neighbour of my father at home; we grew up together there.' 'The two young men were about three years older than myself and had been great friends of my elder brother at home.' 'Whenever we had any sacrifices at home my late father used to invite that young man's father, as he was of our lineage; this is what made me turn to him.' The more people at home are involved (one might say), the more manifold and efficacious are the sanctions emanating from there, and the more confidently can the new-comer depend on the sense of obligation. Any relation between Red *amakhaya* in town—whether they are kin or not—is strengthened by these 'third party' sanctions. You will have to go home sooner or later, and if you have let down a man from home you may be held to account by his people.

This throws into relief the relatively unfortunate plight of new-comers from home areas which send few Red migrants to East London. 'There are very few Cathcart people in town and he was my only possibility': 'he' in this case was a School man and the partnership very soon broke down. Farm people suffer the worst from this kind of difficulty, as their home communities are so small and shifting.[12] They may have to make do with simple person-to-person connexions and slender ones at that: 'I shared accommodation with another young man from the same farming area as myself. We were not childhood friends, but met when we were grown-up boys, because of our girl-friends: his girl-friend lived on "my" farm and mine lived on "his" farm.' In such cases hospitality is not sanctioned by any third party at home and so lacks the moral, obligatory aspect which it has in the case of proper *amakhaya* related by multiplex ties. 'The man was kind to me for the first few days but then he somehow changed altogether.'

While a new-comer is still dependent on hospitality he is sometimes referred to (in Red and uneducated circles) as *inyuwana*, 'new one', a term apparently originating from the Rand mining compounds. Decency demands that he be given his board and lodging free, until he gets a job; but it also demands that he should make acknowledgement of his dependent status and his juniority in the circle. Among Red men the *inyuwana*'s acknowledgement takes a parallel form to that of the *umtshakazi*—the most newly wedded wife of a homestead—in that the heaviest and least popular household chores are allotted to him. *Inyuwana* has to do the cleaning, fetch water, and prepare meals for the room-mates who are out at work. Nobody likes to be treated as *inyuwana* for too long, for seniority is a sensitive spot with Xhosa. 'I left that room because even the two young men of my own age took advantage of my being *inyuwana*. I did not worry about the senior men but I did not like this in my *iintanga*.'

There is also a rural precedent for the 'arrival gift' (*isifiko*) of beer and brandy by which an *inyuwana* usually tries to make himself acceptable to his room-mates. In the country a person who comes to stay after a long absence is

[12] Cf. chapter 10, below.

expected to make *isifiko* to neighbours and kinsmen, but particularly to the young men of his *intlombe*, to re-establish friendly ties. It is not just the gift but the joint consumption of it that matters. 'After *isifiko* has been drunk we can all be free together again.'

When considered in their purely local context the relations between landlord, room-tenant, sub-tenant, and non-paying 'new one' are seen as a hierarchy of power, with the scarcity of accommodation and of money as two dominant factors. Reader has fully discussed the hierarchy in this light, pointing out how the room-tenant as 'boss of the room' occupies an intermediate position between the landlord (as 'boss of the house') and the others, and how he tends to take advantage of his more limited powers in somewhat the same way as the landlord. As Reader's account shows, the room-tenant is considered entitled to domestic privileges. He sleeps on the bed (while the others, like Red men in the country, sleep on the floor); he takes the first pick of food; he may not contribute as much either in housework or in provisions as the sub-tenants do. These prerogatives may or may not be resented by the sub-tenants. Among the other sub-tenants actual seniority (in terms of circumcision-age) may receive normal acknowledgement, but the room-tenant himself is always 'senior' by courtesy if not in years, and cannot be addressed as *kwedini* ('boy').

But in the case of Red, home-bound young men there is another consideration too. The relation in town has to be seen in perspective, has to be set against the background of relations in the country. Here as always the Red migrant has to think 'what will happen when we all go home?' This, if nothing else, puts a brake on tyranny. 'I am careful not to take advantage of my *iintanga* who are living with me here', said a Red room-tenant. 'After all, it is only having the tenancy of this room that has put me in the position of their "leader". If I show no consideration for them here, what will be done to me when we are all at home?'

This use of the word 'leader' to designate the room-tenant—not uncommon among Red informants—is worth considering. The concept of the 'leader' and his 'followers' plays an important part in Red youth organization in the country. Wherever Red young men act together in a group—e.g. in the *intlombe*—they are supposed to be under the control of a 'leader' who is a *primus inter pares*. The leader expects deference from his 'followers' but he also bears responsibility for their good conduct and for the collective good name of the group as a whole. Like a public-school prefect, he is given his prerogative of ordering them about specifically in order that rules should be kept and 'bad things' prevented. He is the spokesman for what are called the 'rules of the *intlombe*'; he is the mouthpiece of the collective conscience.

In town, Red sub-tenants tend to interpret the room-tenant's position in the same way, to include moral responsibility as well as privilege. He is spokesman for certain self-imposed rules of the Red young man, which they call 'Rules of the house', and which are an important concept for them. The rules usually cited as most important are two: not to have sexual intercourse in the room, and not to stay out at night without giving notice beforehand.

The prohibition of sexual intercourse in the room is copied directly from the rules of the *intlombe*. Women are welcome as visitors, even as acknowledged sweethearts, but actual love-making must be done elsewhere. 'If a room-tenant allowed those who are under him to have intercourse in the room, he would be making his room into a kind of brothel.' It is his business to see that each new sub-tenant remains aware that this well-known 'rule of Red young men' applies to the town room just as stringently as to the *intlombe* at home. Red informants rationalized the rule in various ways. The woman might have other lovers in town: one of these might follow her to the room and start a fight. Or the woman might be rendered pregnant 'and the others will be called to give evidence against their room-mate, which is a bad thing'. Or the fact that one man is having intercourse could make the others sexually excited and unable to sleep.

The rule that no room-mate should stay out at night without informing the others beforehand echoes the rural principle that local age-mates must have a care for each other's safety. They 'ought to' side together in fights, and come to one another's rescue in emergency; similarly, they 'ought to' watch each other's movements in the dangerous milieu of town. Staying out at night without notice deserves a severe rebuke on this account: 'Why did you put us in unnecessary anxiety? We had all sorts of ideas about you in your absence. We thought you were arrested, or perhaps murdered by the tsotsis. Obviously you do not regard us as men with the feelings of men.' But this principle of mutual responsibility is given the typical Red home-bound twist: it is not important simply in itself, but also because it has reference to 'the people at home'. 'If anything did happen to you, what could we have said to the elders at home? The blame would fall on us.' 'We know that life is never safe in town. I do not want the senior men at home asking me "What did you do to try to stop him going out at night?"'

Besides the sanctions emanating from home, rules of the house have specific sanctions on the spot. Following another typically Red pattern, the room-mates on occasion constitute themselves a kind of tribunal and carry out a quasi-judicial procedure including the imposing of penalties.[13] This characteristic Red form of internal justice may be applied to quarrels between room-mates when attempts to settle them informally have failed. The procedure of the room-mates' 'court' is modelled on that of the rural *Inkundla*: the 'chairman' (the room-tenant) makes a brief statement, the accuser and accused give their versions in turn, and after discussion a penalty is proposed and carried by the meeting. Many of these 'cases' between room-mates are ostensibly concerned with trivialities, such as who took a bigger piece of meat than he ought, but there may be an undercurrent of more serious accumulated tensions. The hearing and sentence are meant to be cathartic and reconciliatory; thus the procedure is an alternative to the break-up of the group by expulsion or withdrawal. The fine, if a fine is imposed, is something to benefit the whole group—the 'convicted' person must buy food or beer or brandy which is then consumed together. The tone of the proceedings is usually half-humorous, which enables the culprit to feel that he is being chastened 'by those who love him'.

In the last resort the 'town' relation and the 'country' relation between these *iintanga* are one. The fact of living together in town enriches the relation which existed between them already as age-mates, neighbours, kin, and friends in the country. What happens in one context is also relevant in the other. X came to town for the first time and betook himself to the room of a 'man from home', who 'was very kind to me', but he would not stay there for long because he found another sub-tenant there, a man with whom X's family

<hr>

[13] Cf. chapter 7.

would not have been on friendly terms in the country. The trouble was that this man had once seduced X's father's brother's daughter and had failed to pay the full customary damages. 'How could I stay in that room when I found him there? Because of what had once happened he could not look me in the eye. I did not like eating food that he had bought, nor did I like it that he should eat my food.' At the other end, room-sharing *iintanga* bring their town experiences into the country context, having their own new jokes and songs (picked up in town) to introduce to the home *intlombe*, or their special styles of formalized boasting (*ukuchaza*) to practise there. They may associate as a little clique when they are at home; rural people sometimes speak of 'the East Londoners' (*amaMonti*) meaning a local clique of this kind.

UNEQUAL ROOM-MATES

If the *intlombe* provides a model for relations between room-mates who are *iintanga*, the relations between room-mates of unequal age status can better be likened to those of older and younger brothers.

Age differences between Red room-mates in town are rarely very pronounced, e.g. equivalent to a generation difference. As has been said, the older men stop taking room-mates. What may be found is a 'slightly older' man sharing with a 'slightly younger' man. Sociologically, the decisive thing is not the extent of the difference in years but the way in which the parties formalize it. In one case a man two years older (or initiated two years earlier) is formally treated as a senior, in another as an equal. As a general rule, the closer the relation is in the home community, the more the fine distinctions of seniority are likely to be insisted on. It is also the general practice that one who has been *intanga* to one's older brother must be treated as a senior in any circumstances.

It must be mentioned here that in the Xhosa kinship system inequality between brothers is a strong principle. While the brother-relation is conceived as particularly intimate and enduring, it is also deeply imbued with the asymmetry of a senior-junior relation. There is no single Xhosa kinship term corresponding to 'brother'; one is either a man's *umnakwethu* (elder brother) or his *umninawa* (younger brother). There is a marked etiquette of deference to the elder, including a name-avoidance in direct address. The gradations of seniority are observed right through a many-child family so that each brother except the first and the last is *umnakwethu* in one relation, *umninawa* in another. Father's brother's sons are classified similarly.

A senior will hardly accept the status of sub-tenant under a junior except in emergency or temporarily. It would mean casting aside either the rural principle of seniority, or the urban principle of the room-tenant's paramountcy. Conversely, a marked seniority on the side of the room-tenant himself often seems to strengthen the relation. A Red man of about 36, having rented a room of his own, shared it with two sub-tenants, *amakhaya*, in their 20's. He explicitly compared this to a satisfactory brother relation: 'They both respect me very much, and I treat them both just like younger brothers. I love these young men. One of them had an elder brother, who died, who was my own *intanga*.' In another instance a sub-tenant described his room-tenant (a slightly older man from home) as 'very kind to me, as if I were his younger brother'.

One advantage ensues when room-mates regard their relation as that of senior and junior. The formal differentiation between senior and junior is enough, in Red Xhosa thinking, to rule out direct rivalry—for status, for prestige, for women. In groups of *iintanga*, there may be heartburnings about the room-tenant's insistence on eating from a separate dish, or his sharing out the portions of meat in what is regarded as an unfair manner, or evading the more tiresome household tasks. Between recognized senior and junior, these inequalities are normal Red etiquette.

The main danger with a 'senior' room-tenant is exploitation. Here once again it is the thought of 'the people at home' that will constitute the most effective restraint. A Red man of 28 had a junior 'man from home', distantly related, staying in his room. 'I do not take any advantage of him here', said the room-tenant, 'for as an older man, and related to him, I must regard myself as his guardian. If a younger man goes back to the country and there lodges a complaint against you, his senior, the people at home will take a very serious view of his grievance.'

Sharing a room with an actual brother has been mentioned as a favourite arrangement. It seems much more natural, by rural standards, to live and sleep and eat with a brother, than with a mere friend. There is something like the real home atmosphere then, as against the atmosphere of a young men's club. The emphasis is on safety deriving from permanent affection and loyalty. 'I knew that I would be safest with him, with my *umnakwethu*, in a place like town.' 'I am sure my elder brother will always take good care of me. He is not the man to get tired of me in the long run.'

Though staying permanently with an elder brother means permanently accepting a slightly inferior status, this is tolerated cheerfully. One Red migrant who had stayed in town with his elder brother for many years was still cleaning the room and doing most of the cooking, but, he said, 'this does not worry me, because my brother is my senior'. Another pair of brothers had gone on staying together in spite of certain strains. When the younger first came to town he was unmarried, and, as is usual among Red migrants, he used to give his elder brother his earnings to keep safe. After his marriage he had a feeling that he ought to be more 'independent'. The elder, however, was conservatively minded. 'Trouble nearly arose' (as the younger put it). 'One day my brother said to me: "What do you do with your money these days? Are you beginning to copy the town way of life?"' The partnership lasted: the loyalty of brothers won.

FINDING ONE'S OWN ROOM

There are some cases besides those of brothers where two men get on so well in a common lodging that they stay together permanently. But the new-comer, just as he graduated from *inyuwana* to proper sub-tenant, usually wants to graduate from sub-tenant to registered tenant in due course, i.e. to find a room of his own. Case histories showed that this usually happens after about two months to one year. Ideally the parting is amicable and causes no hard feelings. Anyway, there will be no shortage of new sub-tenants ready to take the place of the one who has left.

Sometimes, however, the living together had engendered frictions which became intolerable and were then cited as the specific reason for moving away. As Reader also records, these are commonest where the number of men sharing a room is large. In view of the cramped accommodation, the lack of physical amenities and the emotional strain of the unfamiliar town surroundings, perhaps the wonder is not that some room-mates do quarrel, but that so many get along as well as they do. Many of the quarrels which arise seem to be concerned with food. Catering for themselves is something which *abafana* do not do in the country, and in the unaccustomed task there may be recurrent struggles to enforce the sacred principle of 'fair shares for all'. There is the man who never seems to have any money on him when the room-mates make a silver-collection to buy meat or beer; there is the type who has been seen going off and eating meat in an eating-house, all by himself; there are the two bosom-friends who practise collusion in such matters, to the fury of the other room-mates. There is the room-tenant who seems to take unfair advantage of his position, or to favour one sub-tenant at the expense of others. One way or another, it may be a great relief to get away to one's own room and be at liberty to choose one's own sub-tenants.

Nevertheless—and this is one of the most significant pointers to the strength of incapsulation—the Red man who sets out to look for his own room rarely or never tries to move far away. Even where there has been a quarrel, much more where the parting has been amicable, he will insist that he wants to stay 'near his *amakhaya*'.

Red people practically always look for rooms in the wood-and-iron section. To move across into the better-class municipal houses (as distinct from the old council houses) would be a definite move away from the main stream of Red life. Red people (as Reader also reports) maintain that they like this area 'because there are lots of our people here'. 'When I see the people gathering for a beer drink in the wood-and-iron houses, I can almost think I am at home again.' But the preference for being near actual *amakhaya* is something more specific than this. A School man, at the end of a few months in town, may have made new friends who have nothing to do with his country home. A Red man, even when the first critical stage is over, regards his home-people's protection as essential. To the Red axiom that 'Men from the same home must help each other', he will add 'and they help each other better when they are close together'. 'When I left the *iintanga* who had put me up in Moriva, I found a room in Mekeni, because I wanted to be near my home people.' 'I had to leave the room of my father's brother's son when he got married, but he suggested that I find a place quite near to him, for otherwise it would appear as if we had quarrelled.'

Some owners of house-property in the wood-and-iron section are themselves Red migrants. These like to let their rooms to other Reds and particularly to their home-people.[14] Generally the addresses are already known (or can be found out) at home in the country. (Some of the Red landlords actually live in the country and collect the rents on monthly visits to town, or have them collected by an agent.) Houses full of *amakhaya* form exceptions to the more usual rule that house-mates are not on intimate terms. 'I knew the old man had a hut in the wood-and-iron section. At home he knew my father, and as soon as I came to town I went to his house, where I would be sure to find many Tshabo people.'

Though the location appears to be seething with people coming and going, closer examination suggests that the tenancy of rooms by Red migrants is rather stable. The room-tenant is the constant nucleus of the group; the floating element consists of the sub-tenants who come and go. After his first temporary

[14] For Red landlord-tenant relations cf. chapter 8.

shared lodging, the room 'of his own' which a Red migrant is expected to find 'ought to' be his home as long as he stays in town, or be shifted only once or twice in the course of years.

One obvious reason for stability is the shortage of accommodation. But with Red people this is reinforced by moral feeling. They regard frequent changing of rooms as undignified and improper. 'The spirits do not like it', is the usual rationalization.

'You must remember', said a Red informant, 'that the spirits who have to look after you, are also looking after your brothers and relatives who live far away. Suppose the spirits have been called upon by your relatives at home. Meanwhile you shift away from your room in town which was known to the spirits. From your new room you now call upon your ancestral spirits to come and help you. The spirits go to your former room, only to find that you are not there. They are obliged to trace you. Do you think they are pleased with that?' 'The spirits', said another, 'do not favour a frequent changing of rooms in town. It is a bad thing, showing that you are not capable of keeping anything for a long time. The spirits say that because of this habit you will some day lose or throw away something of real value.'

In more generalized terms, one might say that the spirits are held to be sanctioning the enduring face-to-face relations characteristic of a small-scale community. They 'do not like' the hiding away, the becoming anonymous, for which town offers so much opportunity. They positively require the *amakhaya* to remain in permanent touch.

THE SECOND PHASE OF DOMESTIC LIFE: LIVING SEPARATELY

Once established in his own room, a Red man will almost certainly start off by sharing it with sub-tenants. He has re-created the same kind of group, but now has the dominant instead of the subordinate status within it. One man will enjoy his new elevation and tend to exploit the privileges that go with it; another will be more merciful. 'I remember that I have been a sub-tenant myself before. So I do not like to bully the other men, especially as they are careful not to do anything that will upset me.' But sooner or later most room-tenants give up sharing their room with two, three or more men at a time. After five years in town, there seem to be few Red room-tenants who have more than one room-mate, and most of these partnerships are enduring 'special friendships'. The room-tenant no longer assumes airs of leadership, *qua* room-tenant. As already indicated, many of these enduring room-partnerships are with a younger man who respects the room-tenant as senior.

One of the commonest causes for wanting more privacy is sexual association with women. The 'rules of the house' (as has been said) entail that as long as a man is staying with a group of others, he cannot indulge in love-making in the room. Even if the sexual partner is a man's own lawful wife on a visit from the country, intercourse in the presence of the other men is improper. Many long partnerships between a pair of room-mates break up when one of them receives a visit from his wife for a few days or weeks. (Often the idea is to keep the wife in town until she is known to be pregnant.) 'My room-mate got married and his wife came from Tshabo from time to time. I did not want to inconvenience the couple. He agreed that it was right for me to go; he helped me find a new room.'

As the men get nearer middle age, they begin to value women's company in their rooms not only for sexual but for domestic purposes. A woman will keep the room clean and tidy and do the cooking; tasks which are all very well for young men, but less becoming to a man who grows older. Many Red men have a woman in for a few nights each week in what looks like a kind of domestic partnership, but as long as the woman keeps on her own room elsewhere she is technically only 'visiting'. If the association is regular enough she comes to regard herself as 'his' *inkazana* and to take on certain duties such as brewing beer for his friends.

When a Red man ceases to regard himself as an *umfana* and becomes an *indoda* (mature man), i.e. usually somewhere about the age of 40, he may go the whole hog and take a woman to live in his room as a permanent inmate. As distinct from 'visiting', this 'living together' is characterized as *ukushweshwa*. *Ukushweshwa* is discussed at length in chapter 16. The discussion will show that although at this stage the domestic group appears to resemble a family, its evaluation in Red kinship morality is completely different. The main difference between *ukushweshwa* and all the other forms of domestic arrangement which have been reviewed is that in all other cases the room-mates, one's closest associates, themselves stand for the home community, and the sanctions of the home community govern the relationship. The *ishweshwe* is not obliged to the man's home by anything more than a code of honour, a code (moreover) to which her own self-interest is always opposed, for the less he remembers his duty to his home, the more time and money he will have to spare for herself.

NEIGHBOURHOOD CLUSTERS

One would expect the two Red preferences—for getting a room close to one's *amakhaya*, and for remaining tenant of the same room indefinitely—to combine in producing an effect visible in geographical terms. This is just what has happened. Red people as a whole tend to be concentrated in certain parts of the locations, but also, within this concentration, there are neighbourhood clusters of Red *amakhaya* from particular home places. Generally speaking the districts that appear to harbour proportionately the most Red migrants are the most tumble-down and slummy—parts like those known as Maxambeni, Gomorra, Mekeni, and 'New Brighton'—while slightly more respectable parts, such as Moriva, belong mainly to non-Red people. A similar distinction applies to municipal housing. The old council houses, humble one-roomed cottages, are mainly Red today, but few Red tenants are to be found in the superior sub-economic housing of the New Duncan Village.

The authorities who allot municipal houses and also issue lodger's permits are not concerned that people of one cultural background or one home area should stay close together. (The only exception is a tendency to select the 'better class elements'—which broadly speaking, will mean urban or School people—for the Duncan Village.) Distribution reflects thousands of individual choices on the parts of people buying houses, renting houses, admitting sub-tenants.

Within the Red areas, the clusters of men from particular home districts seemed to be well known to most Red people at the time of the investigation. For instance if asking for Kentani people one would be directed to Gwayi and Mbonisela Street in New Brighton, Bantu Street in Moriva, and Sileku and Nocingo Street in Mekeni. Willowvale people lived along Sofute Street in the old council house area. Men from Tshabo formed clusters in Gomorra,

Moriva, and Mekeni. Nqamakwe people were commonest between 'Lloyds' (the location Office) and Vena Street.

These neighbourhood clusters, it must be repeated, are Red phenomena. It is not Tshabo men as such who congregate in the Tshabo 'area', but Tshabo Red men. The School people from Tshabo might be found anywhere. The neighbourhood clusters belong to the Red pattern of incapsulation.

6

The Incapsulation of Red Migrants

2. RECREATIONS AND FRIENDSHIPS

SETI

The pivot of Red sociability in town, as in the country, is beer-drinking East London having no municipal beer-hall, drinking is done either at home or in the shebeens, where the brewing and selling of liquor is strictly illegal. This account is not concerned with Red drinking habits in town generally, but with the organization of drinking by cliques, *iseti*. *Iseti*, apparently from the English 'set'—some informants say 'We fit together like parts of a tea-set'— is a clique of, say, six to eight people, who habitually take their drinks together. They may be regular customers at a certain shebeen, or may drink by themselves at a member's home, if there is a woman member or hanger-on who can take charge of the brewing. Drinking at home is preferred.

Every *iseti* consists of *amakhaya*. Some of the men may be room-mates in town, some may be work-mates, while others are related only by the ties of home. The female friends of any of the men may be admitted too. The members are usually of roughly the same age, but young and old can be included, if there are 'not enough of our own home-people living near by' to make separate sets possible. Where older men are included, girls and very young women are not. They would be 'shy' to drink with their fathers' age-mates.

In terms of hours, *iseti* is an extremely important institution of Red men in town. Many manage to spend nearly all their free time in it. A set usually meets every evening. As a Tshabo Red man put it, 'when we knock off from work at 5 p.m., we know there is beer ready in the home of one of us, any day of the week'. Otherwise the set will say that they meet 'as often as we can manage', 'whenever we are free'.

The pleasures attributed to the *iseti* are two—drink and nostalgia. 'We get together to have our beer. While we are having it we can talk about our homes.' 'Our topics of conversation, while drinking, are home affairs, stock, or saving money to do things for our homes which we can be proud of.' Thus the bond of being home-people is not only incidental but essential to an *iseti*. Some men rationalized it in elementary terms: 'We like to drink with our own *amakhaya*, so that if a fight should break out we can all fight together.' The woman who supplies the beer should also for preference come from the home place, or be a hanger-on of one of the men. She knows them, she can trust them, and she will give credit if necessary.

Home-people who form one *iseti* are usually those who live nearest together in town, making it easy to drop in and out of each other's rooms, or of the local shebeen, for the daily drink. But different sets from the same home place are also interlinked, by a reciprocal arrangement. If a man visits another man from his home place anywhere in the location, he is entitled to a free drink with that man's set, provided that he himself is known to belong to a set of the same *amakhaya*. Without the implicit guarantee of reciprocity which this common home bond entails, any visitor has to pay a shilling for his drink.

In *iseti* drinking a semblance of rural order, of the Red Xhosa 'rules of drinking', is maintained. The senior man present gets the first drink out of the can and also the last drops (*umqwelo*), and the women are offered sips (*phuzisa*). Financially the principle is strict equality and reciprocity—everyone must pay the same and nobody must drink more than his share, on pain of a fine. Fining really means having to stand an extra drink all round. With some sets it is a great feature, giving rise to prolonged arguments before the verdict of the senior men present is accepted. A member may be fined for all sorts of trivialities: for arriving late without good reason, for 'disturbing the peace of his fellows', for exceeding his share. In one set of Kentani men, a young man who had drunk *umqwelo* tried to apologize, but the seniors refused to accept the apology, 'because we overheard him say something privately to one of his *iintanga*, from which it is clear that he did it on purpose'. He was fined half a bottle of brandy (to be drunk by the seniors only).

While some of the conventions of *iseti* drinking are simply the Red rural conventions, others are adaptations to town drinking specifically. For instance, the beer in town is generally ordered in advance with instructions that it should be left at the room where the drink is to be held that evening. It is regarded as a 'rule' that the host must resist the temptation to drink first before the set has assembled. In a set of Kwelegha men the host one day, getting home early, had drunk about half a mug of beer before the rest arrived. His excuse was that he had only consumed part of his own share. Nevertheless he was fined. 'He knew the rule and had broken it. We allowed him to join us in drinking only on the strict understanding that he would refund the same quantity out of his own pocket on Friday.'

Most members are likely to be fined sooner or later, and while the system nominally stands for keeping order, it also seems to be adapted to secure a rough financial reciprocity over a period of time. Often the whole thing is treated as a joke which even the culprit enjoys. But the principle that the rules are meant to be kept is brought home at the same time. The ultimate penalty for refusing to comply, which will only be applied if the *iseti* do not much like the member anyway, is expulsion. Once a man has been expelled from a set the fact will be made known to the home-people generally, so that they should not unwittingly extend him the privilege of free drinks.

Men who belong to one *iseti* and who are also work-mates may carry on the reciprocal principle in their own lunch arrangements. It may be agreed for one to take a can of food to work one day and the other a can of beer; the next day the obligations are reversed. Besides being a pleasant addition to the lunch, beer can liven up the working hours 'when we may take turns, snatching a chance to go and have a sip'.

It is clear that the sets are not only an important institution for social and recreational life, but also a major instrument of incapsulation. The set brings a man into almost daily touch with his own home-people: it also ensures that the greater part of his free time is spent in typically Red activities. Shut up with his set, drinking according to rule and 'talking about the affairs of home', the Red man gets through his evenings uncontaminated by urban influences.

AGE GROUPS: THE CORPORATE LIFE OF 'ABAFANA'

In Red rural society both the age-grade and the age-set systems are of great importance. Age-grade is here used to mean a grouping according to stage of life, and age-set a grouping according to year of initiation.

The age-grades may be considered first. It is not only that rights, duties, and status in general are largely determined by one's age-grade (junior boy or senior boy, junior young man or senior young man, mature man or old man). Each age-grade in a given locality is also corporately organized for certain purposes, especially for sociability and entertainment. The corporate life of the local age-grade is at its peak with the senior boys and the young men (*abafana*). Clubs of these age-grades function in all rural locations where Red people live. Their most conspicuous activity is the holding of the weekly entertainment known as *intlombe* (or alternatively as *umtshotsho* or *intuthu*, depending on the age-status of those taking part).

As was mentioned earlier, each club or organized group of a given age-grade in the rural community has its 'leader' or 'spokesman', who enforces internal discipline and may also speak for the group in its external relations. Younger *abafana* tend to choose a leader for hero qualities—bravery, dashing personality, success at fighting and love-making; the term *ikalipha* by which they will refer to him is from the root meaning 'be brave'. The older *abafana* more often stress the ability to speak and reason well and give advice. This shift in the concept of the leader often produces an actual change of leader as the group grows older, though a really able man may keep his position from boyhood through till middle age.

In some contexts age-grade mates call each other *intanga* (age-mate, equal), e.g. as opposed to older men or to boys. But the narrowest and most specific sense of *intanga* is based on a different institution—the age-set.

The age-set system comes into the picture from the young men's age-grade onwards. Age-sets are based on initiation; boys, by definition uninitiated, cannot be involved. It is the bond of 'being circumcised together', 'sharing one grass-hut as novices', which constitutes the special relation of *iintanga*, in the narrowest sense of the term.

Within the corporate local organization of the young men's age-grade, accordingly, there is a further gradation according to the *intanga* age-sets. The degrees are small and numerous, for initiations take place almost every year. Theoretically the age-set system stretches much farther than the local young men's club, both in time and in space. The senior/junior relations based on initiation age should nominally endure throughout life. In practice, however, they become of less and less account as men grow older; it is the *abafana*, particularly junior *abafana*, who insist most fiercely on the right to receive deference from age-sets a year or two junior. As to extent in space, the *intanga* stratification is in theory a national system which transcends all local boundaries. But if we are thinking of corporate organization, again, the local community is its effective limit. There is no corporate age-set activity based on a wider area.[1]

---

[1] The local community is the limit of *corporate* organization and *corporate* activity, as regards both the age-grade and age-set. It is not by any means the limit of age principles in *interpersonal* relations. Personal etiquette between Red Xhosa is always affected by age-grade seniority, and to a lesser extent by age-set seniority, even if they are meeting for the first time.

This excursus has been necessary as a background to the discussion of age-groups among Red men in East London.

In town, where Xhosa from all districts meet together, age-grades and age-sets might—perhaps—have been used as a common denominator and basis for associational life, regardless of home origin. They are not so used. The inter-personal etiquette of seniority, of course, is a common code observed as far as practicable by all the Red men in East London, but the corporate organization based on age-groups is practically confined within *amakhaya* limits. It is simply an extension of the local organization which exists in the country.

Thus when Red migrants speak—as they so often do—of associating with their *iintanga* in town, they do not mean age-mates in general, but age-mates from the same home place. We have seen that this applies to sharing rooms: the friend with whom a migrant lodges is a 'home person' first and foremost, and an *intanga* after that. The same principle is the one which forms the Red young men's 'clubs' in town.

These clubs are, in effect, associations between groups of room-mates all of whom are *amakhaya*. Being the local parallel, or shadow, of the *abafana* clubs in the rural community, they are organized for the same functions; namely for sociability in the first place, and secondly for graver matters such as the settling of disputes between members. Each also, like the similar organiza-tion in the country, has its 'leader'.

The size and composition of an *abafana* 'club' in town is determined (of course) by how many home-people of more or less suitable age happen to be available. If there are very few migrants from a particular home place they will probably all form one club with a rather wide age-span; if there are more, it may be possible to form separate groups for the junior, middle, and senior age-ranges. Adaptability in this respect is learnt from the country, where labour migration draws off so many young men. One principle, however, is seen to emerge fairly generally: the farther away the home district, the more active will be the organization of the *abafana* in town. The week-enders can do without it—they go home and enjoy the real thing. It is the Transkeian *abafana* who need their town 'clubs' more than any others.

The actual country leader of the young men may be available in town, or a substitute may have to be chosen. The choice of leader is referred to rural principles. 'It is not enough to be popular among the men in town, one must also be of a character that commands respect in the country.'

Sociability takes the form of *imbutho*, a gathering held on Sundays in the daytime. The members meet in the room of the leader, or of his girl friend. They both eat and drink together (unlike the *iseti*, who only drink), and they 'talk about home'. 'All day long the conversation goes on about home matters, such as the rainfall, the girl friends in the country, and the cattle somebody has bought or hopes to buy.'

Sinandoyi was the town leader of some *abafana* from a Transkeian home (Kentani area). One Sunday morning, three room-mates who belonged to this club were observed setting out for Sinandoyi's room. No special appointment had been made and none was needed: *imbutho* is a matter of course for these men, with their homes too far off for week-ending. On the way, they stopped at the room of two other members, and the following back-chat took place: 'Greetings to you inside, councillors! We are going to Sinandoyi's room to see what he is eating.' 'Let us join them, fellow', said the tenant to his room-mate; 'what is the point of staying here, when by leaving the room we may just be in time to escape an *impundulu* [witch's familiar] that might have been sent to attack one of us?' As they all arrived, Sinandoyi came out to welcome them, shook hands with each and called each by his 'name of manhood' (the name given to a novice by his girl friend when he returns from initiation). Some money was collected and beer was bought. Sinandoyi had also provided entertainment as a leader ought. The meat was ready; he called on one of the company to dish it up. 'Fellows, however little I give you, take it as great, for we are by the roadside here, in the place of the White man.' The expected polite reply was forthcoming: 'Do not worry, Sinandoyi, this that you have given us is great; a man cannot do more than he can do.'

Imbutho cannot strictly be called a rural institution, for although it is entirely based on rural habits and values it does not happen in the country. 'At home one has too many things to do at week-ends, too many people to see.' The *imbutho* is a substitute evolved specially for town 'where there is little else to do'. It is significant of the Red man's outlook that a week-end in town holds, for him, so 'little' do do, whereas for a man with wider interests it is bristling with opportunities—sports meetings, church functions, film shows, dances. The whole associational life of the urban and urbanized people flows alongside the Red man unregarded.

The *intlombe*, which is the characteristic pattern of *abafana* activity at home, does not fit easily into town surroundings. In the country the *intlombe* (or *umtshotsho* or *intuthu*), which lasts from late on Saturday afternoon till about midday on Sunday, is devoted to dancing, singing, and conversation. The more mature people drink more and dance less at their meetings than the younger do. The main function of the girls or women is to provide music and audience; while males dance, females clap, sing, and admire. Love-making on the spot is forbidden, but the *intlombe* is a background from which couples can go off on their own to make love privately. In town, Red *abafana* who are unable to get home for week-ends sometimes indulge in a sort of makeshift *intlombe*.

The country *intlombe*, for young men, is an affair without drink, but the town imitation usually arises out of a beer-drink in somebody's room. It may be an *iseti* which has been drinking together in the evening when somebody gets up and prances a few steps, saying that he feels like a dance, and others join in. In this way it may happen that besides the *abafana*, senior men (*amadoda*) start dancing in the same room—something which would never be tolerated in the country. When a dance gets under way, other Red people may drop in, attracted by the noise. If they are home-people they are welcomed, and can take their share of beer. An 'unknown' Red man—i.e. one who is not a man from home—may also be admitted on request, but he will be told that while the dancing is 'free for everyone' the beer 'has been bought'; meaning that it is up to him to contribute a can or two 'to make friends'.

The nocturnal singing and dancing are likely not only to raise objections among non-Red neighbours but also to attract the attention of policemen. Another drawback, compared with the real thing in the country, is the absence of Red girls. Such girls are rare in East London, and anyway a Red girl (as distinct from a woman) does not attend a place where men are drinking beer. If a female chorus assembles to sing and clap (*ombela*) it will consist of *amankazana*,[2] probably the local 'friends' or concubines of the men. Or the town

[2] For the distinction between girls and *amankazana*, see chapter 5.

intlombe may be held without any women, either because none is available or because trouble is feared from the juxtaposition of women and drink in such surroundings. Alternative music can be provided by one of the men playing a concertina.

Another limitation of the town *intlombe* is aesthetic. Instead of their red blankets and bead finery, the participants have to come in ordinary town dress; nor do they have the sticks which (in the case of senior boys) are held in the right hand during dancing in the country. But however drab in appearance, it does provide an opportunity for the traditional stylized boasting known as *chaza*, which is a great feature of the real *intlombe* in the country. To *chaza* (literally 'explain'), a young man will utter a whistle or high-pitched cry and raise his hands for silence. When the noise has stopped he addresses the company on topics which, he feels, reflect credit on himself. Traditionally a young man might be expected to *chaza* about his success in a stick fight or the big herd of cattle he is assembling. In town a typical *chaza* runs like this: 'I came to East London in 1953 and I have been earning two pounds ten a week ever since. I have managed to buy a plough, oxen, and a harrow. There are witnesses in this room who can tell you it is true. I came here together with X and Y; I do not know what they have been doing in the meantime, but as for me, I am a man. Don't you agree that I am a man, I who have possessions through my own labour?'

Chaza is explained as a way of increasing one's prestige: 'The men will respect the most successful man, the women will love the richest man.' But it may be said to have an important incidental function in that it impresses the 'love of home' as a fundamental Red value. By using the investment of town earnings in the homestead as a typical *chaza* theme, the Red young men at their town *intlombe* stimulate what amounts to a competition in non-urbanization.

Apart from entertaining themselves, age-groups in town meet when there is anything of special concern to discuss. The leader is the one to call the meeting, and is given the chance to speak first. If the leader does not rise after a short silence, or when one of the *iintanga* has remarked 'There is discussion', anyone else may speak. But when a leader does speak, 'though he may not argue better than anyone else, you must mark his words, lest he grow offended and ill-tempered'. No discussion by the *iintanga* can be considered final without some opinion from the leader. A common occasion for such meetings is when a dispute arises between room-mates which they cannot settle among themselves. Meetings of an age-group, that is, can serve as a tribunal for cases between its members. This is copied from rural practice, in which 'matters concerning *abafana*' are settled by the *abafana* themselves. It will be discussed more fully in chapter 7.

URBAN ASSOCIATIONS AND RECREATIONS

A Red migrant who remains orthodox in his outlook will not join in the recreations of urban and School people in East London, nor join the corresponding associations. When questioned, Red migrants said that they belonged to no sports club; that they never attended public meetings or dances; that they never went to a bioscope (cinema).

Many Red men would boast of their thrift in that though they had stayed in town for years they had 'never paid a brass farthing for any of the town functions'. Some Red young men claimed to watch rugby matches in town occasionally, but on the whole gate-money was described as 'a sheer waste of money'. But economy is not the only motive. On their own testimony, Red men would feel out of place in any of those typically urban settings: shy of the smart town youth—let alone scared of the *tsotsis*—and apprehensive of 'trouble' of some unspecified kind. Above all, they regard attendance as a breach of the Red code, a sign of *rumsha* tendencies. One illustration of Red people's intransigence has been mentioned earlier: 'If one said one had been to a bioscope they would never trust one. They said that the bioscope is the main thing that makes School people thieves and robbers.' This typifies the Red attitude to town-style amusements generally.

Drinking, of course, is an amusement practised by all classes in the locations, but it does not constitute the social leveller that might be imagined. It underlines rather than disguises the cleavage between Red and non-Red. Everyone drinks, but the Red man drinks with a difference. He regulates his drinking by rural standards and can only thoroughly enjoy it in the company of Red country people like himself; hence the popularity of the *iseti*. In town both the Red and non-Red people confirm that for preference they 'never drink together'. 'We have nothing in common, our ideas are quite different.' Red people when drinking like to be able to smoke, spit, sing, and talk and swear loudly and freely. All this goes down badly with non-Reds. Red people also like to confine their drinking to kaffir-beer except on special occasions. Brandy, to them, is something too special and important for 'just drinking'. Anyone who knows Red country life at first hand realizes how firmly the drinking of brandy, though illegal, has become entwined in their ritual and semi-ritual practices—how indispensable is *ibhoteli* (the brandy bottle) for weddings and initiations, for 'thanking' and 'sweetening', and how greatly prized by the elders, who will go through many an antic to secure themselves a share. Hence, although Red migrants will sometimes share a bottle of brandy to liven up a week-end in town, they feel that the proper use of brandy is restricted to formal occasions, like the reconciliation following an offence within a group of *amakhaya*.[3]

Still less do Red migrants make a habit of drinking the powerful obnoxious brews of town, such as *isiqandaviki* (fortified with metal polish and carbide) or *inkumpa* (fortified with stale bread and cheap spirits). The strength of these brews is fully appreciated—'the amount that fills a pound jam tin will make a man drunk from morning till night'—but to indulge in them frequently is regarded as aberrant, a mark of the desperado or the down-and-out. 'These things belong to the town people.'

Even more than by any surface differences in drinking habits, a barrier is set up by the different ethics of drinking as such. The Red man sets a positive moral value on alcohol, which for him is an integral part of hospitality and entertainment. The non-Red is no longer able to do this. Because many churches prohibit drink entirely and all frown upon excesses, Xhosa drinkers who are not Red have come to make a great point of secrecy. A remark which one sometimes hears—'Red men praise their sons for drinking, School people blame them'—hits the nail on the head: the School people do not necessarily abstain but are made to feel guilty.

The fear of being given away, then, is an extra and usually compelling reason why non-Red people avoid drinking together with Red people. A highly

[3] See chapter 7.

respectable School man, to illustrate this point, described the following 'terribly embarrassing' incident: 'I was on my way home from church on Sunday when a Red acquaintance hailed me across the street in a loud voice: "Magatyini, you have missed something, we are just come from the place where you and I had a drink the other day, and the beer was very nice." ' It is much better, from the non-Red point of view, to keep to drinking companions who respect the conspiracy of silence. An occasional drink with an old Red acquaintance in a private room—especially if he is footing the bill—is about the limit of mixed drinking that a respectable School man will tolerate.

As regards domestic drinking, the incapsulated Red pattern of the *iseti* has already been described. As regards drinking in shebeens, Red people also prefer to go around in their sets or with trusted Red friends. There is an acknowledged fear of the urban crooks and sharks who may be encountered at shebeens. If Red men who are strangers to each other are thrown together at a shebeen, they may join forces among themselves for a round of drinks (*ibeseti*). Half a dozen Red drinkers may huddle together in one corner of a shebeen room apart from the rest of the company, who are non-Reds, or ex-Reds. Separateness is favoured, too, by the fact that many shebeens have their 'regulars' who will consist of Reds at one place, non-Reds at another. For example there are high-class establishments catering specially for respectable School private drinkers, to which a Red man would not think of going.

To the incapsulated Red migrant it is not just the imbibing of alcohol that counts, but the essentially social nature of the act, the affirmation or strengthening of ties with kin, friends, or neighbours. It is true that town life can rarely afford anything like the free hospitable beer-drinks, great and small, ceremonial or purely sociable, which are a staple of Red neighbourhood relations in the country; nor does it give much opportunity for the faithful mirroring of Red social structure which is practised at those drinks—the allotted places for men on the left and women on the right, the careful assignment of the best seats according to seniority by circumcision-year. Beer in town has to be paid for, and the shebeen-keeper keeps the best places for her best customers, regardless of seniority. But at least, the Red man can and does avoid indiscriminacy: he will not drink 'just anyhow' or with 'just anyone'.

PAGAN CHRISTMAS

An occasion when *amakhaya* organization can be seen in action is Christmas. Christmas (*ikrismesi*) is the greatest festivity in the pagan Xhosa calendar. Now that the traditional public (political) rituals of the pagan Xhosa have practically disappeared, leaving the ancestor cult an affair of kinsmen and neighbours, Christmas stands out both in town and in the country as the single occasion when Red people are celebrating universally. The rural pagan Christmas is a gay affair; the 'native' dress of women and girls is seen at its brightest in honour of the occasion. The Red participants are not, of course, celebrating Christmas in the Christian sense (the churches organize Christmas separately); nor are they tied rigidly to the date of 25 December. (There was seen, though doubtless this was unusual, a postponed Christmas celebration in a Red rural locality in the month of July). What the Red country people are principally celebrating, one could say, is a festival of reunion—the general public holiday which gives them a unique opportunity to have nearly all their migrant relatives and friends at home. 'Everyone tries to go home at Christmas.'

Many Ciskeian workers in East London could get home and back again within the two days' public holiday, but to take a week or two of leave is better still, as the festivities at home may be protracted. Transkeians, needing more time for the journey, have to take some leave: alternatively, before influx control was tightened up, it was common practice to give up one's job just before Christmas. Reader has described the great yearly exodus of labour from East London in December.[4]

For those Xhosa who have to remain in town Christmas is a time of mild licence when normal conventions and restraints can be suspended. People will cheerfully demand small presents of money: girls will be kissed by men they hardly know. Some young girls dance in the streets in men's trousers, hats or caps, while some young men dress up as women. Strangers will enter a house and be offered a drink. None of these freedoms is to be resented: 'nothing is a crime at Christmas.' At Christmas 1957 I found Red and School people, who had never met before, drinking and dancing together in one room. I myself was welcomed with special warmth wherever I went. 'Today is Christmas when we are all happy together.' Men and women who could speak only Xhosa would courteously call out their greeting to me in English: 'Happy, happy.' Even the police, it is said, recognize Christmas as a fit time for relaxing normal severity, and in several past years the much-hated police raids on the location have ceased early in December—not only the raids for permit and pass offenders but those for illegal liquor. Vast quantities of beer are brewed, and bottles of brandy almost openly displayed, for the orgy of Christmas drinking.

As far as the reduced numbers due to the general exodus allow, groups of Red *amakhaya* in town organize their own Christmas celebrations. Naturally, the Transkeians are the most prominent. One such Transkeian group comprises the people from two neighbouring rural locations of the Mqanduli district. These two rural communities are on friendly terms and at feasts in either area 'dishes' (*izitya*) are reserved for visitors from the other. In October 1958 they held a special meeting in East London (as for several years past) on purpose to organize the collection of Christmas funds. They elected a treasurer and fixed a contribution of 10s. from each man, except those who were out of work or had no income. Any man who failed to contribute 'would be cutting himself off from us'. Women were not asked for money, for (as in the country) they contribute by their labour (brewing, cooking, etc.). No School people were involved, and the participants emphasized that none had ever cared to join in, 'not even those who do drink'. 'They are not interested in our affairs. They may have their own organizations, which we do not know about.'

When Christmas came the celebrations were laid on at two houses, the homes of two respected senior men, one representing each of the participating locations (which we will call A and B). For several years running the same houses have been used, one in 'New Brighton' and one in the 'Old Council Houses'. The men usually foregather at one in the morning and move over to the other in the early afternoon. On this occasion the women at both ends had brewed and cooked in abundance, taking care to buy the meat with skulls and internal organs still attached, so that men and women would be able to have the portions traditionally ascribed to them in Xhosa etiquette. In previous years several live sheep had been bought (at £1 10s. 0d. each) and slaughtered the day before

4 *The Black Man's Portion*, chapter 4.

Christmas. 'This was much more enjoyable than buying meat in town as we had to do this year.'

At Mahlantsi's home in the Old Council House area two rooms were available, but all of the men, about forty altogether, were outside, squatting on the ground to eat and drink, some in the yard and some in the street, as men squat around the cattle-kraal in the country. 'We do things here as nearly as possible in the way things are done at Christmas in the country. We thus remind ourselves of our home.' Some of the men had added a 'blanket' over their town clothes. About thirty women sat in a separate group, most of them also dressed in 'best' town clothes, with only the doeks, ornaments, and pipes showing them to be Red. Two or three had ochred blankets as shawls, or paint around the eyes. Inside in one of the rooms a few young women were dancing to the accompaniment of their own singing.

The party at this house had not been allowed to get under way without one of those rather fierce-looking disputes over the distribution of meat and drink, which are also apt to take up endless time at important festive occasions in the country. On such occasions, when two groups are represented, each will argue through a spokesman or spokesmen, with great display of oratory and sophistry. This time the *injoli* (senior man in charge of sharing out meat and drink), speaking for A Location, had offended the second party (of B Location) on their arrival by greeting them with profuse exclamations of regret that they came so late. While the rest of the men squatted down, the *injoli* and the senior man of the lately arrived B party had faced each other standing:

A: (*Injoli*) after formal greetings: 'So much has been eaten and drunk already. The meat is almost cold by now.'

B: (Senior man of second party): 'Attention! We are to have very little meat here, then? As if nobody had known we were coming? As if nobody respects our shares?'

A: 'It is true. We no longer expected you, for we have been here a very long time. We decided to start two hours ago.'

B: 'You expected us, but you did not send for us? Why?'

A: 'Because you know you are expected, you don't need a special invitation. Have you not contributed? Anyway, Mahlantsi did invite you.'

Mahlantsi: 'Nobody is ever invited specially to a feast like this. Each man just tells the other. That's how we have done it for many years.'

After prolonged further fencing peace was restored by the B spokesman graciously accepting what was left. To the host party he said: 'I thank you all for your good words. If you were not men this matter would have caused a split between us. I thank you for the beer you have kept for us.' To his own men: 'I am pleased that you too are real men. You are willing to come to a settlement when the facts are put before you. Here is your share, let us drink and be merry. This is Happy Christmas!'

Besides drinking at the two places where they had organized their own feast these men are entitled to attend similar parties of some other groups with whom they have a reciprocal arrangement for *sara* (each group allowing 'shares' to any visitors who may arrive from the other). A party of about twenty Kentani men and women turned up for this purpose. They rushed forward in close formation, the men swinging sticks, the women singing and dancing. They were received by the *injoli* who offered them a can of beer. The men and women shared this can; afterwards both the host groups kept offering them sips of beer as a gesture of friendship. In the late afternoon some of the younger men struck up a dance indoors, the women clapping and singing for them in rural Red fashion.

INDIVIDUAL FRIENDSHIPS

It will be observed that the normal recreations of Red men in country and town alike—the *intlombe* and stick fight on the one hand, the *iseti* and *imbutho* on the other, and beer-drinks in both cases—are typically of a kind which brings a group of men together, emphasizing the solidarity of this group and the allotment of each individual to a prescribed seniority-ranking within it. Altogether, the emphasis on groups and group structure as against dyadic, person-to-person relations might be called a characteristic of Red Xhosa society. Some of the points at which it appears have been noticed in earlier chapters, e.g. the attribution of wives to 'the homestead' generally, and the idea that social control and discipline are functions of 'the people', that 'we are all each other's policemen'. The emphasis on groups, no doubt, is one reason why individual friendships are rather discouraged by Red Xhosa norms. The idea of special friendships does not seem to be easily compatible with the orderly internal organization of the group or the principle of collective responsibility; friendships could prove disruptive, causing private obligations to be set higher than general ones. Red Xhosa, at any rate, say that instead of having 'private friends' or 'special friends' one should try to be 'friendly with everyone'; that a man risks compromising his independence if he exchanges secrets with any one person; and that it is bad to be swayed by the voice of one friend instead of by the voice of the public. An echo of the idea that special friendships disrupt groups may be seen in the disapproval voiced by Red roommates when two of their number become cronies, and the implication that they will collude to evade their responsibilities towards the others.

Thus Red migrants were not necessarily being evasive when in answer to questioning they denied having any special friends in town. 'I have no best friends, everyone here is my friend.' On the other hand some could give one, two, or three names. The special friendships were usually defined by them in terms of spending free time together, having a common interest or interests, and 'helping one another', especially 'helping with money'. Life in town, especially at work, offers new opportunities for striking up friendships, which might prove to be dangerous loopholes in the incapsulating structure; some Red migrants do escape, or find themselves seduced, by means of their new town friends or sweethearts, as will be discussed in chapter 11. The present question is how friendship relations are handled by those Red migrants who do not escape but keep to the approved pattern of incapsulation.

In these cases, often the 'best friends in town' prove to be nothing more or ress than old friends from home. One of the most intimate bonds in the country is that existing between young men who have been initiated together and spent the seclusion time in the same hut, and sometimes one of these *iintanga* is to be found in town, when he will naturally rank as a 'best friend' there. 'He and I grew up together, and were initiated together, and stayed in one grass hut, and have always been used to discussing our love affairs together.' Or the rural friendship may have been based on something else. 'My best friend here in

East London is W.R. who comes from Dongwe [neighbouring location to informant's own]. We played sticks as boys. He had a sweetheart in my location and I had a sweetheart in his location, which made us great friends.' 'A great friend of mine in town is S.M., who is from my own place, Tshabo. He is quite senior to me, having been circumcised six years previously. We became friends when he was our "supervisor" at the *intlombe* and trained us in dancing as young men.' 'M.S. is my great friend here in town. He is an old friend. We are both Tshabo young men and at home we attend *intlombe* together. The two of us have been very popular at home and have sweethearts there.'

Such friendships, being nothing more than a projection from the rural situation, must strengthen, rather than impair, the migrant's country-rootedness and loyalty to the old cultural standards. But the same can be said of many friendships which are first struck up in town. Any new friend of Red peasant background can serve to reinforce the loyalty to the common value-system of Red peasants. 'M is not from my home place and we first met at work. He is old enough to be my father, but we are great friends. He is a respectable old chap, and he has respect for me as his foreman. During the lunch hour we are always together. He is the type of man one could learn a lot from. His conversation is educative, in that he always emphasizes that we must not waste our money in town, but must send it home.' 'P is one of my best friends. We are of the same age and are both employed at the docks by the S.A.R. & H. Like me, he has his own kraal at home, and a family to support. He has respect for me, and we help each other a great deal in money matters.' 'M.N. is of Mncotsho Location: not far from my own home location. We met for the first time at work under the S.A.R. & H. I have learnt to trust him and he trusts me as well.'

However, there can be no automatic protection against the danger (as it might be called from the Red point of view) of contracting friendships with non-Red men. The sanction is internal: the 'good' Red migrant sees a moral obligation to keep out of the way of other types. This is all part of the self-denying ordinance. 'Many promising young men have become criminals in town, because of their bad choice of companions. I have always been independent here, I have had no best friends at all.' 'Many stories have been told to us about townspeople: they are cunning, they will come to you as a real friend with a broad smile, but you must look out. That smile is meaningless. These stories have helped me to keep close to my own Tshabo friends.'

Not surprisingly, those few Red migrants who claimed to have found a best friend among the town-born seemed to be the irresponsible types. One Red informant said: 'J.D. is my friend, he is an East London man. I drink and he drinks. He introduced me to one of his friends, and now the three of us spend a lot of time going about drinking.' To the 'good' Red migrant such tendencies appear deeply suspect. 'My own closest friends are Red people. In a town there are many crimes people fall into. The Red people are always safe friends. The Red people are always trying to give strong counsel against crimes.'

Although sexual partnerships are more fully discussed in chapter 16, something must be said here about the Red migrant's choice of woman-friends. Usually, he begins his town career young, at an age when he is expected to be sexually active. One who 'has nothing to do with girls' is looked at askance. The question is how and with whom, as long as he is in town, he can conduct the expected affairs. (It must be emphasized that they are 'expected' by rural standards too, and are not a new symptom of urban *anomie*.)

In spite of the demographic factors, Red men in town rarely have—or at least rarely admit to having—steady sexual relations with non-Red women. As a choice between evils, it is better to have a Red woman older than oneself, than a non-Red girl of one's own age. The week-enders would usually say that their 'best sweetheart' was some Red girl at home in the country. A few said that 'Now I am married, my wife is my best sweetheart'. For the young men who can get home only occasionally, and who 'have to' find sexual outlets in town, the maturer Red women have to serve. The older men who take women to live with them under *ukushweshwa* also choose Red women almost invariably.

On rare occasions a School country girl, especially if she is of humble background, becomes a recognized sweetheart to a Red man in town. But the town-born girls are supposed to be avoided like the plague. The final verdict of many Red men was simply: 'There is nothing I like about them.' Some put it on cultural grounds: 'I am a Red young man, I do not wear smart clothes, and the town girls are too smart for me.' And some put it on grounds of moral distaste: 'Town girls are the ones who will not stick at committing abortions.' 'Town girls are immodest. They have extraordinary appetites for sexual intercourse. There are times when a man feels exhausted after a day's hard work. Naturally on a night like this you don't want to be disturbed. But when the light has been blown out, the town girl will poke you with her elbow, and tell you that you are snoring badly. She will go on bothering you until you satisfy her. This is very boring when you are not in the mood.' 'They have private lovers besides you, and if any of these should see you visiting the girl's room at night, you may be killed or narrowly escape death.'

This negative stereotype is set against the positive one of the Red sweetheart in the country. 'I like country girls, I am used to them.' 'Country girls are sometimes a little boring, it is true, but they are faithful and one can trust them.' 'If you have a sweetheart in the country and another man proposes love to her, she will tell you about it the next time you visit her.' 'The country girls are modest and pretend they don't even want a kiss.'

Over and above any such reasons, the town girls are supposed to be avoided by Red men on the specific ground that they constitute a threat to incapsulation. They despise Red ways and have no regard for the country home: thus a man who does not want to be seduced into *ukurumsha* or *ukutshipha* had better have nothing to do with them. 'Town girls are very fond of teaching their lovers this or that. "This is not done in town", they will say, "you must do it that way instead, so as not to look a fool." Once you start to listen to this kind of talk you are finished. I have therefore decided to keep away from town girls.' 'Falling in love with a town girl means that a man starts to neglect his wife and children. He is not given a chance to go home at week-ends.'

Whether the avoidance of town girls is spontaneous, on grounds of disparity or distaste, or whether it is forced, on grounds of incapsulated morality, it constitutes one of the most important bulwarks of the Red migrant community. In chapter 11 it will be seen how non-Red girls and women can, in fact, force Red men who persist in associating with them to become more and more 'civilized', less and less Red.

7

The Incapsulation of Red Migrants

3. THE 'AMAKHAYA' AND SOCIAL CONTROL

SOME CONCLUSIONS: THE RED MIGRANT AND HIS NETWORK

The last two chapters having been largely about networks, it may be as well to summarize the findings under this head (as they emerge so far) before going on to the new topic of groups in action.

We have been concerned with men compelled by economic and administrative *force majeure* to divide their social lives between town and country. For the average Xhosa, migration consists in having to come to town for long periods while never being able to feel that he has come for good. Even if he thinks he may have come for good there are kin and friends in the country who cannot follow him freely. By definition, then, the Xhosa migrant is a person whose network of relations cannot be located in either place alone. The Red migrant's reaction to this common predicament—it will be seen later—is characteristically different from that of the School migrant. The Red man strives to keep his old (country-located) network in as good repair as possible: meanwhile, wherever possible, he uses the *same* individuals for his town purposes as for his country purposes. He does not like having to form new relations. Migration is such a general necessity that any Red migrant can be practically sure of finding in town some Red *amakhaya* (in one sense or another). These can continue to serve him for most of his personal and private needs. The *iintanga* or kinsmen with whom he shares his domestic life, and the members of his *iseti* with whom he spends his leisure time, are his most intimate regular associates in town: they are *amakhaya*. Members of other *iseti* with which his own has reciprocal arrangements, and men from other rooms with whom he can join for *mbutho*, widen the sociable circle: they are *amakhaya* too. It may be affirmed as a general principle, then, that men with whom he shares his leisure hours in town are related by pre-existing ties as well. They are men whom he has known, or known about, since childhood, or who are related to his own 'people at home' in one way or another. The sanctions emanating from the home community are the ones which, in the long run, govern the relations in town. His network has been 'stretched' in a literal geographical sense, rather than 'widened' by the working-in of new individuals.

By this means the Red migrant is protected from the trauma of plunging into an altogether unfamiliar social world; and he is even protected, to a high degree, against the temptation of wanting to plunge.

The values of home and family are exalted by the community-in-exile; home visiting is encouraged; the formation of new social ties in town, with non-Reds, is not only rendered unnecessary but represented as a danger. Kinship obligations, always morally pre-eminent, remain directed towards the country. Parents, wives, and children belong at the kraal, and as the incapsulated migrant will not consider marriage with a town girl, the formation of kinship links with urban families is ruled out. Personal relations with friends and sweethearts are kept, if not within the *amakhaya*, at least within the Red section. The incapsulated migrant refrains from voluntary association with the School and town-bred people who confront him on every side. He refrains from town-style entertainments, creating instead the nearest possible replica of Red rural entertainment that is possible in town, with the help of his own Red friends from home.

THE 'AMAKHAYA' IN ACTION

A group of *amakhaya*—that is, the whole body of 'home men' present in town at a given time—will sometimes act collectively as a quasi-corporate body, raising a levy or disciplining a member. It would be going too far to say that all *amakhaya* groups in East London are permanently 'organized'. What exists is a latent mechanism whereby such a group can be called into action on occasion, and a fairly general agreement as to what kind of occasion is appropriate. Some groups of *amakhaya* have more corporate spirit or proneness to corporate action than others, but all Red men agree in principle that there have to be occasional '*amakhaya* meetings'. These are parallel in form and intention to the *inkundla* of the rural community. That is to say, they are open moots, which every adult male member of the community concerned has a right to attend, and whose decisions are considered binding on the group as a whole. However, in effect they are only for Red people. School people do not attend, or only rarely attend, meetings of *amakhaya* in town, and do not recognize their moral authority. Thus in the case of a location which sends large numbers of both Red and School people to town—such as St. Lukes—the Red men may constitute themselves a working group of *amakhaya* while the School men stay outside.

Some rural locations send a sufficient number of Red men to town at any one time to constitute a quorum (as it were) of *amakhaya* on their own. But if the Red men from a single home location are very few they will attach themselves to the 'nearest' possible group. Among the locations of the Kentani district of the Transkei there are Gqunge and Kobonqaba, each of which in 1955 was able to hold its separate *amakhaya* meetings in town; but there are others which were not—Nyutura and Ngqosi for example: these joined together. The extension of the meaning of *amakhaya* is possible in this context because the locations in question lie near enough to each other for the men to say they 'know each other from childhood'. 'We used to meet at home when we played sticks together.'

It was mentioned that there is a wider sense of the word *amakhaya* to mean any people from the same 'home area'. All Kentani men, in some contexts, e.g. on the occasion of a visit by a chief, might organize something jointly; or the locations just mentioned, Nyutura and Ngqosi, might join in together with Qolora and Chebe. On the whole, however, the organization of *amakhaya* meetings in town seems to be restricted to *amakhaya* in the narrower sense, i.e. men from a single location or a few neighbouring locations.

A group of *amakhaya* in town regards one or more senior men as its leader or leaders. Usually there is one such senior man in each part of the town location who acts as the channel for conveying messages and summonses to meetings. As with age-group meetings, the frequency of *amakhaya* meetings in town is roughly related to the distance from the rural home. Thus, Transkeian men hold them oftener than Ciskeian men, for the Ciskeian men have more frequent opportunities to participate in the 'real' *inkundla*. Even Ciskeian Reds, however, attend town meetings when occasion arises and consider themselves bound by decisions reached there. These decisions may involve submission to a kind of 'taxation' and submission to punishment—both voluntary and backed only by moral sanctions.

One specific function of *amakhaya* meetings in town is to demonstrate continued loyalty to the home chiefs and headmen by planning welcomes for them on the rare occasions when they happen to visit town officially. In 1957 for example, a sub-chief from Kentani, who intended to visit East London for private purposes, sent word to the senior representatives of 'his' locations in town. These men called meetings of the *amakhaya* who were instructed to make suitable preparations for the 'beautiful child' (i.e. member of the royal house). At one meeting the leader suggested 'that we all donate 5*s*. each so that there will be plenty of food for him while he is with us'. Nobody opposed the suggestion. It was also agreed that the leader should act as treasurer and make the practical arrangements.

Visits by chiefs provide the exception to the rule that School migrants do not join in the activities of Red *amakhaya*. Many School migrants from the Transkei, in particular, 'are very proud of their chiefs'. Some Transkeians owned to a feeling that anyone who fails to make a contribution in his chief's honour might run into danger of losing his land at home. Migrants of either section from the Ciskei seemed on the whole to be less interested in these chiefly visits.

A more routine occasion for calling an *amakhaya* meeting is a death or serious illness. Red *amakhaya* meet as a matter of course when any of them dies in town, unless the dead person had entirely lost contact with them. News of the death circulates quickly and it is usually on the same evening that they gather at the room of the deceased. Any *amakhaya* who are prevented from coming must at least send their apologies. The first to address such a meeting is the man who was present at the death-bed. He explains when and how their comrade died, what his last words were, and whether he left any special messages. It is then up to the senior man to take charge of the meeting, and (usually) propose a financial contribution towards funeral expenses. The senior's address on one such occasion stressed the principle of joint responsibility in the following words: 'My friends, you have heard what X says; I will not repeat his words. Now that the son of N has left us, we have a duty to perform. This duty is to see that his dead body is taken home to be buried where the bones of his dead forefathers lie. On such occasions, you all know that each man must contribute as much as he can afford to. There is no fixed contribution. But you senior men must set a good example, and you junior men must learn from the example of your seniors. We are in a strange place here. Therefore we must stand together, on this sad occasion, like sons of one man.'

When a man falls seriously ill one of his room-mates may decide to call a meeting of *amakhaya*. He addresses the meeting, explains the circumstances, and adds his own suggestions about what ought to be done: whether money should be collected to send the patient home, or to get treatment for him in East

London. The senior men must then rise and give their opinion or endorse the recommendation of the room-mate.

The settlement of disputes and hearing of cases is a further function of *amakhaya* which falls to be discussed in the next section.

JUDICIAL PROCESSES

All the social groups of Red people in town which we have been considering employ a mode of internal discipline, directly taken from rural Red practice, which amounts to a sort of 'case-hearing' in prescribed forms. We have already had occasion to notice the 'hearing' by a group of room-mates when rules have been broken or conflict has arisen internally. The *iseti*, the age-groups of *amakhaya*, and on occasion the *amakhaya* groups as such, all exercise social control in the same way. With a little exaggeration one might describe them as constituting a hierarchy of tribunals, whose competence is recognized voluntarily by the Red migrants in town, but ignored by non-Reds. It must be borne in mind that Xhosa in East London have no 'Native' judicial authority to whom they can refer there. There is only the White magistrate; he may hear a case in accordance with so-called 'Native law' but he cannot employ Xhosa procedure.

Whichever group is functioning, all these Red case-hearings follow the same formal pattern. The aggrieved party reports the matter to the leader or senior man of the group, who summons a special meeting of it; he, acting as chairman, briefly outlines the matter at issue; accuser and accused are called upon to state their cases in turn; the meeting is opened to discussion; finally a verdict (the sense of the meeting) is voiced by the seniors and carried by acclamation, and a sentence—usually a fine—may be voted in the same manner. Refusal to submit to the sentence would be tantamount to withdrawing oneself from the group.

This is a basic Xhosa pattern. As a matter of fact, except for the element of accusation, it corresponds to the pattern of the *amakhaya* meetings which gather because of a death or serious illness. In the same way those meetings are summoned, hear the case stated, discuss the facts, arrive at a conclusion which the seniors voice, and vote for some practical (usually monetary) redress. Deaths and sickness, it might be said, are crises which, like serious offences and quarrels, are too severe to be dealt with by the individuals concerned, and demand the joint action of a whole group.

Which 'tribunal' a given case or quarrel will be referred to for formal hearing depends on two factors: the relation between the parties and the gravity of the issue. Normally (for instance) a dispute arising with an *iseti* will be settled by the *iseti*. But if it is grave enough, it may be necessary to call in a higher tribunal, perhaps the whole age-group of *amakhaya*, with 'all the *amakhaya*' as the final resort. The *amakhaya* are the most inclusive unit for the purpose because, after all, the whole system of Red home-made justice in town is a direct extension from the home community. The *amakhaya* in town are the local manifestation of the *inkundla* (location moot) at home; the age-mates in town are the local manifestation of the *abafana* group which at home would 'hear matters belonging to *abafana*'. In town each group applies 'Xhosa justice' to its own members, as nearly as possible on the home model, but the working group must remain the limit of its own jurisdiction. School people from one's home district, who would participate in the *inkundla* at home, are beyond the limit in town, since they do not choose to join in.

The illustrations may start with two petty cases:

1. One day an *iseti* of St. Luke's men, having ten members, subscribed 6*d*. a head for beer. One member, M, was entrusted with the 5*s*. to take to the woman brewer, but came back reporting that he could not find her. During the drinking the woman came in. The senior man of the *iseti* told her that M would bring the money over to her room when the drinkers dispersed. Subsequently the woman returned to the senior man complaining that she had still not received the money. He went to M and demanded the 5*s*. M produced only 3*s*. and said he had lost the balance and 'must have dropped it somewhere'.

With the help of a friend, the senior member produced 2*s*. 'to finish the affair with the woman', and then called a special meeting to deal with M. M was closely questioned but could not give any satisfactory account. The senior put it to the meeting that M must be punished 'because he was spoiling the good name of our *iseti*, and the woman would be justified in looking on all of us as bad men, because of what M has done'. He suggested a fine of half a bottle of brandy, to which the meeting agreed.

M however did not pay the fine. He was a man of questionable character, who drank too much. As the senior man said later on, 'he is the type of man who owes this person 3*s*. and that person 1*s*. 6*d*. and the other person 4*s*.; we knew, really, that he would never pay us'. In consequence he was deemed to have left the *iseti*. 'He has withdrawn himself from us. His name is struck out of our company.'

2. Two young men from Ngqosi in the Kentani area lived near to each other in the Moriva part of East London. One day in February 1958 S began threatening and swearing at B. They came to blows. B reported the matter to the leader of the Ngqosi *abafana*, who called a meeting. About fifteen men turned up (a good attendance). After the leader's outline, B explained at length how S's attack on him had been without any provocation. S admitted it but pleaded drunkenness and tendered an apology.

'We accept your apology', said a member, 'and we hope B will accept it too, for all of us are *iintanga* from Ngqosi. But we have younger men in our midst and I do not want them to get the idea that one is free to break our rules as long as he will apologize afterwards.' Another speaker suggested that S be fined a bottle of brandy. The leader put it to the vote and was assured 'We all say so'. The fine was paid and the meeting shared the brandy.

Like some more serious cases heard in town these two bear the marks of traditional Xhosa judicial process, in aims as well as in forms. Admission of guilt and the fixing of a suitable redress are aimed at achieving catharsis and reconciliation. Tensions are thus released and the group is enabled to remain intact. If the procedure fails, i.e. if the culprit will not confess or submit, the only alternative is fission: he must go.

The rationale of calling the whole group together, and hearing all the speakers in turn, is of course the reaching of moral consensus. The formula 'Do you all say so?'—'We all say so', which usually concludes these hearings, is full of meaning: the group has not only to form, but to record, its collective moral judgement. Where the moral issues are tricky, it is well for the tribunal to include those endowed with the greatest judicial wisdom. Hence although 'matters of *abafana* should be heard by *abafana*', the younger men voluntarily elect to refer certain cases to the full tribunal including their seniors. They resort to the full *amakhaya* meeting in town as they would resort to the *inkundla* in the country. 'A matter like this concerns the *iintanga* but specially needs the help of the seniors.'

On such occasions the younger members do not take much part in the discussion. 'They are there to learn from their elders'—a theme much stressed in Xhosa convention. However, they must signify their assent together with the rest of the meeting; usually their own leader speaks up for them briefly— 'We all say so'.

B was a young man from Kwelegha who called in the senior *amakhaya* to help him to deal with his own *intanga*, D, who lived with B as sub-tenant. B had reasons for wanting to get D out quickly, but felt he 'had to report to the *amakhaya* first so that they should understand and not think I was being cruel to my room-mate'.

The meeting was held at night in B's room. Amid dead silence, B reported that one night two Native constables had come to the room and asked for D. D was not there, but they searched the room for stolen articles. D only came home after they had left, at an hour which was unusually late for him. He could not account satisfactorily for having stayed out so late. When told that detectives were after him he had not seemed surprised, but only said he had not stolen anything. Soon afterwards D was charged and appeared in court, but was released.

B felt that D must go, 'because once your room starts being visited by detectives, the neighbours look at you with suspicious eyes'.

D put his case briefly. The fact that the court discharged him, he said, proved that he was innocent; why should he be forced to move out?

'Son of Tokwe,' said the chairman, a senior man from home, addressing B, 'none of us want our rooms raided by the police. It gives a man a bad name. However, I am not going to tell you to send D away until we have heard what the other men present have to say.' Another senior man from home rose and addressed the chair: '*Intanga*, I must say like you that a man has to be careful in town. If those stolen articles had been found in the room, and D had denied all knowledge, Tokwe's son would have been in trouble now. Thank your *amawenu* [ancestor-spirits], son of Tokwe!'

The younger men remained silent, but eventually, seeing how things went, a sympathizer of D's rose and said: 'You hear our seniors: you had better shift away to a room of your own. Remember that a man must behave himself when he is in another man's room.'

The groups of Red people in town are not only concerned with offences against the special 'rules of Red people'—such as disrespect to seniors, or failure of reciprocity between room-mates or *iseti* mates—though much of their effort, admittedly, is directed to enforcing these. They concern themselves also with offences which would be officially considered worth a civil or criminal action in the courts. In dealing with such matters as theft, debt, assault, and sexual offences, the *amakhaya* justice directly rivals the 'White man's justice'.

In the Red countryside there are no police to speak of, but neither is there very much crime. In the favourite phrase, 'At home we are each other's policemen'. Coming to town, the Red man sees for himself what he knew by hearsay before: that in spite of a considerable police force crime and disorder are rife there. In contrast to the face-to-face community at home with its informal and semi-formal pressures, the urban community seems at first sight to be quite uncontrolled and lawless. 'Mind your own business' and 'each man for himself' are stereotyped ways of summing up the East London atmosphere. The impersonality of this atmosphere—the teeming masses of people not, apparently, united by any moral bonds—is something that the Red man specially fears and dislikes.

The Red communities-in-exile do what they can to go on being 'each other's policemen': *amakhaya* seek to control each other while knowing that they cannot in any way control those around them. They may even be afraid to report on outsiders to the official guardians of law and order. 'In town, if you see some mischief going on and you intervene or report to the police, you may put your own life in danger. There are tsotsis who will do any dirty job for a few pounds and they are always ready to kill you.' The home-made justice, limited to the *amakhaya* and invoked only occasionally, does no more than build up some scattered islands in the sea of urban *anomie*. But that is something.

One of the implicit and often explicit motives for having a serious case heard by home-people is that it saves having to deliver the culprit over to any White authorities. On the one hand Red migrants recognize the police and the courts as allies against urban crime. Only they are adequate to deal with really dreadful crimes like murder, and only they have enough organized physical force at their disposal to counter the tsotsis and ruffians. But on the other hand they are the direct agents of the conquering enemy—the White man—and in town the battle to keep out of their clutches is almost unending. In many cases and especially where a man from home is concerned, it is an act of simple loyalty to keep your fellow-man from falling into police hands. 'We prefer to settle the matter in the Xhosa way.' The Red people claim, perhaps justly, that their own method of justice is more effective in a reformative sense than the 'justice of White men', for the culprit feels morally bound to his judges. 'The very fact that they come together to punish him, shows him that they love him.'

The following case of assault illustrates this sharp sense of opposition between 'White' and 'Xhosa' justice. M, a St. Lukes man, hit his sweetheart on the head with a stick, inflicting a wound which bled profusely. The girl went off to lay a complaint at the charge office. N, an *intanga* of M's, saw what was going on, hurried after her and managed to persuade her to return to her room, promising her that the matter would be dealt with 'in the Xhosa way'. He told her that if she gave M away to the police they would charge him not only with assault but with failing to pay his poll-tax for three years and being without a valid lodger's permit.

'I could see', said N, 'how pleased M was when he saw me bringing back his sweetheart. He knew what a narrow escape it was from *tyala* [charges]. He whispered to me: "*Intanga*, you are a man! You have saved me!" I ignored the whispers and told him I was very much shocked by what he had done; that I was going to bring the matter before the *iintanga* and that he would be fined for cruelty.' (Properly, the woman should have reported to the man's *iintanga* herself.)

At the meeting, where about ten *iintanga* were present, M apologized; he said he had just lost his temper. He was fined a half-bottle of brandy plus a four-gallon tin of kaffir-beer. All this was consumed by the *iintanga*.

In another case which was regarded as far more serious—serious enough to demand an immediate meeting of all the *amakhaya*—the culprit was explicitly given the choice of being reported to the charge office or submitting himself for punishment by his fellows. The senior man who had called the meeting began by saying: 'Fellows, I have called you for a matter which is very serious indeed, though it is not somebody's death which I have to report. It is something which could land a certain person in jail for three years. This boy [indicating an 18-year-old youth] was waiting for me in my room when I came home yesterday, to report that this other youth, his room-mate, had assaulted him sexually. I call on him to tell you what happened.'

A loud murmur of amazement and indignation rose from the meeting, and the accused sat shivering and breathing heavily, as the complainant got up to speak. His account was long and circumstantial. It had been a stifling summer's night: he had lain naked on top of the bedclothes, trying to sleep; had dozed off, and been awakened by the assault. There had been a struggle. In evidence he could produce a shirt which he had used afterwards to wipe off the semen.

Accused said that he had no recollection of the deed, but that if it had really happened he must have been drunk. The meeting then began to cross-question him. Why had he left the room and hidden away? 'I thought the other boy was fetching his *iintanga* to kill me.' Had he any girl friends? 'No, I am not interested in love-making.' Had he a special reason for not being interested in women? 'They are of no help to me, I have no sexual cravings.' Had he ever heard the word *ukushina* (sodomy)? 'I have heard of it in Johannesburg where men sleep with other men.' Did he prefer sex relations with a male or a female? 'I am not interested in either.' Did he never have sexual desires while drunk? 'I do not know what happens when I am drunk, I have no recollections afterwards.'

Finally he was asked if he wanted to be reported to the charge office or to be dealt with by the *amakhaya*. He begged not to be reported; he could only say again that he knew nothing about the offence, because of drunkenness. He asked for the pardon of his 'kinsmen'.

The senior in his summing-up said that although sodomy was an almost unknown offence among Xhosa, he believed the penalty would be the same as for witchcraft, namely death. 'But our nation is under foreign control, and life is confused.' They would therefore be lenient to the accused. They requested him to leave the room while they discussed the penalty. It was eventually fixed at three pounds.

Instead of paying within the agreed period, the accused escaped to his country home. But naturally the news soon followed him there. Eventually he returned to East London and paid up. The money was put into the burial fund. Some of the *amakhaya* wanted to buy liquor with it as usual, but the senior man said that money paid for such a terrible offence should not be used for entertainment.

THE NATURE OF THE SANCTIONS

The Red 'tribunals', staging judicial processes but having no coercive force at their disposal, in effect present the choice: submit voluntarily, or you are not one of us. Membership of the group entails willingness to endure its discipline. The sanctions are purely moral ones. Against refusal to conform, the ultimate measure must be some form of excommunication. Just as the final weapon against a disobedient son is to disinherit him—to cut him out of the family—so the final weapon against unruly brethren in town is to cast them out of the group: out of the *iseti*, out of the age-group association, or, in an extreme case, out of the exiled 'community' of home-people altogether.

If a Red man refuses to pay a fine or otherwise submit to the decision of home-people, he will be 'cast off by the home-people' (*ukhutshiwe ngamakhaya*). This is often described as 'washing off' the relation (*uhlanjiwe*)—the same word which properly means the disinheritance of a son by a father. 'He does not want us and so we do not want him any more. He has broken away from us.'

The thoroughness with which excommunication is carried out will depend on the nature of the offence, and the general attitude towards the offender, but also on the degree to which the particular *amakhaya* group is corporately organized. As we saw, this is directly correlated with distance from home. The Transkeians, who depend so much upon their *amakhaya* in town, are said to be 'very keen to obey their rulings', while Ciskeians may be more prepared to let things slide.

First of all, excommunication involves social ostracism. Two 'police' may be specially commissioned, from among the culprit's own *iintanga*, to go round telling all the home-people in East London that so-and-so has refused to pay the fine imposed on him for such-and-such an offence. The home-people are told 'not to welcome him if he tries to be friendly'. 'He must be made to feel an outcast.' If the rejected individual turns up at a meeting he is not treated as a full person there. Should he stand up to speak (which is every member's right) he will be ordered down: 'Who are you to speak here?'

Further implications are the withdrawal of practical support and assistance, which normally a man could expect from his *amakhaya*. If he is the victim of an assault they need not come to his aid; if he is arrested, no financial or legal help is forthcoming. If he is ill they may not look after him, and if he dies no funds need be raised for his burial or for taking the body home.

In addition, the matter may be reported at the country home. Senior men staying in East London will notify the people at home that 'X refused to obey the laws of this place, when he was in town, and that if anything happens to him we *amakhaya* in town must not be looked upon to rescue him'.

For all these reasons, well-disposed Red people will either try to avoid excommunication or come round after an interval and beg for pardon. 'Nobody from Kentani wanted him as a friend; he felt very lonely; so he decided to pay the fine after all.' Apology has to be tendered formally at a meeting of *amakhaya*, and accompanied by the inevitable drink-offering, usually a whole bottle of brandy or four gallons of beer. If the case involved a personal conflict with another man from home, a public reconciliation may be staged. 'He shakes hands with his victim in the presence of all.' After this he is again regarded as 'one of us'.

Paternal 'washing off' is a moral disaster, implying rejection by the ancestor spirits too. To a right-thinking Red man, excommunication by the *amakhaya* is a moral disaster likewise, implying rejection by the *vox populi* which is also the *vox dei*.[1] Red people recognize that a man who does not take steps to be reconciled to his *amakhaya* after being 'washed off' has repudiated not only their moral authority but (by implication) that of the home community itself. He is an "I-don't-care", and he is soon to become an *itshipha*, for he was ready 'to be separated from his home people.' When all is said and done, such exclusion is only the ultimate weapon of the otherwise powerless, and there is a sad

[1] Cf. chapter 9.

ambiguity about it: it inflicts no smart upon the very people whose punishment is regarded as most desirable. A man who turns his back on the *amakhaya* and their standards 'does not care' that they may turn their backs on him, any more than the hardened absconder minds being 'washed off' by his kin. In fact, often enough, the 'washing-off' is simply the dramatic expression of a breach which had already gone beyond repair. As such, it has no greater punitive effect than a shaking of fists in the direction of the villain who is delighted to be riding away.

Its practical value in such cases, one may say, is to be judged not by its effects on the culprit, but by its effects on his censors, the remainder of the group. Regarded as a gesture of solidarity on their part, as an affirmation of faith, 'washing-off' can be called a significant act.

THE PASSAGE OF TIME

The master-pattern of incapsulation, then, means that the highest value is put on roles either belonging to the country home or derived from the country home. The incapsulated migrant must, at the same time, play certain roles in town at large, but those which take him outside the circle of his *amakhaya* and his Red mates are performed mainly in a passive spirit, without positive ambition.

What is the effect of the passage of time on this pattern of migrant existence? Case material indicates that for most young Red peasants, when first coming to East London, the idea is to stay 'a few years'. The need to continue working in town through most or all of the active life is not a regular expectation. Ideally the young man earns but the mature man goes home. It comes as an unpleasant revelation to the less fortunate to find the stay in town lengthening, year after year, because the migrant cannot get ahead of his financial needs. 'I had intended to stay here for a few years only, but I have still not managed to buy enough cattle to settle permanently at home.' 'I came here to earn money preparing for the time when I would want to get married. During the time I have been here I have bought some cattle and now I am married. But it seems that I shall have to go on working in East London to support my family.'

A prolonged stay in town requires a sort of adjustment, but this is not to say that it requires 'urbanization'. The Red migrant must learn how to keep his end up with the townsmen, but he need not learn to be a townsman. He must learn how to keep a job, but he need not value the job as he values the homestead. On the whole, the main requirement for a satisfactory private life is to learn to function smoothly within the incapsulating circle; that is, to keep on good terms with the *amakhaya* in town and at home.

The years which bring greater skill in coping with the town surroundings also bring nearer the time for final retirement to the country. Red migrants over 45 or so, interviewed in East London, generally spoke of retirement as a definite near objective. And the nearer the retirement comes, the stronger is the feeling of 'belonging' in the country, not in town. The Red peasant migrant, then after fifteen, twenty or twenty-five years in town, may be just as Red as he was after five.

Z left Tshabo nearly thirty years ago to work in Springs, where he became a boss boy (1929–36). He also worked as a labourer in Cape Town from 1938 to 1947; and as a building contractor's labourer in East London from 1947 till the time he was interviewed (1957) at the age of about 46. His intention then was 'to stay working in East London until I can work no more because of old age'. But these many long years in towns, and the less usual intention to stay even longer, in no sense mean that he has become town-rooted. He is still a migrant, not an immigrant. 'My real home', said Z, 'is in Tshabo, in the country, where one is free to keep any number of cattle and sheep, and money does not matter so much. My wife and children are staying there permanently. There is nothing I like about town life. I am only here because this is the place where people come for money. Since I have been in East London I have visited my home every Friday night and returned on Sunday night. I have spent all my holidays at home. When in the country I do what I can on the land, or repair the fences or the house. When I have free time in town, I always spend it visiting the other Tshabo men who are here, and we drink together and discuss home matters.'

Something has been said of the Red fear of sons 'getting lost' or absconding. Clearly, getting lost is not a function of length of stay in town. A misfit or an unruly son may contrive to get lost within a year; a good son may spend thirty years in town without cutting adrift. It is a difference of aspirations and ambitions. The migrant with typically Red aspirations can remain effectively within his home small-scale community, for most of the purposes which matter to him emotionally and personally, throughout his stay in town. The one who will no longer play the game of face-to-face relations finds himself 'washed off' and thereafter ignored. By passing from the small world of his *amakhaya* into the wider world outside, he ceases to count effectively for them.

8

Economic Attitudes of Red Migrants

The labour migrant is usually looked upon as a participant in two economic systems, which are of a sharply contrasted nature, one being a subsistence peasant economy—still largely based on reciprocity and mutual aid—while the other is a full-blown Western industrial and commercial economy. It is obvious that different scales of value are demanded in each of these settings. The first calls for the particularistic attitudes of a small-scale and technically backward community, the other for impersonal, universalistic standards.

But in East London the migrant, it was said, acts in three settings, not only in two. In the third, the urban location, economic relations have a quality of their own. In the peasant economy at home the migrant is a subsistence producer and consumer: in town, in the White economic system, he is an employee and again a consumer: and in the location, among fellow-Xhosa, he acts out economic roles as tenant, landlord, customer, borrower, and lender. This third field of economic activity is ruled by its own standards which partly resemble each of the other two kinds.

RED PEASANT ATTITUDES TO MONEY

The role of money in the Red rural economy is essential but limited. The homestead produces mainly for subsistence; wool is almost the only product that can be used to bring regular cash returns, and then only for the lucky few. Major tasks such as building or sheep-shearing are done with the help of work parties, paid for by entertainment, food, beer, and the acknowledged obligation of reciprocity. The tendency of some forward-looking School people to substitute cash wages is severely disparaged by Red Xhosa.

Thus, in the country, very little money circulates between the Red peasants themselves. Its main use there is to pay White people—the storekeepers and the tax authorities. Because all the money dealings to which Red peasants are accustomed involve White people, they all appear in the light of transactions between the weak and the strong. This power aspect is extremely important in the Red peasant's mind. Because of it he can scarcely be said to have the notion or experience of the passing of money in purely contractual terms, governed by universalistic considerations. Red peasants imply that wherever money is involved the stronger will almost automatically be using his power to the disadvantage of the weaker. Many would not hesitate to use their own power so.

In the country there are unending complaints that the White storekeeper exploits the peasants, overcharging for purchases or underpaying for produce; that the White farmer deducts from his servants' already meagre wages, on account of alleged debts which can never be checked; that the sale of beasts to any White person can fetch only a low price, if the seller is not White. In town the migrant complains that the White shopkeeper, if he gives wrong change, tolerates no argument. Then there is the figure of the White urban employer, paying wages which the worker regards as starvation wages, but which he (the worker) cannot influence either by individual or by collective bargaining. And finally there are the White authorities to whom, in town or at home, he pays taxes and fees.

Once in town the Red migrant feels in danger of being exploited not only by White people but by the more cunning of his fellow-Africans. It is one of his constant reproaches against the more educated Xhosa that to them money has become 'everything'. 'Their weakness is money. They have not got that tradition or love of relatives, that feeling of relationship, which binds together our Red people at home in the country, and binds the Reds even in town.' 'The School and especially the town-born people think in terms of money and do not care how much they hurt a person as long as they get what they want, namely money; Red people would never kill a person just to rob him of money.' Discussions of Xhosa poverty often ended, not without a spark of humour, in the pronouncement that there is no affinity between the 'real Xhosa' and money. 'X went home with handsome savings. A few years later he was back in town. "Why have you come back?" we asked him. He shook his head: "Money is not a thing of the Xhosa. It has returned to its owner, the White man." '

It can thus be said that the Red migrant's attitude towards money is distinctly ambivalent. As money is necessary for getting along in the country and is the direct incentive for coming to town, Red men are greedy for it, bent on earning and saving as much as possible. They are long used to the idea of money and many are skilful and shrewd in its management. At the same time their minds are attuned to a predominantly subsistence economy, and they dislike town not only as the place where they are condemned to work, but as the place where money assumes too much importance. 'Here in town you only enjoy life as long as you have money in your pocket, but in the country you can carry on as long as you have food to eat.' 'The foundation of life here is employment for wages. Without it you are finished: down you go.' 'Even if you are ill rent still has to be paid.'

OBLIGATIONS TO THE HOME ECONOMY

As was said, providing for the needs of the homestead is the only justification of town work in Red eyes. Money earned in town ultimately stands for 'independence' in the country. 'My father has set me an example of what a man should be in his old age—independent.' Very few Xhosa peasant homes can in fact ever hope to be fully independent, in the sense of dispensing with cash supplements from outside.[1] The more modest notion of 'independence' which the Red people entertain is that the family may be able to meet its cash needs regularly out of the current earnings of the current migrant member. Failing this the dread alternative would be to have to sell one's main capital asset, livestock. Thus the Red migrant, in his own view, is putting himself at the mercy of the White employer in order to 'protect the cattle at home', and also to 'build up the homestead' by accumulating money for such things as ploughs,

[1] Houghton, D. H., and Walton, E. M.: *The Economy of a Native Reserve; Keiskammahoek Rural Survey*, vol. II.

oxen and implements, in addition to providing cash for current daily needs.

The Red migrant, needless to say, is supposed to remit money regularly to his parents or his wife, depending on his status in the homestead. One said that he was sending home '£4 or £5 every month'; another '£2 to my wife every second week'. (It will be realized that on the average wage of under £3 per week this requires considerable effort.) 'Not sending money' is the first ominous sign of absconding. The migrant may contribute in kind as well. Many of the regular home-visitors make a point of taking with them *ipasile*, 'the parcel', containing a few shillings' worth of provisions, mainly meat, sugar, coffee and tea. Some men would rather borrow than go home without *ipasile*, which is both a necessary element in the homestead economy and a symbol of the man's role as provider.

To play the role of homestead-head *in absentia* means not only sending money but taking part in the non-monetary economic life of the home. The homestead-head must remain the director of affairs: when necessary he must send his instructions from town by letter or by word of mouth. If he is away for any length of time he needs to have a deputy or deputies on the spot. The wife may be able to cope with routine matters, but some man must be available for men's work (such as ploughing) and for general supervision. The natural deputy is an agnatic kinsman. A Red migrant homestead-head who had been in town for seven years, leaving a wife and three children, spoke of such a kinsman 'living not far from my own homestead. He sees that my lands are ploughed, free of charge. He has one of my goats killed for the *imbeleko* ceremony [after childbirth] and sees that the shoulder is used for my wife. My wife decides nothing without consulting him. If it is important he urges her to let me know; suppose she wants to sell mealies or beans, perhaps I might have money to avoid having to sell at all. Beer will not be drunk at my home unless he has authorized it and explained its purpose, for instance the harvest-home beer' (lit. 'beer for return of the oxen from the lands').

In negative terms, the money earned in town is not used to raise the migrant's status in the wider location society. The appetite for money is not an appetite for town goods or town gratifications. As his social ranking in East London is of little concern to the Red migrant (unless in a few particular situations), he does not care about the externals—clothing, furniture—which mean so much to aspiring School people there. He wants nothing in town over and above his bare living and the means for being sociable in the Red manner. He resists the lure of the town shops: it is the old self-denying ordinance. Few Red migrants have a 'better' suit for use in town, as distinct from their working clothes. For those who sleep on iron bedsteads, sacks may be sufficient mattresses; to sleep on the floor on a mat is all right too. 'We are merely camping here by the roadside.' Expenditure on non-essentials, on anything not needed to keep body and soul together (beer and tobacco being included with the essentials of course), is deplored almost as a moral offence, quickly pounced on or ridiculed by the *amakhaya*. Money—so runs the admonition of the senior men—is not to be trifled away on short-lived pleasures: the man on whom the ancestors smile is the one who looks ahead and builds up his homestead.

The emphasis, then, is on saving, not on spending. There are various modes of saving. Some are provided for by the employers: Red migrants spoke approvingly of the kind of job that offers a pension or gratuity at the end of a

term of years, or carries arrangements for enforced saving, for example a job
with the South African Railways and Harbours, or at a certain sweet factory.
But more often the migrant must manage his saving himself. Before marriage
many young men send a portion of their wages home regularly to the father,
who may try to put as much of the money as possible into cattle. 'I do not
waste any money here. My father keeps my savings and to encourage me has
already bought two young heifers and a young ox for me.' But saving in the
Post Office is already very popular. The idea that money can be made to
increase by bearing interest is commonly understood. Understanding is made
easier, perhaps, by the fact that the word for calves (amathole) has become the
proper Xhosa word for interest. Literally, a Red migrant would say: 'I keep
my money in the Post Office, where it is safe and where it produces calves
from time to time.' 'Calves die from hunger when grazing is scarce in the
country, but the calves that are in the Post Office do not die.' A suspicious
Red migrant who was asked to show his Post Office savings book inquired:
'Why do you want to see the sheep that I have in my kraal?'

The keeping of large amounts of cash in a box is still much practised in the
country, but its disadvantages in town are recognized. 'Wood-and-iron houses
get destroyed by fire, or your room may be ransacked by thieves.' 'If you have
the cash with you in a box the temptation to spend some of it is always present.
Also, other people always get to know of it somehow. Sooner or later friends
will come to you, being desperate, and you will feel obliged to help them
with your money.'

One Red migrant likened regular saving to the accumulation of water in a
tank. 'If you have a water-tank and it is full, it will soon get finished once you
start using it, unless you get fresh water coming in. The Post Office serves as
my water-tank. To catch more water, and keep the tank full, I have to go on
earning and saving money all the time.'

SAVINGS AND INVESTMENTS

It is clear that the stereotype held by most School people—that the Red man
puts all his money into cattle or a box, as against the School preferences for
'furniture and the Post Office'—no longer tells the whole tale. To have some
cattle, including plough-oxen, is the wish of all Red Xhosa, but this is not to say
that all money must go into 'the bank of the ancestors'. The man from a fertile
area and the man from a drought-exposed, over-grazed reserve think differently.
A Red migrant from Cefane in the Transkei expounded the orthodox non-
economic ideas about cattle and goats: 'These animals are good to have
because they are part of our medicines. Death is common among people in
town because they keep no stock to cure their illnesses. Anyone can see that
there are very few old people in town compared to the Reserves.' But a Red
man from St. Lukes had little use for cattle: 'St. Lukes is overcrowded, there
are homesteads all over. There is no suitable grazing. The cattle are thin
because of the scarcity of grass, and when a man sells one of his beasts he
cannot expect to get much. What about the milch cows? It would take several
cows to produce a gallon of milk. During the drought periods you must arrange
for the cattle to graze on a farm belonging to a White man and there you will
have to pay 1s. 6d. or 2s. per head per month. Where is this money to come
from? So why should I invest all my money in stock? Is there any wisdom in
such investment nowadays?'

The indications are that if alternative and less risky forms of investment in the country become available, Red peasants might be glad to take advantage of them. In some parts sheep are preferred to cattle as being more profitable. In the absence of any standard rural alternative many Red migrants were simply keeping their savings as cash put away for a rainy day. Others, both men and women, have chosen another way. They put money into urban property, i.e. into wood-and-iron houses in the East Bank Location.

It is well in keeping with Red values that a man who has to work in town should try to own the property he is living in. 'I did not like the idea of paying rent every month. I wanted a house that was to be my own.' 'I had lived as a tenant among other tenants for some years and I realized that if I could be the owner I could make money. I had cattle at home from which I derive little or no profit.' A house makes for independence in case of sickness or unemployment, and in good days 'it brings in an income every month and you are in a better position to improve your kraal in the country'. But almost invariably the house in town 'is only a tent by the roadside'; 'it is only a business place, not a home'.

The town house is appraised in terms taken from the country. 'As a countryman I believe in livestock, and I have quite a few at home. I have bought this house in town to make money and protect my livestock.' 'A house like this is like a spring that does not die.' Several Red houseowners referred to their town house as 'a cow for more milk'.

Some Red houseowners had accumulated the capital for the house purchase through steady saving from their own pay-packets. An illiterate Transkeian labourer of about 50 said that ever since being in employment with the South African Railways and Harbours he had been saving money in the Post Office. 'I copied saving money from the other workers who had started it long before. Saving money developed into a habit, so much so that if I could not put away any money one month I felt restless, and would make a special effort next month to double the amount.' After some years he had enough in the Post Office to buy a house. He found one in Gomorra for £135—a four-roomed house in a good state of repair. His salary had risen since to £17 12s. 9d. p.m. and he had been able to erect two additional rooms. He let five rooms to tenants for £1 p.m. each and occupied the sixth himself.

In other cases the kin at home in the country had helped. An illiterate man now only 28, from Manzana (Engcobo), came to town seven years ago at a salary of £1 15s od. per week. He decided to put aside 10s. every week, or at the very least 5s. 'After six years I found I had saved £100.' This was not enough for the nine-roomed house he wanted to buy in the Tulandivile area: £200 was asked for it. 'I requested my employer for leave from work for three days, and went home to discuss the matter with my father. My father was not an easy man to deal with in money matters. He had the money, but he decided to come with me and see for himself. After inspecting the house he was satisfied and gave me the difference.' This migrant has now let eight rooms at £1 2s. od. per month each.

In the case of farm servants who had decided to come to town for good (and a few Red peasants also), all or most of the capital for the purchase of the town house had derived from the sale of livestock in the country. In the case of women houseowners (as will be seen in chapter 15) the property had usually been bought out of the saved-up profits of their liquor businesses.

ECONOMIC RELATIONS WITHIN THE LOCATIONS

Red migrants' economic activities in the locations themselves are largely guided by the principle that it is safer to deal with known than with unknown people. While trading with licensed shops has to involve economic relations with non-Red Xhosa, the other prominent activities—such as renting and letting rooms, hawking, supplying liquor—mainly take place within a network of people who know each other, who are related by something more than the cash nexus. Money is the medium in the transactions but they are not impersonal. They constitute a kind of middle term between the functionally diffuse relations that prevail in the country and the functionally specific relations characteristic of a modern town economy.

The business enterprises of Red women are a case in point. Women brewers like to have their regular customers, drawn from the woman's own *amakhaya* or those of her lover. The main business may consist in supplying the *iseti* of which the woman's lover is a member. The women who act as helpers or partners in many of these businesses are often *amakhaya* too. They are offered free board and lodging in return for services.

There is often a sharp competition between liquor suppliers. A partner may try to oust the woman who first took her in and showed her the ropes; making herself independent, she may take most of the clients with her. This may reflect a ruthless desire to make money at all costs, but there is always the limiting factor of Red people's possible disapproval. The women do their business in circles where their conduct is judged personally and morally. Women who deal with *amakhaya* and other known clients need hardly fear being cheated. The good name of an *iseti* would be at stake. Drinking is enjoyed by Red men only among intimates, and where all concerned—including the supplier—are intimates, the moral obligation to pay what one owes is practically inescapable.

Among the relatively few Red men who were found to be entrepreneurs in the locations, some carried on money-lending as a side-line. But they lent mainly to *amakhaya*, whose whole background they knew. 'Whenever I need money urgently for use at home', said a young Ciskeian migrant, 'I have always asked this elderly man from Balasi [his home place]. His interest has always been 2s. 6d. in the £1 per month. I have borrowed £5, £6 and £7, and have pledged a beast at home as security. I would give the colour of the beast and the shape of the horns. He knows my cattle at home.'

Another form of economic transaction with a strong personal element is the forced saving which many migrants undertake in order to be able to accumulate worth-while sums out of small weekly wages. These partnerships are a by-product of wage employment and therefore a typically urban institution, but as practised by Red migrants they are also arrangements between close friends. In the arrangement called *umgalelo*, two or three partners agree to pay to each other, in turn, a fixed sum out of the weekly (or monthly) wage. The partner who pays out this week has to live frugally on the balance of his wages, but next week he will receive something on top of his wages, enabling him to save a 'decent' sum and send it home. Strictly speaking of course, there is no gain in it: the partners are simply acting as one another's bankers and enforcers of thrift. The main thing—as one Red migrant expressed it—'is knowing one another thoroughly and having complete confidence'. Partners, in the case of younger men, were usually *iintanga* from home, preferably in the same employment. 'I have done it for many years', said a building labourer from the Transkei, 'and have never had any trouble with my partner. It has enabled me to send £2 home to my wife every second week, out of my wages of £2 9s. 2d. per week.'

As was seen, there is an economic component in Red men's relations with their *amakhaya* in town. 'Helping each other with money' is a test of true friendship. When *amakhaya* contribute to the train fare of a sick man, or to medical treatment, or funeral expenses, they do so without any financial interest, except the expectation of reciprocity in due course. 'If you did not contribute to funeral expenses you would be considered *igqolo*, that is, a man who gives nothing, and for whom nobody else will give anything if the same should happen to him.'

In that very important economic activity, the hiring and letting of accommodation, Red people showed a strong desire to keep the relation on a personal level. Whereas many School people have learnt to appreciate the impersonal business-like dealings of the Municipality, which save them from having to play up to an often unpredictable individual landlord, Red seekers for rooms prefer to go to Xhosa landlords and if possible to Red ones. Even though nearly everyone has something to say about the arrogance and unreasonableness of landlords, the idea remains that 'a Xhosa will understand', 'one can discuss matters with him personally'. 'There is relationship between us Xhosa.' 'I can always explain to a Xhosa landlord when I am in arrears with the rent.' 'The Municipality is very strict. White people know how to keep a decision. With a Xhosa you may make excuses and he may listen.'[2]

Red landlords, it appeared, often liked to temper the business relation with good neighbourliness of the Red sort. On account of his superior status the landlord can hold somewhat aloof and expect a certain deference from his tenants, but he need not become impersonal. Many Red landlords liked to address their tenants by *isiduko* (clan name). In one house the tenants' women were found in the landlady's room together eating *imifuno* (wild vegetables) with their fingers, amid much laughter and gaiety. Where a woman houseowner's tenants—as so often happens—are also her customers for beer, a sociable atmosphere comes about naturally.

On the other hand there is that part of the relation which has no parallel in rural Red society: the impersonal part, the fact that rent has got to be paid. This hard necessity creates anxieties on both sides; both feel the incongruity between it and the preferred personal touch. The formal 'opposition' over money is translated into terms of a personal battle. 'They [i.e. tenants] have all sorts of evil thoughts about you', said a Red houseowner from Kentani, 'because of the rent which they pay very much against their will.' A Red woman houseowner claimed that 'diviners have diagnosed many a case where an enemy has handed poison to your tenants to be put in your food or beer'.

Not a few Red landlords said that if they failed to get payment they preferred to deal with the situation through an impersonal agent rather than jeopardize 'friendship' by tackling the defaulter directly. Though it cost money in fees they would instruct a lawyer to send a letter of demand. Some had found other ways to reconcile the business and personal relations. One houseowner from the Dallas farm area had tenants who were mainly his own *iintanga* from there. 'They are my great friends. We are always together chatting in the evening

<hr />

[2] Reader has also documented this preference: cf. *The Black Man's Portion*, chapter 8.

and sometimes drinking kaffir beer.' He had sometimes had tenants who owed rent for as much as four months (he said) but in the end none of them had let him down. The arrears had been paid by instalments. 'This is because I take my friends into my confidence over financial matters. Once I had a letter demanding payment of a certain debt of £12. I called my tenants to tell them that I had not been able to pay this account because some of them had not paid rent for so many months. I wanted my friends to understand my very awkward position.' What he still found impossible was to be strict in person. 'I am always reluctant to take drastic steps against friends from Dallas. For this reason I have lately appointed one of the tenants who is *not* from the Dallas Farms to collect rentals. I have authorized him to be very strict. I have called a meeting of all tenants, to tell them that for the payment of rents they are under his control. I did this to avoid direct dealings with my *iintanga* in the payment of rents.'

WORK ATTITUDES OF RED MIGRANTS

Red people like to hold forth on the handicaps they labour under in regard to wage-earning 'because we have no education'. This is not entirely realistic. At least three-quarters of all jobs open to the Xhosa in East London are such that an illiterate can do them presumably as well as the next man. This is shown by Fourie and Lumsden's analysis of Native males employed in the East London urban area in 1955–6. Of the sample of 1,223 males 75·1 per cent came into the 'unskilled' category. Only 19·4 per cent were semi-skilled or skilled workers and only 4·5 per cent clerical, professional, self-employed, managers or officials.[3] This 'bottom-heavy' structure is, of course, partly related to the job ceiling prescribed by South African law and custom. As to income, the same study showed that 86·4 per cent of East London's Native male workers were earning less than £3 10s. 0d. per week.[4]

Schooling will not add anything material to the migrant's qualifications for an unskilled or perhaps even a semi-skilled job. As an illiterate Red girl employed at the Textile Mills remarked, 'as long as you can move fast education doesn't count here'. The uneducated man's handicap, such as it is, lies in his lesser chance of attaining to one of the rare 'good' jobs. But even this can be overestimated. It is interesting to find that (according to Fourie and Lumsden) as many as a third of Native male workers in the *highest* of four income brackets (i.e. earning over £20 per month) were men with no education or only rudimentary education (14·28 per cent with no education; a further 18·09 per cent with education from Sub A to Standard II).[5] It is possible that the Red people's grumbles about their 'handicap' are in part simply a projection of hostility towards the 'educated' category, whom they thus inaccurately accuse of monopolizing all the best positions.

In the course of field-work one came across many Red men who had attained to well-paid positions, relatively speaking. Some, in spite of their illiteracy, were in the coveted occupation of driver; many had reached the top wage-scales in factories or at the South African Railways. It seems fair to say that there are certain characteristic attitudes and personality traits of the Red man

---

[3] Fourie and Lumsden, 'Employment and Wages', chapter 7 in Houghton: *Economic Development in a Plural Society*; table 126.
[4] Ibid., table 129.
[5] Ibid., table 140. This is a combined sample for East London, King William's Town, and Zwelitsha: separate figures for East London are not available.

which help to make him a successful employee; the School man, in spite of his superior education, may actually be at a disadvantage.

To start with, Red men showed an objection to frequent changing of jobs, just as to frequent changing of rooms, and for much the same reasons—it is undignified, unmanly and possibly displeasing to the spirits. Notions like these, much less common nowadays among School men, tend to keep the Red man fixed in one job until he has earned any increments that may be available.

Some of the arguments for staying in one job (apart from influx control) were purely matter-of-fact: 'If you change you may find yourself getting even less pay than at present.' 'All White people are the same, and there is no point in leaving this boss for that boss.' 'One does not like the idea of being a new-comer and having to start all over again from the bottom.' But there were other reasonings which were definitely cultural. 'You stay on at a job because you don't want people to talk about you and say that you stick to nothing, that you are here today and there tomorrow and somewhere else next month. Such a man will be thought of as unable to provide for his wife and children. It is very bad in our Xhosa way of thinking to change one's job. It is like a man shifting his *umzi* from one site to another. We Xhosa say that he must have eaten honey during initiation, that is why he acts like the bees' (which—to the Xhosa—are a symbol less of industry than of restless passing from flower to flower).

'Even if a firm changes hands', said another Red man, 'one stays on because of one's long service. Then one can boast to new-comers, saying, "I have known this firm since its small beginnings". It is an honour to be proud of, in our way of thinking.' A still greater honour is to be holding the same position formerly held by one's father. 'A Xhosa will stick fast to his father's job: "My late father's position", he will say, in a voice of deep respect. It causes him to walk very proudly [*ukwaka amaxhaga*].'

'You must stay on even in a low-paid job', was another explanation, 'because we believe that just when you leave you may have missed your good luck, which might have come to you on that very day.' (The idea of luck is connected with that of the ancestors' approval.) 'Such hoping is not based on reasoning', was the comment of an educated School man.

Secondly, it appeared that Red men on the whole were more willing to discipline themselves to carry on with strenuous and unpleasant jobs. This would be done primarily for the sake of the country home. 'The White people have got the money, which is what we want. To get the money we have to serve them, it does not matter how one feels about it.' It all fits in with the Red habit of looking on labour migration as something like compulsory military service, a period when hardships have to be endured and little mercy can be expected. 'Hard labour does not ruin anybody. The more pay I get the better. Money is the thing that all of us need most at home.' 'Labour is not too hard if the pay causes a smile.' 'I do the strenuous work which is what I have to do to get money because I have no education.'

It should not be thought that this tolerance of hard work springs from a superior work-ethic, or evaluation of toil as good in its own right. If a cushy job comes the way of the Red man he is as ready to enjoy it as anyone else. 'I like my work [in a warehouse] very much, for there is nothing strenuous and no rush. There are piles and piles of goods stacked up, with narrow passages between. The White foreman's job is to move around and see what is going on.

Whenever he is coming we sound an alarm, "Mind out!" [*wabhaqwa*] and the moment he disappears round the corner you can again sit on a soap-box to rest yourself. We all enjoy this work. Some of my *iintanga* whose jobs involve strenuous work always ask me how I got such employment, and I tell them that my ancestor spirits helped and guided me to it.' A really tough job is a matter for complaint: 'I do not like the type of work I do [in the Mechanical Department of the South African Railways]. The heat is intolerable, I perspire as if a bucketful of water has been poured on my body. Lifting up the hammer is a terrible strain; meanwhile the White foreman keeps on shouting "hurry up", and I cannot even stop for a bite of food. I do the job because it would be very hard to get another one and I have a family to support at home.' He said he was earning 5s. 6d. for an eight-hour day. But a Red man is expected to endure such toil, even at such pay, not to quit because of it. It is a question of self-discipline, for the sake of the homestead and family. The main difference between Red and School men, one may say, is that the Red men seem to learn this discipline earlier in life: the young School man, if his responsibilities are not yet pressing, seems readier to leave a job on account of hard conditions or low pay.

Finally, many White employers and foremen tend to like the Red workers better, on personality grounds. The Red type may have been found more respectful: 'You get prompt obedience from them', or (a well-known comment) 'They are not so cheeky'. But it would be far off the mark to assume for this reason that the Red workers lack pride or really favour subservience to the White man. Theirs would seem to be a complex attitude, involving the outward submission shown by a conquered people to their conquerors, but also a hidden intense resentment and aggression. 'If you are in a gang of workers and a White man supervises you, he will pick on one of you to make tea for him at all times, and he will treat you like his real servant. You cannot refuse, because if you do he will give you notice to leave work at the end of the week. . . . It is all part of their intention to keep the Xhosa down.' Some Red men gave as the one reason that would make them change their jobs, 'if the White foreman is so cruel that he sometimes kicks you'. 'Then it is very difficult not to strike back and if you do you will get into trouble. To avoid this you had better look around for another job.' There seemed to be a more genuine subservience, born of fear of immediate reprisals, among some Red farm servants. 'You cannot do anything against the orders of the White boss, not even behind his back. He will find out and beat you.'

As long as their pride is not touched the Red workers are willing to give to the White employer the same respect they are used to giving to a senior man: and they are trained from youth to obey strictly the word of their seniors. It is this which can mislead White employers, and prevent them from realizing the hard core of fierce pride within.

Employers often remarked that they had found the Red workers more 'reliable characters'. And it is true that many Red men cherish the virtues of honesty and truthfulness. But again, it would be rash to say that Red men as such are less prone than other types of Xhosa to steal from their places of work. In this respect the major cleavage between Black and White transcends the differences of Red and School Xhosa. The moral issue involved seems to have been fully sorted out by the men. One heard again and again the same argument: 'White employers are not honest with their Native employees; why should we be honest with them?' 'The old Xhosa rule is (and I believe all races have the same): Be to them what you want them to be to you.' 'If only the employers of the X factory knew what thieving is going on there, they would be shocked. But because the profit they make is more than enough they do not notice any theft. Is it wrong to take that which belongs to you but which is being fraudulently retained by your employer? After all, the extra profit derives from the fact that we Natives are underpaid.' 'A White employer who pays his Native employees a small wage is a very bad man; he is no better than a thief, because he takes advantage of the fact that if you refuse the pay there is another man who will take the job. With this fact in mind you accept the small wage. The thing to do, then, is to steal when the chance presents itself. It is not sinful to steal from another thief. The employer has driven you to this evil, if it is evil at all. You cannot force him to pay you a living wage; all you can do is to get your own back somehow.' 'White employers do not seem to be aware of the fact that Native young men no longer worry about the small pay as long as there is *isonka* [bread], meaning something to steal to supplement your meagre wages. When a worker meets another who had been out of work he will always ask him three questions. Are you now employed? What is the pay? Is there *isonka*?'

Some Red men said they admired those who steal and get away with it: 'If a man takes valuable things from the factory or shop, I regard him as daring and fearless, and if he succeeds again and again, I say to myself: "This fellow will get rich quickly. He is a man." I also say he is "the ox of the sun". He is an ox that will pull a heavy yoke—an ox that will resist the most excessive heat of the sun.' Others maintained that though there is nothing 'wrong' with the stealing (in a moral sense) it may be very unwise. 'I am in deep sympathy with the man who takes away useful things from the factory or shop when nobody is looking. He thinks he is clever. But I should warn him not to steal. He will lose his job and his dependants will suffer. If stealing helped anybody, and there were no trouble to follow, we would all have been thieves—the quickest and easiest way to get rich. . . . When bad luck comes your way you forget about the short happiness, and you feel as if you have never been a happy man. You cannot steal for any length of time without being caught.'

Stealing from an employer, then, is 'not really' stealing. It is a striking case of moral non-involvement. Not only is the employer thought of as someone who exploits and oppresses the Native workers, but the great social distance of the White man inhibits conscience too: 'The valuable things that have been taken are not those of anybody I know. They belong to a White man, whose only connexion with me is employment.' Or the employer may not be a person at all. In the larger industrial and commercial concerns the worker may feel no obligation, because he sees nobody to feel obliged to. 'The White foreman would not suffer if I take home a few things that I can make use of, nor the manager. They get their big wages all the same.' The situation was seen quite differently in regard to stealing from Xhosa-owned shops. 'The business of a Xhosa is always on the small scale, it could be damaged by stealing a few articles. A small-scale business is like a child at the crawling stage, sometimes trying to stand up unassisted. That child should be encouraged instead of being crippled.'

However, the Red men are quick to apply their moral theory on the other side too. If low wages justify stealing, good wages forbid it. 'We often warn one another at work: "Do not excrete on the side from which the wind comes" [Do not do anything that will offend your benefactor].' A certain sweet factory was often cited as a place 'where the pay is good and the employers also help us to save our money' (by an enforced savings scheme). 'Where Natives are well paid', said another Red migrant, 'nobody thinks of stealing. Each employee is a foreman over himself; he says to himself, "I must work hard to keep this good position".'

Further, the Red men are capable of becoming morally involved to some degree with a White employer in circumstances where a more personal relationship has a chance of developing, which is especially the case in smaller firms. 'All the members of the White staff are friendly with us and the White foreman is the same. He is pleased with our work and seems to have confidence in us. Although the pay is small I like the job very much. If you have no cash you could arrange with the foreman to get a bag of mealie grains and send it to your family at home, and pay it off bit by bit. If you cannot pay this week, tell the foreman that you will pay next week; he will be agreeable. If you need money urgently see the foreman who will approach the manager. . . . What I have learnt from mixing with White people is that where they know you very well and you are no wrong-doer, they treat you decently, but if they do not know you, you would think they are nasty to you.' 'I have heard some Native employees say to one another in this firm: "This White man is not the type of man we should offend, for he has done good deeds. Where else in town are Natives as well off as we are? Let us serve him, fellow men." '

ECONOMIC ATTITUDES AND INCAPSULATION

The contrast between the Red migrant's economic roles at home and in town respectively might have been expected to produce serious conflict, but this is averted by 'situational selection', and for another reason which has been indicated—that the positive economic ambitions remain formulated in terms of the rural system. The participation in the large-scale economy as a worker, is after all the *simultaneous* discharge of a more valued rural role, as provider.

Migrancy might also have been expected to induce far-reaching changes in economic outlook at the rural end. Situational selection applies here too. In the rural setting, returned Red migrants did not appear significantly more money-minded than other people, nor more businesslike in the conduct of homestead affairs. Their aspirations continued to run along the conventional lines. Occasionally in the country one found an ex-migrant who went in for market-gardening, or breeding pigs, on a larger scale than is common. There was an ex-garden-boy taking pains with his gardens and another trying to install a tank to catch rainwater; and some returned migrants were said to have developed special business acumen, particularly in selling stock. But these were isolated cases. Other people also pointed out that the innovators were mostly men who for one reason or another would have got along anyway: it was not because they had worked in towns.

Most migrants in town argued that, being absent from home so much, they could not possibly hope to achieve anything more than keep the homestead going, with its patches of mealies and a few cattle and sheep. It appeared, in fact, that most would not go in for much else even if they were at home all the time. When the time for retirement to the homestead comes, the Red men tend to feel they are too old for anything new. They would rather enjoy the familiar scene, and carry on where their fathers left off. There are few lessons learnt in town that could, they think, really improve their homestead economy. Certainly there is little tendency to increase the range of household wants, by introducing the new things or ideas they have encountered while away.

Most significant of all, perhaps, are the tendencies of those whom one might call the Red success-men, i.e. the Red migrants who have risen in town above the average socio-economic level. Private enterprise may have made them rich, by migrants' standards, or they may have been specially successful at work. The former, 'capitalist', type is typified by the houseowner; the latter by the foreman or sub-foreman. Success might, in theory, tend to draw them outside the incapsulating circle; to make them less country-rooted and to change their habits and values.

These two categories, houseowners and foremen, are both privileged, not only economically but in the sense of power. They partly control those two scarce and valuable things which are the concern of every migrant to East London—accommodation and jobs. The houseowner is not only the man who has shown his economic prowess by accumulating more than a hundred pounds of purchase money; he is also the landlord who can give or withhold accommodation, and whose attitudes can drastically affect the well-being of his tenants. The foreman is not only the recipient of higher wages but is often able to put a man in the way of a job; while for those already employed under him he can considerably affect the work-load, and the relations with the employer.

Both houseowners and foremen are accorded respect and are offered presents. 'Bribing' by those who want work or accommodation is almost a matter of course. However horrible the shack, its ownership immediately puts a Red man a cut above his fellows. Even in the country it is admired as a sign of thrift and economic prowess. 'In the country, once they get to know that you have a house in town, you are admired. They say to each other, "that young man obviously does not waste his money on brandy or on amankazana. That young man's father has indeed fathered a male! And now, if we ever have to go to town on business, we know where we can sleep for the night." '

In a position of privilege, such as that of houseowner, the Red man does of course have additional opportunities for making contacts with non-Reds. For example, sometimes a Red houseowner whose own Red wife and family were at home in the country, would have got a School or town girl to come and live with him in his town house. 'He is proud of his School ishweshwe' (it being rare for a Red man to be accepted as lover by a non-Red woman). Or sometimes a Red houseowner who had decided to 'become School' would reject Red tenants and take only School tenants, so as to avoid identification with the Red section. But these did not appear as common cases. By and large, the Red success-men seemed to take little advantage of their special opportunities. Not so much from necessity as from choice, they continued to stick close to other Reds.

Although becoming a houseowner or a foreman is a big step up in Red eyes, it is after all only a preliminary step as far as non-Red ideas of 'class' or udidi are concerned. Neither the foreman nor the houseowner needs to be literate, much less 'civilized'. He may be still 'only a rough iqaba.' Logically his choice seems to lie between remaining in the Red community—comfortably at the top—or taking the chance to break into a non-Red world, and finding himself at the bottom again. It is a common and sometimes painful experience of these Red success-men that their success does not necessarily protect them against the contempt of non-Reds. Even the landlord's own tenants, or the foreman's own gang, may tend to look down on him if he is less 'civilized' than they are.

The ambiguity of holding power over culturally 'superior' people is disliked by most Red houseowners. Rather than run the risk of being sneered at or duped by educated tenants, the man prefers to take only Red tenants and lord it over them. 'The educated type of tenant is very hard to control, when you are an *iqaba* like myself. I don't know how many times I have had School tenants complain about me to the Rent Board, saying I am overcharging. Red tenants don't dare to do such a thing.' 'I prefer Red tenants, because I have lived with Reds all my life. School people can be dangerous, and are always looking for faults.' 'School tenants, are a nuisance. They are very bad at paying and find a lot of things to grumble about.'

X was one very successful young Red man, originally from a farm in Cintsa but now permanently established in East London. Already he combined the two coveted roles of foreman and houseowner. Having found a job (at the Buffalo Harbour) 'under Mr. H. who knew my late father very well', he had been promoted to assistant native foreman within a matter of weeks. He saved £87 at the Post Office, and by adding £77 from the sale of his livestock was able to buy an eight-roomed house. X said he was 'very well satisfied' with his progress in town, and had no longer any ties with the farm. But any tendency to move out of Red circles in town had been checked by hard experience. 'I have had only disappointments in my dealings with School people.' He said he would let only to Red tenants in future.

The Red women houseowners have an additional reason for preferring Red tenants. Most of these landladies are also brewers of kaffir-beer. Their business interests tie them to Red men, who are potential customers, as against School tenants 'who have a lot of nonsense about drinking'.

The tendency of Red migrants to look for rooms with Red landlords, then, reflects a preference which is mutual. The landlord who likes Red tenants better (just as the tenant who likes Red landlords better) is held within the Red community in town, and his contacts with non-Reds are kept to a minimum. He is not under pressure to change his habits or his standards. In the uncommon case where such a man takes advantage of his opportunities to become literate or to 'civilize himself' in other ways, he need still not give up his country roots, his attachment to the country home.

Z was one of the houseowners who had come to feel that the future lay with non-Red ways of life. 'I realize that the Red life does not pay nowadays. Our Red forefathers made their living by keeping large herds, but what are we to live on now, seeing that the White man's government is determined to get rid of our stock?' Culturally Z had changed considerably, since making good in town and buying his house there. 'I have become a School man in recent years. I feel quite at ease among School people now.' He wanted his children 'to become enlightened' and they were already attending primary school. But he still felt very much part of the rural community where he was born. He meant to retire there and he intended that his sons should grow up there, 'as School country men'. 'A house in town', he said, 'is never one's *umzi*, in the sense of the kraal in the country. One's house here in town is simply for business purposes. If anyone gives up his connexion with the country it cannot be simply on account of having bought a town house. It must have something to do with his own character.'

A similar case was S, who came from a Red home at Tshabo. At the age of 34 he had had fourteen years of urban experience—four in the Rand mines and ten in East London. He had made a success in East London, and was a foreman at the East London docks. He intended to stick at the job 'until I reach pensionable age'. S could express appreciation of Western technological achievements: 'I should like to have a lorry, it is more serviceable than an ox-wagon.' 'I should like my sons to use tractors for ploughing.' He said approvingly that 'when Natives are only talking about kaffir-beer, White men are talking about big things'. He would like his sons 'to be educated', and 'wear good clothes'. He had formed a vague attachment to the Bantu Baptist church. But essentially S was still a Red man. He had no doubt about where he belonged. Several times he prefixed a statement with the words 'We Red people . . .'. He was still illiterate, and his belief in Xhosa sacrifices, myths and diviners appeared much firmer than any beliefs he had gleaned from the Bantu Baptists. 'Home', to him, was still Tshabo, where he had his wife, children and mother; he visited them every month. He had joined no organization in East London and did not even attend 'his' church when in town. His town friends were Tshabo men, his sweetheart a Red woman from the country. 'My free time I spend with the Tshabo men, and with my brother and sister who are also here. After my evening meal I keep indoors, in case my sweetheart comes.'

Even these modernized Reds were harder to find than the really conservative Reds whose success had not made them change their habits or values any more than it had detached them from the country. M was one of these latter. He owned and lived in a shack in East London, but his 'real home', he said, was 'a beautiful homestead' far away in Idutywa. To him the town house was just a supplement to the homestead economy; in fact he had bought it from the proceeds of the wool clip. He had never brought his wife or children to town. ('It is a bad place for women and children.') He was sure that his town interests would never be able to detach him from Idutywa. 'I am not afraid of becoming an *itshipha*, just because I have bought a town house. How could I, having my well-established kraal at home, and my wife and children there?' The cultural self-identification of this urban houseowner was quite uncompromising. 'I believe in the Xhosa way of life. When I inherited my late father's kraal I wasted nothing, but looked after the stock carefully. If I had been an educated man I am sure I would not have kept my father's wealth intact. I curse education which has damaged the peaceful life of the Red Xhosa. I myself am Red and will remain Red until I die. My elder sons are already Red men in the country. I mean my younger ones to grow up in the same way.'

9

Spirits and Witches

IN COLLABORATION WITH IONA MAYER

The two main complexes of Xhosa supernatural belief—the ancestor cult and the witchcraft complex—both flourish among Red migrants in East London. As observed in the urban setting, both are directly related to the idea that town life is a temporary exile, and relations in town an extension of relations in the country. Ancestor spirits and witches are both thought of as being based at the country home but reaching out from there to follow the migrant into East London. Only, they reach out for opposite reasons. The ancestors are always pulling the migrant back—back to his home and back to the 'ways of the ancestors'. The witches are always pushing him out: their aim is that he should withdraw from his home and vanish in town. The present chapter is about these specific notions, whereby the moral value of remaining country-rooted as against absconding is dramatized in the strongest possible terms. The embodiment of supreme moral authority is assigned to one side; the embodiment of everything evil to the other.

Both the witchcraft complex and the ancestor cult prove tenacious enough to survive the transplantation to town in cases where Red Xhosa 'lose' their country homes, though the flavour alters in the process. Nobody who is still Red can well stand outside either system of belief. Both in town and country (furthermore) many School people, including practising Christians, are at least partly committed to one or the other. This chapter, however, is mainly concerned with the forms found among ordinary Red migrants.

In Reader's sample investigation of male workers attending for registration in the East London urban area[1] 399 men were asked whether they 'preferred' Christianity or the ancestor cult; 55 per cent replied in favour of the ancestor cult. (This, it should be noted, was a cross-section of the labour force generally, not only of the migrant element.) The men readily detailed 'reasons' for preferring the ancestor cult. Examination of these shows that the younger men, up to the age of 25, mostly favoured simple conservative 'reasons'. 'My parents have taught me that the ancestor religion is good.' 'I like the ancestor religion better because our forefathers used it.' 'I believe in following the customs of past generations.' An allied reason—not confined to the younger men this time—was the nationalistic one: 'The ancestor religion is our own proper religion.' 'It is the root of our Xhosa customs. I believe in it because so many of our other customs are connected with it.' Some men, however, postulated sanctions of a more specific kind. In a few cases the negative sanctions—the fear aspect—took first place. 'If we did not worship our ancestors they would be angry, evil would befall us.' But much more frequently the stress was on the ancestors' power to help, as a positive sanction. This was especially noticeable with the more mature

[1] For an account of these investigations see Reader: *The Black Man's Portion*, Appendix on Method, where they are referred to as Survey II and Survey IV.

men. 'I believe that my ancestors are looking after me all the time.' 'The ancestors can do anything we ask them, our lives depend on them.' 'I believe that our ancestors rescue us whenever evil threatens. We pray to them for the sick and the sick recover.' 'It is a right thing to worship the ancestors who are always doing good for us.'

THE ANCESTOR CULT AND THE RURAL HOME

The Xhosa 'ancestor' cult is primarily a cult of the deceased father and grandfather; its observances are domestic.[2] The spirits are usually termed *iminyanya*, or *amawethu* ('our people'). When properly placated—but not otherwise—they will protect their living descendants from harm. Spirits communicate with one another in the spirit world and also with the living in this world. A diviner has the special gift of hearing the voices of 'his' spirits (his deceased ancestors) directly. These explain to him what is amiss in his client's situation or behaviour, and how the client's own ancestor spirits require to be placated. The traditional way of placating spirits is by animal sacrifices: a beast for major occasions, a goat for minor ones. Beer also helps to placate. It is a routine ritual duty to 'remember' one's spirits by sacrificing on certain occasions. As will be seen, however, the spirits are ethically as well as ritually fastidious, growing offended not only by omission of sacrifice but by lapses from morality in daily behaviour.

The migrant's concept of his town life as a temporary exile is directly reflected in his beliefs about the whereabouts of the spirits. Going to town does not mean disappearing from the spirits' view, for in principle 'the spirits of your father and grandfather are wherever you are yourself'. 'They go with you even to town and to the mines.' 'They are inseparable from you.' 'They will follow a man whether he goes to Johannesburg or Ghana or England.' 'There is absolutely nowhere the spirits cannot reach, if the one they love is there.' 'White men who have come from as far away as England or America also have their ancestors here, though they are not aware of it.' The place which the spirits *prefer*, however, and which they regard as their 'real home', is the homestead in the country. They like to be about the cattle-kraal and to hold their own unseen assemblies (*inkundla*) in the place where the living elders still assemble. They like being among Red country people, 'who are living the kind of life they lived themselves'. It is at the cattle-kraal that the spirits normally communicate with the living, through the medium of sacrifice. 'The father's spirit wants his kraal to be respected.' Thus loyalty to the spirits, and sacrifice in the proper manner, call for a continued loyalty to the country home throughout one's years in town.

The preference of the spirits for sacrifices offered at the homestead in the country applies especially to the important mortuary and commemorative rites for the father—*ukukhapha*, 'accompanying' the father, and *ukubuyisa*, 'returning' the father. These are performed in the cattle-kraal near the grave. Any Red man wants to be buried at his country homestead so that he can have these rituals performed for him there. 'A man who dies in town is like a man who dies by the roadside.' The solemn duty of *amakhaya* to send their comrade's body back to the country for burial is directly connected with the fact that *ukukhapha* cannot be done 'properly' in town.

[2] The best account of the ancestor cult among a Xhosa-speaking people is that of Hunter, referring to the Pondo (*Reaction to Conquest*, chapter V).

These two ceremonies for the deceased father are great occasions in the country, demanding the presence of many kin and friends. On attending several in the Ciskei, it was found in every case that most of the men taking part were migrants, working in town, who had made a special point of coming home for the ceremony.

SACRIFICING IN TOWN

However, a migrant cannot get home every time he may need to sacrifice to his father's or grandfather's spirit. A significant sign of the vitality of the ancestor cult is the way in which the sacrificial ritual has been adapted for use in town surroundings 'if necessary'.

The first adaptation is the extension of the idea of 'home' to cover the town dwelling, in certain cases. The initial question to be asked in determining the proper place for sacrifice is where the dead man's home was, and where he was buried. If a man lived and died in East London it would be correct for his sons to perform even *ukukhapha* there. If the deceased himself lived and was buried in the country (on the other hand), the fact that his son resides permanently in town could still make a town sacrifice acceptable. 'When there is no kraal left in the country, the place where a man lives in town must be regarded as his home, where he has to perform his sacrifice.' It is not necessary that the town 'home' should be the man's own property: it could be a rented room.

A man who still has a home in the country can make an acceptable sacrifice in town instead, if it is a genuine case of *force majeure*. But 'it must be quite clear that you are really unable to go back to the country on this occasion, for no fault of your own'. It is difficult, admittedly, to do a sacrifice 'properly' in town conditions. Old residents of the location could recall days when it had been easier, because there had been no strict control on either the brewing of beer or the keeping or slaughtering of livestock. Under the regulations in force today (primarily hygienic in intention) all slaughtering has to be done at the municipal abattoir near Cambridge, unless a special permit is obtained. Suspicion that the 'sacrifice' may be only a cloak for illegal commercial butchery causes the officials to be wary of issuing permits. Many migrants complained that obtaining a permit is a humiliating and exasperating business. 'Though we fully explained the purpose of the slaughtering we wanted to do, it was of no avail at first. At long last we were instructed to take the beast to the abattoir for thorough examination. There they found many unbelievable disqualifications in the beast, but after a great fuss they gave us a permit. The sacrifice was performed under the suspicious, cruel stare of a Native constable who had been specially told off to watch that there should be no illegal sale of meat.'[3]

It seems that Xhosa who want to sacrifice in town usually take the risk and do it illegally, rather than ask for a permit. Most men being either room-tenants or sub-tenants, the houseowner has to be asked for permission that his yard be used. Few houseowners dare give permission for this illegal use if the animal to be killed is an ox. Then the solution must be to build a temporary 'kraal' on the veld, on the outskirts of the built-up area. The beast is slaughtered in the

[3] There is good reason for the suspicion: illegal butchery and sale of meat is a lucrative business, easily hidden under the cloak of 'ritual'. Once when I stumbled on some migrants carving up a newly killed beast I was told in great detail that it was an *ubulunga* beast, which for such-and-such ritual reasons must never be sold or killed commercially; but in fact, while some parts were being ritually shared out, it was clear that a large portion was being cut up for sale.

open, and meat is divided there. Beer is brewed and drunk among the bushes. The bones are burnt on the spot. By the following day everything is finished and the temporary 'kraal' can be demolished.

Secrecy is less difficult with a goat-sacrifice. Even though the introduction of live goats into the municipal area has now been prohibited—posing an additional problem—migrants manage to carry out goat-sacrifices in East London. *Ukubingelela*, the sacrifice of a white goat to introduce a new-born child to the ancestors, is not uncommon there. The commonest sacrifice of all in town is probably *ukucamagusha*, the killing of a goat as partial substitute for an ox which the spirits are deemed to have requested. *Ukucamagusha* is a kind of delaying tactic frequently used by Xhosa who learn from diviners that their sickness or other affliction is conveying the spirits' urgent request for meat and beer. The man kills a white goat, with an apology and a promise that full satisfaction (including an ox) will be offered as soon as possible. 'People in town, being employed, cannot get leave from their work to sacrifice properly. So they *camagusha*, which makes for peace.' 'After *ukucamagusha* the spirits give relief until one is ready to go to their own home place and assemble properly with the neighbours—the men who used to join the spirits in their sacrifices before death.' 'By *ukucamagusha* a man retains the friendship of his spirits. The ties with them are not broken.'

Whether the sacrifice is done in a yard or in the bush, whether it involves a goat or an ox, the man sacrificing in town cannot afford to relax his guard for a moment. 'You are in the midst of skinning the beast when you see an unfamiliar figure coming down the hill towards you. Immediately you stop skinning, and watch the figure closely to see if you can identify it as a policeman.' Nobody suggested that sacrifices done in town are altogether as good as those done in the country. The makeshift conditions, the absence of relatives, the atmosphere of secrecy and fear, are all negative factors. 'The sacrifices we do in town are a watered-down liquid [*umngxengo*], they are tasteless.' 'Town is not a place where Africans can sacrifice freely. Where is the kraal? If there is such a thing here it is away in the bushes, so that nobody would know it is yours.' 'Sacrifice needs to be done openly and without fear. There must be no disturbances of any kind, there must be perfect peace and calm. Can you get that in town? Definitely not!' The spirits 'shake their heads in contempt when these things are done in town'. 'They come to town reluctantly, because town is the place of *umlungu* [the White man], and they have no respect for anything done at *emlungwini*.' 'The absence of relatives makes the sacrifice in town incomplete. Red relatives matter the most in a sacrifice, because they are the ones living the life the spirits had lived.'

Hence the requirement to sacrifice 'properly' keeps drawing the migrant home to the country. The spirits 'are more pleased with the sacrifices done at home'. 'We are not at home in town: spirits prefer to be sacrificed to at home.' It was emphasized that 'if you sacrifice in town as a mere matter of choice, when you could have done it in the country, it is not acceptable to your father's spirit'. Compulsion is the only legitimate excuse. 'They [spirits] will come to town only when you yourself are forced to be there by circumstances which you cannot control.' 'They are wiser than ordinary human beings, and they understand everything. They are ready to accept a sacrifice anywhere as long as one has explained the difficulties to them.'

Some migrants claimed that the acceptability of town sacrificing was proven by their own inability to think of anyone who had ever been arrested by the police for doing it illegally. It was maintained that the spirits can protect the sacrificers by making the police fail to notice the animal, or quelling their suspicions if they do notice it. Sometimes they can even get the [Native] police to join in. 'By the time we finished our sacrifice we were used to the police tunics. We openly drank the brandy and got out all the beer that had been brewed [i.e. in excess of the amount legally permitted]. What happened? The policemen took part in the sacrifice and the drinking.'

SUBSTITUTE RITUALS IN TOWN

Further specific adaptations to the migrant's situation of exile are the non-sacrificial substitute rituals carried out in town with the object of appeasing spirits temporarily, until it is possible to go 'home' and do things properly. These are extensions of the principle already noticed in *ukucamagusha*. A migrant who feels he 'ought to' offer, or take part in, an animal sacrifice, may be able to compromise by substituting either a beer drink or a purely verbal rite.

All these substitute rituals are based on the notion that migration, employment, and urban rules and regulations add up to a force one cannot resist, an inescapable compulsion. The migrant is not asked to do the impossible—neither to go home for a sacrifice if that would mean losing his job, nor to perform one in town if that is impracticable. The spirits 'understand' and 'know what things are like in town'. Thus far do they sanction conformity with urban requirements and submission to the powers that be. They demand recognition of themselves within the migrant framework, not at the cost of destroying the framework itself. But in any given case, if one would be sure of the spirits' understanding and sympathy, one cannot just sit back and let them discover circumstances for themselves. One must offer a clear explanation and, above all, an apology. The spirits want to be explicitly assured that the good will is there, even if the deed is not. In town, accordingly, purely verbal approaches count among the most important means of placation. A whole technique of prayer has been evolved. 'If one is not able to offer a sacrifice of any kind, it is enough to speak to the spirits quietly. "You see that I cannot help it, it is not that I do not think of you. Do not turn your backs on me, spirits of my father and grandfather." '

A man who has his own room in town will try to have some beer brewed for his ancestors from time to time. He invites his friends and tells them that the beer is a gift to his spirits for having looked after him so well. When the drink is finished, the senior guest bids farewell: 'Peace be with you, son of X. We are returning home now, and we hope that all bad luck will depart from this house. Remain in peace and may your spirits be with you.' The amount of beer legally permitted to be brewed at one time is so small that it might not please the spirits. One could take the risk of brewing more than is allowed; or one could ask the friends to get their own permits and bring their contributions, little by little, so as not to fall foul of the police. But another way is to 'apologize' to the spirits. 'You must explain to the ancestors that you could brew only this small amount on account of regulations that are outside your control.' It recalls the standard apology of the migrant host to his living guests: 'However little I give you, take it as great, for we are by the roadside here, in the place of the White man.' The ancestors, 'kind and sympathetic', may be deemed to answer like the polite living guests — 'Do not worry . . . a man cannot do more than he can do'.[4]

When a man who works in town is asked to attend a sacrifice offered by a member of his lineage in the country, a dilemma confronts him. Not attending dishonours the spirit and 'spoils' the sacrifice, but attending may be incompatible with holding one's job. Here again the solution is to ask pardon. If absence really could not be helped, 'it is enough for him to speak, saying, "Go ahead, for even if I am not there, I am with you in soul" '.

Xhosa sacrifice is often aimed at the removal of a current illness or trouble. Many migrants said that in town, if one cannot sacrifice to the spirits to have one's affliction removed, one can pray to them instead. 'In suffering of any kind all you need do is speak to your spirits in the dead of night, when nobody sees or hears. You get up from your sleeping place and go outside, and talk to them silently, saying, "Why have you forsaken me, spirits of my father and grandfather?" '

Not only when one cannot do what the spirits would like, but when one is forced to do what they dislike, one should ask their pardon verbally. 'Where a thing is really unavoidable the spirits do not take a serious view.' For instance spirits do not like their descendant to keep changing his abode in town, because they want to know where they can find him. If shifting is imperative — if the landlord has turned him out, for example — the migrant should say, 'My spirits, you must know that this is a thing I cannot help'.

THE GUARDIAN SPIRITS, THE COMMUNITY AND THE MORAL CODE

Discussions of spirit beliefs with Red migrants in East London suggested that the role of the spirits as personal guardians becomes additionally important to them there, in the insecurity of town surroundings. 'The spirits look after us here in town and protect us from all sorts of danger and misfortune.' 'When you have to go through the location at night they are by your side, yes, even if you are dead drunk.' 'When you are fast asleep in your room they are there to see that nobody harms you.' 'The father's and grandfather's spirits keep close to a person here, with parental care and ever-wakeful eye.' 'Ancestor spirits are like the bodyguards which great men have. They have no other duty but to look after one and guide one to safety and prosperity.' 'My job involves working at night, when there are no living men around to protect me. My ancestors are my only guards. Anyone who wants to harm me just feels afraid to do so, without knowing why. My ancestors have conferred with theirs, and their ancestors have warned them, through their consciences.' 'If anything is being plotted against me my ancestors will talk to me in a dream, or by making me feel apprehension. They warn one of all dangers ahead. It is when one neglects their signals that one finds oneself in distress.' 'I was at a beer-drink in the East Bank Location not long ago, when I suddenly had a feeling that I must leave and go back to my own room. As soon as I had gone the police came and arrested all those who were still at the drink. Who influenced me to leave just in time? Undoubtedly, my *amawethu*.'

But the spirits' guardianship is conditional, much as that of a living parent is conditional. One has to earn it, by acting rightly. 'When I first went to work in the mines, my father — who has died since — said to me, "Go, my son, and find your spirits already awaiting you in *Erawutini* [Johannesburg], and they

---

[4] Cf. chapter 6, above.

will look after you, as long as you continue to behave yourself well".' The spirits resent insult and neglect; they are quick to feel when a man 'does not want' them, and they retaliate by 'not wanting' him. 'They go on following you just as long as you do not sever your connexion with them.' 'They accompany all their descendants to town, but not those who have nothing to do with them or who ignore them.' Like loving parents, they have the final weapon of abandoning or disinheriting a child 'if he reaches the stage where he is clearly hopeless'.

What do Red migrants conceive to be the moral code which they have to satisfy in order to merit the continued protection of their spirits? From numerous statements it was clear that 'right conduct towards people' is demanded: the moral frame of reference is 'people' or 'the community' generally, not the kin-group as such. The spirits are displeased by anything which causes trouble or strife in a community. 'Ancestor spirits are against anything that disturbs the peace of the community.' 'To be acceptable to his ancestors a person must not be a menace to the public causing the people to be sore-hearted daily.' 'Our ancestors disapprove of wrong things done against fellow-members of the society.' 'They disapprove of wrong behaviour by juniors to seniors, both of their own family and of other families as well.'

Thus the point at which the spirits 'cease to follow you with their tireless care' is 'when you begin to do such wrong things as cheating people, or seducing women and denying responsibility'. Besides cheating and seduction the offences most commonly named were theft and unprovoked assault. In one word, the ancestors were held to condemn behaviour which is antisocial. 'They hate all evil deeds and always warn one against committing them.' 'They disapprove of any wrong action against anybody.' 'They hate all people who live by stealing or cheating or who are a menace to others.' 'If a person old enough to understand does something wrong against any human being the ancestors become cross.' To say that the behaviour prohibited is antisocial is to imply that the ancestors dislike what society dislikes: this too was explicitly confirmed by the migrants. 'The wrong behaviour condemned by the ancestors is the very behaviour that is not acceptable to people in general'; or conversely, 'The things which people do not favour are the things that the ancestors have said to be bad'. 'Whatever is hated in a community is hated even worse by the ancestors than by the ordinary earth people.'

It may seem unusual by Bantu standards that the ancestors should be so closely associated with the peace of the community as a whole, as against that of the lineage or kin group. However, in this case the two concepts turn out to be closely related. What the ancestor spirits particularly care about, in the Xhosa scheme, is the *good name* of their own family—a concept which only has meaning when the family is considered in relation to the community and its opinions. Hence the emphasis on the family's avoiding behaviour which the community would condemn. Migrants' utterances amply bore out this interpretation. 'Spirits do not approve of any member of their family who causes the family name [*undamlonyeni*] to be "news of the mouth".' 'One's ancestors are disturbed when one lowers the name of the family or clan. They are like living human beings who are very proud of their own people.' 'Our ancestors disapprove of any one of us who is a wrongdoer because he brings disgrace to his people and family.' To disgrace the family name is to disgrace the ancestors themselves; a persistent wrongdoer is told, 'You are a shame to your ancestors!'

The spirits are shamed by wrong behaviour in their descendants because the behaviour of those descendants reflects their own (the spirits') moral and disciplinary powers. Just as a father is responsible for the good behaviour and good name of his children, or a leader for that of his set, so ancestor spirits are responsible for those of their respective descendants. Taking this into account together with their requirement for sacrifice and ritual observances, it can be said that spirits are conceived as moral guardians in the same dual sense as living seniors are—interested in 'rules' and ritual correctness (largely for internal relations) on the one hand, but in 'decency' and 'avoiding bad things' (largely for external relations) on the other. 'We who are living here, old or young, are their children, and they hate to see us doing wrong things.' 'A father does not like a child of his to be badly behaved. It defames the father not the child.' Such failures discredit the ancestors in the eyes of spirits as well as of men. 'Wrong behaviour of ours defames our ancestors to the other people in their world of spirits.' If A's ancestor lets A offend B on earth, B's ancestor-spirits are offended too. 'Evil-doers in an area disorganize peace and make other residents flee and leave the kraals of their fathers which have been the favoured haunts of those ancestors.'

Many Red migrants associated with the idea of spirits the idea of a high god (*Qamatha*), in a manner which might or might not have been influenced from Christian sources. Wrong behaviour by living descendants, they suggested, not only disgraces an ancestor-spirit in the eyes of men and fellow-spirits, but also lays the spirit open to reproach from Qamatha. It is to Qamatha, ultimately, that all spirits are responsible for their descendants. 'They are always trying to please Qamatha who is ruler of their world. Anything that is an eyesore before him, they disapprove of strongly.' 'They do not like any behaviour that offends Qamatha who is their superior.' Qamatha's judgement confirms that of spirits and moral men, that is, it deplores all antisocial behaviour which disturbs the peace of communities. 'The ancestors, if they leave their descendants at liberty to disorganize communities, prove themselves total failures before the highest spirit. They therefore try to prove their worth in his eyes by all means', i.e. by rigorously disciplining the living.

The spirits' disciplinary techniques of warning and punishment, and the implications of their repudiating responsibility if or when these techniques fail, must be dealt with later. Meanwhile it is clear that the close identification of 'people's' judgement with spirits' judgement has a bearing on the social organization of Red migrants. The *vox dei* being so literally identified with the *vox populi*, anyone who disturbs 'the community' of the people at home, or their representatives—the *amakhaya*—in town, or who objects to social control by them or defies their opinion, is unmistakably defying the ancestors and also Qamatha at the same time. These Xhosa in no way try to disguise—on the contrary, they loudly proclaim—that the heavenly judgement of spirits and Qamatha is only a transcendental version of the consensus of 'people' around one.

Besides condemning antisocial behaviour in general, the ancestors (like the 'people') demand that a man should 'respect' his own parents, home and family. If he fails in this he is failing in respect to them, the ancestors, who are a part of the home. Forgetting the home and forgetting the ancestors are practically the same thing, and are spoken of in the same breath. Hence *ukutshipha*, absconding, is a crime of crimes in the eyes of the ancestors, and forfeits their regard as well as that of the living. 'The anger of the ancestors is sent against young *amatshipha* who have forgotten them.' 'The trouble today is that too many people are becoming *amatshipha* and forgetting their ancestors.' Reference was made in an earlier chapter to the belief that spirits afflict migrants and cause them to go home if they stay away in town 'too long'. Staying in town against the will of one's senior kin, particularly one's father, cannot but offend them deeply. 'The spirits are proud of the kraal of their descendants. If a man neglects the family kraal they reckon that he has neglected them.' 'The spirits will be with you in town as long as you leave your parents peacefully. That is, there must be a good reason for your coming to town, and for your staying there. If you force your way to town against your father's will, the spirits will not go with you. They disapprove of negligence to one's family. Evil will befall you.' *Itshipha* deserves to be 'washed off' by the dead as by the living.

The spirits stand for moral sanctions not only against *ukutshipha* but against *ukurumsha*. They 'like the Red relatives who live as they lived themselves'. To be loyal to the ancestors is to be loyal to tradition. 'The traditional laws and regulations were invoked by our greatest ancestors who were guided by the greatest ancestor Qamatha.' The ancestors collectively will punish 'a nation' for 'practising a wrong thing that is not in their tradition'. 'Each generation takes [its standards of] what is not acceptable from the one before.' 'The ancestors left us laws which we ought not to break.' In the same way the spirits are Red Xhosa nationalists. 'They disapprove of . . . neglecting one's nationality, e.g. claiming to be a Coloured man when one is a full-blooded Native. In proof of this, a person who does so usually becomes a declared drunkard or a useless jailbird, and dies in shame and disgrace.' Thus living elders at home, *amakhaya* elders in town and dead elders in the spirit world all speak with one voice: be loyal to the country home, visit it often, never forget your piety towards your parents or your Red Xhosa ways. In detesting *ukutshipha*, in approving the man who remains Red in spite of all the temptations of town, the living and the dead are a united moral community.

THE DISCIPLINE OF THE SPIRITS

Ancestors give warning to those who stray from the path. 'They always give a warning to one by minor misfortunes which could have turned into more serious ones, e.g. physical injury, quarrels with one's employer, assaults by one's equals for small quarrels.' If the warning does not bring the descendant to heel it may be necessary for the ancestors to punish him more severely. 'They ask Qamatha for permission to punish us.' This may take various forms: a misfortune sent to the wrongdoer himself, or to his closest relatives (wife, children, siblings), or to those who are 'responsible' for him. The typically Xhosa idea of the 'responsibility' of the moral guardian brings about the likelihood that the sins of the children will be visited upon the fathers. 'The ancestors usually punish the seniors for they are usually the source of the misbehaviour of the younger ones.' Mishaps at home, such as the disease or death of livestock, may therefore be the ancestors' way of warning a father that his migrant son is behaving badly in town. Even more important, the *amakhaya* in town are risking the displeasure of the ancestors (as well as of the 'people at home') if they fail to exercise strict control over their junior comrades there, in accordance with the Red Xhosa principle that 'seniors' and 'people' have a duty to discipline every younger person, not merely those who are related to them by kinship.

A transgressor has two alternatives before him, one good and the other bad. The good way is to admit one's guilt, apologize, and make the redress which is demanded. In relation to the living community, this is expressed by the procedure already described (in chapter 7): summons, case-hearing and public apology, followed by a fine or drink-offering to the company. In relation to the spirits, the summons is a visitation or a troubled dream or prick of conscience; the apology, a whispered prayer for pardon; the redress, a sacrifice or a commemorative beer-party. In either relation, once the transgressor has confessed and has paid up he is received back into favour. The essential sign of grace is to be willing to recognize the moral authority.

The other, bad, alternative is to withhold apology and restitution, which means repudiating the moral authority and thus the relation itself. One then becomes 'cut off'. In such a case both the dead and the living will say: 'He does not want us, so we do not want him any more.' Where the living are concerned (it has been seen) the price of the resulting excommunication is loss of help and protection. ('If anything should happen to him, we *amakhaya* are not to be looked upon to help him, for he has refused our judgements.') A father likewise, as a last resort, 'washes off' his own son and refuses to endow him with his inheritance. Where the spirits are concerned, the consequences of excommunication and repudiation are even more dreadful.

In ordinary punishment of an offender by the spirits, and in ordinary social control by parents or seniors or *amakhaya*, love is held to operate together with anger. 'He is chastened by those who love him.' Discipline is a function of love itself. But when these means fail, love and guardianship are withdrawn at the same time as punishment ceases. Now the offender is left to the far harsher mercies of outside agents, whose inflictions are a just punishment in God's name. 'Spirits let such people [i.e. incorrigible offenders] fall into the hands of other disciplinarians who are chosen by Qamatha at the ancestors' request.' 'Any evil may befall him, for his spirits will no longer help him. As he turned his back on the spirits so they have turned their backs on him.' The consequences may be appalling. Once disinherited by his spirits a man is exposed to untold evils from all sides. 'Their anger is terrible. It results in death, misfortune and poverty.' One migrant who had committed a number of offences against women in town managed to avoid being traced for some time, but eventually the police caught up with him. 'He was charged, but before the case was heard he hanged himself. His ancestors had abandoned him.' 'If one shows no repentance one ends in jail or in the asylum.' On a larger scale, this is the reason why the Xhosa were allowed to suffer defeat at the hands of the White man. 'Africans are subjects of the White people today because they broke the laws of the ancestors very long ago.'

The spirits have an advantage over the living moral guardians: they see further and travel faster. An all-seeing eye enables them to detect impending harm to their 'good' descendants and forestall it by a warning, but also to see any wrong that is being done, 'even when you think nobody is watching'. 'A man may do wrong in town, believing that he is safe because nobody who knows him will ever find it out. He is forgetting something. He forgets that his spirits will know it all. Nothing can be kept hidden from them.' 'The spirits are far wiser than us, they see where we cannot see.' 'Though you cannot see your spirits, they can see you wherever you may go.' In particular, the spirits annihilate the distance between East London and the home community, which for the living is a grievous barrier to the effective exercise of moral guardianship. Spirits are quite capable of watching a son in the Transkei and a grandson in East London at one and the same time. 'Distances are nothing to them, for they are spirits and travel faster than the wink of an eye.' Yet spirits, fast as they travel and clearly as they see, labour in the last resort under some quasi-human limitations too. That they are not completely omnipresent, in the strict sense, appears from the idea that their travelling time is somehow proportionate to the distance. A spirit can reach East London from the Ciskei 'faster than the wink of an eye', but to return from investigations in a place 'as far as America might take them, perhaps, thirty minutes'. More significant than physical distance is social distance. The man who keeps shifting his room, or changing his job, both passes out of the sight of his living *amakhaya*, and makes it difficult for the spirits to find him. 'They come to his former room in town, only to find that he is not there.' It is an offence to evade the face-to-face relations with Red home people—'The spirits like to know where their descendant is'—but it constitutes a possibility of escape.

The omnipresence and omniscience of the spirits, then, are confined within definite limits: initially the limit of the home community (including its representatives in town) and, after that, the limit of Red Xhosa society. Collectively the spirits are 'tribal', in the sense in which one speaks of a tribal deity. In human terms, the concept of the spirits constitutes a fully effective conscience only in proportion as the individual remains an acknowledged member of his community and/or of the Red section.

So once again it is demonstrated that the typically Red sanctions operate, to chastise culprits or restrain potential culprits, only so long as the culprit himself is morally engaged. Anyone who finally snaps his fingers at Red 'rules', Red beliefs and Red people, becomes impervious to the wrath of spirits and *amakhaya* alike. He passes beyond their reach the moment he throws in his lot with something or someone else: a church, a forgiving Jesus, a welcoming circle of town or School friends. It is only to the faithful, who stay within the Red fold, that a tale of personal calamity can spell out the lesson of the might of the Red ancestors and their terrible retaliation.

THE LONG ARM OF WITCHCRAFT

Xhosa in town believe that they can be bewitched by neighbours there, but on the whole those who are migrants associate the evil power of witches— like the beneficent power of spirits—largely with the community at home.

In the present investigation the prevalence of witchcraft beliefs among men and women in town was tested by means of detailed questionnaires and guided interviews. *Inter alia*, respondents were read a list of the principal 'familiars' and other leading figures in the Xhosa witchcraft myth, as found in orthodox country circles, and were asked to say what they knew about each one, whether by first-hand experience or by hearsay (if either), and how far they 'believed' it and how they could prove it. A few respondents declared themselves sceptical on one or more particular points of the witchcraft myth, but few (if any) could be classed as sceptical about the witch-complex as a whole. They either 'knew' or 'believed' that such things as the *impundulu*, the 'snake of women' or the 'people of the river' do exist and work harm. Many said that they knew this to their cost by direct personal experience. Stories and case-histories were quoted in support, few of which (however) would carry conviction to an uncommitted mind.

The Xhosa witch myth[5] follows a familiar pattern in so far as it makes bewitching a function of 'living close together', 'knowing each other very well'. The favourite victim of witchcraft, it is thought, is 'someone of the same family, or a close neighbour'; 'the people the witches know best of all at home'. According to some informants the prevalence of witches at home in the country is the very reason why the spirits stay there too—they have to keep guard. 'The spirits remain in strongest force at a man's home, where there are many enemies of all kinds.' Witchcraft is conceived of as a manifestation of the tensions and conflicts which are an integral part of living together in the close, face-to-face relations of a rural community. The attribution of most witchcraft to the country home is also consistent with the fact that most Red women stay there. Xhosa witchcraft is predominantly a women's affair.

In terms of the Xhosa myth, the witches cannot work across wide social distances because the familiar (by means of which the evil is wrought upon the victim) has to 'know the victim', 'know his smell', 'recognize him perfectly having lived very close'. A familiar sent out to a victim whom it did not 'know' well enough would miss its target, and might be deflected in some unexpected direction, possibly back on to the witch herself. It is essential for the witch's own safety that she should know her victim's circumstances intimately and thoroughly. Otherwise he might happen to be a user of strong protective medicine, which would send the familiar flying straight back 'in great anger' to turn upon the witch. Her own death then might be 'a matter of minutes only'. No wonder witches prefer to persecute their intimates—'it is easier to know what has been done next door'.

But the witch myth has been adapted to labour migrancy exactly as the beliefs about the ancestors have been: social nearness remains essential, but physical distance can be transcended with the greatest of ease. The ancestor spirits follow their loved ones into town 'faster than the wink of an eye'; the witches follow their hated ones 'as quick as lightning'.

This aspect of witchcraft is stated in terms of a number of highly mobile familiars mediating between witch and victim. The familiars are the witch's easy way to project herself into town. Like the distance-annihilating ancestors, they symbolize the notion that the migrant community in East London is an extension of the home community, and that home relationships survive the physical removal of one partner to town.

The various kinds of familiar are credited with varying capabilities for travel, which not all informants assessed in the same order. It was generally agreed, however, that the fastest traveller of all is *impundulu*, which 'goes faster than a bullet and never gets tired'. *Impundulu* may be invisible or may transform itself into any of a number of different forms, including the human. *Uthikoloshe*, another speedy traveller, 'flies through the air like a small hurricane', or 'flies in a lift [*ikhetshi*, from English 'cage'] like the lifts which operate in the high buildings in town'. Either *impundulu* or *uthikoloshe* is ready to be dispatched

---

[5] For a detailed discussion of witchcraft among related peoples, cf. Hunter, M.: *Reaction to Conquest*, p. 272 (referring to the Pondo), and Laubscher, B. J. F.: *Sex, Custom and Psychopathology: a study of South African Pagan Natives* (referring to the Thembu). My own theoretical approach to the subject of witchcraft is outlined in a paper entitled 'Witches' (inaugural lecture, Rhodes University, Grahamstown, 1954).

by a country witch to a victim anywhere: 'they can reach to Johannesburg, they can reach to England.'

It was sometimes said that the witch herself can fly to town in a 'cage'. In addition, she can use the fast-travelling familiars to convey the slow-travelling ones. *Inyoka yabafazi*, for example (the 'snake of women'), and *umamlambo*, are 'lazy' familiars which prefer to work locally. Being snakes they can only crawl. But a witch can put *umamlambo* on the back of a flying *uthikoloshe* or *impundulu*. Failing this she can use an innocent human agent to carry it into town. The familiar's appearance changes into that of some attractive-looking object—a ring, money, a piece of cloth, a fountain-pen. Someone picks it up; when it gets near the intended victim it disappears, 'as if he had dropped it out of his pocket'. After finishing its job it gets itself brought home to the witch by similar means. People often notice that a parcel which they are carrying becomes heavier and heavier, and then they had better throw it away, for it may be *umamlambo*.

If the ancestors defy distance by their supernatural eyesight or insight, 'seeing where we cannot see', the sense with which familiars are supernaturally endowed is that of smell. They have wonderful powers of remembering and following a scent, and they help each other with smell-detection. *Uthikoloshe* may steal away a person's used clothing or belongings, or his hair, blood, sputum, urine or faeces, on purpose to take them home to the witch where one of her other familiars can 'learn the smell'. *Impundulu* may make small cuts in a victim's skin at night, and rub in a strong-smelling substance. 'This smell attracts other familiars like a magnet.' 'They can now sniff his track from his country home right into town, or wherever he may be trying to hide.'

The presence of a familiar may be manifested to the victim by 'uneasy feelings', 'bad dreams', 'a feeling of suffocation', 'waking up at night with a feeling of horror', 'fits', 'choking sensations'. There is a markedly sexual content. The 'bad dreams' are largely of sexual contact in some bizarre form. Both *uthikoloshe* and *impundulu* 'visit' female victims at night in the incubus manner. But these are only warning symptoms: the ultimate consequences (it was claimed) may be loss of health, sanity, and life itself. Often familiars strike without any warning dreams. *Impundulu* is more apt to cause acute illnesses, 'it feeds on the victim's blood and kills him quickly'. Some people said that the symptoms of *impundulu* are so characteristic that one does not need a diviner to identify them: the diviner is needed only to 'sniff out' (*nuka*) the individual responsible. 'A man has rapidly lost weight, he coughs incessantly, particularly at night, and sometimes coughs blood. That is the work of *impundulu*.' T was cited as a victim of *impundulu*, sent by a mother whose sons had turned out irresponsible, and who was jealous of T's care and attention to his own family: 'T went from one *ixhwele* [herbalist] to another but could not get relief. He is now in a TB settlement.' *Uthikoloshe* causes the wasting type of disease, unless it has been specially briefed to choke the victim outright.

THE OPPOSING INFLUENCES OF WITCHES AND ANCESTORS

Witches, according to rural Xhosa ideas, work 'from envy'. Among the special objects of their envy are a thriving family and a thriving herd.

Where the motive is an envy of this kind, the goal—by an overwhelming consensus—is to 'drive away' the objects of envy. A strategic retreat can save the intended victim from further harm. 'The chief aim of witches is to drive

people away.' Once the person is gone the witch will relax, for her purpose
has been achieved. 'Your going away pleases the witches, for you are no longer
near them and have given up the competition with them.' 'Leaving one's home
is regarded by the witches as a compliment to their strength.' 'They like to feel
victorious.' 'Witches are human beings and they have a sense of shame. They
do not wish to become notorious. Therefore, if one goes away, they try to leave
one alone in future.' It is by not withdrawing that one lays oneself open to all
sorts of further evils, including death. 'She will only kill him if he has resisted
her will to get him away.'

For the male head of a family, merely going to town on one's own does not
solve the problem. The objects of envy, the primary irritants—wife, children,
cattle—are still there. The only solution would be to take them away too. A
young man who is not the head of a family or kraal may however feel that he
is escaping from witches if he 'disappears' to town secretly by himself. Perhaps
he, the son and heir, is the very object whose possession the witch has begrudged
his parents. To escape from being killed he may go to town 'without saying a
word', 'so privately that none of the neighbours can know or reveal his whereabouts'. The head of his own homestead strictly cautions all the family against
letting the secret out.

In town the refugee is safe from the witch's pursuit only so long as she does
not know exactly where he is. If he stays at a fixed address which becomes well
known to the *amakhaya*, he risks his whereabouts becoming known to the witch
as well; similarly if he keeps at one steady job. Besides, a full description of his
lodging and place of work will be enough to enable the witch to enlist the help
of a 'bull witch', if she finds the case too hard for herself. Bull witches are past-
mistresses who do not need to know the victim personally as long as his appearance and whereabouts have been accurately described to them. 'It is a good
thing you have moved', observes the diviner to his client in town, 'for *impundulu*
and *inyoka* are wandering all over the place in search of you.' Only after adequate treatment by diviners and herbalists will it be felt safe to show one's
face again in home circles.

A Red young man of about 25 said that he was the son of a headman. His
elder brother and he were still children when their father died. A man of the
same clan but of different lineage was appointed headman, but only to act
until the late headman's heir should come of age, or so many people in the
Reserve believed. When this 'rightful heir' (the informant's elder brother)
grew up and people began to talk of his being made headman, he was attacked
by the *impundulu* of the current headman's wife, with fatal results. 'My brother
was found hanging from the roof of his hut. A diviner was consulted and smelled
out the acting headman's wife. I was still rather young then, but decided to go
in for circumcision that year [1952], so that I should go away for a long time
for *ukutshintsha*, and so escape the headman's wife's *impundulu*. My aim was for
the woman not to know my whereabouts.' He also went to a well-known
herbalist for *qinisa*. 'The herbalist put black powder in the incisions to make
my blood bitter for the *impundulu*. This is the only hope of protection against
impundulu.' In 1956 the young man visited his home for the first time since
leaving. 'At home I immediately fell sick, but I quickly recovered; *impundulu*
found that I was too strong.' He left for East London and this time '*impundulu*
had an opportunity to find out my whereabouts. He was very wild now, because
he had found my blood to be bitter.' One day the man and his workmates

were delivering mealie-bags by lorry for their firm. 'We were sitting on the bags. The lorry was moving fast, when suddenly I was tipped over and a bag of mealies fell on me. I was injured in the pelvic region and had to stay in hospital for a long time. A diviner was consulted and said I was tipped over by the *impundulu*. The headman's wife is still after my skin.'

The superhuman powers of witches, it can be seen, are conceptually related to the bounds of a community, much as those of ancestor spirits are. Once the victim is effectively 'outside' he is beyond the reach of witchcraft, or at least beyond the envy which is the witch's motive. What may perhaps be regarded as an extension of the same idea is the feeling that migrants are safer from witches when they stay on White people's premises in East London than when they stay in the locations. In the locations a person may be struck by a familiar which perhaps was not aiming at him at all, but at his neighbour. Even the smell of the familiar can be dangerous to anyone staying in the same yard as the intended victim. Pregnant women are particularly susceptible to these smells, 'the results of which are seen in the many miscarriages and stillbirths in the location'. But on White premises the familiar is frustrated by its own weapon—smell. Familiars cannot abide the smells 'of the many chemicals and medicines which White people keep in their houses'. These smells are the reason why 'the people who stay with White employers, like domestic servants, are rarely attacked'. One might interpret this belief by saying that the servants live in an environment where illness is less likely to be attributed to witchcraft, because it is more likely to be dealt with by the employers in White fashion.

Logically, the moves inspired by witchcraft fears should be directly contrary to those inspired by ancestor veneration. The ancestors wish their descendant to 'respect' the homestead in traditional ways, which means leaving wife and children there, visiting frequently, and building up a herd. The witches, on the other hand, incite men to stay away from home, to shun the sight of their home people; to remove wife and children to town; to withdraw from the country home, lock, stock and barrel. In town, the ancestors wish the migrant to remain in view of his *amakhaya*, not to 'disappear' by frequent shifting of jobs or rooms; 'they want to know where their descendants are'. The witches cause him to lie low, to avoid having his whereabouts known. It is an unavoidable dilemma that remaining within the social horizon of one's *amakhaya* means being visible to the protective ancestors, but also to the destructive witches.

The effect is that Red migrants who 'believe' in both ancestors and witches can use the witches, consciously or unconsciously, as a device for excusing behaviour on their own part which is contrary to the supposed code of the spirits. The sense of guilt which might ensue when one breaks the ancestors' rules can be dispelled by thus externalizing the 'cause'. A young man uses witchcraft to explain why he has his wife and children in town: 'They are safer here than in the country, where they were always exposed to the threat of *inyoka abafazi*.' A domestic servant uses it to explain why she has picked senseless quarrels with her employer and risked losing her job, contrary to the preference of the ancestors for steady employment: 'Another girl at my country home is jealous of me because of my good job. She wants me to become one of those people who keep changing their jobs from one house to another.'

In general the witch, like the ancestor-spirits, can be said to accept the framework of labour migration and work within it. She aims at turning migrants into absconders, while ancestor spirits aim at keeping them loyal home-visitors. Loyalty to the home, as demanded by the ancestors, has to be paid for by constant exposure to witches. Migrants for whom the price is too high can end by severing ties with home. (Not a few permanently town-settled ex-Red converts attributed their defection to 'witches at home'.[6]) But the rest, the majority, are likely to seek solution in some kind of self-defence or evasion, without severing the relations. In these terms the Red Xhosa dramatize two of the human possibilities of the migrant situation: one, to use town as a permanent escape from untenable relations at home; the other, to reconcile (at a price) home loyalties with migrant opportunities.

[6] See chapters 11–12.

PART THREE

PROCESSES OF URBANIZATION

10

Farm Servants: The Escape to Town

THE STATUS OF WORKERS ON FARMS

A number of Xhosa in East London come from White-owned farms in the hinterland.[1] Most of the farm labour in the eastern Cape—except for seasonal casual labour—is resident not migrant. The farm worker, having been born and bred on a farm, possesses no stake in the reserves: his only practicable move is either to another job on another farm, or to town. To appreciate the ways in which these people may react to town conditions it is necessary to review the status of workers on farms.

Many of the present farm-labour families are descended from Xhosa who took refuge with the White colonists when threatened with starvation after the disastrous 'cattle-killing' episode of 1857.[2] On the whole the peasants still think of farm work as something to which one may be driven by calamity; for preference they keep out of it. According to the customary pattern which still prevails on most east Cape farms, the farmer accommodates and feeds his labourers and their families too. Each regular labourer is allotted a hut—built by himself or by the farmer—where his dependants can live with him, and usually also a patch of land to be tilled for his and their benefit; usually, too, there is the privilege of keeping a few head of stock on the farmer's grazing. The farmer issues weekly or monthly rations, mealies and/or mealie meal being the principal item. The labourer's family serve as a reservoir of casual labour for busy seasons. Neither wages nor conditions on farms are regulated by law or collective bargaining. As a recent study has emphasized,[3] the relation is essentially paternalistic. Depending on the farmer's means and inclinations, the labour may be quite well off or may subsist at a very low level; but in all cases every benefit remains conditional on the farmer's grace and favour—a privilege, not a right. As life is lived under his eye day in and day out, he can also decide

---

[1] The Population Census of 1951 states that Natives on farms numbered 21,427 in the East London district and 5,490 in the King William's Town district. For the difficulty of reconciling these figures with those of the Agricultural Census of 1950, see Fourie and Lumsden, in Houghton (*Edit.*): *Economic Development in a Plural Society*, chapter 7, table 124.

[2] Some of the economic and social implications of the cattle-killing tragedy are discussed in Houghton (*Edit.*): *Economic Development in a Plural Society*, chapter 1, and Reader: *The Black Man's Portion*, chapter 1. A well-documented account of the historical events can be found in du Toit, A. E.: 'The Cape Frontier 1847–1866', *Archives Year Book for South African History*, 17th year, 1954, vol. 1.

[3] Roberts, M.: *Labour in the Farm Economy*.

many things besides the material living standard: how many visits his workers may pay or receive, how often they may brew for a beer-drink, or hold a ritual or a prayer meeting; whether the children may attend a school; whether adolescents can go to town or must hold themselves ready for work on the farm. The word generally in use for the workers is 'farm servants', and this expresses the truth that the White farmer is more to them than an employer, more than a landlord: he is a master. It is an important aspect of this dependence on a 'master' that the farm servant is never left free to make his own decisions about when or whether he will come and go between town and country. He cannot choose between the roles of stay-at-home, peasant visitor, migrant and immigrant as freely as his peasant counterpart can (or could do but for influx control). His choices are necessarily narrower and their implications more drastic.

The same root cause which drives members of peasant families to town—i.e. the need for money—operates as one motive with farm Xhosa too. It is true that they have largely free subsistence on the farm. In the hands of the 'good' employer this may include not only decent rations and some secondhand clothing but free medical attention and elementary schooling for the children. On the farms generally, too, it is rare for wages to be stopped during sickness, or for an old hand to be turned off when he is past work, provided that he can still be regarded as a member of the family of some other worker. But money is still needed; for food over and above the staple mealie ration, for clothing, for poll-tax, for the outlay in connexion with a son's initiation or bridewealth for his marriage. The money wages on farms are distinctly low and cannot meet these demands comfortably. In 1957 the adult male labourer's *monthly* wage, in one east Cape farming district, ranged from below 20s. to 40s., with an average of 31s. 10d. Women and juveniles, when they can be employed at all, receive less.[4] The labour is regarded as unskilled, with wages on each farm at a fixed rate per head. There is nothing to be promoted to; most farmers are against differential wages as being a source of envy and discontent. While money wages are lower than in town, working hours are longer—normally from sunrise to sunset, that is, about fourteen hours a day in summer and ten or eleven in winter. Moreover, there are bad as well as good employers, and the system offers the labourer no protection whatever against exploitation or tyranny.

In return for the privilege of accommodation, children of workers on farms are normally expected to remain available to the farmer as casual labour until they grow up, and then to give him the first option on their services as paid labourers. By the age of, say, 15, most farmers will expect a boy to begin full-time work (though his wage may be paid to his father not himself). At about 18 he will usually be allowed to take a few months' leave from the farm to earn money elsewhere (nominally for purposes of his initiation ceremony). A pattern of brief temporary migration of farm-born youths is accordingly quite well established; but it does not take many of them into East London. With only a few months at his disposal the farm youth is more likely to take out a contract on the mines, or undertake seasonal local work such as orange-picking. (Mining companies, as is well known, make a practice of issuing short labour contracts, and unlike the ordinary urban employer they are legally allowed to recruit in rural areas.)

From this stage onwards migration in the back-and-forth sense becomes still

[4] Cf. Roberts, M.: *Labour in the Farm Economy.*

harder. No longer entitled to a free home on the farm simply as his father's dependant, the grown man has to choose between working there and losing his footing there. Unlike a peasant's son, if he goes to work in town he has no automatic security of being able to return to a country home, either for week-ends or for leave or permanently. Some farm servants do get 'leave of absence' from the farmer, i.e. permission to go and earn in town with assurance of re-employment and re-accommodation when they return. Such leave is often made conditional: the absentee may be required to return within a fixed period, or to hold himself subject to recall at any time when the farmer needs an extra hand, or to provide a substitute worker during his absence.

If back-and-forth migration is hard, so is permanent emigration from the farm. For this the farmer's signed permission is necessary. Since the introduction of the reference-book system, every farm-born Native male over the age of 16 requires the farmer's written discharge before he can obtain the work-seeker's permit necessary for his lawful presence in town (or even before he can be given another farm job). In effect, then, he can have no other means of making a lawful living until released by the farmer. This point is more than academic. Farmers are often reluctant to let their men go, because of the labour shortage which has been complained of for the past twenty years or so, and the (statis-tically confirmed) drift to town. However, to appreciate the full rigours of the situation from the farm servants' point of view, one must think of the dilemma confronting men who have dependants. Even if a farmer is co-operative about granting leave of absence to his servants, with a promise to take them back, there is no reason why he should continue housing and feeding the man's dependants while the man himself is away on a town job. More obviously still, a man cannot go away for good and leave his dependants on the farm. Yet because of influx control he can hardly take his dependants with him either. If he goes to town, he will find it excessively hard to get permits to bring them in; if to the mines, he cannot establish 'residence' in the adminis-trative sense, which means that families are not allowed. In the upshot, then, the farm worker with dependants is taking tremendous risks if he gives up the farm connexion and the farmer's good will. Usually he must either hold down a farm 'place' himself or else make his son or other relative do so while he himself goes to earn in town. Roberts comments that influx control has rendered Xhosa farm servants, like medieval peasants, *adscripti glebae*.[5]

It could be added that the farm servant's job is not tied to him as he is tied to the job. There being no legal contract, the farmer can dismiss the servant at any time and on any grounds. It is true that during the Second World War and for some time afterwards the general labour shortage on farms worked temporarily to the servant's advantage. The pineapple boom of the early 1950's also opened up many new farm jobs. Even some reserve Xhosa were attracted by the relatively high wages then paid on pineapple farms. But falling trends in agriculture have depressed the workers' conditions and prospects again, while at the same time influx control has prevented surplus labour from freely draining off to the towns. The farm servant, one might say, now has more reason to want to go to town but less chance of going.

Some farm servants interviewed in the country[6] went so far as to deny that

---

[5] Ibid.

[6] In Reader's Survey IV of rural workers attending for registration in the East London magisterial district (1955). See his Appendix on Method in *The Black Man's Portion*.

they have any choice in the matter at all: 'I don't prefer farm life, but I cannot get away.' 'I cannot help staying on the farm. I am under control.' 'The owner of the farm will not let me go to town.' 'The farmer forced my parents to bring me back from town, saying that I must work on the farm.' 'It is not that anyone prefers working on farms, but the law will not allow us to leave.'

In spite of the immense obstacles in the way of farm servants trying to move to town, some farmers complain that the drift still continues. It can be seen that it differs from ordinary migrancy. If the farm servant goes to town with the farmer's agreement to keep open a home for him, his future movements are regulated as much by the farmer's as by his own decisions: if he goes without this agreement, he has burnt his boats and can only become a town immigrant as distinct from a back-and-forth migrant. Both circumstances are important for the prospect of urbanization.

THE CHOICE OF EVILS

Xhosa living on one farm, or on near-by farms, have to constitute their own social world. Compared with the peasants in the reserves their social contacts are far fewer, their horizons narrower, their poverty more hampering, their knowledge of the world outside—including town—more restricted. In place of the rich community life of a reserve location, all that the farm can offer is a fairly regular contact with those few families (perhaps ten, twenty or fifty) whom chance has thrown together to constitute the local farm labour force. Contact is kept up by visiting, when off duty, those other families who live within walking distance: if the farm is near enough to reserve land, this may include visits to peasant homesteads. It was found by Roberts[7] that east Cape farm labour tends to be stable in the sense that many farm Xhosa spend all or most of their lives within a short radius of the farm where they were born, and have numerous kinship links there. A son will take over a job from a father, and a family may establish itself on a farm for several generations. But even within its narrow horizons the social world cannot be fully secure. Families come in from the unknown world outside and vanish into it again. Farms change hands: new masters may use less or more labour, or make new rules about visiting.

Within these limits, the eastern Cape farm servants are recognizably brethren to the Red peasants in the reserves. School ways have made even less headway on farms than in the reserves generally. In the East London and King William's Town districts, nearly all farm servants, in spite of the direct relations with White people implied by their status, are pagan and illiterate.[8] Many White farmers explicitly say that they prefer the uneducated type of worker, while few have the reverse preference. Schools for the children of farm servants exist only where they have been set up on the farms by the masters' bounty or consent. The missions have had little direct access to the farm population; church facilities, like school facilities, are limited either physically or by the farmer's not allowing time off for participation.

The habits and values of the farm workers in these areas, allowing for differences imposed by poverty and dependence, not only resemble those of

[7] Op. cit., p. 84.
[8] Reader's Survey IV (of rural workers attending for registration in the East London districts) showed 408 men with no schooling, or sub-standards A or B, and forty-four men with standard 1 or further schooling. The forty-four were mostly not farm servants but brickworkers and other rural employees.

Red Xhosa but have an even stronger traditional flavour in some respects. Farm men (outside working hours) are more likely than peasant men to be seen going about in the 'traditional' dress of ochred blanket and doek, with beads and tobacco pouch. Visiting one another on neighbouring farms, the young people keep up the Red tradition of weekly *intlombe* and *umtshotsho* gatherings. The fact that more young men are working at home, fewer in town, adds to the liveliness of the youth organization: a farm *intlombe* may be better developed than that of a peasant community. Sacrifices and other domestic rituals are kept up, though there are fewer neighbours to attend them. What is missing, of course, is the sense of community and sense of autonomy, symbolized for the reserve location by the *inkundla* and the headman.

Farm servants have basically the same attitudes towards town and country as other Red people. They prefer rural to urban activities, and traditional to 'civilized' ways of life. But while arguments of culture may influence a farm servant in this direction, arguments of status are apt to drive him in the other. This creates a basic difference between the views of the Red farm servant and the Red peasant on possible urbanization.

Red farm servants, like all Red people, set the highest value on the figure of the independent, thriving peasant following traditional Xhosa ways, and measure success in small-scale local terms, rather than by any reference to the wider world. Money, alone among Western imports, is given a positive value, since in these days it belongs to the conception of thriving. Left to himself, the farm servant eschews the ambitions of higher education, Christian religion, or the 'civilized way' of life, including most Western-type artefacts and recreations. On the question of living permanently in East London, farm servants interviewed in the country[9] expressed themselves just as strongly as peasants: they disliked town life as such. Their responses tended to sound more naïve than those of peasants, but the substantial content was much the same: 'We can't grow food in town.' 'In town when you have no work, you have nothing to eat and nowhere to stay.' 'The laws in town are getting very cruel.' 'Town life is rotten. People in town behave like animals.' 'Children get spoilt in town while they are still young.' 'Your daughter will be pregnant as soon as she is ready for the bull.' 'Your wife becomes loose and your children become rude.' 'People become drunkards.' 'If I were in town I would get no cattle for my daughter.' But above all: 'What will happen to me in town when I am too old to work?' 'At the end of town life there is nothing.' 'There is no future in it.'

On the other hand, farm Xhosa interviewed in town also spoke out as disparagingly about life on farms. In this respect their outlook contrasts most strikingly with that of the average Red peasant, who, while speaking adversely of town, will glorify his country home. Even allowing for bias—e.g. that perhaps the most dissatisfied of the farm people are the ones who can be found in town—the loud and universal complaints about 'bad conditions on the farm' make an impression of genuine hopelessness. There is the complaint of poverty: 'On the farms things are very bad. People work hard from dawn to dusk for very little pay. A father, mother, sons, and daughters are all doing some work for the Boss, who pays the father £1 per month, the mother 10s. per month, the sons and daughters 5s. per month each, plus one paraffin-tin full of mealies every Saturday. This is very bad. I do not like to think of it.'

⁹ In Reader's Survey IV.

'The White farmer expects us to do all his work practically free of charge.' 'If you are selling a beast, it must be sold to your master, and you get very little for it. He will first tell you that you owe him so much for bags of mealies taken on credit, and will pay you the difference.' There is the complaint of frustration and insecurity: 'We have no chance of any achievement on the farms.' 'If I had sons I should like them to settle permanently in the reserves, because there is no future for Native servants on farms.' 'The huts I occupy belong to the farm owner, the piece of land I plough belongs to the farm owner. I am only allowed the use of these things while I am still on the farm.' And there is the complaint of personal subjection: 'On the farm you are under control all your life. You are constantly given orders to do this or that, and you cannot refuse.' 'In town I am free in my movements after the working hours, but on the farm the landlord will call upon you any time to perform any kind of duty.' 'On the farm you have to "worship" the master. I mean, to be always friendly with the master, who, if annoyed with you, may terminate your tenancy any time he likes; you are then placed in a very awkward position, having to look for a place on another farm, which it is not easy to get.'

To sum up: in disliking town on principle—in being anti-urban and anti-'civilized'—the two Red types, peasant and servant, are largely in agreement, while both differ from certain more aspiring Christian types. But in the degree of their satisfaction with their rural *status* the Red farm servant and the Red peasant do not agree at all. The peasant normally enjoys, or can hope to enjoy, the kind of independent status which is preferred according to Red cultural norms; the farm servant, idealizing the same status in theory, is debarred from it in practice. The average Red farm servant would much like to change himself into an independent Red peasant, but as the law makes this extremely difficult his only practical way to change his status is to go to town. Thus the special feature of the Red farm servant's attitude to town is its ambiguity: his choice between a town home and a country home appears by Red standards as a choice between evils. To this must be added that the element of unfreedom in his conditions of service restricts his choices altogether.

KEEPING UP THE COUNTRY CONNEXION

(a) Remaining oriented to the farm

Most of the farm people who come to town seem to be determined, initially, to keep open a home on the farm, if not for themselves then for their families. This determination, as long as it lasts, harmonizes with the basic Red principles of preferring the country, remaining Red, and placing the moral demands of the country home higher than all others. The farm servant with extended permission to work 'outside' will explain that the home on the farm remains uppermost in his mind for the sake of the kin above all. 'Because of my father, mother, wife and two children, I regard the farm as my permanent home, although I can get better pay here in town.' 'I am not interested in town friends. Father, mother, wife and children are my constant worry. . . . I want my children to stay there at the farm and learn all the work that is done there. I would not like them to become highly educated, for fear they might leave us and go far away.' 'I have asked the farmer's permission to come to town again and he agreed. If he demands my return at any time I shall return, to avoid having my father, mother, and family kicked out.'

The kin in the country are visited as often as conditions and the farmer will

permit, and as much social life as possible is crowded into the visits. A man of
29 still attends *intlombe* on the farm 'whenever I am there'. Some live so near
that they can go in and out of town for work every day, by bicycle, the farmer
tolerating them as guests or dependants of his resident servants. Others are
week-enders and month-enders.

To say that the farm servant wants to keep the farm as his home, is not to
say that he likes it. While retiring home is the cherished desire of Red
peasant migrants, to the farm servant it may well assume the guise of a sacrifice:
the work in town is often described as better paid and more congenial. The
willingness to make this sacrifice is the acid test of one's devotion to the kin.
It is the price that has to be paid for keeping their accommodation on the
farm. 'If my hut and my dependants were not on the farm, I would stay here in
East London all the time.' 'There is no man who would not rather work in town
than stay on the farm. The only trouble is that every man wants to have his
home in the country.' 'Though we do not like to remain on the farms we are
forced to do so because our families are there.' 'If one could only settle here in
town, one could be a better man than on the farm, where one's whole life
depends on another man.'

(b) Trying for rural security

With some farm people, working in town is a means towards improving the
'home' in the country. These lucky few families, with the help of money earned
in town, manage to achieve something like the peasant prosperity which is the
Xhosa ideal, having a herd of cattle at home on the farm, and savings in cash.
Even so, there is never the ultimate security. Cattle are run on the farm by the
farmer's permission—it is a favour, not a right. A change of hands, or a quarrel
with the present owner, or (of course) a change of job, may mean that the family
can no longer keep any cattle.

What most farm servants would like best, if they could, is to regain the status
of peasant by acquiring a home within the reserve. 'Although I have been
compelled by circumstances to come to town, I am still very much interested
in country life, ploughing, and keeping cattle.' Money earned in town may be
devoted to this purpose. In spite of the overcrowding in the Reserves, the
resettling of farm servants as peasants proceeded on a fairly large scale until
not long ago. It was mainly illegal. A footing could be gained through the
good offices of a peasant relative or clansman, or a well-disposed headman.
One farm servant sent his wife and sisters to stay with his mother's brother in
the Transkei. They are occupying one of his huts. 'My uncle told the headman,
who made no objection, as he had been friendly with my late father. The
headman has already accepted *uswazi* [gift usually of a bottle of brandy]
and has promised to allot me a kraal site. When the site is earmarked for me
I shall give him something more.' Another, born on a farm at Komgha, has a
kinsman at Mooiplaats who put a hut at his disposal. 'I am still just squatting
there, having no homestead of my own. It is very difficult to get a homestead
in the reserve when you come from the farms. But the headman has promised
to do all he can.'

The farm servant with this much hope of a permanent home in the country
settles down into a pattern much like that of the country-rooted Red peasant,
He devotes generously of his time, earnings and thought to the country home.
and avoids getting 'mixed up in town'. 'As I am still a squatter and not yet

fully settled, I go over every week-end to see how things are. The bus fare is 4s. each way. I want my children to be country people. I wish my son might be a headman, and my daughter a teacher at a country school. I have two of my father's brothers here in town, and I spend my free time with them, or with my *iseti* from our farm district.'

Till recently, another possibility has been to become a cash tenant, or squatter, with a White farmer as landlord. This meant holding land under the White owner not in return for services but in return for rent. As long as the rent was paid the landlord could not object to the tenant's absence in town. One or more of the family would obviously have to be away in town semi-permanently, because of the money needed for the rent: an amount from, say, £40 to £90 a year. This situation, therefore, provided incentives to continue working in town for long periods but also to remain country-rooted. Town meant money, money meant rent and security in the country.

H.W., in 1956, described himself as a 'sub-tenant' to his brother who was a tenant on a White-owned farm: that is, he had a homestead of his own on the brother's holding. Their late father had been the original tenant; now the brother carried on, paying £70 a year in rent, and H.W. made certain contributions. He had been in East London for twelve years, working all the time in the same job at a bakery, so that he qualified as 'urbanized' under the Urban Areas Act. In appearance, however, he is readily recognizable as Red. When interviewed in town he was wearing an *ubulunga* necklace (of cow's tail hairs, sometimes prescribed by Xhosa diviners). The brother looks after his wife, children, and cattle on the farm. 'I regard it as my home, though of course the land is only ours as long as we pay the rent. Here in town I am only concerned with money. I am not interested in town life, only in the farm.' He goes back there every time there is a long week-end, and on his annual leave.

The presence of such squatters on White-owned farms was strongly discouraged by an Act of 1956.[10] Under the law now in force, it is extremely difficult for a Native to be permitted to reside on a farm unless he is bona fide and continuously employed by the farmer. In most cases farmers therefore had the option of either giving the squatters full-time (not merely seasonal) work, or telling them to leave. Displaced squatters could apply for homes in one of the two rural centres for homeless people (one at Chalumna, the other at Soto, Komgha district), which are near enough to East London for daily trips to work. Or they could try to move directly into the East London locations. The legislation has, in fact, produced a flow of ex-farm residents as legal or illegal immigrants into East London during 1956 and 1957.

GIVING UP THE COUNTRY CONNEXION

Unlike the Red peasant, the Red farm servant who chooses to give up his footing in the country is not necessarily a deviant or misfit by the standards of his own people. One is doing no wrong by moving to town to escape from the dependence of a servant, so long as one does not jeopardize one's family. 'I could no longer tolerate the conditions of farm life, especially after the death of my father, so I came to town.' 'I came here because I could not see any future in farm life.' Farm servants may be obvious candidates for urbanization.

A decision to transfer to town as a permanent immigrant may be taken early and consciously. In such cases there is sometimes a history of acute tension

[10] Roberts, op. cit., pp. 127–8.

between the servant and his former master on the farm, which may reflect personality difficulties on either side. Other farm servants accept the *ultimate* loss of farm accommodation as inevitable but try to put off the day. They hedge their resolution around with contingencies: 'I will settle permanently in town unless I can get a homestead site somewhere in the reserve.' 'I shall come to town for good when my father dies.' It may be that some, in due course, will recant and convince themselves that it is better to go back to farm work after all.

Two cases may be used to illustrate different phases of the uprooting from the farm. B.M. came to East London four years ago when he was about 19. Besides his parents, he now has a wife and two children on the farm, which is in the East London district and very close to town. He cycles home most nights after work and is back in town for work in the mornings. He spends week-ends there, and enjoys the *intlombe*. He is still much attached to his parents. 'My parents are Red people and so I am still under their control myself. If I got into any trouble here I would send word to my mother on the farm: I have nobody in town who would help me.' B.M. has the farmer's permission to stay away in town, as long as his young brother works in his stead. But he is not prepared to make the decisive sacrifice. He 'hates farm life' and wants to make his 'permanent home' in town. 'If the farmer ever says that I must come back to the farm or else clear out, I would definitely leave the farm altogether. The pay is too low there and the conditions too hard.' He has vague aspirations towards 'a town job with a *pinsholo*' (pension), or preferably a business; though unfortunately, he says, 'the White people value business so much that they do not allow us to run it without first obtaining licences'.

S.S., who is now about 30, has his family on a farm in the East London district. Apart from one year in the mines at Springs, he has spent the last ten years working in East London. 'I was young when I came here and I regarded the farm as my permanent home, because my father was there, as he still is. Father urged me to go to work in town because the 10s. cash per week was too little to support our family. I have since changed my mind. I now think I will make town my permanent home.' He still goes every week-end to his father's place, by bus, to see his wife and children who are under the father's care. But, 'I cannot see any future in farm life. When my father dies, that will be the end of our country home. My wife and children will have to join me in town, unless I can get a kraal site in one of the reserves. I shall never go back to farm work.' This man's preference for town is entirely based on status reasons: 'A White farmer takes advantage of his servants. He will give you an order to do something which is not part of your work, and if you refuse or argue, he shouts: "Out of my farm, you are cheeky." A farmer has no sympathy when a Native servant has died on his farm. If you ask for permission to attend the burial, he grumbles: "My work is now to be at a standstill." ' In town, on the other hand, 'there are chances for you to get rich if you are intelligent and not lazy. People here sell firewood, milk, empty bottles, and they buy fruit and vegetables on the market and sell it to make profit. If a man could stick to any of these he would be well up in no time, and in the end he may be able to buy his own hut.'

RESISTANCE TO TOTAL URBANIZATION

In town, farm-rooted people from one area tend to mix with one another where possible as neighbours, friends and drinking companions. 'My friends live in the part of the location called Tulandivile. They are servants from Dallas farm area, like me. Some of them are my own age-mates, we grew up together.' 'My best friends in town come from my home area, the Orange farm area. I am always together with them, or with my younger brother.' 'My *iseti* are men from the Komgha farms. I spend my time with them. We drink together. We chat about country matters. We are customers of a certain woman brewer, and have a standing order for *iseti* beer every day.' What is missing—by comparison with the *amakhaya* organization of the peasant migrants —is the tight social control, the submission of junior to senior, the sense of a functioning parent community as the ultimate moral referent. The people of one farm area cannot parallel the organization of *amakhaya*, simply because the community life at home has never been the same thing.

Perhaps more interesting than the farm-rooted is the section of ex-farm population which is not attached, or is only doubtfully attached, to the country. It remains to be seen how these uprooted and transplanted Red people order their social life in the town which is now their only home.

Many of them show a willingness to move in the direction of urban habits and values as well. Then they *ipso facto* become totally urbanized. Something will be said about these in the next chapter.

But there remain others who, even having lost their country connexion beyond recall, resist total urbanization. They will not go back to country life as farm servants, they cannot go back as peasants or squatters, but they persist in trying to live as Red men, within the urban setting.

A.M.'s father, born on a farm in Queenstown district, became a servant on a farm at Amalinda (East London district). He later went to work in East London, leaving his wife and children (A.M. and a brother) on the farm. When A.M.'s mother died the father decided to 'abandon farm life', and both sons joined him in town. This was twelve years ago when A.M. was about 24. A.M. is married to a Red girl from a farm. She is staying with him in town, not earning anything: the couple live in a municipal sub-economic house.

There was no doubt from the outset that A.M. was going to town for good. 'I had come to stay permanently, and I have not changed my mind. Town is my real home. I have no other home to go to or even to visit.' But A.M.'s dress and manner immediately proclaim him as Red. In spite of heavy drinking he is an intelligent and orderly person. He has nothing much positive to say about town life to balance the usual criticisms of its anxiety-producing features (permits, arrests, overcrowding, etc.). Nor does he like urban people. The only people he cares to mix with are 'Red men from the country, with no education, who drink—because I drink heavily myself. I like these people because there is no nonsense about them. A younger man respects his senior.'

A.M. spends his time visiting his Red friends, 'seeing if they have anything to drink, and if not, we move about in the location, looking for places where they sell kaffir beer or brandy'. He belongs to no church or organization in town. Bioscopes and newspapers do not exist for him. A.M. is proud of his Red rustic values. 'I do not like to cheat anyone, I do not take anything that does not belong to me. This I have copied from my late father.'

It might be suggested that illiteracy, in A.M.'s case, is a factor preventing him from moving outside Red circles. However, one can find a basically similar pattern among some literate immigrants from the farms.

M.G. was educated to standard III. He has married a School wife who belongs to the Bantu Presbyterian Church, and nominally adheres to it himself. M.G. emigrated to East London from Iseli farm area, King William's Town district, sixteen years ago when he was about 25. His wife is with him, and has a job at a well-known local textile mill. 'I could not make a living on the farm, so I came to town to stay here permanently. As we are not allowed to shift from the farm to a reserve, town was the only alternative. I have no home anywhere but East London.' His widowed mother is also in town, 'but I don't see her often, because after my father's death she became too loose: that is, she has since lived with another man as husband and wife, very much against my will'.

In spite of his schooling and his nominal Christianity, M.G. looks like a Red man, and he regards himself as belonging to the Red section. 'My brother and I are Red men.' Most of his free time is spent attending beer drinks of Red men. 'Certainly,' says M.G., 'I live under better conditions here than on the farm.' He has no intention of going back to a farm job. And yet he still feels, after sixteen years, 'new to town life'. He belongs to no organization, and does not attend church, sports gatherings or bioscopes.

It amounts to a sort of shadow version of incapsulation when the new-made 'townsman' continues to move within the social world of country-rooted Red migrants to town, though he has no longer any country roots himself. Preferring these people on account of their Red habits and values, he keeps up the old relation of aloofness in regard to School people and real townspeople. 'In town', said a farm immigrant of 50, with no rural connexion, 'I like to belong to the Red people. I trust them. These people are not cunning, they do not like to do anyone down.'

Sometimes the principle is to go on associating with men from one's original farm area; sometimes the immigrant picks up new companions in the promiscuous urban manner, merely making sure that they are Red. Perhaps he will not even inquire about their rural home of origin: to him as an immigrant it may hardly matter. 'G.M. has been my friend since I first came here [1945]. He was employed at the harbour, like me, and we were in the same *ispani* [gang]. I only know that he was born of Red people, and had never been to school, and that his home was somewhere in the King William's Town district.' 'X.M. comes from Peelton, I believe. He has been my next-door neighbour here in East London for many years. We are age-mates. He is also born of Red people, and has no education. He also has his wife in town.' 'T and myself are *iintanga*. We are employed in different firms but we have our lunch in the same eating-house, where we hold conversations on different matters. Like me he has no education.' As a mere isolated couple of friends, not incorporated into a Red sociable group, such men may find no better occupation for their spare time than drinking together in a rather dissolute fashion. 'We go about in the location together looking for beer, often until late at night.' 'Z is my next-door neighbour, and is a Red man a few years my senior. He is a widower and his house is therefore most suitable for drinking purposes. My wife complains that I spend too much money on drink. To evade my wife, Z buys brandy or kaffir beer and keeps it in his house. He will then give a sign indicating that I must come over.'

A network of acquaintances with whom one can spend one's free time in typically Red ways, serves the same function as true incapsulation on the *negative* side. It prevents a man from becoming culturally urbanized. He keeps aloof from town people and town activities and takes as his reference group the 'Red people in town'. But it will be clear that the significance is not the same as that of true incapsulation on the *positive* side. In the case of a peasant migrant still oriented to his country home, the activities of town are means subordinated to an end—to the well-being or betterment of the country home. Morally the life in town is only a part of the total 'way of life', even if very little time remains for the country home. But in the case of the immigrant, as the rural 'home' recedes and vanishes, the life with other Red people in town—such as it is—becomes the whole way of life, the end in itself. It is not related to anything outside itself. In particular, it is not related to any other coherent structure. It does not re-create in town such social features as the submission of junior to senior, the 'keeping the rules of Red people', the solidarity between home-people or age-mates. The desire to exercise social control, and the willingness to accept it, both hinge on the common loyalty to a community at home, which these immigrants no longer have.

Some Red immigrants, however, not content with confining themselves to individual Red friends, make a point of attaching themselves to a functioning circle of Red *amakhaya*, on the strength of a personal connexion (such as a kinship link) with one member. By doing so, an immigrant who has no direct connexion with a rural community can taste its life at second-hand. He is now a hanger-on to what is in itself a projection of a rural community. A serious-minded immigrant from a farm gave as his explicit reason the fact that such circles of *amakhaya* are the only effective agents of Red social control in East London: 'I mix with the Red people who come from Mooiplaats reserve. These people still observe the rules of seniority. The most senior man among them is respected by all the younger men and if he says "No" the *abafana* cannot force their way. I like them for this reason in particular.'

The Red farm immigrants themselves, even while they prefer to practise their own brand of Red culture, mostly face the fact that they will not be able to transmit it to their children. They accept the prospect that the children will go to school and grow up as urban children. A.M. is illiterate and pagan, but he says that his children are going to be 'School town people'. He has already made up his mind that 'when my infant daughter reaches school-going age I will send her to the Salvation Army School, which I like the best'.

II

Red Migrants outside Incapsulation

AVOIDING THE 'AMAKHAYA'

The Red notion that the 'real Xhosa' way of life is basically superior to all others, and is worth the price of some self-denial, has been seen at work both in the country and in town, helping to protect the Red section against wholesale erosion. In cases where this internal source of moral strength gives out, the Red section as such is, of course, powerless to keep a hold on its members. The painful dilemma of the censuring *amakhaya*, mentioned in chapter 7, epitomizes the Red dilemma as a whole. Moral censure for disloyalty will make the least impact on those who do the most to incur it: they need not stay to hear the reproaches of the orthodox. On the other hand there are external factors in town which help to reinforce the internal ones. Influx control could be called one in so far as it reminds every migrant that his only permanently secure home is in the country, where his kin and friends will expect him to continue in the old ways. No less important are the social and cultural barriers in town which make it difficult for an ordinary Red migrant to become accepted in non-Red circles there.

This chapter will examine some aspects of life among Red migrants who do not remain within the incapsulating circle; in the process it may help to show why incapsulation is still so much favoured. Some of the men to be considered are Red migrants who, as it were, forestall incapsulation. They defect at the critical moment of first setting foot in town, when out of reach of home influences for probably the first time in their lives. Deliberately avoiding their *amakhaya*, instead of seeking them out as Red norms require, they find themselves at large in an anonymous town society, free to adopt new habits or even to give up visiting home. There is also a slow wastage of Red migrants who, although they start off in the orthodox way, drift off gradually in the course of their town careers, becoming less and less Red and/or less and less attached to home. For them, breaking away has been a process not an event.

Broadly speaking, one can distinguish two themes in the life-histories of self-confessed ex-Reds in town. One is the theme of having renounced old friendships to gratify new cultural ambitions. The other is the reverse—renouncing old cultural preferences for the sake of new friends. These broad categories can serve as a guide through all the rich variety of actual experiences to which ex-Reds themselves may attribute the decision to change—a family catastrophe, a religious experience, an economic ambition, a nervous collapse, a hankering after smartness or after education, a love affair or a jilting, a snub by a relative, a quarrel, a disappointment, an unexpected kindness, an act of witchcraft.

Changes away from the orthodox Red pattern of migrant life are reflected in the individual's network in various ways. First there is the question of the original relations in the country. The special nightmare of Xhosa peasant families, as has been said, is *ukutshipha*, absconding—the 'vanishing' of a man in town, leaving his kin at home without money remittances and without news of him. *Ukutshipha* implies that the individual becomes entirely detached from his old network of relations in the country. Fear of *ukutshipha* helps to inspire Red people's mistrust of *ukurumsha*, the learning of 'town ways', which they regard as the thin end of the wedge. But not every migrant who learns town ways need drop out of his rural network. There is the man who—as migrants say—becomes 'School in town', i.e. lives in a non-Red way in town but eventually returns home and lives in a Red way there. Then there are those *amarumsha* who also return to the country but take some of their newly learnt non-Red ways back with them. Their most likely destiny will be to join the School section of their rural home community in due course. Even in this case the immediate result, from the home point of view is not so much a discarding of old relations as a change in their content.

There is the further possibility that a Red man—either with or without any special cultural ambitions—may become town-rooted, but without the flagrant disregard of rural obligations which *ukutshipha* implies. In such a case the network as a whole will change, old rural ties will be loosened or dropped, but in a gradual and relatively harmless way. The migrant—for instance—may contrive to bring his wife and children into town, before he ceases to visit the country.

But any kind of change towards 'urbanization', whether gradual or drastic, must spell change in the town-located network too. For the old friends dislike innovation and believe that the man who prefers life as an old-style Red peasant is the proper type of man. The emphasis being on the unique relation between culture and group, a Red migrant appears to his *amakhaya* as disloyal if he either adopts White-inspired habits or chooses to live permanently at the 'place of White men'.

As long as one persists in associating with *amakhaya* or even with other Red people in town, one is subjected to social controls aimed at keeping everyone orthodox. For this reason a migrant bent on change cannot well endure the usual type of *amakhaya* network. Lapses from home-visiting will hardly be allowed to pass as long as the room-mates and other members of the network are *amakhaya* exercising the moral guardianship expected by people at home. Nor can fundamental changes in habits occur. The pressure to conformity is almost physical. It must be vain for one room-mate to aspire to 'civilized surroundings' while the rest want to live in the spartan Red manner; impossible to entertain a new friend 'smartly' while they insist on holding *iseti* or drinking and singing through the night; futile to try to discuss church matters or sports while they are mainly interested in the mealies and the cattle at home. Moreover these conservative principles are not confined to any one group of *amakhaya*. Wherever Red men are gathered together in town, a migrant will find disapproval if he is known to neglect his people at home and distrust if his habits appear too obviously non-Red. No Red circle will want to keep *irumsha* as an intimate.

Restrictive as they may be, however, the *amakhaya* (and to a lesser extent the generality of Red people in town) do offer a migrant a kind of social and emotional security. On the one hand stands this ready-made circle with its comforting solidarity and its familiar patterns: on the other hand, the rest of the town world, strange and often hostile, not eager to take a 'rough *iqaba*' to its bosom. This must be borne in mind when considering the attitudes of Red migrants to the cultural novelties encountered in East London. Any Red new-comer who starts to feel attracted by the refinements of non-Red ways as against the coarseness of the Red: any who thinks that dropping Red habits might help him to get a better job, or get on socially, or cut more of a dash with the women, or 'help on the progress of the nation'—anyone tempted by such feelings has also to reckon the high price of acting on them, the price of losing the only friends he knows he can count on in town.

FORMING NEW TIES

It belongs to the stereotyped Red view of East London that town people are supposed to be waiting on every corner eager to teach 'their' ways to the innocent new-comer from the country, and it is part of the protective armour of incapsulation that the new-comer has to learn to resist their overtures. 'Getting mixed up with the town people' is always represented as a most imminent danger. Yet, inconsistently enough, many Red migrants speak from experience of finding just the opposite—that it is extremely hard to become accepted by non-Reds in town. For some it is so hard that they give up. Disappointments and rebuffs drive them back into the Red fold. Others who are cleverer or luckier (Red people would say, sillier or less lucky) manage to pull it off in spite of the difficulties, and graduate to a new *milieu* where they are permanently accepted.

These inconsistent pictures can both be true, because what holds good at some levels of urban society does not hold good at all levels. Unless he could perform prodigies of 'civilizing' himself, a Red man would aspire in vain to the company of the 'better' classes. It may be easier to drift over into the company of non-Red but still humble people, who as regards education and sophistication are hardly above the level of the Reds themselves. Widening his network by means of one or two personal friends in this category, a Red migrant can be induced to join in their associational activities: to go to church, or join a sports club, or attend dances. In the process he meets more new friends and so widens the network still further, and also learns to leave off most of what was distinctively Red in his appearance and manner.

Highly important is the difficulty of making successful personal contacts in the very place which one might expect to afford the easiest entry into respectable non-Red society, namely in the churches. The churches in East London, though theoretically glad to make converts, are not all very welcoming to a Red recruit in practice. After initial explorations many would-be Christians fall by the wayside for this reason. There are a few church congregations—mostly revivalist in tone—which really do welcome in the heathen with open arms, but these also require him to 'change' drastically and all at once: to 'start a new life' and renounce everything that is Red. Conversion, therefore, is apt to entail the serious difficulty of a radical and immediate breach with one's former friends. This will be discussed in the next chapter.

In relation to the possibility of changing allegiance, the role of the churches may be said to constitute one of the most significant differences between Xhosa rural society and East London society. In the country, people who are not Red are almost bound to have either a real or a nominal link with a church. The School peasant need not be a practising Christian himself, but at least his wife or daughters will be adherents. In town on the other hand there are many non-Red circles where church participation does not matter, and the Red man finds a new possibility of ceasing to be Red without becoming at all Christian. From the point of view of the more orthodox country man he will be entering a kind of limbo peopled by individuals who are 'neither one thing nor the other', i.e. who do not pay allegiance to either of the two familiar moral systems.[1] Some of the urban representatives of this category come high in the social scale—e.g. free-thinking intelligentzia or well-to-do sophisticates—and are therefore most unlikely to draw Red recruits; but some are ordinary middling people, and others again come very low in the scale, constituting the urban riff-raff of loafing, criminal, and tsotsi elements.

It was often suggested in East London—and there seemed no reason to doubt the truth of it—that this urban riff-raff draws recruits from among Red migrant young men who desert the company of their 'own' (incapsulated) people. In terms of the network, a Red man who takes this plunge may fare rather like the one who plunges into a revivalist church. The riff-raff and the zealous proselytizing churchpeople have in common that both tend towards 'closed' networks, self-sufficient circles, whose members have few or no voluntary contacts outside. The church zealots shun outside company, while the riff-raff find themselves shunned. A plunge into either *milieu* must mean a decisive break with the old Red friends from home, and an overt opposition of interests or sentiments.

It may be the strong internal camaraderie that specially appeals to a Red person casting around for new bearings. The revivalist church congregation on the one hand, and the street-gang or underworld clique on the other, can both offer him the prize of 'belonging'. Provided he will really throw in his lot with them, they will not—like some other kinds of town people—sneer when he tries to copy their diacritic habits, but will encourage him on. He may respond with all too much zeal. It was common consent that the ex-Reds who decide to 'become something else in town' are conspicuous for 'overdoing things', for 'exaggerating'.

In effect, when the Red person joins in with the zealous churchpeople, he is exchanging one kind of incapsulation for another, just as rigorous; and almost the same might be said about joining a street-gang. If he wants security comparable to the security he renounces when he leaves his circle of Red *amakhaya*, these seem to be the two possible alternatives.

We have now touched on four of the most common patterns of 'getting lost': (1) refusing incapsulation from the outset; (2) drifting slowly away into non-Red habits, under the influence of ordinary non-Red friends and associates; (3) joining in with a gang of town riff-raff; (4) joining a church. It remains to illustrate these four ways one by one: the fourth requires a chapter to itself.

THE REFUSAL OF INCAPSULATION FROM THE OUTSET

Red migrants who avoid their *amakhaya* from the outset constitute a special case. They must already have been alienated from their home, family or culture in some important respect, or they would not start their town life in a way which by Red standards is so peculiar and reprehensible. The seed was sown before: town provided the environment where it could sprout.

[1] For similar attitudes among Zulu cf. Vilakazi: 'A Reserve from Within', article in *African Studies*, vol. 16, no. 2.

Several of these case histories revealed abnormal people, whose desire to make a fresh start in town had sprung from a deviant or neurotic personality. Such an individual comes to town to move away from something, rather than move towards something. Decisive signs of personal abnormality, by Red rural standards, are a young man's failure to get on with his age-mates or to enjoy their regular pleasures of drinking, smoking, and sexual adventures. Some youths even funk the critical test of circumcision. Running away to the anonymous world of town provides a way of escape from the shame and ridicule at home; but to make the escape permanent one must avoid the home people in town too.

J.M. from the King William's Town district was brought up Red but 'never felt very happy until I became a Christian'. He came to town in his early 20's and avoided his home people from the start. He did not want to drink or smoke with them. He had no dealings with girls. There are signs that he is sexually abnormal. His family got him married to a Red girl—an unmarried mother—but she had no children by him. Eventually she left him. In town he joined the Apostolic Faith Church; he is now a very active member. He is lost to the Red section, and is not likely to go home.

T.S., from the Transkeian district of Butterworth, ran away to town to avoid circumcision, when his age-mates at home were getting ready for it. On arrival he pretended to be an *umfana* (circumcised young man), and carefully kept away from Butterworth people, who might have known better. He stayed with a relative, a cross-cousin, who came from another district (Tamaha) and had never seen him before. This relative was a School man. 'In his company I learnt to dress in the town way and to mix with School people.' After three years T.S. plucked up enough courage to be circumcised, but rather than go home he went to his relative's place, Tamaha, for the purpose. Coming back to East London he took up with a town-born sweetheart. She has taught him to read and write.

Then there were cases of personal trauma. A dread of home itself and of home-people in town may develop after bereavement or other disasters, or a series of quarrels may make life seem pleasanter elsewhere. Often an individual explained his avoidance of home people by saying, or hinting, that he was trying to escape from witchcraft. The following are four cases of migrants who refused to attach themselves to their *amakhaya* in town for reasons such as these. They were all Red men without any schooling or cultural aspirations, but the result, in each case, seems to have been a drifting away from Red culture and a permanent detachment from the country home.

B.M., from St. Lukes, said: 'I was happy to make new friends here in town, because I was fed up with the people at home. My new friends are School people, and I may be joining a church myself one day.' He never goes home to St. Lukes. 'My elder brother has succeeded as head of the homestead and I do not want to share with him or be under him. He has always hated me. He always thought I was favoured by our mother. I am probably of a different father because I look different and, I am told, was born after the death of my father [i.e. of the legal father]. But nobody has a right to say this to me. I am a son of my [legal] father's widow, and should have the same rights as any son of his. My mother always stayed at his kraal as long as she lived.'

C.M., from Gwaba, had a dispute with his father who would not let him marry a certain girl on account of her parents being suspected of witchcraft.

'Father was rich in cattle and did not want me to go to town to work. But because I loved the girl and she loved me, we eloped to East London. I had a guilty conscience, for I had forced my marriage very much against my father's will. I did not go home, neither did I mix with home people. I mixed with young School men in town—they were illiterates like myself, but went to church.' Later he parted from his wife, only to marry a widow to whom his new friends had introduced him.

A.D. was about 28 years old, living an ordinary Red life in Kentani, when the successive deaths of his father, mother, and younger brothers deeply upset him. 'I believed in witchcraft and these deaths in my family worried me very much.' He came to town and attached himself to some members of the Old Apostolic Church. 'Now that I have learnt to reason I doubt the existence of witches after all. However, I feel happy and free from trouble since I came to town. I have no enemies around me here.'

D.L. is also from Kentani. When he arrived in town at the age of 21, he attached himself to some Christian young men. 'They lived in the same street, and immediately took an interest in me and visited me after work. Since then we have remained great friends. It was one of them who found me a job. Like me they have no education but they are members of the old Apostolic Church, and have influenced me to join it too.' D.L.'s reason is that he feels 'safer' with them. 'With my friends in town I feel safe and free from trouble, I will probably stay here.' He has brought his wife and children into town— although there is still a family kraal at Kentani, with the father at its head— and he means to keep them there. 'I am happy with my wife and children here. There is less witchcraft here than in the country. I should not like my children to live in the country, for a child's life is not safe there; they are easily attacked by *inyoka yabafazi* ['snake of women', a familiar of witches].' What gave him the feeling of danger in the country he has not disclosed. It is now fifteen years since he left.

If all Reds were faithful Reds, the category of those who forestall incapsulation would be exhausted by cases like these, where there is an abnormality or a disastrous life-history. But sometimes Red men admitted to having run away from home influences for reasons of genuine cultural preference. They had 'always' had a hankering after School ways but could not express it at home. It was in order to be free to indulge in church-going, or in Western-style entertainments, that they had gone straight for other friends when they landed in town and steered clear of home people. By other standards, perhaps, this is being strong-minded; by Red Xhosa standards it is one more kind of deviance.

The seed of cultural aspiration may have been sown in the country by a few years of school attendance, or by the example of church- and school-going neighbours. Often it was found that while one parent (usually the father) had insisted on the son remaining Red, the other had been encouraging his School ambitions privately at the same time. G.G., aged 41, was the only son of a Red family at Mncotsho, King William's Town district. G.G.'s father sent him to get some schooling, but ordered him to leave school at Standard I, 'because learning how to look after sheep and cattle was more important than reading books in school'. But the mother 'sometimes said she would like me to go on until I became *utitshala* [teacher]'. After leaving school G.G. seems to have been divided in mind. 'At first I went on associating with School boys. But I had not got the right kind of clothes. So I gradually got used to Red friends again.' Then he went to Johannesburg for *ukutshintsha*, 'where for the first time I earned money. And I remembered my mother's ambitions, to make an educated man of me. I bought good clothes. I kept away from the Red home people. Now I have become a School person for always.'

Another migrant, Z.M., had been brought up in a Red family in a mainly Red community (Chalumna), but had been sent to school for a short time. The teacher, who was also a Methodist preacher, made the schoolchildren go to church on Sundays. 'When I got to standard III I was taken out of school, as I had had enough education, being able to read and write a letter in the Xhosa language. From then I lived the life of a Red boy again. I attended *imitshotsho* and played with sticks.' But at the age of 19 he came to East London for *ukutshintsha* and immediately reverted to School habits, avoiding Red circles. 'I bought myself good clothes, and started going to church again. I am now a School man.'

DRIFTING AWAY: PERSONAL CONTACTS

Perhaps it is never again quite so simple for the Red man to break away as it was at the beginning when he first set foot in town. If he has once submitted to incapsulation it will be a problem to get away from the *amakhaya* without creating too much ill-feeling. There will also be the problem of living down the identification with the Reds in town, which needs to be done before he can become acceptable in non-Red circles. There is likely to be a long period of tension and indecision; an interplay of pushing and pulling forces, and a doubt which will win in the long run.

Needless to repeat, all Red Xhosa realize that in town *some* changes of habit are inevitable. If we want to identify those who are drifting away, the question is how far a man changes beyond what is regarded as inevitable, and—more important—how deep the change goes; is it simply an outward concession to the demands of the moment, or has it become a thing desired for itself? This should be qualified by adding that not every further change of habit in town—over and above the necessary minimum—must be taken to indicate a decisive breach. It appeared that some Red migrants who by and large remain faithfully Red do pick up a number of new habits or attitudes in town; they still called themselves Red but, one might say, were Red in a modernized way. Even in the country, after all, not all Red Xhosa are equally orthodox.[2] In town a little dabbling with a church, a little inclination towards a 'better' style of life, does not necessarily mean the end of Redness.

Two particular facilities in town may be considered with regard to their 'urbanizing' effects on Red migrants who make use of them. These are night schools and municipal housing.

Red Xhosa in town who stated that they go (or have been) to night school included some energetic, enterprising people, already fairly successful in their town careers, and hopeful of bettering themselves through literacy. They included former farm servants to whom the better job in town was all the more important because of the doubtful prospects in the country. A.S. for instance is a delivery 'boy'; he attends night school every evening after work. He comes from a farm only a few miles out of town, where his mother and his children still are. He still visits the farm weekly, but has his wife in town and regards it as his 'real home'.

[2] Cf. chapter 2.

If becoming literate was part of a scheme for 'getting on' generally, other changes may follow. The new literate may begin to cast an eye on School business people as a possible reference group, perhaps, or to toy with Christianity for pragmatic reasons. 'I should like to belong to the town people who attend churches, because these people would advise me about the ways of success', said one Red pupil. As another put it, 'I think Christianity is useful in a place like this, because it keeps people away from drunken gatherings and evil things. You go to church on Sundays. That is all.'

But literacy, as such, does not seem to be very effective in detaching Red people from the Red network. What those interviewed were mostly after was an elementary knowledge of the three *R*'s with the object of earning better wages, or possibly rising into independence as petty traders. They were not aiming at white-collar jobs, still less at mastering 'civilization' through books and papers. When they have achieved literacy (it would seem) they mostly go on living the same kind of life as before, with the same friends. 'I like to keep to the Red people', said one new literate, 'because I feel most at ease with them.' 'My real home is in the country', said another night-school pupil, 'and my best sweetheart is a Red girl there.' There does not seem to be much effect on the traditional belief system either.

In a previous chapter it was said that the great majority of the Red migrants in East London are concentrated in the wood-and-iron section, where they can be nearer to their *amakhaya* and other Red people. Normally it is the person with middle-class aspirations who may be tempted to leave the wood-and-iron section for the municipal houses. There is always a waiting list for municipal housing. For a Red person, to put one's name down on this list is a deliberate step away from the *amakhaya* and from the main stream of Red life.

T.N., a Red migrant from the Transkei, had to be on duty on Sundays selling milk in the location. When he came home on a Sunday afternoon he would find that his three room-mates had left him no meat. 'They pretended to be fast asleep, snoring, but as I took the lid off I noticed that they were laughing quietly in their throats. I could no longer stand it. When I complained they would only laugh and make light of it. I looked round for a better kind of accommodation altogether.' He now lives in a municipal sub-economic house. Two significant changes have followed. First of all, T.N. has begun to feel quite at ease without the neighbourhood of his Red *amakhaya*. 'I used to prefer staying with men from Gcaleka country; I no longer mind who my neighbours are.' Secondly, he has brought his wife to stay and work in town. Up till now, however, this young couple still look Red, and they make no pretence of being anything else. They have contrived to move outside the *amakhaya* circle without ceasing to use the Red migrants as their reference group.

Generally, the standards in 'Duncan'—the sub-economic housing area—are set by School people. 'This kind of house whispers to you that it needs more furniture', as a Red new-comer aptly said. Some hold out under the pressure. They remain recognizable as Red by the scarcity and simplicity of their furnishings and utensils, and at the same time limit their more intimate contacts to Red people. Some sublet (illegally) parts of their houses to Red lodgers, creating an echo of the incapsulated life of the wood-and-iron area. On the other hand there are those who change into School people. It seems fair to say that there is usually some additional reason—the move to the municipal house will not simply 'cause' the change unless the person was ripe for it in other ways. 'I like School people better than Red people, now that I am staying mostly among them', said a young man who is buying his four-roomed house under the Home Ownership Scheme, at £4 10s. 0d. a month. 'There are some other Red people here', he added, 'whom you could no longer distinguish from School people.' But he is a former farm servant, unable to go back to the country and determined to make East London his 'real home'.

The Red men who let themselves be 'civilized' by women constitute a familiar case of drifting.

A Red migrant may happen to make a conquest of a non-Red girl who at first, seeing him 'dressed for town', did not realize that he was Red, but interpreted his awkwardnesses as those of a School country man. Having discovered her mistake, the girl, to silence the teasing and sneering of her friends, will set to work to give her young man the missing polish. This is precisely what Red people expect to happen in such cases, and is why they caution their young men so earnestly against consorting with non-Red women.

The task of the girl who wants to 'civilize' a Red young man is in danger of being frustrated by any mishap which touches too sorely on Red sensitivities and causes opposition to flare up again. N.R. came to East London as a young man, after circumcision, and bought himself some shoes, a hat and a suit. 'A School fellow whom I knew at home before we were circumcised had a nice sister. I fell in love with her.' They went to a dance one evening. 'I did not know how to dance, so my girl was taken by a chap whom I did not know. One of my friends whispered "You must refuse him next time". When the same chap came to ask my permission again for the next round, I refused. He pulled at the girl, and I told the girl to sit down. The girl sat down. He started slapping and kicking the girl.' A fight started, and fists and knives were used. They all ran away but were caught by a policeman. 'These fellows spoke to him in Afrikaans but I could only speak Xhosa. They said I had started the fight. We were all found guilty and fined 10s. each.' That was not the end of the Red man's troubles: 'I paid the fine for one of the men, because he begged me to, saying he had left his money in his room. When we were out he said he had no money, but would repay me at the end of the month. He never did. He thought he could fool me because I was simple.' 'I changed my mind from then', says the still-Red young man. 'I saw that these new friends would only get me into trouble. I moved to Maxambeni, where there are mainly Red people, and there near my old friends I have never got into such trouble again.'

However, if the man loves the girl enough, or if there is already latent in him some discontent with the Red life, he may be willing to swallow his pride and learn from her. Under her influence he changes his way of dressing. She brings him new ties and shirts. She criticizes his way of speech and tells him how he ought to speak in town. When she feels he is presentable enough she will ask him to take her to the jive sessions at the Peacock Hall. At first he can only watch her while she is dancing. Soon he is jiving himself. He starts being included in the party when she goes out with her girl friends and their lovers. They go to drinks and other social gatherings together. Under their influence he may join a sports club. Gradually, through his contact with the girl, he is able to find a new circle of non-Red companions. And as he grows more at ease among his new friends, the intimacy with his old friends suffers. Neither he nor they can find the old satisfaction in each other's company. One day he will be ready to say: 'I used to be a Red, but now I am a School man.'

INTERMARRIAGE

It is rarer for Red men to marry School girls met in town than to have them as sweethearts. For good reasons, not many self-respecting School girls will consider marriage with a professed Red migrant whose roots are still in the country. Difficulties about how to conduct the marriage negotiations and the wedding would only be the start; there follows the deeper difficulty of how a School daughter-in-law is to make her home in the Red family circle. In the Red kinship system it is demanded that the girl who marries into a family shall start by 'learning its ways' and bend all her strength to pleasing the husband's senior kin by her willing service. The School bride would have to do as her husband's Red kin do. She might perhaps feel she is justified in doing her wifely duties at sacrifices and beer drinks, but she will not like changing to Red dress. (In this respect she is worse off than Red girls who marry into School homes and who usually adopt School dress without much demur.) One does occasionally meet, in the country, these square pegs in round holes; for instance the Cape Town-born woman who is married to the eldest son of one of the outstanding pagan men of Tshabo. They lead difficult isolated lives.

The cultural destiny of a 'mixed' couple partly hangs together with the question of their return to the country. If they go back to the country the wife must expect to be the one who makes the adjustments. If they are prepared to stay in town indefinitely, either may make the adjustments. But field-work suggested that only a few men leave the Red section and their Red home connexions because of marriage to School wives.

Not surprisingly, the School girls who had married Red men in East London often appeared to be marginal types. The girl might be not from a pure School but from a mixed home, with a potential readiness to change back to the Red ways of the other parent. Or she might be of very humble School background, and illiterate, so that she did not feel the 'descent' too keenly.

Nevertheless, even in town, let alone in the country, the accounts these women gave of themselves bristled with human problems and frustrations incidental to trying to adapt themselves to the requirements of a Red marriage. 'My husband, who is Red, is very strict in that he does not want me to associate closely with School women like myself. He thinks this will lead to dealings with other young men. On the other hand, I myself do not like to associate intimately with the Red women; what can I discuss with them?'

Where a couple were found to have solved the problem by cutting out the rural network altogether, it generally turned out that the husband (irrespective of his marriage) was already pretty far gone along the road that leads away from the Red section. One young School woman said of her husband that 'all of his relatives are Red, and he is Red himself, but he wears School clothes here in town and looks so much a School man that I only discovered he was Red after I had accepted him as my lover. He does not seem very keen that I should visit his home at Kwelegha.'

In some of these cases both husband and wife were now zealous Christians, so much so that perhaps the Church—rather than the marriage as such—should be regarded as the main severer of roots. P.N. was a 'proper Red man' when he came to East London from Kentani, though he had been to school as far as Sub. B. He got to know a School girl in town, from Middledrift, and eventually married her. They and their children have stayed on in town. 'I have been converted and become a Christian', said the husband, 'and I feel I am a better man for it. I should not like my children to be Red like my late father and I used to be, I want them to be educated and religious.' M.Q., illiterate and Red, came to town from the King William's Town district and met a girl from a Christian country home (in the Transkei) with standard VI education. He joined her church and they were married by 'special licence'. 'My sole aim is to be a permanent resident in town, for I want to be near my church. I am only happy when I am with the people of my church.' He has never introduced his wife to his family, nor has he paid any bridewealth to her parents.

JOINING THE URBAN RIFF-RAFF

Joining in with the urban riff-raff does not entail the effort which is needed to rise in the social scale, but entails other changes in the way of life. The 'low-class' East Londoners and the 'low-class' country-born migrants wear their poverty with a difference. The glaring contrasts in dress, in speech, in manners, are only the outward signs of completely different values.

There is a 'low-class' town-bred society which puts an accent on smartness, or rather on trying to be smart. Work plays a relatively small part. A high proportion of this riff-raff are chronically unemployed, or work only spasmodically. Born and bred in town, they fail to make a respectable living there—not necessarily through their own fault, for it is well known that there are not enough suitable jobs in East London to keep all the juvenile male potential workers employed all the time.

Some country-born women—unmarried or widowed—have proved unequal to the task of rearing respectable families in town single-handed. Sons of Red women brewers, for instance, are said to 'grow up speaking very bad language', and are not welcome companions to the better-class location children. There are also sons of School working mothers, women who have been too busy earning a living to keep their children off the streets.

Low-class young men who are employed only sporadically may spend a good deal of time going around in gangs or cliques, loafing and amusing themselves, and occasionally venturing into crime. By way of amusement they can drink, play at dice, or smoke dagga, or hold night parties. To keep themselves when not in work, they may resort to swindling or petty theft. One described his out-of-work days as follows: 'We stole from shops, especially in the location, and we also cheated young children when they were sent to the shops on errands. We played dice for hours. Sometimes we had part-time jobs, which we liked better than full-time ones. We might be caddies on the golf-course for a while, or dig gardens for White madams.'

Some of these youths, it appears, harden into the real tsotsis or criminals. They go to the shebeens at night on purpose to rob the drinkers, or beat up people in dark streets, using knives, stones, bicycle chains, sharpened bicycle spokes, and suchlike. In these gangs the town-born youths provide the superficial smartness and know-how, while Reds from the country add roughness and daring. A Xhosa member of the local C.I.D. maintained that among the really troublesome town criminals a high proportion are country-born Reds, and that the tsotsi type who go in for American-style or exaggerated clothes will often turn out to be Reds in disguise. Ordinary people said that 'the worst people in town are the half-Reds,' meaning the ex-Reds who have taken to gang life or crime.

However, a Red migrant who falls in with a clique of low-class town-born people is not necessarily making for a life of crime. The main significance of the change may be simply the new veneer of smartness and the repudiation of Red standards in favour of typically urban ones. A town-born man who had had some experience of this flashy and irresponsible (rather than criminal) kind of life said that in his own set 'many of the boys were Red boys from the country' and that many of the others were from Red homes in town.

The appearance aimed at in these circles is characterized by a kind of dress which was once fashionable among smart people but has since become the badge of the tsotsi or near-tsotsi: tight trousers, tapering towards the ankles, and jackets with heavily padded shoulders. They also like 'very fancy clothes, such as white shoes and white hats, and green, yellow or orange jerseys'. The girls too go in for smart styles, though sometimes combining these with beads worn around the ankles; some like to use lipstick, and to powder their cheeks with pink face powder. The general effect is not very elegant. 'These girls look shabby', as a hostile observer said, 'and you can see they are the rough type of girls who run around with men.' By migrants' standards they are noisy, crude and uncontrolled. 'These girls make a point of being rough. They shout in public places. A man could use any kind of language in their presence.'

It is recognized that Red youths get into this kind of company through unemployment; but to say—as one migrant informant did—that they 'really prefer' an idle life, is probably an expression of hostile feeling rather than an accurate statement of fact. Many could not find work if they would. Any migrant who cannot find work becomes an illegal resident in town, and having consequently to dodge the police may be drawn into the company of those who dodge the police for more sinister reasons as well. Some, after a time, manage to find jobs and settle down to a respectable life.

The frustrations engendered by the orthodox Red way of life may provide one of the motivations. Incapsulated living makes severe demands of a young man. He is required to limit his pleasures, to endure perhaps years of discomfort for the sake of his obligations to his family, and to submit to the dictation of the older *amakhaya*. By joining up with the urban riff-raff he can rid himself all at once of the triple authority of family, seniors, and employers. The life may appeal to him precisely because it is irresponsible and self-indulgent.

Without becoming an actual criminal, a Red young man estranges himself from decent Red society in town simply by the act of taking up with low-class urban friends. The rejection is mutual and compromise impossible.

On the one hand the decent Red migrants regard the youth with the distaste reserved for the turncoat. 'He is *irumsha* by choice and on purpose.' He has flouted the self-denying ordinance and all the injunctions of his seniors about avoiding town company and town ways. On the other hand, and even more notably, the ex-Red recruit to a town clique will fall over backwards in his own eagerness to cut himself off from everything that is Red. Whether out of insecurity or of ineptitude, 'half-Reds overdo everything'. In his own room the young man may be living with the rough-and-ready furnishings typical of poor Red homes, may still be sleeping on a mat on the floor, but with the gang he is all out to impress. To this end he exaggerates in his dress; he is all for using the special slang of the town; to him a girl is always '*icherry*' and a detective '*iturkey*'.

As the whole object is to be taken for a really urban person, ex-Reds of this type particularly resent being called *amagoduka* (home visitors) or *amaGcaleka*. It must be borne in mind that the low-class urban people—their new reference group—are of all Xhosa the ones who have least use for Red traditions and Red virtues. Peasant thrift, piety, family discipline, do not impress them as they may impress the more middle-class non-Red Xhosa; nor does national (i.e. tribal) history hold any charisma for them. Inevitably, then, a Red man who joins into such company grows ashamed of his Red background. 'These ex-Reds are always trying to be what they are not. It is clear why they exaggerate; anybody who does not want to be discovered as what he really is, will always try to prove his superiority.' 'The ex-Reds of this type will always try to show off. Wherever they go they are anxious not to be looked down on. They use force to end an argument; for if they cannot impress by their speech they want to be feared. They want to be praised by their girl friends.' Thus did two Xhosa observers describe over-compensation.

The wholesale repudiation of Red ways in favour of the ways of town riff-raff goes together with a wholesale rejection of Red company. 'They want nothing at all to do with Red people and avoid meeting them. . . . They are specially vulgar and rough when they feel that we [i.e. Red migrants] are watching, so that we should not dare to divulge the great secret that they are Red people born.' They go in for town-born girl friends, or for those who can pass as town-born. 'To them even the roughest town girl seems more desirable than any country girl.' Some of these low-class 'urban' girls may be Red girls in disguise, who find it possible to keep up the pretence in low-class company, but not in 'respectable' circles where they constantly risk being given away by small points, such as their inability to serve tea in the proper manner. (School Xhosa both in town and country have a custom of asking a female visitor to serve the tea, 'to make her feel at home'.)

As a result of the complete breach with the Red home-people in town, no restraining influence is left. No new moral code takes the place of that represented by family, *iintanga* and *amakhaya*, except the rough code of the gangs themselves. Far from having any lingering feeling of moral obligation towards fellow-Reds, some of these ex-Reds (out of guilt or insecurity perhaps) turn to fleecing Red victims with special gusto. Their own knowledge of Red ways and interests makes this an easy matter. Red migrants are particularly afraid of these ex-Reds, while the ex-Reds for their part see the 'stupidity' of the Reds as a ready-made target.

One Red man new to town asked a 'smart' acquaintance to help him to sell a town house which he had inherited from his late father. They agreed on a commission of 20 per cent, but when it came to the point the smart friend kept back more. Not satisfied, he took the Red man to his room, to celebrate the deal with much brandy, and in the night robbed him of the whole remaining amount. 'I will never trust a School person again', the poor Red man is said to have exclaimed, 'they are all robbers'. 'He did not know', adds the narrator, 'that his "friend" was actually as Red as himself, except for his smart clothing and the wickedness he had acquired in town.'

Even if the story were apocryphal—which there is no reason to think—it would reflect the common feeling of Red migrants, who like to draw comparisons between their own straightforward behaviour and the cunning disguise of the ex-Reds 'always pretending to be something else'. 'The actual Reds in town do not come in for criticism. They are not snubbed or treated with half-hidden contempt by the School people.' (This, of course, is not always true.) 'Real Red people, those who declare themselves Red even in town, are the right people. They are in town what they are in the country. Their friends in town are Red, and their lovers. These are peaceable well-behaved people.' In Red eyes the moral guilt of 'pretending to be something else' adds a decisive touch to town-style delinquency.

12

Red Converts to Christianity

THE CHURCHES AND THE RED PEOPLE

The category now to be discussed are the Red migrants who fall under the influence of a church in East London. Given that they become permanent converts, they must return to the country—if they return at all—as School people.

There are ample facilities for would-be church-goers in the East London locations as compared with most country places. Twenty-three recognized church denominations operate there: in addition a recent investigation has confirmed the existence of ten unrecognized bodies and the likelihood of there being several more smaller sects.[1] On the other hand—as has been said—Red migrants who have leanings towards 'progress' need not necessarily bother about church at all, in town. By and large it appears that the headway made by Christianity here is very slow. That Red Xhosa are not easily drawn into the main established churches would be agreed by most local missionaries, clergy, and Xhosa Christians. It can be added that not much is seen or heard of nativistic churches, such as the Zulu have for example. Here among the Xhosa, Christianity still bears the prestige—or the stigma—of being the White man's religion.

In town as in the country the ordinary Red migrants are easily put off by the many negative requirements—in particular the prohibition of alcohol—which in too many cases seem to them to be the main content of the Christian teaching. Nor do they see any important social compensations. That going to church will not enhance their prestige among their Red fellows goes without saying, but it will not necessarily do much to win them acceptance among non-Reds either, as long as other 'civilized' attainments are neglected. It is in situations involving White people that the Red migrant is most likely to feign more church interest than he really has. In both Reader's and the present investigation it was found that illiterate Red migrants would sometimes name one of the established churches when questioned as to their religion, but would reveal (on further questioning) an almost total ignorance of Christianity and an absence of any real connexion with the church.

If church dabbling is made easy in East London, conversion in the proper sense is not. The Red migrant may make the experiment of attending services without there necessarily being any lasting consequences. He may find that he cannot follow the service, or that what he does understand of it makes little sense to him. Even if a Red new-comer musters enough interest to become a nominal member of the church, moreover, he may well feel disappointed in

[1] Cf. forthcoming publication by A. A. Dubb, whose investigation of semi-independent Bantu churches in East London has arisen partly out of the present work. His monograph will deal with the Bhengu Church in particular. For Bhengu see also Schlosser, K.: *Eingeborenenkirchen in Süd- und Südwestafrika*, Kiel, 1958.

his relations with the rest of the congregation. He finds that they are mainly people with a different cultural background from his own, people who make him feel out of place and ill at ease. In such cases the church 'membership' may become nothing more than a symbol to be invoked in appropriate situations, as a token of one's civilized aspirations.

Out of the many denominations in the East London locations there appear to be only four or five that win any significant numbers of converts from the Red section (as against converting Christians from other churches). With one exception, all of these have predominantly poor and uneducated congregations, and might be called 'low-class' churches. Such are the Old Apostolic Church, the African Methodist Episcopalian Church, the Apostolic Faith Mission, and the Jehovah's Witnesses. These contrast with (say) the Anglican and Methodist Mission Churches in not having a conspicuous element of highly educated, highly Westernized members to set the tone. Case-histories revealed not a few men who had come to town Red and subsequently joined one of these churches. It is significant that many were former farm servants, dispossessed people, struggling hard to keep head above water. Such people, with few ambitions except to make a living, do not demur at low social status in town.

By common consent, however, the conversion records of all other churches (where Red people are concerned) have now been surpassed by that of 'Bhengu's Church', whose atmosphere is not predominantly low-class in the same sense. This church came into existence only at the end of 1950, but eight years later, with 3,000 members, it was the largest in the locations. It seems worth while to consider who the Red people are who have joined the impressive flow of converts into Bhengu's Church, and what are their motivations.

BHENGU'S CHURCH

Bhengu's Church is part of a Pentecostal church of (White) American origin, the Assemblies of God, in which every local assembly is allowed almost complete autonomy. While formally the American church is still the mother church, to most of his followers in East London Mr. Bhengu is the undisputed head. Nicholas Bhengu most definitely belongs to the 'wide-scale' world. He was born in Zululand in 1909. Before deciding to devote himself to religious work entirely (at the age of 29) he had taken an active part in the I.C.U. and the Communist Party, and had held posts in a lawyer's office and the Department of Health. He has travelled extensively abroad. His outlook has always been non-sectarian. He has been under the influence of several different churches: the American Lutheran Mission (which first trained him), the Roman Catholics, Sabbatarians, Full Gospel Church, Salvation Army, and Union Bible Institute; even since joining the Assemblies of God some twenty years ago he has indicated that he belongs as much to the Plymouth Brethren and the Baptists as to the Pentecostals proper. An interdenominational mission campaign in East London was the origin of the present 'Bhengu's Church', which came into being to accommodate the converts. Bhengu's own career, then, has taken him across tribal, national and racial limitations as well as those of sect; and he clearly does not fit either of the tradition-influenced patterns of Bantu church leaders —the 'prophet' or the 'chief' pattern—which Sundkler has documented for Natal.[2]

East London, the birthplace of 'his' church, is still its main stronghold, though

[2] Cf. Sundkler, B.: *Bantu Prophets in South Africa.*

flourishing congregations have been built up in Durban and elsewhere. An enormous church building, capable of accommodating 2,500 worshippers, now stands as visible tribute to the extraordinary and rapid success of the movement here. Adherents proudly claim it to be the largest church building (for any race) in all South Africa. Bhengu's campaigns have followed some familiar revivalist patterns: the call for public repudiation of one's sinful past, the promise of release from sin and/or affliction on condition of absolute faith, the underlining of the emotional and ethical content of Christian religion, rather than the intellectual or philosophic content, and the use of the mass-meeting technique which magnifies the emotional impact. American-style campaign equipment—a huge tent, loudspeakers, and electric lighting—has been put to good use. But this church keeps converts as well as making them: a fact which must be attributed largely to Bhengu's special understanding of the needs of the urban African and the raw migrant alike. Special effort is made to win over pagans. In preaching (to use his own words) he is applying 'an African approach, suited to African psychology'.

A survey[3] of all the people attending one of Bhengu's Sunday services—a total of 767—showed that 29 per cent were of Red origin. A relatively high proportion of these ex-Red converts—over a third—were men. (All Bantu churches in East London tend to have disproportionately high female membership.) On further analysis this Red element was found to consist of farm people and peasants in fairly equal proportion (58 per cent of the Red men and 43 per cent of the Red women came from reserves; 40 per cent of the Red men and 50 per cent of the Red women came from farms; the small remainder did not answer the question properly). There was also found to be a high proportion of widows among the women converts. Farm people and widows are among the most underprivileged or least satisfied elements of Red rural society; it seems fair to say that Bhengu's Church has not as yet made very great impact on the hard core of Red migrants with still-secure roots in the country. Again, more of these Red converts were people with some schooling than one would find in a representative cross-section of Red migrants generally. (About half the men and a third of the women said they had attended school.) Thus, although Bhengu has drawn many Red individuals into Christianity where other churches have failed, he cannot be said to have succeeded notably in the main strongholds of paganism. He himself has expressed disappointment on this score.

One of the things that attracts Red migrants into Bhengu's Church, rather than into other churches, is undoubtedly Bhengu's great gift as a preacher to the unsophisticated. 'He has a wonderful tact and a gift for converting the rawest people', said one ex-Red Christian. 'It makes me think he was sent by God to start this church.' Another former Red man explained how he was won over by a single sermon, which he happened to hear when on his way to a beer-drink. 'The service was in the open air and I stopped out of curiosity. As a result of hearing Mr. Bhengu speaking I did not go to that beer-drink, and I have never been to one since.' In his deliberately straightforward preaching Bhengu draws on parts of the Gospels and Old Testament which he maintains are specially congenial in language and setting to people with a rustic background like the migrant part of his audience. At the same time, he deals with his listeners' everyday problems and experiences in town too.

Besides preaching, two other important weapons of conversion in Bhengu's

[3] Dubb, A. A., unpublished data.

revival campaigns—namely healing and confession—have each made deep impressions on Red people. Informants recounted how, in 1950 and 1951, young men and girls could be found at Bhengu meetings unashamedly confessing to evil things they had done. Even tsotsis were confessing and handing in their knives and stolen goods. 'The convert would burst into a cry, he prayed out loud and during this prayer confessed to the evil life he had lived. Theft, rape, burglary, murder, all were admitted.' Bhengu would then pray for forgiveness. Such scenes rightly impressed Red people. Here, it seemed, the demons of the town were being tamed by a higher power. All decent people hated the savagery of the tsotsi and the immorality of the town women; but where others could only hate and fear, Bhengu—apparently—could conquer through the power of God. It was equally impressive that those who confessed seemed to be protected against the worldly consequences of letting their crimes be known. 'The police have not taken criminal action against any of the converts.'

In the days of Bhengu's great revival meetings healing was even more prominent. His church was widely known as the 'Healer's Church' (*icawe kamphilisi*). Long queues of sufferers formed after every Sunday service, to kneel before him as he prayed that their affliction might be lightened. Cures are still talked about, mostly stopping short of the out-and-out miraculous or incredible. 'None of the blind men who came forward regained their eyesight, nor did any of the hunchbacked people have their backbones straightened. Probably these did not have any faith. But some of the chronically sick were healed. One would be cured of fits, another of asthma.' The fame of Bhengu as a healer spread far outside East London, and people from remote districts of the Transkei would come in on purpose to try for a cure.

Red people have no intellectual reasons for being sceptical about faith healing. On the contrary they may have been specially willing to listen to a religion which—like their own ancestor cult—made relief from sickness a prime object of appeal to the supernatural.

The motivations of some ex-Red individuals who have joined Bhengu's Church may now be reviewed. Many, it is clear, have been won over in the first place by the promise of relief from some personal trouble, either physical, mental or spiritual. One cannot properly call their conversion an adaptation to the town environment. It is true that most of them would probably not have become Christian if they had stayed in the country, but it is equally true that even in town they would not have become Christian if not for the previous personal trouble. Statistical data on motivations were not collected: all that can be offered here is a selection of case material.

First there are the seekers after healing. In the quest for a cure, either for himself or for some member of his family—so the typical account runs—the person had gone the rounds of all the agents known to him as a Red man in the country: diviners, herbalists, and perhaps White medical doctors. Everything had failed. And then he heard that in East London there was a wonderful healer who did not even have to use medicine but who cured simply by prayer. He came, attended, and was cured. Thoroughgoing conversion is represented as a necessary accompaniment of cure in all these cases: 'It cannot be done in the spirit of testing God's power.' 'Before praying and laying hands on our heads, Bhengu would warn us that all his prayer was futile unless we would co-operate by believing.' Most of the stories of cure are told five or six years after the event, for Bhengu has given less time to healing lately, but the person will say that he has been strongly attached to the church ever since.

One such convert said that when he was still Red he suffered from pains all over the body, with swellings on his neck, which discharged, and paralysis of his right arm. 'Then someone told me about Mr. Bhengu. Sunday after Sunday I joined the long queue; one after another we knelt before him and he prayed for us. . . . I did not become cured all at once, but after some weeks the places on my neck healed up, and nowadays I am completely cured.' Some of the cases are probably neurotic; some give a family history of mental disorder too. Bhengu himself, when asked about his converts, has said that they include 'many who are a bit crazy'.[4] On the borderline between mental and physical disorder was the Red young man on a farm in the Brakfontein area who suffered from 'the feeling of some invisible person choking me at night', eventually resulting in what he calls 'fits'. These attacks, he says, were caused by *impundulu*, which nearly every night suffocated him in his sleep by pressing him down on the floor. 'Diviners and herbalists were consulted but none of them could cure my illness. The fits were so frequent that I had to be watched. Then I heard of Mr. Bhengu, so I came to town and I joined the church in order to be healed. The feeling vanished and I have not had any more fits since.'

One Red young man from the Transkei came to town to earn money for his ailing mother and younger siblings; the father was insane and under treatment at a mental hospital. In town he happened to hear about Bhengu as a healer. 'The first time I heard him preach, he was saying that God had the power to remove any illness. These words reminded me of the money I had paid out to herbalists, trying to cure my parents, and to the diviner to smell out the witch responsible for my father's mental disorder. From what Bhengu said I became convinced that I had wasted all that money. . . . Next night when he called for people who had heard God's word I held up my hand. He asked for people who wanted relatives healed. . . . He prayed for my mother (who had chronic stomach trouble). She had been sick for twenty-two years. Drs. X and Y in Umtata had given her up. I sent my mother a letter to tell her what I had done. Soon I got an answer, saying she was actually cured.'

Other Red people have joined the church not for physical cure but for emotional or spiritual relief. The beneficial effect of public confession in crisis situations is known to traditional Xhosa culture.[5] For many converts confession at Bhengu's revival meetings has lightened powerful feelings of guilt engendered during the previous Red phase of life. Although one must allow something for backward projection of Church concepts of sin, it is clear that the guilty feeling must have been well developed beforehand.

As confession in Bhengu's Church is held to give relief from sin for ever after, the emotional reward is great. 'What I like very much about Bhengu's church', said one formerly Red man, 'is that once your sins are forgiven you can no longer sin. You are holy, you have been washed in the blood of the Lord Jesus, you have conquered the devil.' 'Other churches preach that no man is perfect, that we sin and must pray for forgiveness all our lives, but Bhengu's Church says this is not true.' A good many converts explained that Bhengu's Church had rescued them from a downward path and given them back their self-respect,

---

[4] Schlosser, K.: *Eingeborenenkirchen in Süd- und Südwestafrika*, p. 36.
[5] Cf. Hunter: *Reaction to Conquest*, pp. 148, 283 ff., 325 ff.

by helping to overcome such faults as sexual over-indulgence, excessive drinking, constant quarrelling. These failings even by Red standards deserve a sense of shame or guilt. It was often implied that coming to town had started the rot which only Bhengu was able to stop. In this limited sense the conversion might be called an adjustment to urban life.

A Red woman from a reserve in the King William's Town area was made pregnant in town by a man who did not marry her. After this she became 'morally weak' and had 'dealings with several men who were all my lovers. I drank kaffir beer and brandy heavily. I became rough and vicious, and when drunk had no respect for anybody.' The feeling of shame was strong enough that she felt she 'could not return to my brother's homestead'. Bhengu's Church 'has shown me the way to live in town and not become morally weak. I am now a woman of God. I do not drink and I have conquered lust. I am able to make a living. I polish floors in town and do some ironing; I buy fruit and vegetables and sell them in the location. I have followed the best way of life in this world of worries. I have no more worries of any sort. I dispel them by vigorous prayer.'

A young girl, coming to town with her widowed Red mother, was sent to school and at the age of 16 was made pregnant by a teacher. 'I joined Bhengu because he showed me how in my terrible disappointments and confusion over love matters I could be saved by devoting my life to Jesus. I have given up love affairs and am able to resist any temptation. Jesus is in my heart now. I love all people alike, even the school-teacher who seduced me and did not marry me. I will remain in town all my life and worship God in Bhengu's Church. I have the ambition to go to night-school and further my education.'

It was unexpected to find, in some cases, that the remorse derived allegedly from misdeeds which were well hidden and which nobody would ever have known about but for their confession to Bhengu. By their own accounts such people seem to have experienced, in the Red state, private feelings of guilty conscience which they had not externalized as 'ancestor spirits' or otherwise.

Two examples may be given. The first is of an illiterate Red farm servant who on his parents' death had passed into the care of the father's brother. 'This uncle was very cruel to me and my sisters, forcing us to do the strenuous work on the farm for the White owner, while his own real sons and daughters had it very easy. I had nobody to appeal to, but I did feel very bitter.' When the young man went to work on a nine-month contract at the Natal Collieries he bought from a herbalist there 'a piece of deadly root to kill my uncle. . . . The herbalist told me not to let anyone open the box, because merely inhaling the smell might cause instant death. When I got home I privately warned my wife and sisters. But to my surprise, I found that my uncle was very kind to me, calling me "son of his *mninawa* [younger brother]", and telling all the neighbours that "*umninawa*'s thing has come home at last". His welcome made me hesitate about using the root. I put it off indefinitely.'

Some three years later, in East London, the young man happened to pass one of Bhengu's Sunday morning open-air services. 'I stopped to listen, and what the preacher said went deep into my heart. He said, "Pray to God for our sins. I may not know your sins, you may not know mine, but, friend, all our secrets are revealed to God, who knows the evil in your heart and in mine." This made me think at once of what I had been contemplating doing to my uncle. I had to confess my sin then. And after I had confessed, I also felt obliged to go to my uncle on the farm and tell him about the root.'

Another case also concerns a farm servant, a woman now about 35. She was living with her parents when her elder brother took ill. He had epileptic fits, and became insane. 'The White owner of the farm was a Roman Catholic and advised my father that the case could not be cured by medicines—it was a case for praying hard to God, who could easily remove the illness if all the relatives would wholeheartedly join in. But my father was a drunkard and did not believe in praying. I was very young then. I loved my brother but nobody had taught me how to pray.' The brother died and she was 'terribly distressed, because I believed that if we had all prayed he need not have died'.

Later she was made pregnant by a married man. 'In fear of the shame, I committed abortion and pretended to be still a virgin.' In 1945 a School young man, 'who thought I was also School', made her acquaintance in town, and they were married. 'He genuinely believed I was still a virgin. But my guilty conscience worried me continuously since the abortion.'

During Bhengu's religious campaign in 1950, 'it reached my ears that converts were making confessions to Bhengu, and that after his prayers they felt great relief of conscience'. One Sunday 'I actually saw several young women of my age confessing to abortion. The abortion committed so many years ago worried me as if it were only yesterday. I felt I could never be happy until I did what the other converts had done.' She confessed, and became a firm convert.

It would be wrong to give the impression that *only* afflicted or unhappy people are found moving away from Red circles into Bhengu's Church. For such Red migrants as become ambitious to 'get on' in urban terms, and particularly to mix with School people of a decent class, Bhengu's Church offers opportunities that are unique in East London or nearly so. In most of the associations where he might rub shoulders with respectable School people, the Red migrant is made to feel humble and inferior. Alternatively, if he finds a set of School people who welcome him without making him feel inferior, these are likely to be humble '*Gcaleka*' or low-class urban people themselves, offering not much hope of social advancement. Many of the associations, and the established churches, suffer from the first drawback; the 'low-class' churches from the second. In Bhengu's Church, by contrast, owing to the stress laid on wooing and welcoming Red converts, a Red man can meet self-respecting School people who receive him courteously and are not out to shame him in any way. The neat appearance which Mr. Bhengu demands of his followers, and now the enormous new church building, set this congregation above the few other churches which also try to cater specially for Reds.

EFFECTS OF JOINING BHENGU'S CHURCH

(a) *Habits and values*

Xhosa talking about Bhengu converts stress that 'they are entirely changed', that 'it alters the character of people'. Red people who have been converted bear out this impression subjectively: they speak of 'having been born anew', of 'living an entirely different life'.

For the converted member, church and religion are supposed to become —and often do become—the supreme values, with first claim on loyalty, time, and money. Ex-Red Bhenguists generally display both the ardour and the sincerity of the convert. Many Xhosa can excel at Christian-sounding verbalizations when they want to, but with the Bhenguist the impression of genuine feeling is often conveyed. The atmosphere of the church is puritanical, but with emphasis on energy and success in this world rather than 'pie in the sky when you die'. That 'Christians are saved while alive, and not merely after death', is a doctrine which Bhenguists like to quote as a supposed distinction between their own church and others.

The Red convert finds that in Bhengu's Church drinking, smoking, and irregular sexual relations are strongly condemned. The worldly amusements of town, such as dances and bioscopes, are forbidden. On the positive side a high value is set on thrift, prudence, neatness, cleanliness, education, and industrious pursuit of one's living, as well as on the spiritual duties of prayer, bible study, and spreading the gospel.

Comparing their Bhenguist present with their Red past, converts dwelt on the feeling of moral and spiritual enlightenment. 'Today I believe in the existence of God Almighty and I fear him, for I have learnt that the fear of the Lord is the beginning of wisdom. I am no longer what I used to be, *udlalani*, an aimless lover of women.' 'Now that I have joined the church my conscience tells me that I must not only do good when I am seen by people. I must do good when I am all by myself too.' 'I am true to my wife now, I love my neighbours, I do not forget God my shepherd either morning, noon or night.' 'My marital life has changed greatly since I joined Bhengu', said a woman. 'My husband used to be in love with concubines whom I hated bitterly. When I got any ailment I used to think I was bewitched by one of his concubines. I would approach a diviner who would tell me all sorts of lies. . . . I would be so offended that I would go to see my husband and his concubine at Moriva. I would shout at them, and my husband and the concubine would make a fool of me and agree that they had bewitched me because they wanted to be relieved of me. I would tell them every bad name I could think of. My husband stayed with the concubine for two years. Now he has returned to me.'

No great changes are demanded on the intellectual side. Perhaps it may be one of the reasons for the success of the Bhengu Church with Red people that determined frontal attack on Red intellectual concepts is avoided. Though the Red man may well come away from a Bhengu service with a feeling that herbalists have cheated him or that diviners are not much good, he is spared the intellectual insult of being told that ancestor spirits mean nothing or that the whole notion of *impundulu* is ludicrous. What he may feel he is being offered, in the first place, is a superior technique for mastering the *impundulu*, or for obtaining blessings that the ancestors alone could not dispense. The idea of God is first introduced, as it were, over the heads of the existing members of his Red supernatural hierarchy. 'The spirits of the ancestors may indeed be watching our steps, though they are subject to God.'

But the religious, moral, and intellectual aspects are only half the story, since, as was said, Bhengu also has a great deal to tell his followers about the way to manage their daily practical affairs. As one Red man succinctly put it, 'Bhengu teaches us love and cleanliness'.

With Red migrants in particular, the effect may amount to a startling outward transformation. Appearance, personal habits, values, are all remodelled. Though some of the Bhenguist values, e.g. thrift, are underlined in Red culture too, the total effect produced is quite new. In making self-advancement a matter for praise or even a duty, the Bhengu Church destroys the passive acceptance of low worldly status (in town) which with most Red migrants is a matter of course. In some other churches the poor are taught resignation but not here. 'Everybody can improve himself. There are no *amaqaba*.' Bhengu tells them to get some education, or to improve on what they have: 'Some of you are like a good car without headlights. It is not enough to be a Christian. He may be good, but he is useless for enlightening the night of his fellows. He who cannot read his Bible makes a poor evangelist.' Education is necessary for being respectable as well as for doing justice to religion. With such encouragement, a number of Red converts start going to night-school, and take it very seriously. Other symbols of moral and of social advance coincide too, e.g. good clothing and hygiene.

In heaven the streets are shining gold and the dresses shining white. 'Let us, as good Christians, be as clean and shining in our appearance as we can, even here.' 'It is difficult', said Bhengu at a Convention of the Assemblies, 'for people to break away from their old customs. Africans in the country like to relieve themselves in the bushes, but here we have lavatories. Use them. I shall not be pleased to hear that dirty paper is lying about in them. I see that you are even too lazy to flush the lavatories. That is being very dirty. This church, too, is cleaned every day, but look at it just now, with all these papers lying around. It is this kind of thing that makes the location streets unnecessarily dirty too.'

If the most commonly emphasized differences of appearance between Red and School people are quickly eliminated by these means, a barrier is put up at the same time against assimilation of 'smart' or would-be-smart town habits. Town amusements and town frivolities are thundered against in church. In this regard, of course, the Bhengu Church is only repeating a lesson which the Red man learnt in his incapsulated days. 'I have never had any opportunity to get to know bioscopes, dances or concerts because now I belong to Bhengu's Church, and before that I was Red.'

On the other hand drinking and smoking, which for Red people are legitimate amusements, also have to be given up. For some converts the main compensation is one that appeals to Red and Bhenguist feelings alike—the increased possibilities for thrift. 'I have given up drinking and smoking, so I do not waste money unnecessarily now. I have learnt how to save it at the Post Office instead.' 'Before I joined Bhengu I spent my money on brandy, kaffir beer, tea parties, and buying presents for my boy friends. I wasted money on diviners and herbalists. Now I spend my money on buying good clothes for my family; on good things to decorate my house; and on church affairs. I give some money to my husband, who makes a small saving at the Post Office.'

Abstinence not only saves money, it also helps to keep one out of trouble. 'The Christian kind of life, which I am leading now, is quite different from my old pagan life. It is very pleasant to live as a Christian. No crimes, no debts, no contagious diseases, no raggedness, no fights, no extravagance, no worries.'

(b) The social network

There is a strong corporate feeling among Bhenguists, which is reflected in their social life. It is well known that they like to keep together. In some houses nearly all the tenants belong to the Bhengu Church. A landlady, a young widow, commenting on this, explained that as a Bhenguist herself she 'naturally' prefers tenants of her own church, and that she regards them as her equals: 'In the eyes of God we are all on the same level, and the fact that I own this property does not make me any better than them. The human value is far more important than money.' As regards friendships generally, it was a common saying of Bhenguists that 'I cannot get on well with friends who are not religious'. Social and recreational activities are concentrated within the church. Besides the three services held on Sundays, there are prayer meetings every evening; in addition the girls' and mothers' *imanyano* each meet once a week, 'to preach and pray and sing, and teach one another about the need to live a pure life'. There is Sunday school for the children. In their spare time many Bhenguists like to go around in small groups or singly, preaching to the unconverted.

Thus there is a tendency to the 'close-knit' type of network, in which most of the people whom ego knows also know each other. The Red convert—like others—may meet the demand for cultural reformation more willingly in that he is offered in exchange a sense of 'belonging', of solidarity within the church itself. Unlike the Red migrants who say that they have tried various churches but 'never felt at home', the Red convert to Bhengu's Church will often stress that he felt at home from the outset. The fact that there are many other ex-Red members may be one factor, but in addition the Bhenguist congregation as a whole will welcome each new-comer in a way that makes him feel a person of some consequence. There may be special references during the service, as when the minister in an opening prayer mentions 'Red people who have left their pagan dances and joined the flock of God'.

It is true that even here some Red converts seem to be sensible of their disabilities. It is significant that, in Dubb's sample Bhengu congregation referred to earlier, the proportion of ex-Red women who admitted to never attending *umanyano* meetings was considerably higher than the corresponding proportion among other women. (31 out of the 89 ex-Red women who answered the question said they never went to *umanyano*—that is, 35 per cent; among the other women only 44 out of 309, i.e. 14 per cent.)[6] But on the whole, taking all contexts together, Red converts to this church will speak gratefully about their feeling of security, in terms exactly opposite to those used by ordinary Red migrants about the generality of Christians: that is, instead of alleging 'deceit' and 'lack of openness' they praise the complete sincerity which engenders mutual trust.

'In Bhengu's Church I feel most at home, for I can trust the other members. I know my feeling is shared by them. I feel relieved of my sins here, I really feel the presence of God.' 'I love being a member of Bhengu's Church because of the trustworthiness of the members. With Bhengu's people you know that if they swear before the minister that they have left off a sin, they really have left it off for good.' Some echo the Red 'group' type of friendship by extending affectionate feelings to the whole Bhengu congregation as such. 'I love all our [i.e. Bhengu's] people alike.' 'At Bhengu's Church we are all very friendly to each other, like real brothers and sisters. It is for this love shown by all its members to each other that I like Bhengu's Church most.'

The price to be paid for this new brotherhood is the renunciation of ties elsewhere. It is for this reason that many Red people, though interested in

6 Dubb, A. A., unpublished data.

Bhengu's revival meetings, say they took several months before they rallied the strength to become open converts. It is impossible to take up the Bhenguist way of life and at the same time keep up with one's still-Red friends on the same level of intimacy as before. The Red man who joins Bhengu's Church typically finds a wall growing up between himself and his *amakhaya* in town, and—very often—ultimately in the country too. The consequences as regards urbanization may therefore be important.

Bhengu's Church expressly disapproves of social contacts 'with non-religious people'. 'Our church does not allow its members to mix with people who are not believers. If we mix with them they are sure to talk about matters which are not for us.' When a Red man joins this church, the breach with his Red *amakhaya* is apt to be more obvious than if he drifts away from Redness in other ways, for as a Bhenguist his objections to Red social life are moral and not only snobbish. The old network in town therefore quickly disintegrates. The convert will frankly admit that he and his old Red friends no longer interest each other much. 'My old friends are like strangers to me nowadays.' 'There is now no link connecting me with my relatives and former friends. I am devoting all my time to religious matters.' 'When I meet any old friends the only conversation I have is to ask them about the health of the other people whom I have not seen for a long time.' 'With my old Red friends there is always kaffir beer and drunken noises.' The feeling of estrangement is mutual: 'Once people get to know that you are a member of Bhengu's Church, those who used to be your friends sort of hold back from you. They don't actually run away on your approach, but will not start any conversation.'

Even the closest kin ties are not proof, and converts may find themselves drifting apart from their own family. 'With my brothers and sisters I am not as intimate as we used to be. I meet them in the town or in the street; I ask after their health. They have criticized me a great deal for joining Bhengu's Church saying that Bhengu is an uncircumcised person [a reference to his Zulu origin] and that a "boy" cannot be trustworthy; or that all new churches are only after money.' 'My brother and three sisters are Red and not interested in Christianity. . . . Right enough I still love them as a brother, but we are not as openhearted to one another as we were. There is a stiffness on their part as though I am a stranger to them.'

What strains relations above all is the missionary zeal of the Bhengu convert. He is mindful of his duty to preach to the heathen; the heathen are mindful of their duty to resist. They get out of his way to avoid being preached at. The keen spirit is not discouraged but carries on with his thankless task in a spirit of willing martyrdom. 'We are taught that we must make allowance for those who criticize us, for "they know not what they do".'

'My friends avoid me as much as they can. They fear to stay with me, because I will blame them for remaining in sin. My concubine hides herself when she sees me, for instead of other things we did when I visited her before, I now pray for her. She always promises me to join the forces of repentance and salvation to the eternal life.' 'Many of my *amakhaya* here in town take me to be a nuisance for preaching the good news about our God to them. I don't blame them, I keep on visiting them in their houses, for I know that at last they will follow the way.'

That the repulsion is genuine, and not a projection from the Bhenguists' own imagination, was suggested by the comments of still-Red migrants.

Once again the ex-Red came under fire for 'exaggerating' and 'making an exhibition of himself'. 'Those Bhengu converts who used to be Red, are preaching at you every minute you are talking with them.' 'Some of these people wake up early in the morning and go and preach in the streets by themselves!'

If the Bhenguist is cut off from the Reds he is kept away from most other elements of town society too. The dislike of mixing with 'unbelievers' applies also, of course, to secularly minded town society. All the normal associations and recreations of urban life are disapproved of accordingly: sports clubs, dances, bioscopes, and ordinary private gatherings, not to mention drinking parties which are automatically out of bounds on temperance principles. There is in fact practically no organization in town to which a Bhenguist can belong, consistently with his church principles.

Nor do the Bhenguists even mix as freely or happily with the rest of the professed Christians in town as they do among each other. It is not that there are any important conflicts on doctrinal or strictly religious grounds, but rather that the Bhenguists seem to have a different concept of the relation between church life and everyday life. Ordinary people of other denominations like to say that the Bhenguists are 'over-religious'. 'They have no other news except for talking about religion.' Their proselytizing zeal is also complained about. 'The Bhenguists, always wanting to collect new converts, go about preaching together. It is very rare to find enlightened people going around the streets preaching to everyone, as they do. I have never seen our own Mr. Godlo preaching in the street.'

BHENGU'S CHURCH AND COUNTRY-ROOTEDNESS

In general terms, any man from a Red country home who becomes a Christian in town will find it hard to take his Christianity back with him. Perhaps this is one of the reasons why Red people expect the *irumsha* to become *itshipha*. If a man becomes really committed to School ways, staying away from home may seem the line of least resistance.

Whether one can comfortably carry on as a Christian in the country depends partly on how strong the Christian element happens to be in the neighbourhood, and especially whether there is a branch of one's own denomination. Lone Christians in all-Red neighbourhoods need something of a martyr's endurance. Even if the neighbourhood is mixed, with other Christian households within reach, the convert will still have the opposition of his own Red family to deal with. Very few Red men will venture to come home as committed Christians if they have a Red father still alive.

Knowing all this, many town Christians evidently resign themselves to becoming pagan again if or when they return home. Church-membership is accorded its place as part of the migrant life in town, but at home it seems pleasanter to play the prodigal son and return to the embraces of the familiar pagan life. Still less would one risk trying to Christianize one's pagan neighbours.

The alternative—to hold on to the Christianity and let the home connexion go—may be all very well if the ex-Red man is a farm servant whose connexion with the country is precarious in any case. But a peasant, with reasonable hope of retiring to a normal peasant life, finds it hard to have to surrender this for the sake of his Church activities.

With the Bhenguists, the dilemma for the time being is particularly sharp, because of the fewness of Bhengu congregations in country places and the extreme antipathy between Bhenguist and Red ideals. 'I still go home every week-end, but I do not find it very pleasant there. There are no services, which revive my soul.' 'I do go home but I no longer attend the *intlombe*. I have learnt to pray at all times, I know that God is watching me everywhere and always.' Difficulties of personal intercourse invade the country-located as well as the town-located network: 'It makes it difficult to keep up with my old friends in the country. We meet as strangers. I am no longer interested in the things we used to be equally interested in.' The convert meets with the usual Red suspicion of all converts: 'I visited my home to tell the good news of how I regained my health [through Bhengu]. Though they could not help being impressed, they said I had joined the church because I wanted to be an absconder.' 'When my friends at home asked me to go to beer-drinks I told them that I had stopped drinking, and when they talked about girl friends I did not take any part. They suspected me and they left me alone one by one.' The content of relations is likely to change also in that the staunch Bhenguist makes each one an opportunity for missionary effort. Success in this uphill work is rarely claimed, but the convert makes a virtue of perseverance. 'I keep visiting my home, to talk to my relatives about the word of God and try to convert them, and make them feel I still love them.' 'At first I was shy when I went home, knowing that they were going to mock at me. I did not even talk to them about religion. Now I am bold about it. I just preach to the Red men and women. I am very happy in Jesus and fear no man about it.' 'When I go home I find there is a difference in my friendship with the people there. I do all the talking myself. I talk about godly matters. They keep quiet, they watch me but show no interest in what I say. Occasionally a remark will come from one of those listening: "My son, young as you are, you think you can teach us who are your seniors." However, I do not let such remarks worry me.' There are cases where relations become strained to breaking-point: 'When I visited my country home in 1951, my mother, wife, and brothers and sisters thought I was slightly mad, all my conversation being about religious matters. When I started preaching in the open air, in the mornings and evenings, my relatives and neighbours became convinced of my being insane. My wife deserted me as a result.'

It is too early to say how far this will make for town-rootedness in any individual case. The Bhengu Church has not been long established and few of its ex-Red converts have had to make the decisive choice that influx control makes necessary—whether to work for the status of 'permanent resident' in town, or accept the fact that one's real home can be in the country only. Meanwhile, both trends seem to be emerging. Some of the formerly Red Bhenguists are people who feel that they now belong in town, either for independent reasons or because of their religion itself. For instance there was a former farm servant who said he could not go back to the farm and therefore intended to stay in town permanently. 'My church friends have advised me about opportunities in town, e.g. that I might take up vegetable hawking. They are now my only friends here and I spend all my free time with them. My old friends from the farm knew nothing about town life.' Another, from a quitrent area, said that he had sold his land and decided to stay in town 'because I think I am happier when I am with my church members. At home in the country I am the only saved person.' The wife of a man from a peasant home said that he meant to stay in town 'to be nearer the church, to be attached to the church for good', and that she was pleased because 'in the country we might lose somewhat of the holy spirit which I have at present'. But on the other hand there were found converts who kept up their rural connexions and consoled themselves with the thought that they would spread the light in the country when they retired there. 'Country is my real home in that I have a mother and younger sisters and brother to look after and many cattle and sheep there. But more and above all, if I really mean to be a faithful servant of God my services are most needed at home, where the demand for the light is greatest.' The missionary ardour of the Bhenguist may actually reinforce the rural attachment of the peasant: 'My great wish is to have a strong branch of the church at home. In town I will only work and collect what I can, and then go home to start a branch.' 'I am not pleased that I am the only one at home who knows the Way, and I am trying to influence fellow-members to hold revival meetings there so that we could have a congregation. This would help me to bring many lost sheep to God.'

To sum up, it appears that conversion brings the Red migrant into line with School people in making him more receptive of urban cultural influences, but that there is a significant difference. For the ordinary School migrant, church is a main link between country and town: for the new Red convert, a main barrier. Bhenguism, in particular, has of all forms of *ukurumsha* the greatest explosive force, blasting away not only old values but old networks. Case histories show that it is hard to say whether Red migrants reach the point of no return 'because' they joined Bhengu, or whether they join 'because' they had reached that point. In either case the changes are too drastic to appeal to any but a small minority.

13

School Migrants

School migrants are a less homogeneous element in the East London population than Red migrants are, and it is harder to generalize about their way of life. Occupationally, while most are concentrated in unskilled and low-paid jobs (like those of Red people), there are individuals who have made their way into clerical work and the professions, in so far as these are open to non-Whites. But even the unskilled worker is more open to urbanizing forces than his Red counterpart. The School peasants, on the whole, do not come to town equipped with a stock set of responses to protect them against town influences. The values they set on town life and ways are equivocal. While they deplore absconding (*ukutshipha*) in the sense of abandoning one's rural dependants, and while they share the general country view of East London as an 'immoral' place, they are not ready to censure every move in the direction of urbanization. In fact it may be counted all to the good, if it appears to be a move towards a higher degree of 'civilization'.

Thus in the migrant situation the School man enjoys greater moral freedom. His morality does not enjoin him to remain a countryman at all costs. It does not necessarily discourage him from bringing his wife into town, or rearing his children there, or staying on in town when—financially speaking—he is able to go back to the country. Field-work showed that many School migrants are quite prepared to become urbanized in these senses, the limits being set only by the external forces of influx control. Again, School morality does not discourage changes in the style of life in town, participation in urban institutions, or friendships with townspeople as such. The School migrant can make choices decently, which in the case of a Red migrant would be insults to the home people and ancestors. This chapter shows how different network patterns result.

Apart from the question of moral sanctions, it is clear that there exists an overlap or common field which makes the School migrant better able to participate in town life and enjoy himself there (outside the circle of home-people) than the Red migrant is. The overlap exists almost by definition in that the diacritic institutions of the School peasant in the country are precisely the ones he has received from the White man, who has transmitted them to town-dwelling Xhosa too. Church and school, the two most prominent of these institutions, are adapted equally well to town and country settings. In both contexts they have a social significance as associations, over and above their primary significance in transmitting common teachings. They carry such patterns of activity as club meetings, sports meetings, committees, concerts. Their common patterns of activity bring about some face-to-face contacts between town Xhosa and School peasants even in the country. Ministers from East London pay formal visits to country church congregations; town choirs come and sing at rural 'concerts', and rural choirs at town ones; country teams meet town teams at various sports. When the School peasant comes to town, accordingly, he finds common fields of activity in which he can easily make the acquaintance of individual townspeople. For all these reasons he is relatively free from the dependence on home-people which marks the ordinary Red career. He can 'widen', not merely 'stretch', his network.

Another kind of overlap which needs to be considered is the overlap between town and School ideas of 'class'. There is no real counterpart among Red people. Even at home, School peasants pay more attention to differentiation by style of life or cultural accomplishment than Red peasants do. In the country all Red peasants including the wealthiest live in much the same style; all mature Red men are supposed to understand the main disciplines of their culture, such as law, ritual, and the management of land and cattle. Far more important than 'class' criteria, in Red rural society, are the notions of seniority based on age, sex, and kinship, and of prestige based on economic and personal success within the peasant way of life. The idea of cultural or social climbing hardly exists. In the rural life of School peasants, on the other hand, one can trace without difficulty the rudiments of something like class-consciousness and cultural aspiration. The School person's experience of East London only develops and reinforces the tendency to think in terms of udidi,[1] it does not have to implant it. A School countryman is familiar with the concept of 'getting on', in the sense of culture and not only of economics. He may define it as becoming more civilized, or sophisticated, but most commonly as becoming more educated. The educational ladder is a potent symbol.

In School rural society a person's accomplishment can be socially measured and graded according to the point he has reached in his schooling. Such labels as 'Passed Standard IV', 'Junior Certificate', 'Matric', are familiar and meaningful ways of assessing individuals. The most highly educated person, the akafunde ugqibile ('finisher of education'), is conceived of as 'the one ahead of others' (ingcungela); as a 'bird that perches the highest' (ingcungcu). These attitudes were also found in town, where illiterates and the lowly educated would be ranked at the bottom of the scale of udidi, 'half-educated' in the middle and the 'finishers of education'—especially teachers, doctors, lawyers, white-collar workers—at the top.

Cultural differentiation in School peasant society has other aspects too. Where the Red countryman is a pagan, the School countryman may belong to any of a dozen different churches; where the Red countryman lives 'like a real Xhosa', the School countryman's demand for varied European-style artefacts is limited only by his means. Dress and ornament, possessions and style of living, which in the Red world mainly indicate age and family status, function in the School world as insignia of wealth or poverty, fashion or old-fashion, smartness or shabbiness; as insignia of something like class. They function like this in the town world too.

In town, the School migrant's lesser dependence on his home-people combines with his greater perceptiveness of udidi or 'class' difference to produce a much greater variety of possible reference groups than exists in the case of Red people. One question put to migrants in town in the course of field-work was 'What sort of people would you like to belong to here?' Red informants rarely got beyond a stereotyped kind of answer reflecting the incapsulation ethic: 'I

[1] Explained in chapter 4.

should like to belong to the Red people in town', 'Red people who are in town only for work', 'Red people, those who drink kaffir beer', or, more simply, 'Red people from my home place'. School migrants produced a wide variety of answers: 'I should like to belong to the business men in town'; to 'sportsmen'; 'those who attend church regularly', to 'people with professions', or to 'property owners'; to 'the educated town people, because of identity of interests and outlook in life'; to 'those who are civilized and eager to make progress in life'; 'the younger men, who are ambitious to succeed in life'.

If Red migrant society in East London is like the ghost of a segmentary system, with Tshabo men contraposed against Middledrift men, or Dallas farm men against Cathcart farm men, School migrant society is much more like the embryo of a class-stratified system, contraposing high against low *udidi*, 'the well educated' against 'the illiterate', or 'sports people' against 'church-going people'.

Town, which constitutes a narrowing of opportunity from the Red home-bound point of view, may constitute a widening of opportunity from the School point of view. Subject to the usual reservations about 'White oppression' and unsatisfactory living conditions, the School migrant was found to be readier to say that he enjoyed town for this or that reason, while the Red person 'likes nothing about town' and 'is only here for the money'. A School peasant of 33 with standard VI education, Anglican by religion, who is a messenger in town, said that he likes his job 'very much', and also enjoys town for 'the company of young men like myself who are anxious to succeed in life. We discuss matters together, exchange ideas, and advise each other.' A standard VII man (Ethiopian Church), who works in a textile factory, praised town life as 'the life of progress and competition. There are opportunities here for individual independence. I should like to belong to the business set of townspeople. These people make a lot of money. The harder they work the more money they make. They do not look to anyone for an increment of salary as I do.' Another factory worker in his twenties, also with standard VII education, said that 'there are fine opportunities in town for a man who has an aim in life. I should like to find work here in a lawyer's office or Native Administration office.'

School migrants often expressed their liking for town in terms which had nothing to do with work or money. Many dwelt on the facilities for sport and entertainment. No ingrained conservative morality threatens the School man with human or divine retribution for enjoying these pleasures of the town. 'Life is less dull here than in the country. I attend church services regularly. I like to go to concerts in the Peacock Hall also. I read *Imvo* [Xhosa-language weekly newspaper] fairly regularly. My children will be townspeople and will be able to speak English and Afrikaans besides Xhosa.' (Aged 28, Methodist, standard III.) 'I am used to town life altogether. When in town I attend bioscopes about twice a month, and I attend all popular functions unless I am out of cash—we sometimes have to pay 5s. or 7s. 6d. at the door. I am a member of the Thembu football club, though not a player, and I attend church regularly on Sundays.' 'The following are good things about town: I play rugby for the Swallows Club, and tennis for the ex-Coegans Tennis Club. I attend all social gatherings in town, such as dances and concerts. I go to the Vigilance Association meetings, and I go regularly to the bioscope. I like all these things. I read the *Daily Dispatch* every morning, and the *Sunday Times* and *Imvo* weekly.' (Age 27, standard VII, factory worker.)

Before going on to illustrate some School ways of forming ties in town, something must be said about that element in the heterogeneous School migrant population which comes nearest to the Red type in outlook and level of attainment. School people themselves recognize, and define as 'low' or 'humble', a particular type of School migrant who is unresponsive to the attractions of town and remains conspicuous there by his rustic appearance and habits. Men of this type are commonly spoken of as '*Gcaleka*', as was explained in chapter 4. The rather naïve and fearful attitude towards town which distinguishes '*Gcaleka*' produces among them as among ordinary Red people a distinct preference for keeping together with 'one's own kind'. When questioned about their friends in town they would refer to the bond of home, or of belonging to one church, or of being 'illiterate though Christian, like myself'. School migrants of this type laid much stress on sending home most of one's money, on visiting home when possible, and on bringing up the children within the rural setting. Not all of them were Gcaleka in the geographical sense: some were humble School rustics from Ciskeian districts. They differed from Red migrants, however, in not having the full *amakhaya* organization. The School migrants' abstinence from formal 'meetings of *amakhaya*' in town was referred to in chapters 5–7.

Because of their typically rustic attitude and their lack of accomplishment in urban terms, School migrants of this special type are sometimes tempted to mix with Red migrants in town, particularly with the Red girls or women. An attractive Red girl may find a humble School lover, while the attractive School girl is probably aiming higher. There may even be intermarriage. P.N., an Anglican with standard II education, had married a Red girl of farm origin. Since the marriage, he explained, she 'has become a School woman and wears proper clothes'. Such contacts seem to be rarer between men, however. It is notable that while the Red man takes a pride in being addressed as Gcaleka (because it is 'his own tribe'), the School man is apt to be offended. He minds, as the Red man does not mind, the derogatory implication of being not fully civilized.

ROOM-MATES

The School migrant arrives in town with the same problem as the Red migrant, that of having to find somebody 'to look after him'—his kin or else his friends from home. However, on the whole, School people make less of the staying-together phase. It is rarer to find the larger groups, of say four or more men, living together in one room, unless as a very temporary arrangement. School people tend to regard prolonged staying-together as a sign of low class. The ideal is to have one's own room as soon as possible and then to keep it to oneself, with or without dependants of one's own family.

The first lodging in town is more likely to be with kin than it is among Red migrants. This is related to the tendency of School wives to go into town with or after their husbands—a tendency only lately interfered with by influx control. Because of this tendency a School new-comer may find kinswomen and affines as well as kinsmen in town. The first host was sometimes described as 'my mother's sister, staying here with her husband and children'; 'my sister who is married to a man working here'; 'a couple who are related to me, because the wife is the sister of the girl whom my brother married last year'. A Red migrant, of course, might easily have affinally related males in town too, but owing to the absence of the women who constitute the link, he is much less likely to find entrée into their homes.

Where School migrants do go to stay with male 'friends from home', as against kin, there is much less emphasis on the *intanga* relation. The word *intanga*, indeed, figured only rarely in the accounts of School migrants describing their first lodging. On the other hand there was often a reference to having been at school together.

It is highly relevant that the School migrant does not (or did not) necessarily come to East London as an unaccompanied man. In terms of the home moral code the married School migrant has a comparatively free choice, whether to bring his wife with him or to leave her behind in the country. If it can be confidently stated as a general rule that Red peasants do not think it right to bring wives into town permanently, the only recognizable rule in the School section is an absence of rule—men may do as they think fit in the light of their particular circumstances. Up till 1957—when it became harder for a migrant to get his lodger's permit endorsed to cover his wife too—the School man had both moral and practical liberty. Now, such choice must be practically limited to the 'exempt' class (whose status carries the right to bring dependants to town) and to those whose wives will be allowed in as workers in their own right.

Field-work done in 1956–7, before the tightening of this particular regulation, revealed something about the wishes and motivations of the School migrants themselves. It also gave the impression that School migrants who had brought their wives to town formed a substantial minority of the School section at that time. A sample of 80 School informants who gave full details about their circumstances and life histories supported this impression: 29 of them (36 per cent) were found to have their wives in town and 51 (64 per cent) to have their wives in the country.[2]

The theory and practice of School men in this respect seemed to deserve special consideration, being so unlike those of Red men. Factors which appeared from their various life histories will now be discussed. Similar factors, no doubt, would still be seen among those whose 'exempt' status leaves them the power of choice today.

SCHOOL MEN'S WIVES: TOWN VERSUS COUNTRY

Certain themes came up again and again when School migrants were explaining why they had or had not brought their wives to town. Three of the most frequent were land tenure, money, and kinship considerations. But these could not be characterized as objective determinants, for each one could motivate different individuals in different directions. One School migrant would say that he had brought his wife to town 'because' the land rights in

---

[2] Mere statements about the wife's whereabouts are often suspect. They need to be checked by lengthy personal investigation, as in these 80 cases. Even before 1957 many men were contravening regulations in one way or another. A man who has named his town concubine as 'wife' on his lodger's permit will not at first admit that his real wife is actually in the country; another may be slow to reveal the fact that his real wife is actually in town, because she is there illegally without a permit. Decency makes it almost imperative for a man to describe the concubine with whom he shares a room as his 'wife' when questioned by strangers, and especially if the woman is present during the questioning. Thus house-to-house survey methods could not and cannot give reliable information on the question how many migrants have their wives in town. (See Reader: *The Black Man's Portion*, Appendix 2 (Method).) The difficulty is illustrated by the discrepancy between Reader's Survey 2 and Survey 3 results. According to the former the proportion of men having wives in town was 37 per cent; according to the latter, 74 per cent.

the country were uncertain; another would cite exactly the same uncertainty as the reason which 'compelled' him to leave his wife in the country. One man would explain that the high cost of living in town forced him to leave his wife in the country, where she would cost nothing; another, that it forced him to bring her to town, where she could earn something. To a certain extent, perhaps, the various 'reasons' were being invoked as rationalizations for preferences which were purely personal, and beyond the reach of statistical analysis. Among the Red section on the other hand all arguments will be bent to rationalize one general cultural directive, that wives must be left at home.

To a large majority of migrants, in present circumstances, the maintenance of land rights or prospects in the country must be an important consideration.[3] This could affect the decision about the wife in various ways.

Prima facie, there is a class of peasants who, tenurially speaking, can easily afford to take their wives to town; they will not thereby risk losing their land or prospects of land. Freeholders, and those who hold by quitrent, need only arrange for the land to be utilized meanwhile by a squatter or a kinsman. Among men who hold by communal tenure (a much larger category) many are almost equally safe. The instalment of a deputy to look after the homestead and land, an occasional visit home to keep the headman's good will, and perhaps an *uswazi*[4] now and again, is usually sufficient.

On communal-tenure land an eldest son has a clear expectation of succeeding to his father's holding. A younger son, without this prospect, may have to watch out carefully for a possible allotment somewhere else in the neighbourhood. It may be as well for him to leave his wife in the country, otherwise he might easily miss his chance.

The younger sons of quitrent holders have an even bleaker prospect than the younger sons of communal-tenure peasants, for it is exceedingly hard to get an allotment in a quitrent area, except by inheritance. Plots that fall vacant are put to auction, but the chance to bid for one may occur only once in two or three years, and a successful bid may involve a capital outlay of £75–£90. To some School migrants this seemed sufficient reason to bring the wife into town and try to stay there permanently: it was simply 'too difficult' at home.

But while recognizing the significance of tenurial factors, it must be repeated that their total effect does not amount to determinism. Different peasants respond to similar tenurial situations in different ways. In St. Luke's for example (not far from East London) one can observe the different responses of Red and School peasants all holding by quitrent, and also of different individuals within the School category. Some School men from St. Luke's have taken their wives and left for town 'permanently' because of the land difficulty. Others in the identical difficulty have contrived to keep the wife 'at home' somehow or other, perhaps by illegally renting (*qesha*) the land of someone else, or by undertaking to cultivate on an *isahluko* basis (a kind of share-cropping) the land of somebody who has no cattle or implements of his own. And Red people at St. Luke's, in the same circumstances, have found another—a typically Red—answer. The Red younger son builds a homestead near to that of the elder brother who inherited the land; the holding is divided unofficially between the fraternal households, so that there is a place for the

---

[3] For social effects of different land tenure systems in the Ciskei, cf. Wilson, M., and Elton Mills, M. E.: *Land Tenure, Keiskammahoek Rural Survey*, vol. 4.
[4] A gift, usually a bottle of brandy.

younger brother's wife to cultivate. School people, it is interesting to find, declare against this solution, saying that it 'would lead to quarrels' between the wives or the brothers.

Many School peasants when questioned said that it was economically wasteful to bring a wife and children into town, because the whole family will have to live on the earned income there, whereas in the country 'they eat mealies which they plough themselves'. 'In the country a wife needs only matches, salt and paraffin.' 'If I had no mealies at home, I could not afford a family at all.' But the opposite argument could also be heard: it may seem more economical to bring the wife into town than to keep spending money on fares for the husband to visit her in the country home, or for her to visit him in town.

A particular aspect of the economics of bringing the wife to town—especially now that influx control excludes most non-working women—is that she may earn money herself. From a merely economic point of view this could be a distinct asset, and some School men regard it as such. 'We cannot come out on my weekly salary, and her earnings bring some relief.' 'My wife must work to improve our standard of living. If she did not earn we should not have enough. We are School people who are supposed to have well-furnished houses, and good clothes, and our children should be well educated. . . . My wife has never been out of employment except when she had to go to hospital for confinement. Our children are looked after by someone whom we pay monthly.' (School migrant aged 35, Junior Certificate.) In most cases the preference expressed was for the wife to work as a waitress, shop's employee or office cleaner, rather than as an ordinary domestic servant.

If economics were the main point at issue, the lowest-paid men should show the greatest willingness for their wives to work. But field-work suggested the contrary. Forty migrants gave detailed answers to questions about whether wives ought to work. On the whole it was younger School men of somewhat higher educational standard, higher income and higher aspirations who said they were glad for their wives to earn. The poorer, the more ignorant, the more rustic migrants often seemed prepared to go short rather than allow it. If the wife was actually earning they would make some excuse: 'When we came to town we never meant her to work. She has to work now because of money troubles.' Now that the working wife is favoured by influx control these arguments might be heard in different forms.

School migrant husbands who opposed their wives' working in town often explained that working 'spoils' a woman, but they might mean this in either of two different senses. Some meant a moral spoiling: 'If my wife earns money she becomes too independent and does what she likes. I cannot control her.' 'A married woman who takes employment of any kind becomes cheeky and disobedient to her husband.' Others meant physical spoiling, with implied fears for fertility: 'My wife is not to work because I cannot get any suitable employment for her, light work that would not ruin her health and thus ruin the chances of expected offspring.' 'My wife has been working very hard as a housemaid, which is a very strenuous job, especially for young women who still get children.' Some men admitted that their wives worked in defiance of the husband's will: 'My wife is employed as a cook-washerwoman, and to look after a three-year-old child, very much against my will. She has forced her way. She gets £4 10s. 0d. per month, and what she does with it I do not know; she does not give it to me. . . . It is my conviction that a married woman should depend entirely upon her husband.' 'My wife drinks, both kaffir beer and brandy, and I think it is because she is employed.'

Nevertheless, wage-earning by the wife could not be used as a simple index of departure from rustic ideals. There were cases where, on the contrary, it was associated with the couple's specially strong determination to get back into the country as soon as possible and resume the kind of life they both preferred. A young woman of relatively high educational standard explained: 'I have no future plans here in town except to work and so help my husband to save money which we shall use for building a home in the country. I like the country because if you have built a beautiful homestead there it will be your own property, and the property of your children when you are deceased.'

Although the obligations of a woman towards her husband's kin were less emphasized among School than among Red people, they would still be cited by some School migrants as a strong reason for leaving the wife at the country home. It was often said that the eldest son's wife (who will one day be the senior woman of the homestead) ought to stay there permanently 'in order to learn the ways of his family'. There might be a more specific duty also: 'My wife is at home to look after my aged mother, who is a widow'. 'There is no other senior woman at home to take care of my two sisters.' 'My wife, besides running the home, is looking after my sickly elder brother.' In School families, though not as frequently as in Red families, two married brothers may stay on together in the parental homestead after the death of both parents. If both brothers go into town for work the two wives may stay behind together 'to keep each other company' while running the household jointly.

But logic such as this—it seems—appealed to School people only where personal relations were tolerably good. Where personal relations were not good, the School man might be found quite ready for a solution which Reds would hardly commend—to resolve the tension by removing the wife to town. Resentment of the elder brother's wife was named specially often by School wives in town as a reason for having left the homestead. 'I did not like being under her.' 'One detests having to take orders from another woman who herself is only married into the family. One might have taken instructions willingly from the husband's mother, but not from his brother's wife.' Another not uncommon kinship argument was for a couple to say that they 'had no real home' in the country because the husband since childhood had been with foster-parents.

SCHOOL MARRIAGE MORALITY AND THE WIFE'S MOVE TO TOWN

The School concept of marriage offers a number of conflicting ideas as to whether or not it is good for a wife to accompany her migrant husband to town. The role of a Christian spouse, one might think, cannot so conveniently be discharged *in absentia* as that of a Red spouse; the 'teaching of Christ that man and wife are one' was sometimes quoted as a reason why wives should go to town. On the other hand many School people said that 'marriages are spoilt in town'. Like the Red Xhosa they regard town as a bad place for sexual morals altogether. On the other hand, again, they see a threat in separation itself, having no great confidence in the average wife's ability to remain faithful during separation, and still less in the husband's.

Complication is increased by the fact that the School husband's attitude to the ideal of marital faithfulness tends to be ambivalent in itself. The Christian ideal of marriage is not identical with the accepted social code of School Xhosa, and this is particularly true of the teaching on extra-marital chastity. School people repudiated the Red idea that a husband may take lovers openly (while requiring his wife to remain submissive and faithful), but they evidently did not regard complete extra-marital chastity as a practical proposition either. Adultery by husbands is rather like drinking—it is practised by both Red and School men, but the School men have more sense of shame or guilt and care more for privacy. There are some School men, no doubt, who refrain from adultery on Christian principle, just as there are some who genuinely abstain from drink, but this does not seem to be the general norm. Many School men said that a man's extra-marital affairs should not be regarded as 'adultery' at all unless the woman involved is a married one. 'Christian marriage is something new in the life of us Xhosa, and with some of us it is rather boring, for we are required to resist some of the demands of nature in which we feel most pleasure.' As for the wives, the Christian idea of something like equality between man and wife has been given a particular twist in some School circles, as if it entitles both spouses to be equally unfaithful. Quite unlike Red husbands, School husbands said that 'you cannot expect your wife to be faithful to you while you yourself are being unfaithful to her'. School wives are popularly supposed by all types of Xhosa to be less faithful than Red ones.

If danger to the wife's morals is made the main issue the argument may turn either way. To leave her alone in the country, according to some School husbands, is to ask for trouble. 'There are certain men in any country district who are most attractive in the eyes of women, especially the minister of religion, the teacher, the headman, and the agricultural instructor.' 'I could quote at least five cases at my home place where the married woman is not a bit worried by her husband's absence because she has a private lover permanently there.' But others dwelt on the dangers of town: 'The temptations here are too great for a woman to resist. Town is no place for a married woman.' 'Any man can see that here in town there are men more attractive than himself, and holding better positions; and his wife, he knows, has no will power.' One highly educated migrant, an Anglican, combined Christian and Xhosa feelings: 'Any married woman who stays with her husband in town is in danger of losing her reputation, because such a life is not favoured by the ancestor spirits.'

It is the unattached man, however, who is most notoriously exposed to temptations in town. School morality does not expect him to be able to resist indefinitely. 'The town *amankazana* are experts in tempting a man when they know his wife is in the country; at times the temptation becomes too great to resist.' 'It is absolutely impossible to resist the temptation when the town women will knock at your door any time of the night, under the pretext that they want to know where so-and-so is living in the location.'

There are certainly some School men to whom, for this very reason, town seems more attractive when the wife is not there. 'Freedom of behaving as you please' was sometimes cited as a main reason for leaving the dependants in the country. 'In the country' (the speaker was a middle-aged husband and father, of high educational standard) 'a School married man, like myself, is supposed to live an exemplary life, the life of a Christian, and stick to his wife. His movements, especially at night, are restricted; he is expected to tell his wife where he is going, why he had been kept out so late at night. Freedom to do as you like is the main factor which influences a man like me to leave the wife and children in the country.' Others cited temptation as a reason for bringing the wife to town: she is a protection. 'Coming back from work very late at night I always find the girl helper indoors [a girl hired by the informant to clean and cook for him] and I have noticed that I will be greatly tempted if my wife is not there to help my self-control.' 'Very few men can hold out against female temptation. My wife's presence is a great help.' A man of 35 with standard VII education said his wife saved him from a girl whom he had seduced at home in the Transkei. The girl, being pregnant, followed him to town and stayed with him nearly two years. 'She was extravagant and wasted a great deal of my money. I got tired of her. I went and fetched my wife, to make her go away. Now I am keeping my wife here so that she should safeguard me from any other temptations. I have repented. I agree that the wages of sin is death. When my wife arrived I had nothing in the house, whereas now, thanks to her coming, I have a dining-room suite, two oak beds, a wardrobe and a lot of kitchen things.'

Sometimes it may be the wife who insists on keeping her husband under observation. 'The real reason that has brought me to town is jealousy', said a Transkeian woman. She described how she had originally come to town for a short visit only, when her suspicions were aroused. 'One night my husband had gone to church. I heard a loud knock. I opened the door and saw a woman standing there, with hands on hips. "Is this the said Dickson's wife, this?" she said, looking at me very contemptuously. "Yes", I replied, "I am the rightful owner of this room, I and nobody else." I closed the door, I heard her grumbling outside. "East London is ours, with the men in it", I heard her say, "and we will not tolerate being kept from our men for days on end by such sickly little country creatures". . . . I wept all night . . . . Back in the country, I was tortured by jealousy. At night I would always imagine that woman in my husband's room.' Not liking to reveal her real motive to her husband, she wrote to him that she must come and take a job in town so as to help financially. 'Now because of the good income and the dinner and supper I bring him from the hotel where I work, he is very pleased with me, and has no more to do with concubines.'

Other factors within the marriage relation, besides that of sexual jealousy, may inspire the struggle to 'be together' and live a normal domestic life. Some School men emphasized the domestic comfort of having the wife in town 'so that now I need do no cooking, no washing, no sweeping, no cleaning of dishes'. Some said that the wife could be useful in the business, or in 'guarding the room when I am away at work all day'. Or it might be financially prudent: 'If I left her alone in the country she would be too extravagant'. Or, typically, from a School convert to the Bhengu Church: 'I brought her here because I noticed that it was not good for me to be of one denomination and herself of another one. I wanted her to know my church and to hear the word of God herself. I am very pleased that now she has joined my church of her own accord.' Then there is the wife's own point of view. Some School women, born and bred in the country, are quite willing to stay there as long as the husband supports them financially, but others object to the hard and lonely life. 'My wife does not stick at home, she always wants to be where I am.' 'My wife had been used to town life before her marriage and could not be content in the country.'

Another personal reason often mentioned was 'ill health'. This, one suspects, may sometimes do duty among School people rather as witchcraft does among Red people, namely in providing a blanket to cover all kinds of physical, mental, and social malaise. 'In the country my wife looked unwell. I thought perhaps she needed a change. Native people stick too much to old traditional customs. . . . Having brought her here I found she recovered her vigour in three months.' 'I want my wife to stay in town to be nearer to doctors and the hospital whenever her health requires this.' 'She came because the baby always had eye trouble in the country.'

Whatever the alleged or real circumstances—it may be repeated—their implication for an orthodox Red couple could hardly be the same as for a School couple. The Red wife's fidelity would be the concern of the senior kin at home, and the husband's a matter for his own discretion; his domestic comfort could be left to room-mates and concubines; while ill-health, rather than requiring any move to town, might well seem to demand more frequent and careful rituals for the ancestors at home in the country.

SCHOOL MARRIAGE IN THE TOWN SETTING

Transplanting married domestic life from the rural homestead to the single shack room, or to the municipal house which most School people would prefer, is a dramatic change in itself, and it helps to bring about other profound changes in the pattern of marital relations. In town, behaviour which would normally be proper in a School country home may become either impracticable or ludicrous, or both.

School families in the country vary more than Red families in the degree of their insistence on traditional Xhosa marriage etiquette, but most of them preserve a good deal. Like her Red counterpart the School wife is said to be 'married to the homestead', and has to observe the successive stages of *umtshakazi* (new wife) and *umfazana* (young wife) as a condition of being accepted there. In more orthodox School families the *umtshakazi* wears distinctive clothing; in the less orthodox she may be allowed to dress for her part more subtly, by keeping to styles that are proper rather than smart. The disabilities of the School *umtshakazi* include not being allowed to go out to weddings, funerals, concerts or other celebrations. To make an exception so that she can go to church, a special ceremony (*ukusa umtshakazi ecaweni*) may be staged soon after the wedding. The School *umfazana* is allowed out to celebrations but has to be back before sunset.

The principle of the subjection of young wives to their seniors, male and female, is likewise affirmed in the country by School as well as Red families, with the difference that its enforcement may not always be as strict in practice. The School *umtshakazi* is assigned the hardest household work. She cooks; the *umfazana* dishes out. Even among the better-educated the submission of women may be openly demonstrated at meals. There may be a dining-room suite, but most likely the male head of the homestead sits at table in solitary splendour; women eat sitting on the floor, ranged on mats in order of their seniority. Children eat in the kitchen. Only a really senior woman, such as a widowed mother, eats at table.

Hlonipha (respect) of the senior male kin, especially the father-in-law, is demanded of School women. The universal wearing of the head-covering is one manifestation of *hlonipha*; others are name avoidances, avoidance of physical contact, and not sitting on the bed. *Hlonipha* lies heaviest on the new wife, who until she passes out of this status should 'talk only a little' and use a subdued voice.

All these patterns drop away in town almost inevitably. The joint household has vanished, and with it the occasion for much of the traditional etiquette. The School wife in town is an autonomous housewife responsible for her own arrangements, not a junior member of a hierarchy. Even if there happens to be a senior kinswoman at hand it is soon made plain that 'you cannot teach or order about an *umtshakazi* in town as you do at home'. The wife in town goes about freely, and may accompany her husband to church and social gatherings, whether she is *umtshakazi* or not. 'In town you cannot tell an *umtshakazi* from a woman who has been married three or four years', neither by dress nor by manner. 'In town a young wife thinks she can take part in any conversation. If there should be anything to laugh about she will laugh freely.' *Hlonipha* dwindles to vanishing point. 'Young wives in town will talk to the father-in-law quite freely, if politely.'

The taboo on sexual relations for mothers with suckling children is another aspect of traditional kinship morality which does not survive the transfer of the wife to town. School women in the country said, like Red women, that non-observance of this rule would weaken a child, or give it diarrhoea. Some younger women compromised by saying that such harmful effects need only follow if the sexual partner is a man other than the child's father ('his blood is not the same'), but older women still stood by the principle of separating the spouses until the child is weaned. In town, many younger School migrants had dropped the observance or were rendering it no more than lip-service. 'I do not observe this rule' (said a young man with his wife and child in town) 'although the baby is only six months old and not weaned. My wife objects to my going out at night. I take her objections to mean that she is willing for me to have intercourse with her, and I have had it.' Another School migrant in his early 20's said that he was married but had a sweetheart who was rendered pregnant by another man. 'After she had the child I saw her walking past my room at night and called her in, and we had sexual intercourse. She did not object and nothing happened to the child.' A fairly common opinion among School migrants in town was that a man can sleep near his wife immediately after a baby has been born, and can resume sexual relations with her after six months, as against the two years or more demanded by traditional Xhosa morality. Care should be taken not to make her pregnant too soon: *coitus interruptus* will serve the purpose.

Of course, some School young men in town find the suckling taboo convenient as an excuse to have a free hand with their girl friends, and then they may pay homage to it in the strongest terms.

VOLUNTARY TIES

(a) Friendships

The School migrant finds no shadow home community, no ready-made circle of *amakhaya*, waiting to receive and envelope him; to entertain his leisure, help him in trouble, sympathize with his complaints or chastise his errors. For companionship and help School migrants may look partly to kin and friends from home, but for companionship alone they also look elsewhere—to friends met in town, to churches, clubs and other associations. As regards social ties in town they have more freedom, but less security, than the incapsulated Red man.

Personal friendships between two individuals, as distinct from clique or group relations, seem to loom larger for School migrants than for either the Red migrants or the real townsmen. School migrants when questioned were almost always able to name one or two 'special friends', whereas Red and town people, for their different reasons, would more often disclaim having special friends at all, or else would name several friends all equally 'best'. The Red migrant—as has been said—is more interested in the multiple friendships of the sets or the home *abafana*, while the townsman—according to popular stereotype—'has no friends', 'trusts nobody', 'is a friend of everybody and of nobody'.

Where School migrants do keep up intimate contact with their home-people in town they do so mainly by way of individual friendships. 'We grew up together at Pirie. He came to town in 1940, and when I followed in 1946 I found him here and we continued our friendship. We neither of us drink, we both play cricket and have joined the same club.' 'His home is close to my own home at St. Luke's. We grew up together, though he was circumcised a year later than me. . . . He is a single man like myself and we are always together. Sometimes we spend a night together in his room or in mine with our sweethearts.'

But in many cases the School migrant's best friend was said to have been chosen irrespective of previous acquaintance. He might come from anywhere, might be country-born or town-born. Many friendships are struck up at work: 'My best friend in town is of my own age and used to be employed by the same firm. We would have our lunch together in the same eating-house and would help each other out if perhaps one did not have money to pay for lunch; we always repaid the money on pay day.' 'We became friends through work, and now I visit him at Cambridge location where he has a room, and he comes to my room in Duncan Village.' Others have not even the steady background of a common place of employment. The acquaintance may be struck up by merest chance. Some School informants seemed to take a positive pleasure in this. 'I met my best friend for the first time in 1945 when I first came here. We were both looking for work and met at an eating-house after having moved about the town. Our friendship started through conversation that day.' 'We met for the first time in 1953 as passengers on a train. He had lost his luggage and I helped him to find it again.' 'He was in the police force and came to East London on transfer, knowing nobody here. I happened to meet him and I offered him temporary accommodation in my room. That was in 1948, and since then we have been firm friends, and have helped each other in many ways.' 'We became friends through girls. We met one night when both on our way to town. I introduced myself to him and he told me who he was. It happened that we were going the same way, because our sweethearts were employed in two white people's houses nearly opposite each other.'

It is not only in its origins that School friendship differs from the Red pattern: its content is different too. The shared interests which make a Red friendship are interests of the country home; School migrant friends on the other hand claimed common interests of various kinds in the town setting. A 33-year-old delivery 'boy' mentioned two best friends; one was a town-born man with whom he 'sings in the Church choir and attends concerts', the other a fellow-cricketer of country origin. A 32-year-old messenger said that he 'attends dances, concerts, and football' with one friend and drinks with another. A young clerk claimed a best friend who belongs to the same 'cultural organizations' as himself; sharing his interest in music, tennis, and sports generally.

There seems a tendency for the friendships to narrow down in middle age: the man in his 40's or 50's usually seemed to have difficulty in naming more than one best friend. It was the older men, too, who more often mentioned religion or church as a basis for friendship. 'C.N. and I were trained together as lay preachers for our church; this necessitated our meeting in spare time and discussing points in the Bible. The church has kept us friends till this day. He is a very religious man and is not interested in things like dances or bioscopes.' (School migrant of 49.) 'I have one outstanding friend. He helps me with money and I help him. He is a church steward like myself, and we meet often to discuss church matters.' (School migrant of 51.)

Whatever the ages, whatever the interests, the friendships of School migrants in town tend to lack something of the compelling, axiomatic quality which is found in the relations of Red *amakhaya*. Because they are *only* friends and not *amakhaya* as well, the friends met in town cannot be ultimately relied upon for help in time of crisis. Few only of the School men declared that among their friends in town they had one whom they could turn to with full confidence on any occasion: 'I know that my friend the churchwarden would always help me.' 'I have one friend whom I first met in town thirty years ago, I know I could trust him.' The more guarded view of the majority, especially among some younger men, might amount to distinct cynicism: 'Your friends in town are excellent as long as things go well, they will help you with money and in all possible ways. But as soon as you are in trouble they are gone. Now you are a nuisance, a parasite. They avoid you. Your mere appearance is like a call for help, even if you don't say anything. They know your troubles. So whenever they see you they turn away and start walking in a different direction.'

(b) Churches and clubs

Younger School migrants, especially the better-educated, did not always hide their doubts about certain aspects of organized Christianity. 'We listen very critically to the teaching and preaching of half-educated church elders threatening eternal hell-fire.' Nevertheless the churches provide a great number of country-born School people with their first and easiest opportunity for active participation in town activities. The women especially, besides finding the familiar patterns of church service and worship, will find the equally familiar half-social half-religious gatherings which are popular in town and country alike, namely the *iimanyano*. The member pays a subscription and (in the case of women or girls) wears a uniform for the weekly meetings, which provide for singing, tea-drinking, and conversation, as well as prayer. The *umanyano* may also organize special events now and again: a concert to raise funds, a visit to another congregation, an outing on a public holiday. A migrant moving from country to town can usually get a ticket certifying that he or she was a paid-up member of the local *umanyano*, and providing an introduction to the corresponding *umanyano* in town.

Some churches encourage, or even oblige, lay members to propagate the Gospel themselves, singly or in groups, by house-to-house visits, singing in the streets, or revivalist gatherings. A walk through the location any Sunday will reveal many such activities going on at the same time. There is nothing to stop the School migrant from taking full part. A fair number of migrants hold office in town churches. There are many offices to be filled in the organization of most churches, between the simple lay member and the minister. A humble old migrant, a clothes-pedlar, now about 70, said that he not only sings in the choir of the Ethiopian Church but 'is a member of the committee of what we call our church brigade, composed of the younger male and female members who march through the streets singing hymns and playing bugles while one man beats the drum'. A Tshabo man of 50, with standard V education, was a lay preacher in the same church 'and also a member of the church quarterly meetings, for which reason I attend all services every Sunday, morning, evening and afternoon'.

To the religious and organizational activities of the churches must be added the more purely sociable ones—receptions and farewells for ministers or important visitors, tea-parties and concerts with a collection in aid of church funds, and the weddings, baptisms, and funerals which are occasions for sometimes lavish display. Taking all of this together, it is justifiable to say that the churches organize more spare-time activity than any other category of associations in East London, and for more people, including School migrants.

Recreational clubs and associations are the next most important. While Red migrants keep out of these, School migrants join in eagerly. The sports clubs are the most prominent. 'I am particularly interested in all sports. It seems to me that sport forms part and parcel of life in town, and I usually spend my free time in town playing cricket, or watching rugby, according to the season. I have joined the Try-again Cricket Club'. In the field of sport a migrant may be following up what was already a strong interest in his country home. Some rural areas are specially known as centres for particular sports: Middledrift and St. Luke's for cricket for instance, and certain parts of the Transkei for soccer.

To be an active sportsman, in town, means being a member of one of the many clubs. 'When in sport you have many friends; if you are good at it they all want you to join their own clubs. If you are out of work they all try to get you a job so that you should not think of leaving town.' About twenty-five separate sports clubs were counted in the location in 1956 (eleven rugby, four or five soccer, six cricket, four tennis). They are organized on the lines of White clubs but often play a much greater part in life, for the sports club—like the church—provides a welcome outlet for the ambitions and rivalries of the location-dwellers. Each club has its president, two or three vice-presidents, a secretary, a treasurer, and four to six committee members. The clubs are combined into four unions—one each for the rugby, soccer, cricket, and tennis clubs. The four unions are combined in the sports board. The politics of the various clubs, the unions and the board, with endless jockeying for positions on committees and executives, and much accompanying intrigue, provide quite an exciting game in themselves.

Reader has compiled figures for the Gompo Rugby Football Union (the Union of the eleven rugby clubs) which differentiate between East London-born and other members (though not between Red and School in the latter category). According to these figures it seemed (1955) that over a quarter of all available migrant men between 15 and 24 years old claimed to be members, and about a sixth of those between 25 and 39 years. If we could exclude the Reds (who certainly do not join in any numbers) these proportions would be much increased. The School migrants might then be found to approach the town-born figure of nearly half the available males joining the Union.[5]

Some sports clubs, a minority, are formed on a regional principle. They draw their members from the week-enders or month-enders of a particular home district, with the idea that games and practices can be organized in the country when the migrants are at home. The Black Lion club recruits members mainly from Middledrift and King William's Town. The Thembu United Rugby Club recruits migrants from Queenstown, Lady Frere, and Glen Grey districts (Thembuland). The Black Lions at one time were somewhat notorious for their behaviour on the local train, when going home for week-ends. 'They would treat other people on the train, who did not wear Black Lion uniform, in a most disrespectful manner, boasting and heckling, so that many Middledrift men have joined this club just for the sake of peace.'

But the majority of sports clubs are formed on some other principle. Occasionally the idea is to cater for people who live near together in town. This is not only for the obvious reasons of convenience, but (according to informants) to keep an eye on the treasurers and other officials and prevent them from embezzling funds. A more frequent and significant principle is that of 'class'. In 1957 two out of the four tennis clubs catered mainly for particular classes: the Highlanders for teachers, nurses, and clerks (with a sprinkling of 'ordinary people'), and the Silver Star for labourers and domestic servants (with a sprinkling of teachers). The Stone Breakers Club (Rugby) was well known to cater for the most educated players, including Native Affairs Department clerks and other civil servants: 'It can be taken for granted that everyone who joins our team is educated.'

Whether formed on a regional principle or not, the sports club in town is a very different matter from a Red migrant organization of home-people qua home-people. It may bring home-people face to face but its objects are wide-scale and not small-scale. The fact that the clubs are integrated into 'unions' in town speaks for itself. At times the sports unions have received serious consideration from political bodies in town, for their form is such as to enable large numbers of supporters to be brought together easily, quickly, and without incurring suspicion. The A.N.C. Youth League is said to have gained control of the Gompo Rugby Union in 1953 before turning its attention to the more recognized organs of local government.

Organized dancing is another recreation in which 'class' distinctions are noticed by location people. Jiving is the normal way of dancing for young School migrants; they may have jived in the country as well. In East London all classes of School people from the labourer to the professional worker (such as teachers and nurses) go in for jiving. But ballroom dancing is a rather different matter: it has become a fashion with those who specially wish to 'civilize themselves', including servant girls, messenger 'boys', factory workers, commercial travellers. A leader of a prominent dance band, formerly a social worker and secretary of the social centre, summed it up in these words: 'Ballroom dancing is an outlet for the lower classes, aimed at raising their social status. Tail-coat and bow-tie give status. Jiving seems cheap entertainment by comparison. Ballroom dancing appears to these people as a short cut to

[5] Unpublished tables.

achieving civilization. The competitions, with White audiences and judges, give them great satisfaction.'

(c) Drinking together

The *iseti* or *mbutho* drinking parties which figure so prominently in the domestic life of Red migrants in town, and which keep them in such regular contact with home friends, have no counterpart among the School migrants. This is not only because many School people are obliged by their churches to drink secretly or not at all. It is also because when they do admit drinking companions they select them on a different principle. Only people who 'have a lot in common' are welcome. For School people, this means that the cliques of drinkers should preferably be drawn from similar educational and occupational levels.

Not all denominations forbid the consumption of alcohol. The Anglicans and Roman Catholics, among others, are permitted both to brew and to drink. But even here the constant warnings and preachings about the evil of excessive drinking act as a brake on the full enjoyment of drinking in public. Above all, drink is not given a high positive value, as it is among Reds: 'Red parents are proud when their grown-up sons drink; Christians, angry or worried.'

Among the rest of the School people, whom their churches forbid to drink, some are genuine abstainers, but a high proportion are secret drinkers. A whole system of conventions has been built up to make discreet 'private drinking' possible, and it is well known that the private drinkers include many of the best-educated as well as the urban riff-raff. A certain degree of secrecy is a necessary precaution against getting into trouble with the police for infringement of the liquor laws. But for the respectable School person it remains a pressing need to conceal his drinking even from his fellows, for fear of losing face. It is easy to see how this consideration would inhibit the development of regular drinking parties like those of the Red migrants.

More educated men generally prefer brandy to kaffir beer. In explaining this they would refer to the supposedly unhygienic habits of the Red women (who are the main brewers of kaffir beer), but would also give the significant reason that brandy is easier to hide, because a small amount satisfies at a time. Those with the necessary certificates often preferred to drink in hotels in town rather than in the location.

Ordinary School men, like Red men, rely mainly on kaffir beer. They may send children to fetch it in cans, not wishing to be seen carrying it themselves. The beer is drunk in one's own room or in the room of a close friend, often at night, behind locked doors, for fear of being seen. Those with wives in town sometimes let the wives prepare beer and call a few trusted friends to join them after work. 'It is a matter of conscience', said an informant, 'not of law. All Church people, even Anglicans, have a conscience about drinking, and keep it private, and do not want it to be publicly known. We all know that drink is self-ruination.'

There is a special feeling of embarrassment, of degrading oneself, about the idea of being seen drinking by inferior people. Hence the strong tendency for School people to choose their fellow-drinkers by 'class' or social set, rather than by home origin. The upper-class School informants expressed themselves reluctant to attend an 'ordinary' drinking-place. 'At those places, the lawyer would have to drink with the low type, and this embarrasses a man of the more elegant set.' 'At common beer-drinks there are always fights, and you are degraded by being involved in fights with the low types of ruffians who attend those drinks. I should not like Mr. X to see me drinking with such a one.'

There are private drinking-places that cater especially for the upper set. A widow, Mrs. B, whose late husband was a teacher, and who herself possesses a teaching certificate, holds high office in the woman's *umanyano* of a church. She sells liquor, 'which is very risky, I know, for a person of my position and prestige. But I do not sell liquor to just anybody. I sell it only to teachers, preachers, and other decent people who I know are afraid of being known as people who drink.' She said that there are many in her church, 'but they will never mention the fact to anybody. Each has his or her own friend with whom they drink. I have my friend near by, also a member of the *umanyano* and also selling liquor. If I am short of supplies when any of my customers come, I approach that friend and nobody else.' This lady explained the advantages of restricting her clientele: 'The church people usually drink quickly, so that not even a child in my place should see them. If the children are there, or someone whom they don't know, they won't drink at all. Actually, there are even Ministers who come to my house at night for drinks.' 'I myself [she added] drink quite a lot, but not if there are many people present.'

Informants regarded it as a clear distinction between School and Red people, that the former drink 'by *udidi*' while the latter do not. 'The Red people in town have no "grading" in drinking whereas School people "grade" themselves. Doctors or teachers will not drink with "men in the street" whether they are Christian or not.' Many humbler School migrants were strongly aware of, and even annoyed by, the class-distinctions which excluded them from drinking in the company of their betters. 'Those lawyers and doctors will drink only among themselves, or at most sometimes with gentlemanlike men of the teacher or clerk categories.' Some mentioned the exclusiveness without rancour, as right and proper. 'These men must be respected for their prestige and great talents and education.'

14

School Migrants between Town and Country

DOUBLE-ROOTEDNESS

It has been found possible for purposes of discussion to distinguish two separate types of Red migrants—those who want to resist urbanization (the incapsulated) and those who do not. In the case of School migrants it would be much harder to apply a corresponding distinction. While some of them clearly feel as countrymen in exile, and others equally clearly have leanings towards urbanization, there remain a large class who seem intent on keeping a footing in both camps. They tend to become town-rooted and urban-cultured to a considerable degree, without ceasing to be country-rooted at the same time.

From the School point of view, life in town—as has been said—may constitute a widening of opportunity: not only in terms of money to be earned, but in terms of friendships to be made, recreations to be enjoyed, and civilized tastes to be indulged. At the same time the School migrant cannot be insensible to its many uncertainties and unpleasantnesses. The attitudes to town and to the country home both become ambivalent. The home is the blessedly cheap place 'where one can live without money', but in the eyes of many School men in town it also begins to seem 'boring', 'a place without pleasures'.

In this situation the School migrants are not, like the Red migrants, provided with an ideology and a form of social organization designed to secure the permanent paramountcy of rural interests. As the previous chapter has shown, a School migrant's network in town is not typically a displaced portion of his country network. His comrades do not artificially limit his interests in town, nor insist that he must visit home as often and retire there as early as he possibly can. There is no supernatural sanction for preferring the country: if Red men's ancestors demand that sacrifice be made in the country, it is in town that the churches of School people are usually better represented. Neglecting one's dependants would always be wrong, but this consideration does not tie a School man to the country either, as he can take them into town without offending anyone. Thus, from the internal viewpoint of his own society, he is morally free to become urbanized.

On the other side of the balance, however, there are all the considerations arising out of influx control. Here—rather than in the internalized moral code—compelling reasons now appear for not giving up the country home. The town network, the town interests and activities, may seem to make up the most important part of a School man's life for the time being, but today he must know that a hammer blow could fall on him at any time, forcing him to give them up perhaps for ever. Almost equally important is the feeling of economic insecurity. A man may make a satisfactory income in town as long as he works, but old age brings almost insoluble problems. House-property, the one apparently sound investment which could also become the inheritance of one's children, is safe no longer. 'We Natives hear that we are all to be shifted to the new location, and not be able to own any houses to let for profit.'

Thus the School migrant, like the Red migrant, may stay in town for long periods being 'in' it but never wholly 'of' it, only for quite different reasons. The Red man, having been shielded from town influences, is tied to his country home by moral and emotional considerations above all, where the School man —in many cases—may be tied by nothing more than stark practical necessity. It can be said that nowadays, owing to influx control, the more a man wants to become urbanized the longer he must submit to remaining doubly rooted. To become urbanized he will have to achieve 'exempt' status; to achieve this status he must establish the necessary record of ten or fifteen years' continuous employment. But throughout this initial period his fate still hangs in the balance (for he may not succeed in establishing his record), and the country home has to be kept open at the same time.

When School migrants were questioned in 1958 about their attitudes to town and country life, some had positive things to say about the country, but many others frankly admitted that they only thought of returning there for reasons of security. It is too early to say whether or how far the practical necessity will produce a new ideology, a higher valuation of the country apparently for its own sake. At present one's impression is of regulations deflecting what would otherwise be a rather powerful drive towards urbanization.

SCHOOL MEN AND THEIR COUNTRY HOMES

In the matter of home-visiting, the School migrant's attitude was not noticeably different from that of the Red migrant, though fewer School men had the chance to be week-enders (the near-by districts being predominantly Red). It was when one came to the question of eventual retirement that they expressed themselves very differently. The Red man would say he 'wants to go home as soon as possible'; not necessarily the School man. This was demonstrated by investigation of a sample of eighty School men (1957). The question was put in an open-ended form ('When would you like to retire to the country?') The category among whom the difference was most noticeable were the younger School men (up to age 39). Of the fifty-one in this category, only nine expressed an intention of retiring as soon as possible, or at some specified date fairly close at hand, or indicated that they would prefer to be living at home. Nearly all of these were eldest sons of well-established peasant families or other lucky individuals with thriving homesteads in the country: 'As the heir and eldest son I shall not be staying in town long. All I need is to earn for a few years.' 'My father is well established, with many cattle and over 100 sheep, and the time for me to work in town is only so long as my father is alive.'

The remaining forty-two School migrants in their 20's and 30's—that is, four-fifths of this age-group—either mentioned a vague or distant date for retirement, or seemed unconcerned with the matter altogether. It was noticeable that among them the idea that '*abafana* must earn' seemed to have developed into the idea that 'town is the right place for *abafana*'. Many argued from this consideration of age-status rather than from financial considerations directly. 'I suppose I shall retire when I am no longer *umfana*, that is when I am about 40.' 'I am too young to return.' 'I am still only an *umfana* which means that

I must learn to work here before settling in the country again.' 'My late father worked in town until he was quite old and I think I shall do the same.' Others left the whole matter quite vague. 'Nobody knows when he is going to return home.' 'Retirement to the country is a thing that will happen to me one day without my knowing now.' Further, out of those who set themselves a distant though definite date for retirement, many sounded as though concerned with town objectives rather than rural ones. They would be aiming at a pension, gratuity or other benefit to be attained by long service in town. 'It will be twenty years before I can get my pension from the South African Railways and Harbours. I should not like to leave before then.' 'Having been with my firm [a department store] for ten years I must stay another fifteen years so as to get my gratuity.' A few men who had taken out insurance policies on their own may be put in the same class. 'I have had my insurance for four years, and have another sixteen years to work in town before it matures, when I shall draw £300.'

Among the older men (from 40 upwards) impending retirement seemed to have become more of a reality, in so far as nine out of twenty-nine men in this category (almost a third) had fixed on retiring 'soon'. These got down to reckoning in hard practical terms: so many livestock, so many implements, to make retirement possible. 'I shall be able to retire in a couple of years, now that I have about twenty cattle and thirty goats.' 'I need about five more years in town, by which time I hope to have enough oxen for ploughing, and perhaps three heifers. Then I shall be able to live by ploughing and keeping sheep.' 'I am saving to put up my kraal and buy my land [in a quitrent area] and I hope to be able to retire in five years.' 'I propose to retire in ten years, I should have bought enough ploughing implements by then. I have bought a few beasts already.'

The remaining twenty of the older men gave vague or distant dates. 'I keep postponing my return, though truly speaking I am well-to-do at home.' Drought was often invoked as a reason for not being able to fix a date more precisely. 'I cannot say when I shall return, for good, because there are always droughts that force us to earn in town.' 'I have seen other men retiring but coming back again after some months because of drought. The same may happen to me.' Though drought is a real bane to farming in many areas, one suspects that in the mouths of some informants it serves like 'ill health', as a convenient formula covering disinclination to go back.

These data seem to indicate that School men are relatively more willing to stay on in town 'for the time being' than Red men are, or, at least, that they have fewer inhibitions about admitting it. But a willingness to stay in town is one thing: willingness to give up the country home is another. With many School people, infrequency of home-visiting or apparent unconcern with the date of retirement may be misleading as an index of the strength of country interests. A great deal of effort may be put into the country home *at the same time as* the migrant himself stays contentedly on in town. Correspondingly, a verbal statement that 'my real home is in the country' cannot be taken at its face value; for with School men it may represent anything from a powerful motivational drive to conventional lip-service or sentimental illusion. What we have to consider, therefore, is the *actual* effort put into the country home.

A genuine intention to retire must imply a genuine preparedness to fight for, or in defence of, one's land-rights in the country. Depending on the type of land-tenure, different measures are necessary: collecting money to buy freehold or quitrent land, or paying annual visits to the headman to protect communal tenure rights; provision for relatives or friends to look after the land in one's name (i.e. as caretakers not successors); leaving, perhaps, at least one very close relative *in situ*—a wife, a parent, a brother—to make sure that rights do not go by default.

The actual economic condition of the country home, and the amount of economic effort devoted to it, is the other main consideration. Behind the stereotyped picture of the country as a place of blessedly cheap living—'you just eat your own mealies, and milk from your own cows'—lies the stark need for capital investment to keep the country home productive at all. Unless sufficient has been done to provide buildings, livestock, implements, the question of retirement will become academic sooner or later, and the man will admit, in his 50's, 60's or later, that he has got to stay on and earn his living in town 'as long as I can work at all'.

School migrants' life histories in their various forms might be symbolized by a few typical curves showing the changing intensity of this rural pull at different times of life: (*a*) In some cases active energy has been put into the country home throughout the worker's stay in town. (*b*) In others the active interest has weakened for a time (especially if the wife is in town), then revived at middle age, when much effort will be devoted to establishing or re-establishing the homestead. (*c*) The weakening of the rural pull may have been progressive; in his late middle age, or past it, the man may still show more concern with his town 'home' than his country 'home'. The idea of going back 'some day' is not exactly repudiated but seems rather academic. The man appears to be town-rooted, though in theory he has not stopped being country-rooted. (*d*) Only when the curve has sunk to zero, and the idea of a country home been repudiated altogether, are we justified in calling the person town-rooted and not doubly rooted.

Nominally, many of the School young men in their 20's or 30's who said that they thought they would stay in town 'a long time', or indefinitely, were arguing from country economic reasons. Over and over again one heard financially prudent remarks from School men: 'You can only think of retiring when you have saved a lot of money.' 'Our salaries in employment are so small that after paying out weekly or monthly bills nothing or very little is left for saving; so how can we retire to the country?' 'Even if a man has got land of his own, and the actual home has already been built, I should think that a family with several children, like mine, would need to have saved at least £75 before they could think of retiring.'

True as these statements are, in a sense, they may not convey the whole truth; there may be a personal factor as well. After all, one can find other School migrants for whom return to the country has remained axiomatic so that financial reasons are not allowed to interfere. 'It will not be long before I go home', said a man of 48, 'for I am getting on in years. It doesn't matter whether I have enough money or not—I shall just force my way. What I have at home is my kraal and land, six head of cattle and ten sheep. I know that this is not enough: all the same I shall try to make it do.' Or here is a man of 55: 'I am now tired of town life. I feel I must go and join my family at home. I have my kraal and land, cattle and sheep and fowls, and somehow I shall just manage to make a living.'

With some men 'saving' seemed to be used by way of a formula; the man talked about the need to save, but could not show that he in fact devoted any savings to the homestead. With others words were borne out by deeds, i.e. a real effort was clearly being made. 'We men of a certain type', as one man put it, 'really are eager to retire to our country homes, and if we stay in town it is only because of circumstances over which we have no control. If you are such a man you improve your country home by buying the things it lacks; perhaps a planter this year, a harrow next year; or if you have not enough oxen, you may be getting them from a White farmer, paying by instalments. We know that our friends at home are ready to admire us for this; in the country a man is admired for his deeds, not for appearances.'

If a declared intention to stay in town for fifteen, twenty or an indefinite number of years seems to indicate a tendency to become permanently urbanized, the impression may be corrected by looking at the further intentions of the School men who were waiting for pensions, gratuities or insurance benefits. Almost without exception they stated that they meant to use the proceeds for farming at home. The department-store employee quoted above said that when he gets his gratuity he will 'retire and start seriously on ploughing my lands'; another employee of the same firm, that he will 'retire home and live on ploughing and poultry farming'. The holder of the insurance policy said that he will 'retire home and concentrate on sheep, which I regard as the most profitable thing at my home'. They were planning to stay in town 'a long time' but not to 'become townspeople'.

A priori one might expect the wife's presence in town to make a migrant town-rooted. This proved to be correct up to a point, but not universally. The man with his wife in town (it seemed) was not necessarily going to give up his rural interests. Some couples would be working together solely because the wife's wages helped to hasten the day for permanent retirement to the country. Some would be arranging that though both parents worked in town the children were returned to the country to be reared in rural surroundings. Fourie and Lumsden's data on wage-remitting seem to support the contention that couples in town are not necessarily town-rooted, for out of all the men in their East London sample who claimed to remit money to the country, almost 19 per cent described themselves as having their wives in town (25 per cent as being unmarried or widowed, and 56 per cent as having wives away from town). Thus out of all *married* men who remitted money to the country—to adapt the same figures—just over 25 per cent remitted in spite of having their wives in town.[1]

That willingness to stay in town is very different from willingness to give up the country home, may be illustrated by two cases drawn from different walks of life.

(1) M.N. is a Tshabo-born man of 64, who has almost forty years' continuous experience of town life (Johannesburg 1914–21; Cape Town 1921–4; Port Elizabeth 1924–6; East London twenty-nine years 1926–55). He reached standard V and belongs to the Ethiopian Church. Though only a delivery 'boy' he finds much to enjoy in East London: 'Town life is an education by itself. There is progress here, which needs to be taught in the country.' He was

[1] Cf. *Economic Development in a Plural Society*. Ed. by D. Hobart Houghton: Fourie and Lumsden, chapter 7, table 165. However the objection to 'survey' data on the wife's whereabouts may apply here also. Cf. chapter 13, footnote 2.

an active member of the Vigilance Association, and is still a life president of the Try-again Cricket Club, and a member of the rugby club. He also has a 'regular woman friend' in the location with whom he spends much of his free time. He has two sons who, he says, 'should live under modern conditions'; he would like one to become a teacher and the other a tailor.

But his homestead at Tshabo has remained a special interest and pride. 'I have managed to put up a homestead of my own, even if I have not made any great achievements otherwise.' His wife is there, and he goes there almost every week-end and during annual leave. 'I like spending time on the mealie lands and in the vegetable gardens, and visiting friends and relatives.' He looks forward to settling there himself in due course. Country is my real home. I believe in ploughing the lands. In three years or so, I shall settle permanently at home. I think I have had my innings here. I must return home and resume country life while I am still physically fit.' He bases his preference for country life on the usual Xhosa reasons—independence and security. 'In the country you can manage with little money, as long as you have your crops and your sheep. Also, I like the country because it is peaceful there: no passes, no police raids.'

(2) William S. has only standard II education. He came to town from Peelton in 1933 at the age of 21. During his twenty-three years here he has become a prosperous man, with a flourishing grocery business in the East Bank Location. He has sent his eldest daughter to Port Elizabeth to study for her Junior Certificate; his wife and younger children are with him in town.

William S. has no great urge to live at Peelton. 'I keep staying on in town of my own accord, that is, I have postponed my return to the country, although truly speaking I admit I could easily afford to go home if I wanted.' He has left his brother in charge of his affairs at Peelton. But he is actually putting most of his money into building up his Peelton home, for he intends to retire there 'one day'. He has bought some freehold land there, a larger parcel for himself and a smaller one alongside it for his brother. He has bought a 'ploughing jeep' and other expensive ploughing equipment, and cattle. He has a fowl-run and is selling the eggs through the East London egg circle. 'I go home every week-end to inspect my stock and fowls, and other possessions, for most of the money I have made in town is invested there.'

GIVING UP THE COUNTRY HOME

The intentions of younger School migrants must (broadly speaking) nearly always be considered uncertain. Few were found—outside the 'Gcaleka'—whose expressed attachment to country on the one hand or to town on the other was so unequivocal that one would be justified in guessing it can never alter. The man in his 20's and 30's is still (by School standards) 'too young' to make up his mind about going or staying. But the man of about 40 needs to make up his mind, having little time left to prepare against retirement. Some finally cut loose from the country 'because I like town best'; others, because they 'had bad luck', 'could not help it'.

B.P., a Methodist, aged 42, comes from Victoria East. He holds a teaching certificate and had taught in various country places before he was offered an appointment in East London. 'I am getting good pay here, I am very popular and everyone seems to be friendly with me.' His wife (also country-born) is earning too as a nurse aid. 'We occupy a comfortable house with our children,

I should say that town is my real home now. I don't even visit the country any more, except once in two or three years to see relatives.'

In a different category altogether is the absconder whose stereotype runs as follows: 'He has spent many years away from home, has not been of any help to his relatives, has not taken any trouble to improve his country home, and has entirely neglected his wife and family. To console himself this man will say, "There is no difference between town and country life, it does not matter where a man dies; the grave of a man is by the roadside".' Since the absconder (in this sense) is condemned by School morality just as much as by Red morality, it is not easy to come face to face with actual cases. The person being questioned will take care not to identify himself with this negative role.

It is easy, on the other hand, to obtain 'hard luck' histories explaining why a man 'could not' get back to the country in spite of his efforts. There was for instance a man of 55 whose livestock had died off through drought and who, being already in late middle age, saw no hope of re-establishing himself as a peasant. 'I am under poor conditions in the country. It appears that I shall have to continue working here in town as long as I am physically able to work at all. If only I could get some money today, I would get home at once and settle permanently.' 'I am really anxious to retire home', said another man of 44, 'especially because I have children in the country, who have now reached the stage to need a father's care. But because of poverty I must continue working here.' 'I have practically nothing at home except the land', said another middle-aged man.

Then there is the stereotype of the man who never managed to marry but spent his years in town living with a woman or with several in succession. 'In town he finds that his salary is so small that after paying his weekly accounts there is nothing left over for him to pay into the Post Office. Year in and year out, his financial position does not improve. His ambitions to raise money for marriage cattle cannot materialize and he becomes desperate. The chances of a decent marriage, as he had wished for, are not visible, and he admits to himself that the only way now is *ukushweshwa* [concubinage].' The end of this man's life is unquestionably 'in town where the rule of "mind-your-own-business" is observed'.

The School man who 'missed the bus' home may express regret in his later years. 'I am not satisfied with what I have achieved in my life', said a School man of 71. 'I wasted my money on nothing. As a young man I spent many years in the Orange Free State and Transvaal, and when I returned home I found that my kraal had collapsed. I was too happy in the Transvaal, and did not think "the time will come when I shall need a home". Presently I found it was too late for me and my family to start from scratch in the country. So I decided to make East London my permanent home.' He is a hawker in the location. 'I have no home to retire to in the country. Now the time is approaching when I shall not be able to raise money for the rent.'

URBANIZATION FRUSTRATED: THE INSECURITY OF TOWN

The fact that so many School men remain doubly rooted is a product of two forces, both of which derive from the White part of society. On the one hand there is the cultural preparation by school and church, and the reception of many Western values (especially Western-type economic aspirations), which makes the School Xhosa adaptable to town conditions. Such people do not feel as the Red person so often feels, rejected by the urban Xhosa community; they are not fish out of water; the country home is not the only place where they are subjectively 'at home'. But if the location does not hold them at arm's length the authorities do: this is the second of the two forces. The policy which is designed to prevent urbanization and integration has achieved its aim to this extent, that not many School men nowadays feel secure in town. The opportunities for 'good' jobs and money-making, and the varied social life, rarely outweigh the desire for political and economic security, which now seems attainable only in the country.

Three case histories may be quoted in conclusion to illustrate the effects of insecurity on School men who would otherwise have been willing candidates for permanent urbanization.

A is a man of 49 with standard V education who has been in East London for most of the past thirty years. As a young man he inherited a homestead; his wife stayed behind to look after it. On the death of his wife he tried entrusting it to various neighbours but encountered many difficulties. 'They did me down so much that I saw it was a waste to carry on.' A bought a six-roomed house in town. He married a second wife there; unlike the first she 'was never used to country life'. But for the opposition of his eldest son, A would now have sold out entirely in the country. His aim was to save up for a business in town. He had his wages at the store where he is employed, and the rents from his house. He put his two eldest sons through 'college'.

A has been disappointed financially. 'Owing to the rise in school fees and the cost of living generally, I now see no hope of being able to start a business.' But without a business he cannot face the future in town. The house by which he had set so much store no longer gives him a sense of independence. 'Now the town council have decided to shift our location altogether, and I am afraid to own any property in town. It will become profitless. All Natives will have to live in municipal houses instead of renting rooms from other Natives. We are told we should rent a site to build our own house, or buy a house under the Home Ownership scheme, but what is the good of that? You will still have to keep paying out for it until you die, and after your death your children will not inherit anything.'

A has regretfully decided to go back to the country. 'I must use what I have left out of my wages of £4 a week to buy stock and to build or rebuild a hut. In the country a poor man can survive, but in town today he cannot.'

B is a man of 50 who came to town about twenty years ago. He was first employed as a Native constable, but resigned (he says) because he was held to have acted wrongly in putting handcuffs on to a White man whom he wanted to arrest. He held a succession of other jobs and saved up enough to buy a five-roomed house. He now found he need not be employed any more, for he received £7 10s. 0d. monthly in rents and also did very well out of illegal butchery (buying sheep and slaughtering for sale). He told his younger brother that he would not be returning to the country. He brought his wife to town.

B is a flourishing man by location standards. 'Out of the profits of the illegal butchery I educated all my children and put the last one through college.' After jealous people had informed on him to the police he felt that the risks in butchery were too much for him and switched over to being a self-employed craftsman instead. 'I have never been without business for a single day.' For some time now his wife has been busy too, 'selling meat again and also brandy on a big scale'. They are accumulating money to build on five more rooms for letting; he also means to buy a municipal house under the Home Ownership scheme, and to apply for a butcher-shop licence in the neighbourhood.

B says he is sure 'I shall prosper more than any man who depends on farming in the country'. His whole ambition is 'to keep on as I am doing'. But doubts have appeared. 'Today no Native can say he is permanent in an urban area, since we are being deported every day without a reason. Any thoughtful Native sees trouble when he thinks of the laws affecting us in urban areas.' Accordingly, he has sent his children to the country to his younger brother 'to learn country life', and has decided that 'my country home must not be neglected entirely. If things turn against me I will simply have to sell out here and go back there.'

C is a man of 50 with standard IV education. He was born into a well-to-do Methodist family not far from King William's Town and established a prosperous homestead of his own after marriage. Financial difficulties drove him to East London, however, and he brought his wife and children with him. He worked as a storeman; his wife was in domestic service. The country home was allowed to disintegrate altogether. 'I had no more stock, my lands were allotted to other people. Today there is nothing on the spot to show that once a well-established kraal stood there.' He had 'left the country for good'.

In town C bought a three-roomed house where his seven daughters grew up. One after another they became old enough to work, 'and there was no difficulty at all about maintaining the household, for they all helped me'. The daughters all married and settled in East London.

'I am in a great dilemma now because the new regulations in East London make one think of the country.' His specific fear is that 'we are going to be transferred to the new location where I shall have to pay monthly rent', and also that 'when people become unemployed they are often sent away from the urban area'. The wife and the sons-in-law, however, do not agree with him that it would be wisest to return to the country immediately and start building up a new homestead. One son-in-law has offered him a partnership in his fruit shop and comforting assurances 'that he will look after my wife if I die first'. C's mind is not finally made up yet: 'Perhaps after all it is better to stay than to go back and start from nothing in the country. I am old to start a new life. I may stay and struggle here in town like the other old men.' But of one thing he is sure: 'Had I known that things were to be made so difficult in town I would never have neglected what I had in the country.'

PART FOUR

WOMEN AND CHILDREN IN THE MIGRANT SITUATION

15

Girls and Women in Town

The preponderance of males usually associated with migrant-labour centres applies in East London only to the older part of the population, and is offset by a preponderance of females among younger people. For the East Bank Location (1955) the masculinity ratio was reckoned at 140:100 in the age-group 40–49, but 103:100 in the 30–39 group and only 78:100 in the 20–29 group. The total ratio for all ages, for the locations as a whole, was just under 100:100. To this it must be added that female domestic servants (not resident in the actual locations) apparently outnumbered male servants by about ten to one. It is clear therefore that the flow of country-born women into East London exceeds (if anything) that of men, for the town-born population itself is demographically normal.[1] It is also clear that a majority of them are unattached women, since relatively few male migrants can or do bring their wives with them to town. This chapter is concerned with the unattached women.

School women seem to predominate on the whole. Among the older women the field-worker can easily collect Red samples; but if he wants to interview Red girls he has to hunt for them, while School girls are in evidence everywhere. Reader has data suggesting that only 17 per cent of the non-town-born female population as a whole is Red.[2] Other indirect confirmation comes from the respective figures for Xhosa and Mfengu. Mfengu people are predominantly School and their masculinity ratio in East London is only 87 per 100; whereas the masculinity ratio for Xhosa—the category including the great majority of Red migrants—is 104 per 100.

TOWN AND THE STATUS OF WOMEN

Town can be expected to attract people who have little to lose in the country. If this applies to certain categories of men—dispossessed farm servants, drought-stricken peasants, unhappy or deviant personalities—it tends to apply even

---

[1] For demographic data cf. Reader: *The Black Man's Portion*, chapter 3.
[2] Based on responses to a question about religion. Those replying 'Ancestor religion' or 'no religion' were taken to be Red. As remarked in chapter 4 above, judging by this criterion is likely to produce an underestimate of the Red proportion.

more widely among women, whose disabilities in the rural social system are more pervasive and general. Even the most fortunate rural woman has to go through a long period of subjection to men and to older women; the least fortunate, such as widows and unmarried mothers, may suffer deprived status permanently. Many Xhosa women seem to use East London as a semi-permanent escape. Most agree that it is a place 'to be free', 'to be independent', 'to get away from the rule of the people at home'. In different terminology, women have reason to like this new environment where status depends less on ascription and more on achievement.

That females *can* be more independent in town all Xhosa, both male and female, both Red and School, seem to agree: but how this independence is valued remains another question. Neither Red nor conservative School men like the idea of an emancipated woman, other than the senior woman who is acting head of a homestead. It is realized that when girls and women can 'run away to town' the whole structure of the patriarchal family and the maintenance of its basic values is threatened.

That women and girls can keep their own economic and social footing, not by virtue of their relations to men, but in their own right—this of course is one of the great novelties of town life as compared with the Xhosa countryside. Living in the country means, both for Red and for School people, living in a domestic unit that is defined patriarchally. The woman's right to live in an *umzi* (homestead) depends upon her relationship to some man, alive or dead. The definition of her household duties also depends on this indirectly, in so far as this determines her seniority relative to the other females of the homestead. Moving to town frees her from both the men and the senior women. Age and sex distinctions, without ceasing to be relevant in interpersonal relations, lie much lighter as a whole. At least money may be earned, lodgings hired and property acquired, regardless of sex, seniority or marital status.

Prima facie one might expect many Xhosa women to break away from rural society permanently, but it must be considered how to define the break, to identify the 'real home' of a husbandless woman. Property-rights in the country, which are a good index of country-rootedness in the case of men, hardly apply. Under communal tenure women cannot inherit land, though widows may retain the use of their deceased husbands' fields. The transfer of land to unmarried women, e.g. daughters with illegitimate children, is frowned upon by the authorities.[3] On quitrent land there is theoretically no legislation to prevent a woman from acquiring land by purchase, but it has been official policy to prevent such acquisition.[4] Town, in fact, is the only place where women can acquire real property. A woman can earn money which, though it could not buy her an *umzi*, can buy her a location house or shack.

In judging whether a woman is giving up her country-rootedness, perhaps one should regard her 'residence right' as the closest parallel to a man's property right. As men can hope to inherit or acquire an *umzi*, women can hope to marry into one, or else remain acceptable in the parental one. The question of whether a woman hopes or aspires to become the 'wife of a homestead' is therefore relevant, and also the question what close kin she has in the country and how much effort she makes to keep a 'home' open with them. A younger woman or girl would, for example, have to send a proportion of her earnings home, instead

---

[3] Mills, E., and Wilson, M.: *Land Tenure*, pp. 18, 24, 124, *Keiskammahoek Rural Survey*, vol. IV.
[4] Ibid., p. 148.

of spending them for personal gratification; to obey the senior kin whenever they may require her to go back home; to avoid attachments to people who would involve her too closely in town life, including would-be lovers or husbands; to be willing to send children home so that they can be brought up by the grandparents and lend a hand in the homestead.

As a woman grows older her closest ties in the country are less likely to be with her parents, more likely with siblings or her own children. Her closest ties in town, at any time, are likely to be with the most regular lover or husband-substitute, and/or her children.

By such tests as these, relatively few of the women in East London appeared to be country-rooted exclusively. While a few Red women were found to remain incapsulated like Red men, the temptations to develop important interests in town seemed less easy for them to resist, and a more usual pattern was the doubly rooted one. The woman has not cut herself off from the country decisively, but she stays on in town and admits to enjoying life there more than life in the country. There were other women, both Red and School, who had let slip their rural anchors, and had drifted into a town-rooted existence, in which *inter alia* they were rearing children as recruits to the community of the town-born.

GIRLS AND 'AMANKAZANA'

As wives are not under discussion here, two female categories have to be considered, namely girls (*iintombi*) and maturer non-marriageable women (*amankazana*). Definition of these categories is necessary.

Every Xhosa girl is initially an *intombi* (pl. *iintombi*), and as long as she does not pass out of this category she is still, technically speaking, marriageable. The *intombi* stage may be terminated in either of two ways. One way is by marriage, which promotes her to the status of wife(*inkosikazi*), whether through Native marriage (*umdudo*) or through church marriage (*umtshato*). The other way (principally for Red women) is by entering into the status of *inkazana*, in which—although unmarried—she is permitted to have full sexual relations and bear children.

Inkazana (pl. *amankazana*) is often translated by some English word with a strongly sexual referent, such as 'concubine', but another of its meanings, equally basic, is that of a woman who, being ineligible for marriage, will not bear children out of her parental home. She and her children (if any) will always belong there, will never be transferred to another homestead or lineage.

Sometimes a woman who has actually been married returns to her parental home to live there henceforth as an *inkazana*. In town, *inkazana* is applied to some widows and deserted or runaway wives, who are living as concubines with married or unmarried men. Strictly speaking, however, a woman who has once been married is always entitled to the status and appellation of a wife (*inkosikazi*), even if she chooses to play the role of an *inkazana*. The *inkazana* in the strictest sense is the woman who remains outside marriage. It is rare for a man to marry one, even one with whom (as often happens in town) he lives together 'as man and wife' for many years. Once an *inkazana*, always an *inkazana*, is the general rule.

Amankazana are socially equated with mature people as against the immature and the unmarried. An *inkazana* dresses like a woman, not like a girl, and is accorded seniority over unmarried girls. She is supposed to associate sexually with mature men (including married men), never with boys or unmarried youths.

In discussing Red Xhosa attitudes towards pregnancy of the unmarried, one must always remember to distinguish between *iintombi* and *amankazana*. Pregnancy of an *intombi* is a severe disgrace. It destroys the girl's chances of honourable marriage and automatically relegates her to the status of *inkazana* for the future. But a woman who is already an *inkazana* may go on bearing children without further reproach.

In itself the status of *inkazana*, while less dignified than that of a wife, is by no means to be despised. Many Red women become *amankazana* for not dishonourable reasons, such as reaching their late 20's without being sought in marriage or returning to the parental kraal after a marriage which has been found insupportable. In such cases there would be no disgrace even about the first pregnancy.

Among School people the position is different. According to the Christian sexual ethic, the *inkazana*—who by definition is not married, but has sexual relations, preferably with married men—combines in her own person the two sins of fornication and adultery. The word *inkazana* is rarely heard among School people, except in a pejorative sense. The fact remains that many School girls—probably far more School than Red girls—do become pregnant while still young and under full parental control.[5] And many of these go on, like the Red *amankazana*, to have a succession of illegitimate children. If they are not to be termed *amankazana*, they have got to be fitted into the social structure under some other guise. There would seem to be two alternatives: they can act as if they were still girls, or as if they were already wives.

The former solution is, on the whole, the more approved. Church authorities in particular do not condemn an unmarried mother for still claiming to be a girl, but they may condemn her for trying to pass herself off as the lawful wife of her child's father. The churches also affect the situation through their rulings about the *iimanyano* (women's and girls' circles attached to churches). In most church denominations there is a clear separation of 'girls' and 'mothers', each category having its own *umanyano* with distinct uniform and separate meetings. In most churches a young unmarried mother, after a period of suspension from the girls' *umanyano*, will be received back into it, not made to graduate to that of the mothers. Even two or three children are not necessarily a bar.

Church teaching, again, encourages the view that a girl who has had a 'fall' is not unmarriageable; she had better marry than continue having further 'falls' as a multiple unmarried mother. Here the Christian and Red evaluations are significantly different, the Red people not finding it proper that the status of wife should ever be accorded to a 'fallen' girl.

The classifying of School unmarried mothers together with girls is made easier by the fact that many of them are very young in years. School girls often give birth in their teens, while Red girls rarely allow themselves to conceive (and so launch out on the career of *inkazana*) until they are too old for marriage, in their middle or late 20's. This is directly related to School people's abandonment of the *metsha* (external intercourse) technique, which Red people consider proper for young girls.

It is in town that the confusion of unmarried mothers and girls among

[5] Cf. chapter 2.

School people reaches its peak. Being socially classified together with 'virgins' in the country is one thing; pretending that one actually *is* a 'virgin' is another. For School people, who do not stick close to *amakhaya*, town life can be truly anonymous, and motherhood easily concealed. The child is left with the mother's own parents at the country home; the voice of the home community does not follow a School girl into town as it follows a Red girl. One who is a little older may pass herself off as a 'widow' for town purposes.

The tendency of School unmarried mothers to extend their own girlhood—as against the Red mothers who accept the maturity of *amankazana*—is often mentioned by Xhosa. Red people strongly disapprove. 'Among us Red people a girl who once had a baby has no right to carry on friendships with virgin girls, but the School girls let *amankazana* go around with them and attend their social gatherings. I should not like to be a School girl!' School people are not always easy about it either—still less about the trick so common in town, of 'pretending to be a virgin'.

Girls' reasons for coming into town can now be discussed, and afterwards the reasons of mature women.

REASONS WHY GIRLS COME TO TOWN

Neither Red nor School peasant families normally expect their young daughters, as they expect their young sons, to go to town to earn money. The daughter's role is to stay at home and then get married. She discharges her economic obligations to the homestead first by working at it, under her mother, and then by earning bridewealth for it.

If a young girl absolutely must earn, the Red families—in particular—usually prefer her to do seasonal work (e.g. pineapple-picking) on White-owned farms not too far away. Such work, undertaken by a number of girls in a gang, is thought of as relatively harmless, though it is sometimes said that 'too many pregnancies' result. But East London is another matter. Country parents, both Red and School, distrust it profoundly as a place where 'girls get spoilt', and mere financial reasons are not supposed to count compared with the threat to the girl's virtue. Except with some educationally ambitious School families who send their daughters in to East London for high-school education (not normally available in country districts), there is no decent reason for kinsmen to encourage or even permit a young girl to go to town, short of a real emergency. Thus a girl who was in town by permission—as distinct from one who had run away or forced her way—would generally tell a story of crisis: 'I have to help my old mother and my sisters, for my father has died, and I have no brothers. I have to earn clothes for us. Mother said I may come.' 'Both my parents died at Nqamakwe. My elder brother is away working in Cape Town. The only relative who could take charge of me is my father's sister, who is employed here in East London.' 'My mother is elderly, my only brother is deaf and dumb. We are really very poor at home.'

A parent who lets a daughter go to East London usually insists that first she should stay with some senior relative or other family acquaintance, and then get herself a job as a living-in domestic servant. It is fondly believed by the country mother that at both these stages there will be some control over the girl's movements. But experience shows that in many cases this hardly delays the almost inevitable pregnancy. The more worldly-wise among the country parents realize that there is nothing they can do about it.

In the Red section any girl who goes to town, unless for a brief visit only, seriously compromises her chances of marrying. She needs to stay at home during her brief marriageable years if she wants to be married, for unlike a youth she cannot be married *in absentia*: marriage will require her actual removal to the husband's homestead. But over and above this, Red girls who go to town become suspect as loose livers. It is assumed that all girls have sexual relations in East London as in the country, with the difference that country limitations cannot be enforced in East London. There will have been no supervision by the girl's kin or age-mates; no guarantee of her limiting herself to *metsha* as against full intercourse, or to one lover at a time as against many; no fear of the parents' wrath to keep her lovers from impregnating her.

The loss of eligibility at home is not offset by new chances of marriage encountered in town. Lovers whom the Red girl may find in town may be culturally suitable Red men, but hardly any of them—even of the unmarried ones—will be likely to end by marrying her, unless there is some connexion within the home society as well. As has been said, the parents of a Red young man would hardly countenance the introduction into their *umzi* of a bride who was simply 'picked up in town'. The essence of proper Red marriage is the formal transfer of a girl from one homestead to another, and the parents have the last word, and often the first.

Thus Red girls who go to East London cannot well find husbands either there or at home, and are felt to be all set for the career of *amankazana*. This displeases the senior kin, if not for prestige reasons, then for bridewealth reasons. Loss of potential bridewealth cattle is a serious matter in a Red peasant family. 'Town is a bad place where marriage cattle get lost.'

Town does not seem to interfere with a School girl's marriage prospects as directly as with those of a Red girl. It may even extend them. Rural School men do not necessarily fight shy of girls with town experience as possible wives, and many actually prefer them, as being more 'up to date'. In town, too, a School girl may find a town-born husband, or a School husband from another rural district. Such marriages are less unthinkable in School peasant families. Some School migrant men said approvingly that 'you can make discoveries in town', i.e. find a wife superior to the girls at home.

The argument about bridewealth being lost, in so far as it applies, does not mean the same in economic terms to a School as to a Red family. The Red family regards the marriage cattle as a real access of wealth, even after the customary distribution and deductions for gifts and entertainment. But the School family benefits little or nothing by the marriage payment for its daughter, for School custom tends to convert this from a true bridewealth to an indirect dowry. The parents will use the money (or sell the cattle if paid in kind, and use the proceeds) to buy all the things a School bride is expected to bring into her new home: furniture, crockery, sewing-machine, and so on. This change of emphasis has much weakened one of the moral pressures which a girl's senior kin used to be able to exercise in regard to her pre-marital conduct; indirectly, it weakens the sanctions against her going to town.

But if School parents' views on their daughters' going to town are less directly concerned with marriage prospects than those of Red parents, there remain similar general objections on the grounds of 'going to the bad'. The School girl, not unlikely to have a premarital child even if she stays at home,[6] becomes

[6] Cf. chapter 2.

far more likely to have one once she goes to town. It is undoubtedly more honourable and convenient for one's daughter to get married as a 'virgin', i.e. without having borne a child. Or if she has one illegitimate child already, it is certainly undesirable for her to have a second, third or fourth, which will be very likely to happen in town. One advantage of delaying the daughter's childbearing until after her marriage is that responsibility for her offspring will then be placed somewhere else. Premarital children often become a burden to the mother's parents, with what may be sporadic contributions from the mother's own earnings. A husband is not expected to take responsibility for his wife's premarital children by other men, and whatever the girl herself contributed while she was still unmarried, she will become less likely to contribute when provided with the status and duties of another man's wife.

So much for the official reasoning, the parents' reasoning, which leads them, whether Red or School, to be wary of their daughters going to town. The motivations of the girls themselves may be very different.

The Red peasant girls, with relatively few exceptions, seem willing to obey; witness the scarcity of marriageable Red girls in the locations. Rather more Red young girls are found as domestic servants living on employers' premises, but these are mostly of farm, not peasant, origin. They tend to be concentrated in the West Bank suburbs, where they can keep in close touch with their near-by farm-homes.

Sometimes, however, a Red girl was found who said she had run away to town in defiance of her family, perhaps with a girl-friend of the same age. 'We came to town so that we could earn all the time, unlike the work we used to do together for the farmers, a few months a year. We came to the husband of my father's brother's daughter, who is here in town, and told him a lie, saying that our mothers had agreed on our coming here because of the better pay.' The stated motives usually included a desire for 'freedom' in one form or another. It might amount to desire to break away from Red life altogether, as with a young girl from the King William's Town district: 'All my family are Red and I am the only one who went to school, where I passed standard VI. Then my father wanted me to strip off my School clothes and become Red again. In this I did not want to obey him, for what he was after was to get me married quickly. I disappeared and ran away to town. I shall go to night-school here and I want to pass my Junior Certificate and become a nurse.' This handsome and determined girl was still governed by the Red sexual code and insisted that she would not allow herself any lovers in town. Others, less scrupulous, seemed to look forward to enjoying sexual freedom there as a prime consideration. An 18-year-old Red girl grumbled about the 'very strict' chaperonage exercised by her father's sister with whom she was staying in East London and who 'is not too pleased about my having come'. The girl complained that she can sleep with her lover only once a week, for an hour in the afternoon, as she always has to get home early.

Some Red girls were found to have run away to town in revolt against the traditional right of the parents to marry them off without their consent. Among Red Xhosa this right takes an extreme form. Parents can privately authorize a suitor's kin to *thwala* their daughter, that is, take her by surprise somewhere in the bush and carry her off by force to the suitor's home, where she will be made to put on the clothes and insignia of a newly married wife. This form of 'marriage by capture' is liked by some parents since, among other reasons, it saves them the heavy expense of a formal wedding (*umdudo*). But it is essential that the girl must be unaware of the plan beforehand. At the least she is kept unaware of the day and place fixed for her capture; at the most she does not know for which 'husband' she is being captured, and may never have set eyes on him. It is not uncommon for a *thwala* bride to run away the same day, or try hard to run away, and if she has a sweetheart of her own she may choose this moment to elope to him. East London is a welcome refuge for these thwarted lovers.

A Red woman now in her 30's said that as a girl she had a sweetheart who was working in East London. One day she noticed her father and uncle engrossed in private discussion with two strange men. When a bottle of brandy changed hands she 'became nervous, realizing that this could have no other meaning than marriage. . . . I questioned my mother but she only told me not to be inquisitive.' Next day four men *thwala*'d her as she was drawing water from the river on her mother's orders. She met her new husband for the first time and found him 'old enough to be my father'. Running away the same night, she boarded a train for East London; she was still in her Red clothes. 'Here I found my sweetheart and told him of my escape. How pleased he was! Since then we have been living together as husband and wife; he has paid *lobola* to make peace with my parents.'

Turning to the School girls one finds a different picture. It is no longer a question of occasional runaways but of hordes of young girls, from the age of about 17 onwards, coming into town deliberately, with or without their parents' consent. Many School girls live in the locations, mostly under the protection of their lovers; many others are living on White employers' premises. It does not take a specific quarrel or crisis at home to send the School girl townwards. She is usually running towards something she likes, and not only away from something she dislikes. Of all the types of migrant Xhosa in East London it was these young School girls who had evidently started out with the most favourable preconceptions. Many said that they 'specially liked the thought of town'; 'came because I thought it would be nice here'.

The idea of earning and spending one's own money holds a particular charm for School girls. Among Red people, money is mainly an interest of men and of mature, economically responsible women. But School girls have personal wants of their own which can only be satisfied through the medium of money. Most of them are keen on clothes to an extent which a Xhosa rural family can ill afford. Going to town, for what the kin at home hope will be a limited period, is often expressly related to this: 'I came to town to dress myself' is a stereotyped formula. 'When you come to town, the money you earn is all your own, and you can buy what you like with it, unlike the country where you work hard all day and hardly see any money for it.' The School girl who is keen on money has an initial advantage in that she usually knows a little English, which gives her a wider choice of jobs in East London.

Sometimes the resentments against the home life, as with Red girls, were formulated in terms of a particular battle of wills. 'My father was trying to make me marry a man I didn't like, a man without education—indeed he was of Red background—and I am going to stay here in town until the *lobolo* he paid has been returned to him.' But often enough there was nothing specific, just a general complaint that the country life which the parents favoured for their daughter is 'dull', 'old-fashioned', 'without enjoyment'. It must be remembered that a young girl in a School peasant home tends to be allowed fewer pleasures than a Red girl. The morality of the School home—at least the one to which the parents pay lip-service—stresses the importance of temperance and chastity, and the sinfulness (for girls) of lapses from a prudish sexual code. Parents' attempts to enforce 'Christian standards' on their daughters may easily lead to tension. 'My father would not let me attend any social gatherings which took place after dark, and he would drive off any young men who came to our home to chat with my brothers. He always suspected that their real motive was to make love to us girls. Sometimes he was right, but often they were quite innocent. This was a thing I did not like about my home.' 'There is life in town, and by life I mean pleasures', said another young School girl.

In the 'dull' country the School girl is able to form a picture—however distorted—of other lives which go on in the world outside, particularly in cities and among sophisticated people: a picture gleaned from school-books, from newspapers and illustrated magazines, and above all from the tempting accounts of her age-mates who have been in town themselves. 'Girls who had been in East London before, told me the most interesting things about it, especially the freedom that one enjoys there—a room to yourself, and earning money and buying anything you like.'

If the mass movement of School girls into East London reflects (as it seems) their own inclinations, as against parental or social expectation, it illustrates a general trend mentioned before—that School parents seem to find more difficulty than Red parents in controlling their own children. 'Discipline' will not necessarily keep the girls at home as in the Red family where thrashings are the accepted order of the day. Red parents are strict by divine right; the strictness of School parents is open to question by their offspring as just another irksome old-fashioned trait. Even the mothers, sometimes, desert to the side of their daughters. 'My mother was opposed to my father on grounds that he was too strict. She used to explain that by being too strict one just makes the children want the forbidden things all the more. My father's excessive strictness is one of the things which has made me come to town.'

REASONS WHY WOMEN COME TO TOWN

Going to town as a woman—mother, widow, *inkazana*—is more socially acceptable by rural standards than going as a girl. All Xhosa, whether Red or School, think that town is quite a suitable place for mature females who have no primary claim on either father or husband in the country. On the one hand they can be entrusted with the conduct of their own lives. 'They are not children any more. We can let them make their own decisions.' And on the other hand their removal from the country scene may be a relief to those who stay behind.

(a) Widows

Widows are at a disadvantage in both Red and School families. It must be remembered that as the Xhosa peasant economy depends on wage-earnings as a necessary supplement to agriculture, the loss of the husband's earnings may cripple the widow economically. The luckiest is an elderly or old widow who can carry on as *de facto* head of her late husband's kraal, with her adult son to contribute as wage-earner.

Problems both economic and social face the widow of a man who was neither homstead-head nor heir to a homestead, but only a junior member. Her status is anomalous in itself. The Xhosa have no institutionalized levirate and seem never to have had one. Jural obligations and the function of guardian can pass to an elder brother of the deceased, but sexual privileges cannot. The widow may have love affairs with other (non-related) men but must conduct them discreetly 'to respect the husband's relatives'. This sharp division between the jural and the sexual succession does not seem to be comfortable for the widow. Sometimes a young widow with a growing son makes a special effort to hang on at her late husband's place because she 'does not like to take her boy away to another place where he has no inheritance'. But many widows who are still young choose to go back to their own parents' home. Here the sexual freedom is greater, but the widow's presence may soon become an irritant similar to that of a mature unmarried daughter, with status rivalries vis-à-vis the 'wives of the kraal'.

For School widows there is an added complication as regards the taking of lovers. The Christian expectation that a widow should remain chaste (short of remarriage) runs directly counter to the Xhosa expectation that she should have regular and authorized lovers. This clash of two moralities has never been resolved. Young School widows in the country do, in many cases, take lovers, like their Red counterparts, but with an extra burden of shame and secrecy.

Red or School, the woman seeking escape from the disabilities of a widowed life in the country was found to be a common figure in East London. 'Town is the best place for a widow like me.' 'I could not support myself at home once my husband had died. I put the two cows and some fowls under the care of a senior relative, and said I must come to East London at least for a short time.' 'My husband's death ended my life at his homestead. I did not like returning to my own people's place, for both my father and my mother had died, and the homestead head was now my younger brother. I could not stay there to be under children.' 'I was 25 when my husband died and left me with two young children. There was nobody to support us except my own mother who works in Johannesburg. When my younger child was weaned I left both children with my mother's sister and came here as a domestic servant.' 'After my husband's death I first tried staying on at his place with his elder brother and family. The wife of this elder brother bullied me, and used to order me about as if she were a mother-in-law instead of only a sister-in-law. Here in East London I can work and support my little son.' 'I struggled from 1953 to 1957 to continue life at my late husband's homestead. Since I had nobody to help me it was extremely difficult. In the end I left my three children with my own brother and came here.'

This is one side of the picture: the irritation caused to the rest of the household by the widow's presence is another. 'To be a widow in the country', said one informant bitterly, 'is to be made responsible for all the misfortunes of the neighbourhood. A widow is always being suspected.'

Similar to the disabilities of being a widow in the country are those of being a divorced wife, or—what is commoner among Xhosa—a wife who has deserted or been deserted without formal divorce. Such women can go back to their parental homes where they are allowed to take lovers; but going to town offers more hopeful prospects for independence.

(b) Unmarried mothers

In this large category a difference of emphasis was found as between the Red and the School women.

Red unmarried mothers in town dwelt on the shame and disgrace which pregnancy had brought upon them in the country. One said that she had been seduced by a man who was married and could not marry her, but paid five head of cattle as the customary damages. She stayed at home only until the child was weaned. 'My chances of getting married were very small indeed, as I was now *inkazana*. I could no longer mix with the girls of my own age, which made me very unhappy. All these thoughts pushed me away from home. I felt I must go to town.' Above all there is the anger of fathers, brothers, and senior kin generally. A second Red woman said she had come to town as soon as the child was weaned 'because of the unhappiness at home. My father's brothers and my own brothers were annoyed with me all the time.' A third was an orphan who grew up under the care of her mother's brother. As a senior girl she was seduced by a young man. He never paid customary damages but ran away to Johannesburg instead. 'As a result my home life became very unhappy. Neither my uncle nor any of the family were ever kind to me as soon as my pregnant condition was known.'

Such strong arguments of disgrace were rarely heard from School unmarried mothers. Occasionally a very respected School family will have taken its daughter's pregnancy hard: 'I was rendered pregnant while still in standard IV and this early pregnancy came as a great surprise to all who knew the N family well. We are very much respected at home. I became very unhappy and secretly decided to run to town.' (It may be added that this informant became pregnant again almost immediately after she reached East London.) But on the whole, the School girl can live down the shame at home. Anger and protest about a 'fall' in a School family will be sharp rather than long-lived. Pregnancies of girls are so common that School parents have come to accept them in a sense, and the daughters know exactly how to behave during the temporary fury.

Nor is their position so anomalous vis-à-vis their age-mates as that of the Red girl who has had a pregnancy. At the worst the School unmarried mother may sometimes not feel quite at ease with the 'virgins' of her age. 'She will not dare to say much, and has to control her tongue for fear at being snubbed as an *inkazana*.' At the great occasions in the life of rural locations, such as singing competitions, she may think it better not to join her local team: 'The relatives of "virgins" do not like it if their location is represented to outsiders by girls like her.' Her own parents too may advise her 'not to make a fool of herself' by joining in. But the local community usually includes several other girls in the same position, and they are all accepted among their age-mates in due course, and readmitted to social gatherings.

Hence it may not be so much the disgrace which drives a School unmarried mother to town, as the positive hope of making a new start, supporting her child, and perhaps finding a new lover.

Both School and Red unmarried mothers often said that they had run off to town to join the father of their child. Sometimes it was an arranged elopement, sometimes the lover sent for the woman and sometimes she came without telling him beforehand. 'I decided to follow the man who had rendered me pregnant', said a Red woman of 25. When she arrived in town she shared accommodation with some women of her own age from home. 'I expected them to know the whereabouts of my lover. I was in fear of town women, and asked my home women to inform my lover that I was about. He might be staying with a town woman who might be a dangerous sort.' The lover came to fetch her, and they are still staying together under *ukushweshwa*. Cases of pre-arranged elopement with lovers sometimes shade over into a kind of *thwala* marriage. But for both Red and School couples the majority of these affairs seem to end in an *ukushweshwa* arrangement rather than in marriage.[7]

THE TENDENCY TO STRIKE ROOTS IN TOWN

In one way or another, then, most women and girls who come to town feel they have 'more future there than in the country'. To this extent they have the strongest motives for staying and making good. It is true that a return to rural life would usually be less difficult for a woman than for a man. If he is ever to go back to the country, a man needs a right to the use of land, whereas a woman needs only some kin who are willing to receive and befriend her. Some women, defeated by town, do go back to relatives in the country; some are pulled back by the thought of the children they have left there. But going back again means embarrassment, and the necessity to take up again a kind of life that was found irksome before.

The women's tendency to become town-rooted (or at least doubly rooted) was particularly noticeable in the Red section because of its contrast with the men's attitude. Whereas the average Red man spoke longingly of 'going home' and hoped to bring his retirement as near as possible, the Red woman often expressed herself as perfectly content with a life in town. 'Why should I be anxious to go home?' asked a Red unmarried mother of 32, who works as a pineapple packer. 'I am a woman, a mother, but I am not married. I have no homestead of my own. If I went home I would be under orders from my brother or his wife. Here in East London I am free. I do as I please. I have my own room. My lover is at liberty to come and sleep with me at my room, or I can go and sleep with him at his. You cannot find such freedom in the country. There, your lover will have to walk on his toes if he visits you at night.'

Town has been seen to confer two new freedoms on a woman—to earn money, and to consort freely with lovers. Both these freedoms have to be discussed with reference to their bearing on urbanization; but first the earning of money.

A woman can earn money in East London either by accepting employment in the White-dominated economy (as a domestic servant or in some industrial or commercial undertaking) or else by carrying on a business enterprise within the locations. Both these ways of earning seem to have a tendency to 'urbanize' women, in one sense or another, more effectively than the men's jobs are likely to 'urbanize' men. To make a broad generalization, one may say that the women's paid employment is very often of a kind (domestic service) which fosters new cultural aspirations; while their self-employment within the location is very often of a kind whose rewards are substantial enough to constitute a strong town-located interest.

(a) Employment and urbanization

Red and School girls compete for domestic and factory work, but School girls have some additional openings. A girl who is literate in English and/or Afrikaans may become, say, a waitress in a White café or boarding-house, or a

[7] Cf. chapter 16 below.

shop assistant in the poor North End district. Such jobs are rated somewhat higher than domestic service, though they do not necessarily pay better in terms of real wages. There are two particular occupations which rate much higher still and also pay far better, namely teaching and nursing, but both of these are restricted to a small, highly educated fraction of the School female population.

With the exception of factory work, the common run of women's employments are such as to develop or encourage town-style personal habits and wants. In the case of domestic service the living-quarters are furnished in some semblance of White style, and the employer sets a premium on the servant's accurate understanding of White domestic habits. Over and above any pressure from the employer, the consumer goods which constantly have to be handled and viewed, whether in a home or in a shop or café, seem to exert an influence of their own: not only on the School girl who already had a penchant for them, but on the Red girl fresh from her ochred skirts and rough rustic surroundings. From Red as well as School girls came comments like the following, showing that personal aspirations as well as external pressures are involved: 'I do like the White people's clothes, and the kind of food they eat.' 'I like being a domestic servant, for besides earning money, I am also learning how to keep a house nicely.'

What enables these cultural pressures to have full play on Red girls is the absence of any incapsulating social circle like that which surrounds the average male Red migrant. The conditions of domestic service are unfavourable both to incapsulation in town and to frequent home-visiting. There is no week-ending, for Sunday afternoon is the usual extent of the servant's free time. A fortnight's leave enables her to go home once a year, unless she throws up her job for the sake of going more often. At work she lives, usually, in a detached room at the end of her employer's garden or adjoining the garage. This situation, while it enables her to receive visitors fairly freely, prevents the formation of *amakhaya* clusters and the voluntary restriction of social contacts to people of one's own cultural background. She is thrown into the closest contact with other servants working in the same household, with whom she may have to share a room. She is likely to make friends among girls working near by, close enough for them to drop in and out of each other's rooms in off-duty hours. Her new friends often induce her to join one or other church. They also introduce her to School men, through whom she may be drawn further and further away from the Red life.

One class of Red servant girls in East London forms an apparent exception to the foregoing. In the West Bank suburbs one can see girls who look Red, and who clearly want to look Red. Many wear an interesting combination of town-style dress—often quite smart—with blatant symbols of Redness, such as heavy brass coils right up the forearm, or anklets and bracelets of brass wire; their doeks are brightly coloured and twisted up in the elaborate fashions of Red girls. But these girls, socially speaking, are not really 'in' town, for they come from farms only a few miles away, and are still effectively attached to their homes. A free Sunday afternoon is enough for such a girl to visit her farm-home; she travels by bus for a few pence, perhaps with her *intlombe* outfit in a parcel. It is because of its geographical nearness that the West Bank attracts these girls. The farm, not the location, is the place where they have their homes, parents and boy friends, for whose sake they remain Red.

Apart from these, a few Red peasant servant girls were found who had managed to remain anchored to their home community and their Red cultural standards. D is an example. She is about 23 and comes from Tsomo. Though able to visit home in person only once a year, at Christmas, she keeps up an active connexion: 'I ask friends to write letters for me. There are also *amakhaya* going home by train or taxi sometimes, to whom I give messages for my relatives and sometimes money to hand over.' In town, she submits to the guardianship of her mother's sister, who has been working in East London for some years, and who, she said, 'is watching my movements here. She visits me every day, or if not I go to her place.' D gives her free time to 'friends in the location who are other girls from my home'. On Sunday several of them meet in the room of one; they sing songs. Her best friend in town, T.R., also comes from Tsomo. Her father's father and D's mother's father are brothers. She also has no education. 'Most of the time when we are together we chat about home matters.' D has a regular man friend (married) who is from Tsomo; 'at home we buy from the same shop'. She has been sleeping in his room in the location 'whenever I can', but ceased to do so because of the arrival of his wife for a month or two over Christmas.

D has resisted the acculturating influences of town as far as can be managed in her kind of employment. She dresses like a School girl of the poorer type, but the kind of doek she wears indicates her Red background. She has 'never attended any dances, concerts or meetings, nor been to any bioscope'.

This case, though not unique, did not seem to be typical of the majority of Red servants. Another Red girl of 19, though in town for only nine months, showed that her loyalty to the Red way of life was no longer unquestioning. She was still giving most of her monthly pay to her brother to hand over to 'mama' at home; she still allowed a Red young man from her home area to regard himself as her lover; and she accepted—like a good Red girl—the moral guardianship of her employer's middle-aged cook. ('Whenever I disappear from the house for a while she asks me very searchingly where I have been, and I respect her for that.') But she admitted to finding life pleasanter in town, for the time being, than at home. When she was out of work for a while, she did not go home to see her mother, but stayed on in the location with a friend, 'because I enjoy being here very much'. She was dressed in good taste, like a well-educated School girl, and had discarded any outward signs of her Red background.

What applies to the Red girl applies with even greater force to the School girl. Her greater initial proficiency in 'civilized' ways gives her fuller opportunity to enter into new circles and new activities, while—very often—her predisposition in their favour, and her impatience with her home, give her stronger motives for doing so. These girls, if not soon town-rooted, can be very soon doubly-rooted. A girl with standard VI education from Shilo regards Shilo as her home, 'because my mother and sister are there', but at the same time she made it clear that she is well content to be away from home. She had been in town six months, looking for a job in a café, so far without success. Her mother had confided her to the care of an elder married sister: the attempts of the sister's husband to act as moral guardian were resented. 'He is of the old-fashioned type, and is against evening entertainments, saying that young girls learn all sorts of bad things there. It is his fault that I have only been twice to the bioscope since I came to town.' She much preferred the influence of her girl friend, S.H., who, though from the same rural home ('we played together as children'), was steadily drawing her towards town ways and involving her in a circle of town friends. The two went to 'concerts' together and attended various gatherings in the location together with their boy friends. (Each now had a sweetheart in town as well as one in the country.) S.H. had also introduced her to another girl friend who was born in East London.

(b) Self-employment and urbanization

In considering the women who make their livings by self-employment in the location, one is mainly considering the mature women. That is to say, while females of all ages take paid employment, the self-employed category includes few young girls. However, the Red people, who classify a girl as inkazana after her first child, are also ready to let her have the privileges of maturity that go with this status. Thus Red women may start off in independent business while still rather young. One unmarried Red mother aged 22 had already been in business for two years. 'The father of my child used to give me money for my support, and I used it for brewing beer, as assistant to another woman. He died in an accident and I decided to carry on with brewing, realizing that I could live by this business. I gave up all thoughts of being employed in town. I am working on my own now and my prospects are quite pleasing.'

Some women entrepreneurs liked to contrast their own independence with the dependence of the employed woman: 'The business is your own, the profit is your own, there is nobody to say to you "Hurry up!" Stand on your own feet, I say, do not be like a suckling baby!' 'Holding a hawker's licence, as I do, is better than being in the employ of anybody. I am satisfied. I feel that my amawethu (ancestral spirits) have been with me.' It was characteristic that several middle-aged women had something positive to say about life in East London which scarcely any Red man ever said, namely, 'If you are ambitious there are chances here to get rich'. Vegetable hawking, and the making and selling of fatcakes or the kind of bun called irostile, are common enterprises mainly in the hands of women, both Red and School. Some other businesses are mostly run by School women, e.g. dressmaking, sewing and mending, peddling secondhand clothes, and hawking meat and offal. There is general agreement, however, that to make 'real money' and make it quickly there is no better way than by selling liquor, and this is a women's business too. School women are no less involved than Red women.

That a widow or mature woman should undertake an economic enterprise of some sort—especially if it be brewing beer—is not strange in itself by country standards. Brewing is women's work in any case, and the regular sale of beer (imbara, 'bar') is now a feature of many peasant communities nearer town, though not an old Xhosa tradition. The 'bar' run by a woman might be called a common institutional pattern that runs through town and country life alike, at least in the Ciskei. The novelty in town is the greater scope and greater possibilities: brewing is no longer an adjunct to subsistence farming but can become an economic mainstay in its own right.

All these types of women's enterprises serve their necessary functions in the economic life of the locations, but the brewing business has a special social importance of its own. As has been seen, the entire social life of the Red migrants in town depends on beer, while School people also need their liquor suppliers who know how to observe the School convention of secrecy. Some women brew on a small scale and mainly for their own lovers with their *iseti*, but others build up a large clientele. Everyone seems to agree that in this business 'the competition is very strong compared with competition for jobs in town'. Success requires strong personality.

Women brewers have to cope with their customers, rough, half-drunk men; with their competitors; and last but not least (since the business is strictly illegal) with the police. Some are bold: 'I do not worry too much about the police. I am getting used to them. In order to be successful one has to be careful not to be arrested; but at the same time bold and undaunted.' Others are wily: 'I was friendly with the police. If they came near my room and I had no brandy, I would give them 10s. to buy anything they liked, so I was only arrested once for one half-bottle of brandy and I paid £5 Admission of Guilt.' In some of these women the pride of independence extended into the field of race relations and politics: 'Work hard, but make your own start quite independently of *uMlungu* [the White man].' One highly intelligent Red woman brewer of about 50 told us that 'the independence of the African people' was her 'day and night dream'.

But the businesses of the self-employed women, whether small or large, are hardly of a kind in which accumulated savings can well be reinvested. Because of this, and because of the necessarily precarious nature of illegal enterprise, nearly all self-employed women have the ambition to buy a wood-and-iron house as soon as they have saved enough. Owning a house in her own name may give a country-bred woman a very special satisfaction as well as an assured income. 'A house here is the best possession for an unmarried mother like myself. The property is registered in my own name and it is I who collect the rentals. There is no fear of a brother who, in the country, could claim anything that belonged to his unmarried sister. Here I can do what I like.' (Red woman, aged 32.)

As compared with self-employed women, few ex-domestic servants were found among the women houseowners. This cannot be entirely explained by relative earnings, for the domestic servant is normally fed and housed free, and can put her money wages to other uses. That it is economically possible for servants to acquire houses was proved by a School woman from Idutywa, who on the death of her husband twenty years ago 'came to East London, the place for widows' and found a job as cook. Her wages of £2 10s. 0d. a month were almost all saved up in the P.O. Savings Bank; lately her wages rose to £5 per month and she saved even faster. In 1950 she bought a house in Tulandivile for £140, 'built of good second-hand iron, with five big rooms'. There may conceivably be personality reasons why this remains rare among servants, i.e. the women with the initiative to buy their own property may be the ones inclined to go in for self-employment rather than service. At any rate, the landlady who made her fortune as a brewer appeared to be much more typical. X came to town from Qumbu in 1941, three years after her husband's death. She joined another Qumbu woman—Red like herself—who already had a beer and brandy business. After three months of helping this friend she found her own room and started her own business. 'Some of her customers came to drink in my room, and I also got new customers. On Fridays I would go to town and get an intermediary to buy me some bottles of brandy, which I would bring home concealed under my dress in preparation for week-end business. You become very popular if your customers know they can buy both kinds from you.' X soon opened a savings account at the Post Office. In 1948, after seven years, she was able to buy a nine-roomed house for £230.

How far does this life in East London as entrepreneur and/or property-owner conduce to urbanization? To begin with, the self-employed woman has a better chance to keep up her rural connexions by frequent home-visiting than the domestic servant. Further, she has more chance to remain incapsulated within a circle of her own choosing. She is not forced to mix intimately with non-Red workmates nor required by an employer to adopt urban dress and manners. And it has already been shown that a house property in town does not necessarily mean a home in town; it might be 'only a place by the wayside'.

Here and there, accordingly, a woman entrepreneur was found to have remained strongly attached to her country home, to be still discharging roles there, sending remittances to her kin, and making frequent regular visits. 'My real home is in the country, at my late husband's homestead. My late husband's elder brother looks after the land while I am away and his wife takes care of my children. I go home myself every month-end. I go other times too, whenever anything important requires my attention at home.' (Red widow.) 'I have no property of my own in the country, being a widow and having returned to my own people. I have left my children, including three sons, under the care of my mother. I regard her homestead as my real home, particularly because of my children. I am always there every month-end.' (School widow.)

For some women the economic prowess they have shown in town shines all the brighter for its reflected lustre at the country home: 'In the country I have my late brother's widow, and her sons and daughters, who have deep love and respect for me. They think I have plenty of money. I help them a lot in money matters.' 'My brother's son, at home in the country, will always be good to me, for he has one eye on my assets after my death.' (This woman has a Post Office savings account and a copy of her last will and testament.)

But such tendencies are more likely to indicate double-rootedness than exclusive country-rootedness. Normally these Red women did not, like the typical male Red migrant, lay *all* the moral emphasis on the continued ties with the rural community at home, and represent the town life simply as a necessary evil, a means to an end. Setting a high value on the business in town, and the independence which it affords, they appeared to prefer staying on in town 'for the time being'.

Some mature women referred to the comfort and convenience of town compared with the drudgery of a country homestead. 'Life is much easier here for a woman in my position', said a semi-invalid widow in her 50's. 'I do not have to go and collect firewood, for I use paraffin to cook my food. I do not have to carry water from the river—the tap is only a few steps from my door. The dairies are near by too: "Milk, milk!" I hear the milk boy shouting very early in the morning.' Many more emphasized their pleasure in 'being independent'. This was not only a point scored off the domestic servant in town—it was, and more importantly, a point scored off the women of similar age and status who stay at home in the country: 'In my hut at East London I am both the head and the wife. I do as I like. I have nobody to consult.' 'I do not like the idea of being under somebody else's rule. That is why I only go to visit my brother's family at Tshabo, and do not live there permanently.' 'A woman here is independent. You are free to do as you please. There are no homestead people watching you.'

In the pursuit of independence from home, many Red women in town were found to have turned their backs on their (parental or marital) *amakhaya*, or at least avoided seeking them out. Unlike the Red male houseowners who said they prefer to let their rooms to *amakhaya*, the landladies often disliked this. 'I do not wish that too much should be known at home of what I am doing in my room here.' The widow does not want to feel that her husband's people are still watching and carping; the unmarried mother, that her own people still try to control her movements. When she takes a man as sexual partner in town he is likely to be Red, but not from home. Similarly with other personal friendships. It is true that sometimes two women who had already been friends in the country were found to be friends in town too, perhaps running a business together. But often enough the 'best friend in town' was simply another woman in similar circumstances, without any common home background: 'My best friend is a Red woman about as old as myself; she is like me, too, in that she is a widow and has no education. Her home is at Qunira, somewhere in the Transkei way I believe.' 'We became friends through business. She would come to me every day to buy potatoes, cabbages, and onions on credit, and I would visit her to collect the money on Saturday.' An independent woman may be closely attached to a particular circle of *amakhaya* in town, but most likely these are not her own *amakhaya*. The link has been established through some man. As his town concubine or close friend, brewing beer for him or running his household, she is drawn into relations with his *iseti* and the rest of his group. Of course she is only a local hanger-on, and has no standing in the man's rural home community itself.

Many independent women emphasized that their participation in urban life had come to mean a great deal; here is their business, here alone is the possibility to maintain themselves by their own efforts. 'As far as I am concerned, I shall never leave off my business. If I did, who would look after my children? I shall die brewing here.' If in spite of all this they do not become real towns-women, and surrender the connexion with 'home', the reasons seem often to be bound up with the interests of their children. Either the children are actually in the country being reared by kin, or the mother intends them to live there when they are adult, for town cannot offer them the same degree of security. 'When my sons reach manhood I want them to be permanently settled in the country, and to have their own homesteads, land and cattle. Although I myself am happy here in town, I know that this happiness has no foundation. It is like a grass fire, which burns bright but does not last long.'

With Red women, over and above this, there often remains an emphasis on 'Red people' generally and an attachment to the values of Red culture. Those women who have been quoted as expressing their satisfaction at being in town did not necessarily aspire to the urban culture. Their lovers and friends, their tenants and customers, were all or mostly Red. Even the kind of Red landlady who did not want to be 'watched' by people from home would insist in no uncertain terms that she 'wants to have Red men in the house'. The Red people were still those she felt she could deal with: the non-Red those whom she still distrusted. Only women who were in the process of breaking away said that they 'take either Red or School tenants, as long as they pay'; only converts said that they 'prefer School people, of my own church'. Some appraised their urban success, itself, in terms of Red cultural concepts: 'I am satisfied here, for I am better off than many of my own people, Red people. I feel that I have not offended the spirits of my late husband.' 'I am financially well off here; I can say that my *amawethu* have looked after me.'

Red independent women may therefore be likened to Red farm people in that they tend towards an intermediate type of incapsulation. In this intermediate type, as compared with incapsulation proper, the bond of home is less stressed, but the network is still contained within the Red section of society. In addition, attachment to the *amakhaya* circle of some male friend may produce something very like the incapsulated atmosphere, in town. What this pattern does not provide for is the continued sense of 'belonging' in one's own rural community at home.

16

Sexual Partnerships

It has been shown that while most of the men who flock to town for work are parted from their wives, many of the women have lost or missed the benefit of marriage, as widows or as unmarried mothers. This conjunction of deprived men and unattached women in a tight-packed urban slum is bound to favour sexual liaisons. Such liaisons proliferate all the more on account of the Xhosa philosophy of sex. All Xhosa, including the Christians, regard sexual satisfaction as a normal requirement of every adult, whether married, unmarried or widowed. Sexual contacts (they feel) have to be regulated not because they are intrinsically evil or dangerous, but in order to avoid infringements of existing rights.

There is much sexual competition in the locations, though it does not follow a single pattern. In the younger age-groups there tend to be too many women chasing too few men; among older people the reverse. Red-School distinctions are also relevant. The Red section is the one where men most often have to compete for women's favours, not only because Red women are relatively few in town, but because the Red man rarely goes outside his own cultural section for his love affairs. The abundance of other kinds of women in town does nothing to offset the scarcity from his point of view. The older Red women, particularly if they were financially well established, often suggested that they could have their pick of men. 'I hope my present lover stays with me, but if he leaves me I will find another in his place.' The School people's problem, on the other hand, tends to be a problem of surplus women. Not only do non-Red females at the most sexually active ages considerably outnumber non-Red males: they are exposed to some competition from Red girls too, because non-Red men do sometimes like to take Red sweethearts. Some of the more educated School women referred to the surplus of females as a fact that justified them in 'forward' behaviour. The right to sexual gratification was implied as an axiom. 'I do it with a free conscience, because there are more women here than men', said an unmarried woman of high position—a teacher—who was having an affair with a married man of equally high position (a clerk in the Native Affairs Department).

In point of fact few Xhosa in East London, whether male or female, young or middle-aged, Red or School, need be deprived of sexual satisfaction in a physical sense. Although statistics may be against them, there is the saving fact that many people are prepared to 'carry on' with a number of sexual partners at various times, or even at the same time. However, it would be unfair to speak of promiscuity, except among certain sections, e.g. young men of a particular type, usually town-born, who notoriously 'go to a different one of their girl friends every day'. What the migrants would mostly prefer, especially as they grow older, is the satisfaction of a stable secure relation. It is not finding a lover, so much as keeping a lover, that causes the concern and heartache.

The lover tends to be relatively more important to a woman's than to a man's well-being in town. If to the average male migrant East London primarily means money, to the average female it means money and a lover. But, except in the cases where the woman runs to town expressly to be reunited with her (ex-rural) lover, her first consideration—almost always—is to work and earn her own living. To appreciate the sexual freedom of town is not the same as deliberately planning to pick up men there in order to be supported for nothing. It may be added that prostitution, as a regular means of subsistence, is hardly known in the locations.

That Xhosa regard town as a sexually immoral place has been indicated already. The accepted stereotype is that country people 'can control themselves' sexually, while in town 'people do just as they wish'. Yet sexual liaisons—outside marriage—are practised and tolerated in the country hardly less than in town. They are part of Xhosa tradition. It is not because fornication (as Christians would call it) arouses any horror in itself that town gets branded as an immoral place. Rather it is because of differences in etiquette and in the degree of supervision and regulation. The conventions proper to extra-marital affairs, the rules of fair-play (as country Xhosa see them) are apt to go by the board in town. This is the only sense in which one could properly speak of 'moral breakdown' in connexion with the sexual life of the locations.

The most significant symptoms of moral breakdown in the sexual life of town are two, according to Xhosa ideas. The first is the discarding of regulations by which country people (Red especially) try to prevent premarital sexual activity from resulting in pregnancies. This slackening is felt to contribute to the enormous illegitimate birth-rate for which town is notorious. The second arises from the fact that unmarried lovers, in town, can do something which is virtually impossible in the country, namely stay together under one roof as a domestic unit. This institution of migrants in town, the sharing of bed and board by unmarried partners, is known as *ukushweshwa*. (A politer term, preferred by School people, is *masihlalisane*, 'let us stay together'.) In School eyes, 'staying together' is intrinsically improper; in Red eyes it is decent enough but may easily lead to consequences which are regarded as immoral, viz. a man's neglect of his home and relatives in the country.

IMPREGNATION OF GIRLS IN TOWN

In the days when Xhosa girls were regularly inspected by senior women to ascertain if their virginity was still intact, the word *intombi* meant both girl and virgin. A girl whose hymen had been ruptured could be called *inkazana* (though in a general way the benefit of the doubt was extended to all girls who had had no pregnancy). However, the official Red morality, while still demanding virginity (unbroken hymen) until a girl marries or is old enough to turn *inkazana*, does not expect her to be sexually abstinent: nor did it in olden days. The object of inspection (a practice now almost obsolete) was to discourage girls from indulging in full sexual intercourse as against *ukumetsha*,[1] external intercourse. In *ukumetsha*—intercourse 'between the thighs' as Xhosa say—the girl is not supposed to take off her undergarments, and her technical virginity should be safe.

[1] This verb can also mean 'being lovers' in a generalized sense.

The rule is still current among Red Xhosa in the country that intercourse with penetration is only proper for wives and *amankazana* but that younger people can freely indulge in *ukumetsha*. This distinction is hammered into the awareness of the Red male from boyhood onwards. 'We are told', said a Red migrant of about 35, 'not to have our sexual relations with girls in the same way as with women who are married. First we heard this from senior boys, at the time when we were growing up. Then we would hear more of it from young men when we were old enough to discuss such matters with them. At circumcision further warnings would be given by the men.'[2]

Meanwhile the School people (as described in chapter 15) have come to extend the *intombi* concept to include young unmarried girls in general, even if they have had one or more illegitimate children. But English-speaking School people have made use of the existence of two separate English words, 'girl' and 'virgin', to express a distinction within the ranks of *iintombi*. 'Virgin', as used by them, does not mean being sexually untouched, but means having never become pregnant. This extension of meaning may appear ironic or comical to local White people, who perhaps see it as the telling reflection of hopelessly debased standards. It is not so much this, however, as the expression of a particular concept of chastity, logical within its own cultural setting.

It has been seen (chapter 15) that official School Xhosa morality gives strong preference to girls remaining 'virgins', in this extended sense, until they marry: i.e. a young girl's duty does not include refraining from sexual intercourse, but does include avoiding pregnancy. In contrast to the Red girl, however, she is given no clear guidance as to *how* pregnancy is to be avoided. *Ukumetsha* is out of fashion. It has been condemned by Church teaching as obscene, unnatural, and sinful, while at the same time the young School people themselves have learnt to disparage it as old-fashioned, 'dirty', and 'not much fun', compared with full intercourse. A School girl who wants to safeguard herself by limiting the sexual contact to *ukumetsha* will be stigmatized as 'blind' (old-fashioned). Her choice, then, is between complete abstinence (as enjoined by the Church) and full intercourse without benefit of contraceptive techniques (except *coitus interruptus*). Modern contraceptives are unknown unless to a tiny handful of highly Westernized women.

Then there are the town-born Xhosa. Their standard for both sexes, it appears, is to practise full intercourse from puberty onwards. Abstinence and *ukumetsha* are almost equally out of the question. This picture of uninhibited sexual relations is not simply a hostile migrants' stereotype. Town-born informants themselves confirmed it freely. They insisted that 'play' (*ukumetsha*) cannot possibly be a substitute. 'In these days both young and old, here in town, have full sexual intercourse. We do not even start with "play" as older people used to do at our age.' (Girl of 21, with illegitimate child.) 'In town children grow up having sexual relations as if they are married people. We hear about the country practice but we think it is a waste of time'. (Boy of 17.) 'Since I was 13

[2] Red women informants denied that *coitus interruptus* is generally known in Red country circles. Most said they knew of only two possibilities—*ukumetsha* where pregnancy is to be avoided, and normal intercourse where it is not. *Coitus interruptus* as a contraceptive technique was sometimes mentioned as 'a thing learnt in town'. 'Since going to town I have realized that what we were taught ourselves—that intercourse with penetration always leads to pregnancy —was only a device to make us control our behaviour while unmarried. However, I shall teach the same to my children. If they knew what I have discovered in town they might try it out. And then they might accidentally become pregnant, like the daughters of School people. I could never divulge it to older people at home either, for they would regard it as very immoral.'

I have felt the need for full sexual satisfaction, and not merely "playing" with girls. If a girl is in love with you, she knows that she must give you what you want.' (Boy of 18.) 'We do not refuse full intercourse for we know that if you refuse your boy friend he will beat you till you agree.' (Girl of 17.)[3]

Older informants who disapproved tended to lay the main responsibility on the importunity and unscrupulousness of the males. But while the attitudes of girls differed greatly from one individual to another, it was clear that many would not require any threat of a beating to make them fully co-operative. Most town girls, it seems, begin full intercourse at 15 or 16, and are saved from correspondingly early pregnancies only by their adolescent infertility. A not unusual age for the first birth is 18 or 19. Even with the enormously high infant death-rate, unmarried mothers abound in the locations.

Plunged into such an atmosphere, migrants from the country show different moral reactions according to their cultural and personal standards. To the Red young man it is still largely an issue where both sexes 'ought to' consider their moral duties more than they do. 'Even today, boys and young men know full well what is right and what is wrong', said a young Red migrant, 'and though there have always been a few young men who would want full inter-course the girls used not to allow them. When a woman refuses, a man stops bothering her. But there are girls here today who lack resistance. The men are to blame because they persuade the girls, but the girls are foolish to submit, and not report them to the seniors afterwards.'

With School migrants such outspoken disapproval was mostly restricted to the older generation. Christian sexual morality has not proceeded far enough to create any strong feelings of guilt among the young about pre-marital intercourse as such. It is still only the pregnancies that count.

But moral scruples, such as they may be, stand little chance of carrying the day in town. Over and over again, migrant informants explained how they had 'had to' conform to the town sexual standards themselves, or else forgo that sexual gratification to which every Xhosa considers himself or herself entitled. The other party (of course) is usually held to blame; but behind the other party stands the dreaded public opinion, which would make a fool of the overscrupulous person and leave him or her at a loss in the race for sexual partners.

Many Red migrants maintained that when they first came to town they had tried to continue the practice of ukumetsha but had found themselves derided. 'Our girls made fun of it, and as a result other girls would not accept our proposals either.' A young, formerly Red, convert to Bhengu's Church recorded that 'here in town I never bothered about the country practice, because I thought the girls would look on me as a "Red blanket". Here, it isn't only men who want full internal intercourse. Even the girls who come from the country want it too. They think they have wasted their time without full enjoyment otherwise. It may be a disgrace for a girl to have a baby, but girls in town are very keen on men.'

The School migrants are even more exposed to the pressures of town opinion, and the fear of being despised very quickly converts any who were not already of the same mind. A young educated School man, a teacher at a school in town,

---

[3] This account of School and town sexual habits is also supported by about forty histories of senior schoolgirls in East London collected in 1955 by Miss Laura Jacob (then African Nuffield Research Fellow with the Rhodes University Institute of Social and Economic Research).

explained with great seriousness that he 'had to' have full intercourse with his girl, aged 16, because otherwise she would tell all her classmates and friends that he was 'no good'.

A similar point was made to explain why even the most timid and discriminating country girls have illegitimate babies when they come to town. Girls too are afraid of being considered 'no good'. 'It is not only bad girls who have babies here. Many good girls fall victims too, because they love their boy friends and want to please them. If they refuse, they know that the same problem will arise all over again with one lover after another.'

The position was summed up by a 16-year-old town girl: 'I am told that in the country girls control their feelings and rarely become pregnant. But in town girls do what they have seen others do. We all want to be regarded as up to date.'

Sanctions for respecting virginity can emanate only from the home community. For a Xhosa girl who comes to town, almost the only hope of remaining a 'virgin'—even in the extended sense—is to confine herself to a lover from her own home community, whose fear of home opinion may overmaster the fear of local opinion and cause him to 'be careful'. The common formula in both sections is that girls become pregnant in town 'when they no longer fear their parents'. 'I think the unmarried girls here get babies because people's parents are far away.' 'They fear nobody here. They do not think of going home.' 'The men are careless here, and make the girls pregnant, because they have no respect for the parents.'

Even the remote sanctions emanating from home, it must be added, are largely lacking in the case of girls who—like many of the migrants—come from broken homes, as orphans or illegitimate children themselves.

Plainly, then, there is much foundation for the country belief that 'girls will get spoilt' in town. In fact it appears to be the destiny of almost every country girl who comes to town to bear one or more illegitimate children. Girlhood—except in the sense in which School people pass off unmarried mothers as girls—is a short, fleeting thing there. Soon enough the girl who came to town as an *intombi* has been admitted to the ranks of the *amankazana* and the unmarried mothers.

STAYING TOGETHER (UKUSHWESHWA)

The practice of unmarried couples staying together (not merely visiting each other) was mentioned as the second great difference between town and country sexual behaviour.

In the country a man cannot introduce a girl into his parental homestead, or his own homestead, without immediately becoming involved in bridewealth debt and the obligations of legitimate marriage. Repudiation of the intention to marry would be just as much an insult to the ancestors by Red standards as a grievous sin by Christian standards. In effect there would be nowhere for an unmarried couple to stay together.

In town, by comparison, staying together seems excessively simple; it is merely a matter of finding a room and paying the rent. Every couple can make the choice, whether they will live on in their separate rooms and visit each other, or whether they will move in to share one room. In Xhosa terms they can choose whether the woman will be merely her lover's *inkazana* or his *ishweshwe* too. The term *ukushweshwa* is applied to all the town unions in which the woman comes to stay with her man without being married to him, and they live in his room as one domestic unit.

In accordance with the patriarchal ideas of the Xhosa, the room for staying in together is always supposed to be his, not hers. (This is kept up, by way of pretence, even in cases where the woman is the actual provider and furnishes the money for the rent.) The man involved may be unmarried or may be a married man who has left his real wife in the country.

Ukushweshwa more often involves Red than School men. It is specially favoured by Red married men, whereas self-respecting School migrants rarely take to it unless they are unmarried. For a married man *ukushweshwa*, according to School people, 'lowers one's character', 'gives one a bad name'. It clashes too flagrantly with the official morality of church marriage. The prime consideration of School people in their extra-marital affairs is secrecy, and *ukushweshwa* cannot be kept secret for long. It would expose a married School man to possible sanctions from his church; a teacher might be dismissed by the school committee. Even to have a son or daughter flouting marriage vows in such a way can adversely affect one's position in church circles.

In particular, School married men are more afraid of detection by their wives. The Red wife is brought up to accept her husband's extra-marital affairs, as long as she herself is not neglected. Red women said that it is ill-advised to visit town unexpectedly so as to check on the husband's behaviour; 'it is not our business'; 'it offends the husband'. The School wife, on the other hand, is encouraged not to tolerate any open association of her husband with another woman. If a School man is not sufficiently circumspect in town, some of those School people who are great letter-writers will no doubt pass on the news, and the irate wife will soon be on the spot demanding redress.

The other form of *ukushweshwa*, in which neither partner is married, is practised more freely by School people (as well as by some Red people), though it still causes head-shaking among the elders. It always carries the possibility that the couple may marry; some couples do so in the end. It is a regular thing when a girl who has been impregnated in the country comes to town to join her child's father. She goes to live in his room, the child is born there, and the family situation is normal except that the marriage has not yet been legalized. Many of these cases are on the borderline between *ukushweshwa* and marriage (of the *thwala* type), and it may remain uncertain for a considerable time which is the more correct interpretation.

In general, the moral ideas attached to *ukushweshwa* constitute an important example of the tendency for School and Red people to look down upon each other for complementary reasons, as 'shameless' on the one hand, 'furtive' on the other. School people advance the expected arguments about decency and keeping up one's good name; but according to Red people, *ukushweshwa* —if properly conducted—is a much more moral institution than the 'visiting' which School men and women practise instead. Red men prefer living together as being wholesome and honest, in contrast to visiting, which is usually covert and somewhat shamefaced. Another Red argument is that '*ukushweshwa* prevents one from falling in love with too many women'. 'I stay together with my *inkazana* so that I should not make a fool of myself with women whom I don't really love and who don't love me really.' Also, 'if I do not live with my *inkazana*, other men will keep proposing love to her, and we do not like to share our women, nor do we like to fight over them'.

Ukushweshwa has grown up specially to meet the needs of the isolated migrant men and women, and its practical conveniences to them may be great. If a couple are fond of each other and want to be mutually helpful, the simplest and cheapest way is to join forces in a domestic unit, with only one rent to pay, only one set of meals to cook. It is also each partner's insurance against destitution in times of illness, unemployment or pregnancy. Living together under *ukushweshwa* provides many of the same co-operative advantages as living with *iintanga*, but is acceptable to men who have passed the age for *iintanga*.

The self-employed woman who runs her business in her own room may be glad to have a man's protection. It appears that many or most Red women brewers live under *ukushweshwa*. This has its advantages for the man too. He may derive benefits from the woman's business. Apart from this, a man may be entitled to a cost-of-living allowance from his employer if he can prove that his wife lives with him in town. He will go with his *ishweshwe* and make a sworn statement that she is his wife 'by Native law and custom'.

Pass laws are another reason for living together. A man making nocturnal visits to his girl, who stays in a White district as domestic servant, runs risks of arrest if the police find him without a night-pass. A woman runs a similar risk if she is found sleeping in a man's room without a lodger's permit: this has caused many a man to include his *ishweshwe* in his lodger's permit under the guise of 'wife', when permits for wives were easier to get. Another motive for this pretence may be supplied by the fact that the desirable sub-economic houses are normally reserved for married couples.

Ukushweshwa is also favoured by some men on the ground that it safeguards them against deceit by their women. Perhaps the lover suspects that the money which the woman has squeezed out of him, saying it was for taking a sick child to the doctor, is used for her own clothing instead. The best countermeasure is to make her live with him. 'A man gets fed up with daily demands for money. Taking the woman to stay under his eye gives him some control.'

Practical considerations apart, living together may give great satisfactions on the personal side. In the rough-and-tumble of location life a woman has reason to value the steady countenance of a male protector. 'Once you are staying with your lover, there is an end of other men saying and doing just what they like with you.' A man will value the domestic comfort of a woman to prepare his meals and to wash and iron his clothes. For both partners, *ukushweshwa* can provide an intimacy and human warmth like that of a conjugal union with a shared domestic life—something which the young may not always miss, but the older people greatly appreciate. If there was much hard self-seeking and much careless expediency to be found in *ukushweshwa* arrangements, there was also much genuine personal regard.

THE DECISION TO STAY TOGETHER

Except in cases of elopement, where a country girl follows her lover directly to town, a couple will usually have had a period of 'visiting' each other in town for sexual purposes before they start staying together. One common reason for making the change is that the woman finds herself pregnant and is forced to give up her job. 'I shared a room at my employer's place with another girl, who had a lover already. Presently an *intanga* of this lover proposed love to me. After about three days I accepted him. I used to visit his room every night. On becoming pregnant, and having to give up my job, I stayed with him permanently.' Or it may simply happen that the woman wants a more convenient place to live. For migrants of both sexes the first accommodation in town is often inconvenient: the man leaves when he 'gets a room of his own', but the woman leaves when she 'finds a lover to stay with'.

One Red girl said that she had run away to East London because of a pregnancy she incurred on a White-owned farm, 'where I had been hoeing mealie land at one shilling a day'. She first stayed with a woman from home, very much her senior, who was engaged in brewing. As the girl's condition made her unemployable she helped in the business in return for food and accommodation. The hostess 'was very much inconvenienced by my presence because she was so much senior, and because her lover often wanted to sleep in the room. She did not say anything but I could feel it.' The girl gave birth to a dead child three months after her arrival. Two weeks later she started looking for work and was taken on at a canning factory. Through contacts at work she found a lover. At first she would go occasionally to sleep with him in his room. But soon she decided she should relieve the older woman of her presence, and joined him as a permanent arrangement.

A young widow from Kwelegha first shared a room with another woman, a rural neighbour of her own, left husbandless by desertion. She too assisted her hostess in return for food and accommodation. 'I had to get used to town life before looking for domestic work. I had never worked for White people.' Soon the new-comer had a lover, and started visiting him by night in his room. 'Immediately my friend's attitude to me became nasty. Almost every day beer had to be strained at cock-crow. I could not do this now, because my lover would not let me leave his room at 3 o'clock in the night. My friend and I quarrelled over this. I asked her who had done this work before I came. She got furious and ordered me out of the room. I then went permanently to join my lover in his room.'

THE MORALITY OF 'UKUSHWESHWA'

In a case involving an unmarried man, the morality of *ukushweshwa* turns on the question of marriage prospects: whether the parties intend to marry, and what their parents' attitude to the marriage is. Those *ukushweshwa* cases which result from the elopement of a country couple in the face of parental opposition seem only a little immoral by Xhosa standards—only in so far as one offends the parents by insisting on a spouse not of their choice. The couple stay on in town hoping that in due course they can return to the country as man and wife. Sometimes the man says he is saving up hard for bridewealth.

A Red girl from Mooiplaats (an orphan staying under the guardianship of her elder brother) was rendered pregnant in the country, and the man responsible did not pay the full customary damages. She joined him in town, has been living with him for some years, and now has three children by him. She has never visited home because of her brother's hard attitude. They live together 'as if they were married'. The woman brews in a small way. She keeps the profit herself, but tells her lover how much she has made that day. Her lover pays the rent and gives her household money. She hopes that they will become wife and husband openly and properly. 'One day he may take me to his kraal at Kwenxura and kill a goat to *dliswa amasi* [lit. 'to be given milk to drink'— an important ritual of marriage]. Only then will my lover's relatives recognize me as a married woman.'

A School girl joined her lover in East London after he had rendered her pregnant when she was doing standard V. 'His parents did not want him to marry me so we privately agreed that I should come here.' The child was born in town, and when the girl started work at a textile factory she employed an elderly woman to look after it. She said that she gives all her money to her lover 'the same as a married woman does. I tell him what we are short of and should buy, and he gives me the money for it.' His father, who was against the marriage, has died recently. 'I hope he will really marry me now. We love and respect each other, and he seems very proud of his little baby boy.'

The moral situation is far more complex in the cases where the man staying with his *ishweshwe* is already married. Since this is primarily a practice of Red men the question is to see how *ukushweshwa* fits in with Red concepts of marriage.

Ukushweshwa is particularly convenient for married men from the Transkei, who cannot easily visit home or be visited by their wives, but Red men from nearer town practise it too. It will be shown that *ukushweshwa* is on no account to be confused with polygynous secondary marriage. The Red men who practise it are simply claiming the customary Xhosa liberty to conduct relationships with other women so long as the wife's rights are not directly affected. Red Xhosa say that it is 'not the wife's business' to know too much about such affairs. Ideally, *ukushweshwa* is intended to help the migrant men and women in town without infringing the rights of anyone else. It is supposed to be temporary in the same sense that town life itself is supposed to be temporary. The years may lengthen, but the moral content should not deepen, for the country home in the background must keep first claim.

Thus, where School people find *ukushweshwa* (of a married man) immoral in any case, Red people find it immoral only to the extent to which it may turn a husband into an absconder. An *ishweshwe* is behaving immorally when she fails to 'respect' the prior rights of the wife in the country. Morality demands that she must move out without protest when the wife comes to town on a visit to her husband; that she must recognize the husband's prime duty to support his family; that she must therefore strive to earn her own money and to demand as little financial help as possible from the man; and especially that she must accept the essentially temporary basis of the relationship, and not attempt to make it permanent by using her wiles 'to oust the wife'.

In practice the situation may be highly complex. *Ukushweshwa* with a married man usually produces a situation in which the man is legal head of one elementary family, and domestic head of another. But the woman too, when she joins the man, has often already had children either by a deceased husband or by a previous lover. The woman's previous children, like the husband's legal children, are normally in the country. The children arising from the *ukushweshwa* relationship may also be sent to some relation of the woman in the country after they are weaned, but some or all of them may remain in town.[4]

The inherent weakness of all *ukushweshwa* relations with married men is that the long-term interests of the man and his *ishweshwe* cannot coincide so nicely as their short-term interests may do. The man will, or ought to, leave town ultimately and go back to his wife in the country; the *ishweshwe* will probably (though she ought not to) object to his going. She knows that there is no hope for her to keep her man anywhere in the country. The chances of his marrying her polygynously are almost non-existent. Even if polygyny were not rather

4 The children of *ukushweshwa* partners will be discussed in chapter 17.

unusual nowadays, she is not in the marriageable category herself. An *ishweshwe* who wants to keep her man therefore has the task not only of ousting the wife in his affections, but of making him ready to forgo return to the country altogether. The victim of the 'bad' *ishweshwe* becomes an absconder. He stays in town for good, and, with the *ishweshwe*, may rear a family of town children (without legal paternity) who have no claims at his rural 'home'.

Red people are wide awake to these dangers of *ukushweshwa* degenerating into something which is obnoxious to their moral code. Though there are undoubtedly women who try to live up to the standards demanded of the 'good' *ishweshwe*, and though there are men who impose this role on the woman whether she wants it or not, the 'bad' *ishweshwe* and her wiles are almost proverbial in the locations. The triangle is delicately poised at the best of times. The *ishweshwe* has two lines of attack. One is to put off the man's departure indefinitely; the other is to make hay while the sun shines, getting as much money out of him as she possibly can, against the day when he will be here no more. In view of this second possibility the morality of *ukushweshwa* is largely a question of economics.

ECONOMICS AND MORALS

All Red people, men and women, agree that an *ishweshwe* 'ought to' contribute to the domestic expenses, 'ought not to' divert much-needed money from the migrant's lawful family at home. But the actual economic arrangements differ greatly, from cases where the man is obliged to be sole provider, to cases where the woman keeps the man and perhaps contributes for his family too.

At the beginning the man will usually assume responsibility, especially if his *ishweshwe* is young and not self-employed. This means that he goes on paying the rent of his room himself, and buying the food, as he did before. Or he may hand over a weekly sum—perhaps 15s. or £1—for her to lay out on house-keeping.

At this stage the man may in effect be subsidizing the woman by a good deal more than the amount of her keep. Many women said that they managed to save something out of the housekeeping allowance for their own benefit. 'There were always a few shillings over and I kept those.' 'He buys some of the food and he gives me 18s. every Friday for the rest. I know how to buy enough food and still have something left, so that I can keep back five or six shillings.' 'Besides keeping me, he gives me money when the child is ill; 2s 6d. for the location clinic, or 7s. 6d. for the doctor or our own "doctor's" [*igqira's*] fee which is 10s.' The little weekly sums saved by a thrifty *ishweshwe* out of her lover's money may become the capital that sets her up in a business of her own.

But the man should not be expected to keep up such generosity for long; if he does, it is most likely a case of the *ishweshwe* having ousted the lawful family —'he treats me just like a real wife'. More often, the *ishweshwe* must go back to earning—with minimum interruptions for pregnancy and childbirth—and contribute in cash or in kind, or both. Some women make it their special responsibility to buy the meat, tea, and coffee. Some give the lover his pocket-money for buying liquor. Gradually, things even out until the contributions can be considered roughly equal.

There remain the cases where the woman is the main provider. These run apparently counter to all rural Xhosa tradition and practice. Every rural youth is taught that it is the man's duty to maintain his wife and children and make his homestead prosper; translated into terms of the migrant situation, that he has to earn money for the family's support. Indeed, as we have seen, many Xhosa migrants interpret this patriarchal division of roles so narrowly that they try to prevent their women from earning any money at all. But some Red migrant women have managed to square town practice with rural theory by a different interpretation. They pointed out that as women have to work for their husbands in the country, they have to work for their men in town too.

Motives of many different kinds may induce an *ishweshwe* to take on herself the burden of supporting her man. Sometimes affection predominates, sometimes fear; there may be the weakness of a girl who cannot stand out against exploitation, or the strength of a dominating woman who likes to keep men under her thumb.

One young Red woman, aged about 25, had been keeping her ne'er-do-well lover for several years. While still in the country she had had an illegitimate child, fathered by a married man; a year after arriving in town she was made pregnant again by this present lover who is also from her home place. 'I was anxious to get away from the uncle I had stayed with in town, who would be worried about my pregnancy. So I gave my lover money to find us a room where we would be far from my uncle and all other Dongwe people.' They moved in together. But the lover was 'the type of man who does not stick to a job long'; soon he was out of work, and the girl 'bought all the food for both of us'. To this day she is still paying for the rent and food. 'I also give my lover a few shillings for pocket-money, and if he needs clothes I buy him a second-hand suit when I come across one.' Recently he was sentenced to a term of imprisonment for horse-stealing, but as soon as he came out of jail she took him in again. It can be said that two typically Red virtues—fear of the uncle and faithfulness to one lover—have prompted this girl to carry on the un-Red role of a man's regular supporter.

With another Red woman, it was a history of ill-usage by many men which made her 'extremely anxious to keep my present lover's affections'. She came to town many years ago, leaving behind an illegitimate child fathered by a married man. Her first lover in town deserted her after making her pregnant again. All her next attempts turned out badly. Now she has a married man from the Transkei, and will make any financial sacrifice to keep him. 'I give him money whenever he needs it; if I had none I would borrow from my employer for him.' For appearance's sake she lets him pay the rent and buy some food, but she takes care that the sums of money she gives him from time to time should add up to a good deal more than he spends.

With older women who are well established in business, this keeping the lover as a kind of hanger-on may add to the welcome sense of power and importance. It is a far cry from the subjection of women to their men in the country. One widowed landlady in her 40's, originally from a farm, said—no doubt with truth—that her present lover 'will never do anything to hurt or offend me, because he is always hard up and I am the one who is supporting him'. Her previous lover of many years' standing died, but she easily found this replacement, a casual worker at the harbour. She pays the rent of their room (her own seven-roomed house is all let) and buys all the food for them both.

All of the women just cited are of the 'good' *ishweshwe* type whose intentions, at least overtly, stop short of ousting the man's lawful family. At the other extreme is the type of *ishweshwe* whose generosity springs from the golden rule of wicked women—'Give him money if you want to oust his wife'. 'Give money whenever you are employed; the bead-work is useless in town.' 'Make him feel that you are a help and not a burden.' Men warn each other of the over-generous *ishweshwe* on this account: 'They take advantage of the fact that men will stay on where life is easy and free of charge. Married women always tell their husbands about bills that have to be paid, or money needed for this and that. *Amashweshwe* don't ask, they give.'

UKUSHWESHWA AND URBANIZATION

It would seem that staying together, being officially only a device for cheering up town life 'while it lasts', need not interfere with Red people's remaining country-rooted and Red in outlook. But its actual tendency to urbanize a man or woman depends on the circumstances and the balance of personalities in the given case.

Most of the older women questioned were philosophical both about their men's probable return to the country, and about their own futures in or out of town. They agreed that *ukushweshwa* is temporary in the nature of things. 'I should like to stay here with my lover all my life, but if we quarrel or he leaves, there is another man ready to propose love to me.' 'If my lover leaves me I'll just go on working. As long as I have money there is nothing to worry about.' 'I have only come here to work for my children in the country. When they are grown up I shall go home. After all, my lover won't be staying here for ever either.' Such women might perhaps not go to the length of helping to support the lover's family, but neither will they stoop to seducing him perma-nently away from his wife and children in the country. 'It is not every woman's aim to oust the wife', said a widow of about 40. 'A woman likes to have a lover in town for the sake of protection and also for financial help sometimes. I have had no intentions beyond these.' 'I do not want to oust his wife', said a pathetic and unattractive *ishweshwe* also in her 40's, 'for I have always been ousted myself, and I know what it is like.'

Younger women, however, perhaps because the demographic sexual balance is against them, often expressed open defiance of the *ishweshwe* code. 'When your married lover is the father of your child', said a woman of 25 from Kentani, 'you think of yourself and not of anyone else. You always want to have your lover as your own husband. You do not care what happens to the wife in the country.' One unmarried mother from St. Luke's had followed the father of her child, a married man, to town. She earned money by brewing. Now she has two more children by her lover. 'My position is safe now,' she said, 'I regard myself as his wife. He has abandoned his real wife and children, who have returned to her people's kraal in Kwenxura. It was a competition between me and the wife. One has to be very clever about it.' In form she gives the man her beer profits, but in practice she obviously rules him and his purse together.

In such cases both parties seem set for becoming town-rooted. The woman cannot go home, the man will not. His end is *ukutshipha*, absconding.

There is a whole lore about these designing women and how they attain their goal. Red men tell stories to younger men by way of warning; medicines are said to be employed to keep a man bound; women discuss certain well-tried recipes in a matter-of-fact way. Few—if any—of these recipes have a specifically sexual content. The seductiveness of the bad *ishweshwe* lies not in physical charms but in economic, domestic, and social deftness. An *ishweshwe* of 45 can, if she wishes, prove a far more dangerous rival to the wife than one of 25. 'If you want to oust a married woman in the country, be very fair to your lover about money, and tell him that you can manage without any more just at present, you still have a few shillings to carry on with.' 'Always have beer and brandy ready for him, and drink it with him and his friends.' 'Notice what his favourite food is, and take care to cook nicely. His acquaintances, when they meet him in the street, must be able to tell him that he looks better and has put on weight since you have been living with him.' 'Talk to him pleasantly and do not bother him with things which would be a worry.'

A migrant who is holding stoutly to the Red ideal of incapsulation should be able to resist such designs. Some men told stories of how they had 'just managed' to break free at a critical moment, or had 'nearly made fools of themselves' by staying with an *ishweshwe* 'too long'. One Red railway worker of about 35 had started innocently enough by 'visiting' a country-born sweetheart. She bore a child by him and presently moved in to stay. 'The child seemed to be requiring treatment by doctors all the time. I suspected that she misused much of the money I gave her for this purpose and that in fact she was letting the child's health be ruined.' They began to quarrel and in the end he told her to leave his room. She refused. 'I asked the owner of the house to drive her away, but he said he could not because I had brought her in without his permission.' The owner and his wife were both on her side. 'I got very cross. I took all her clothes and possessions and threw them outside. When she returned she broke the door open; she was swearing and threatening to have me arrested. She put all her things back into the room. So I went to report her at *loyiti* [the Location Office]. I was told it was entirely up to me to get rid of her, because I had written her in the lodger's permit as my wife. I then told her to go away because my real wife was coming to East London on a visit. She only retorted that she would give her a good hiding if she came to disturb her in "her" room with "her" (the *ishweshwe's*) husband (meaning me). There was nothing I could do but leave her in the room and move out myself. I have decided never again to stay with an *ishweshwe*, for in the end they will try to rule one and pretend to be one's wife. I shall only visit an *inkazana* when I fall in love with her; I may stay in her room daily, but never again will I take her to stay in my own room. That is the way to make a fool of oneself.'

'UKUSHWESHWA' AND MARRIAGE

It remains to show briefly how and why *ukushweshwa* remains distinct from polygynous secondary marriage. In the traditional Xhosa system, as in other patrilineal Bantu systems, women and their offspring are supposed to acquire legitimate status in the husband's family, lineage, and clan by way of bride-wealth payment. But today, while Xhosa marriages still normally involve bridewealth, no payment at all need precede the actual transfer of the bride. An understanding that bridewealth 'will be' paid is enough. In the interim the husband's kin group is given the benefit of the doubt as regards rights over the wife and children. The Xhosa go still further: almost the last vestige of ceremony may be dispensed with. This happens in the widespread institution of *ukuthwala* marriage, referred to in the previous chapter. *Ukuthwala* procedure consists in the man's representatives abducting the girl and installing her at his home, where she is required to perform the duties of a wife. In the country very many couples live together permanently as man and wife on the basis of *ukuthwala*, and no query is raised about the status of either wife or offspring. It might well be asked whether setting up house with an *ishweshwe* in town would not have a similarly binding effect.

In fact there is no such effect. The reason is the non-involvement of the kin. In *ukuthwala* marriage the real binding force is an agreement between the two groups of kin (as distinct from the couple themselves). The girl's parents must have come to a private understanding with the suitor's kin. Just as in more ceremonious marriages, the *ukuthwala* bride is being transferred from one homestead and one group of kin to another. Anything else would be mere illegitimate abduction or elopement. The consent of the couple themselves (which forms the basis of *ukushweshwa*) is quite irrelevant.

Thus, as a rule, *ukushweshwa* does not and cannot solidify into marriage. (The exceptions are those cases of eloping rural couples who have merely anticipated their parents' consent by coming to town together.) The point at issue is not whether the parties are 'free to marry'. After all, not only the Red bachelor is free to marry: a man who is married could still theoretically marry his *ishweshwe* polygynously. But this does not happen, because only kin can make a marriage, and here no kin come into the picture.

It seems fair to say that *ukushweshwa* is not modelled on marriage arrangements of any kind but on something quite distinct, namely *amankazana* arrangements. In rural society the *inkazana* is never for one moment confused with a wife. The relation is purely personal: no kin are consulted. The institution is complementary to marriage and not parallel to it, catering specially for men who already have wives and women who will never have husbands. It is characterized by an almost complete lack of formal obligation. A country Xhosa man and his *inkazana* owe one another nothing jurally, even while each expects occasional gifts or services from the other as a token of personal good will. In spite of the novelty of joint housekeeping these concepts continue to apply to *ukushweshwa* in town. The migrant and his *ishweshwe* are not 'bound'. They interpret everything that passes between them as a voluntary gesture of good will, without jural basis. This affects both the relations of the couple themselves and—as the next chapter will show—the status of their children.

VISITING LOVERS

Out of the many casual liaisons bred by the conditions of the locations, some develop into more lasting relationships without the couple going so far as to set up house together. The steady 'visiting' relation is specially popular with School migrants and might be called their alternative to the predominantly Red *ukushweshwa*. It can be regarded as a major institution of the East London locations. This typical School pattern has many variants. The partners may be members of entirely separate households, or their housekeeping may become joint in some respects while remaining separate in others. They may meet for nothing more than sexual satisfaction, or may intermittently enjoy the intimacy of a shared family life. Only the passage of time marks the transition from the first casual encounters, through the courting period, to the established steady relation. Many Xhosa women in East London, dependent for their happiness on some visiting lover, never get to know how much the relation means to him and how far they can depend on its continuance.

During the early or courting stages the man's room rather than the woman's

is supposed to be used for sexual purposes, unless he has a wife there. Freedom
to receive girl friends was given as a reason why most School young men like
to have their own rooms as soon as possible. Sometimes women employed as
living-in domestic servants like to receive men in their own rooms, where there
is the attraction of comparative privacy (though also the risk of prosecution,
in that the man has left the locations during curfew hours). In the overcrowded
locations privacy is at a premium and subterfuges of all kinds may be necessary.
A girl of 20 with standard VIII education was staying with her elder sister; her
lover had a room of his own where they met two or three nights a week and
had sexual intercourse, but the girl had to explain her absences to her sister.
She did so by saying she had worked overtime at the cannery where she was
employed. In the case of another couple, both man and woman were hampered
by sharing their rooms with two other partners. The woman's two room-mates
had lovers of their own; all three lovers would be invited to the room for visits,
but it was useless for sexual purposes. The man's room was also ruled out
during the week; they could only sleep there on Saturdays and Sundays when
his two male room-mates were visiting the country. Luckily the man had a
younger friend with a room of his own, who was always willing to go out to
oblige him. They met at the friend's room two or three nights a week.

This kind of thing is, of course, not the monopoly of bachelors. It is practised
both by married men whose wives are in the country, and more circumspectly
by those who have wives, *amashweshwe* or other regular female associates in
town. It is widely accepted among School as among Red people that a man can
have one 'main' sweetheart and several 'private' ones at the same time, the
'private' ones being those who pay or receive occasional visits by stealth. The
only difficulty is for a woman to determine which class she belongs to at any
given time. Some of the younger School men claimed that they appointed
fixed days for each of their sweethearts, and said they would send away any
young woman who dared to appear at the room out of turn, for being
unwomanly and interfering.

When a visiting couple become deeply involved in economic as well as
emotional obligations, the arrangement may come very near to *ukushweshwa*.
A young deserted School wife from the Transkei was officially sharing a room
with the daughter of her mother's sister, but spent hardly any time there.
At work all day, she was in her lover's room every night and over the week-ends.
Usually he bought food for supper and she added a contribution, especially
for the more elaborate week-end meals. She cooked and they ate together.
The woman had her blankets, sheets, and pillows in her lover's room, and had
supplied the crockery. Similar arrangements were reported by a young School
widow from the East London district, who officially 'lives in' as a domestic
servant, but actually spends most nights in her lover's room in the location.
In these and many other cases the housekeeping had become essentially joint,
though the partners kept their separate addresses.

In other cases the daily housekeeping is still distinctly separate but the couple
recognize a mutual obligation to 'help each other with money', extending
beyond the presents (cigarettes, shirts, etc.) which many women buy for their
lovers 'purely out of love', and which the men may reciprocate by occasionally
paying a taxi for the girl when it rains, or taking her to the bioscope. In such a
case both partners may be prepared to take full financial responsibility if the
other is out of work or ill, or even to help with each other's kinship obligations.

'If my mother writes to me to ask for some money and I have not got it, I ask my lover. He has given me as much as £2 for her at one time.'

Some visiting couples appeared to find sustained satisfaction in their relation and to have remained involved together for a number of years. In other cases the man begins to neglect the woman, yet without letting her go. He may appear at her room only when he feels a need for sexual relations, especially when he has been drinking. Some women spoke of the wisdom of keeping up a second string as insurance against possible exploitation or abuse by the first lover. Some women did little but wait for the visits of a man who hardly came any more.

Paradoxically enough, visiting relations often seemed to be most stable and satisfying in cases where the man was already married, having his lawful wife at home in the country. The woman will have early resigned herself to the fact that the man cannot marry her, and the man will feel secure in that he cannot be 'trapped'. Despite the acknowledged right of School wives to resent adultery, a few cases were found where a School wife in the country actually gave her blessing to her husband's affair in East London, visiting the 'other woman' when she came to town and even offering to have one of her children for a visit in the country.

A critical moral test for the relation of visiting lovers is, of course, the occurrence of a pregnancy. Very many women complained that 'my lover disappeared as soon as I told him I was pregnant'. 'It is strange how they stop loving a woman when she is the mother of their child; one would think they should love her all the more for it.' Legally the natural father is liable for one of two alternatives: either damages for seduction, or support for the minor child at the rate of about £1–£2 a month. It is not usually complained that men deny paternity if actually charged in court. (One man who did so was already maintaining the mother's previous four children, and she admitted herself that he had been 'saddled with more than enough'.) But the court case itself signifies a personal or emotional breach. Many women would rather refrain from going to law, in the hope of somehow keeping or regaining the man's affections and his unofficial support for the child. The unlucky woman is the one who finds herself finally left without either love or money.

The duties which a man 'ought to' accept vis-à-vis his sweetheart once he knows she is pregnant by him, are fairly well defined. First of all, if she has no secure *pied-à-terre* with relatives or close friends, he ought to provide her with a room where she can stay when no longer able to work and where her baby will be born. As 'staying together' is not contemplated, this means renting a separate room for her for a few months. Thereafter it is regarded as right that the man should continue supporting mother and child to some extent. But how much he ought to give them will depend on circumstances, e.g. on whether he is a bachelor or has to divide his support between two families, and also on the relative earning powers of himself and the woman. A mother would proudly speak of the visiting father of her illegitimate children as 'a good man' in cases where he was giving her money for food with some regularity and in addition paying the doctor's bills for the children and herself. It is much appreciated if he also 'dresses her' (gives money for necessary clothes and shoes), and occasionally surprises her with the gift of some piece of clothing. But hardly ever did a woman in this situation say she expected to be *fully* maintained. Probably the main burden would remain her own.

Reciprocity is expected too. A woman who is receiving help from a visiting lover 'ought to' cook for him whenever she can, and look after his clothes, as well as helping him in turn if he falls out of work. Meanwhile it is clearly understood that his contributions to her are for the children and not for herself. Among the more rustic type of women a characteristic wish was 'that the father should buy some sheep or a calf for the children', so that they 'will have something of their own when they grow up'.

If the woman does not send the children away to the country,[5] but keeps them in her room in town, the man will become inclined to visit her there instead of expecting her at his own room. In these cases the matrifocal 'family' with the visiting lover/father may become established. Even when the children are no longer small, a School man may continue to visit and sleep with the mother in the same room, a curtain round the bed or in front of it representing the one pathetic attempt at privacy. The position of the lover/father vis-à-vis this type of household tends to be marginal, as he has never been and never will be a permanent resident member. Many respectable working women in the location have borne a man two, three, or more children but have never known even a short spell of the kind of common domestic life one associates with 'normal' marriage. They often maintained that they feel no sense of deprivation, that they could not imagine what it would be like to have to live with a man always, in one room. They appeared to prefer their freedom.

On the other hand, there is one strong argument which makes the woman —ultimately—more dependent on the man in a moral sense than he is on her. Any 'decent' woman feels that she must try to keep the affections of her children's father as long as she possibly can, because to bear illegitimate children to more than one man is unworthy of a self-respecting woman. Xhosa women still like to use the phrase that 'children must be of one kraal' (*abantwana bomzi omnye*), i.e. must have the same descent on the father's side. They may say that children of different fathers will have different 'customs' (*amasiko*) or will be likely to quarrel and fight. From a practical viewpoint there is the fact that a new lover will hardly have great liking for the children of his predecessor.

Most women with young illegitimate children, therefore, appeared ready to humble themselves towards the father if necessary in order to prolong the relation. One sensible and feeling woman was found still putting up with the occasional visits of a man who came to her drunk and sometimes insulted and maltreated her. 'I stick to him only because I don't want to bear children by another man. As soon as I become unable to bear children I don't want to have anything more to do with him.'

These arguments, it must be added, amount only to the woman's not liking to terminate the relation *herself*. If the father takes the initiative and deserts her, nobody will blame her for taking up with another man, and having children by more than one father.

Not infrequently the relation between the visiting lover/father and his children is a happy one as long as they are small. He will play with them and bring them little gifts. Sometimes the mother refrains from sending a child to relatives in the country, because the father wishes it to be near him in town. In such fond relations the children may be encouraged to call their natural father *tata* (father), and the mother may quell a naughty child with the threat

[5] See next chapter.

of a punishment from 'father' when he comes. But this phase rarely seems to outlast the children's early years. Sooner or later the man's effectiveness both as a partner to the mother and as a father to the children starts to dwindle. It is clearly recognized that the relation has few outward props and depends mainly on one single precarious factor—the continuance of some affection, however diluted, between the parents. 'He will come to me as long as he still has some love for me.'

As the woman grows older, the fear of bearing illegitimate children to more than one man loses its force. At the same time she tends to become less dependent in an economic sense—better able to work regularly, less involved in supporting the children, perhaps even able to count on some financial help from them. By this stage the visiting lover/father may have vanished from the scene altogether. However, this need not be the signal for the woman to find her own way back to the country. The need to earn money, and the limited prospects she would be faced with in the country, may keep her feeling that he is better off in town.

17

Town Children and Country Children

IONA MAYER

SENDING CHILDREN OUT OF TOWN

The roles of migrants as parents have to be considered. In town there are country-born fathers, couples and 'unattached' mothers, whose preferences as to where and how their children should be reared help to determine what proportion of the next generation will grow up as townspeople. That many migrant fathers leave their children in the country when they leave their wives —either by preference or because of influx control—needs no special explanation. But the married couples, and also the unmarried mothers, might be expected to rear in town the children whom they produce there. Field-work showed that this is by no means justified as a general assumption. Many migrant couples and many unaccompanied mothers deliberately part from their town-born children so that the children can be reared in the country by foster-parents. The effect is that an unexpectedly high proportion of the next generation has an almost complete rural background until adulthood brings the individual to town to start the migrant cycle over again.

Reader's one-in-ten survey of the locations in 1955 included data on 'persons away', i.e. having moral right to houseroom with the respondents but not actually living with them. Two-thirds of all 'persons away' were found to be children under 15. The gross total of all children claimed by all parents in the survey was 2,744: out of these 797—i.e. almost 30 per cent—were 'away'. The true proportion of *migrants'* children away is higher, as this survey included town-born parents too. It must also be remembered that many migrant mothers would have been likely to suppress particulars of illegitimate children whom they were keeping in the country. These figures, it must be added, related to a time just before the tightening up of influx control regulations against migrants' dependants. Presumably more children as well as more wives are now in the country.

When Reader's figures are broken down, the percentage of children away is seen to rise with age (e.g. 25 per cent of male children away between ages 0 and 4, for the wood-and-iron housing section, but 37 per cent between 5 and 9, and 42 per cent between 10 and 14).[1] This tends to support the field-work evidence that many children born in town are sent away 'when old enough', either after weaning (about two years) or when their moral and educational needs become more pressing.

If most migrants reared their children in town, the distinctiveness of the Red and School categories in this setting could be largely obscured within a generation. Children brought up in town can hardly fail to be town-rooted and also town-cultured. Even those Red migrants who determinedly remain

[1] Reader, D. H.: *The Black Man's Portion*, Appendix 1, table 6.

incapsulated in spite of having lost their country homes realize that they will not be able to transmit Red values to their town-born children. But with perhaps a half of all migrants' children being rediverted from the stream of town life the prospect looks different. These may be the migrants of ten, fifteen or twenty years hence but not the cockneys; they may prove to be just as country-bound, or just as determinedly incapsulated, as their parents before. Influx control is largely responsible for this situation, of course, but so are the parents. In present circumstances many of them, both Red and School, are determined not to rear children in town even where opportunity allows.

ATTITUDES TO TOWN-REARING

That the ordinary Red father prefers not to have his children brought up in town was explained in chapter 5. He has no right to take them away from the homestead where they belong. He would also be doing himself a disservice economically: children are productive workers in the homestead economy whereas in town they are only so many mouths to feed. Above all there are the considerations of moral danger. Conservatively minded School peasant parents, and even the more sophisticated, mostly agreed with Red parents about these. 'Town is no fit place for a child.' Rearing children there was supposed to mean loss of parental control, with disastrous consequences for the child's morality, especially in the fields of sex, work, and crime. As might be expected, each section also feared that town-rearing would expose its children too much to the influences of other sections. Red migrants felt that the children would quickly lose the 'real Xhosa' ways; School migrants with more genteel ambitions feared the loss of refinement which would follow from 'mixing with all and sundry'. Both with one voice united in blaming the children of the real towns-people. 'Town children are no good. They teach the knowledge of gambling, stealing, cadging for pennies. It is hard to keep your own children away from their evil influences.'

School migrants who set store by formal education sometimes explained that the country is a better place for rearing children on this account. 'In the country the children like going to school. They prefer the five hours in school to the harder work in the home.' 'Because my daughter has been reared in the country she really loves school and is now entering high school.' But in town school-going children 'are always tempted to dodge school'. 'They escape and loiter on the streets.'

Many migrant parents told cautionary tales about their own disastrous experiments with town-rearing. One educated School wife said that at first she had welcomed the chance to follow her husband into East London with the children. 'I did not heed my mother-in-law who warned me that town would be no good for children.' A few months' experience changed her mind. 'My elder son [aged 13] had been very meek in the country. He liked working for me or for the neighbours, and he liked school. But in town he changed at once. He started going out early and coming home late. He played dice games; he stole pennies for gambling or for sweets and ice-cream. The younger children became a nuisance too. They were always in the room with older people. They got into the way of laughing at older people's jokes. I soon saw why my mother-in-law disapproved of town for children.' All the children have now been sent to their paternal grandmother in the country.

However, unlike the Red parents who spoke in favour of country-rearing on all accounts, the School parents often tempered appreciation with regret. Children reared in the country will benefit morally but may suffer mentally: 'If parents could control their children here in town we would not have been so keen to send our two back to the country, where they will undergo the mental setback of country children.' 'The only reason I regret sending my girls away is that in town children gain a wider knowledge and seem naturally cleverer. They are brighter at school because they are not so shy.' Ambivalence also emerged from statements about physical health; some School parents maintained that 'children grow up weak in town' but others that 'in the country they are underfed'.

Several School parents qualified their denunciation of town-rearing with the proviso that it is all right for certain categories of age, sex or temperament. 'Boys are always difficult in town, but town life is good for girls. It teaches them things a modern woman needs to know, such as taste in dress and good cooking.' 'Girls growing up in town are always a big problem, more than boys. Girls should be kept out of town altogether till they marry.' 'It is best to send children to the country between 5 and 9 when they are ready for school.' 'There is no need to send girls to the country till the age of 15, when they are always in love and in danger of seduction.'

The histories of School migrant families often reflected these ambivalent attitudes. The siblings would have been separated, some staying in town and others going to the country; or they would have been sent hither and thither, according to how the parents happened to feel at the moment. One School migrant man was married to a town-born woman. During the first pregnancy she went to his country home, and their son was born there. For some years mother and child stayed there, the husband visiting them at week-ends. Two more children were born. Then the mother and the children moved back to town. But again, after a while, 'we sent our first-born back to the country again. We want him to learn country ways.' The two girls are still in town for the present: 'Girls are less apt to learn filthy habits.' There was another School man's wife with an urban background who had 'never tasted country life till my husband took me to the Transkei at marriage', but who found herself so much impressed by 'the excellent behaviour of country-bred children' that she left her first son there, with the husband's parents, when she followed her husband back to town. Two younger children were born and reared in town. Some years later the son was sent for also. But now the parents have decided to send all three children back to the Transkei, 'where we hope they will learn good behaviour'. 'Our son when he came here was quite different from our two town-born children. He had more respect altogether. But town life has made him start dodging school and even visiting girls at night, though he is only 14. Even my daughter seems to be receiving lovers and I believe the next thing would be a pregnancy.'

Behind their agreement with the Red parents about the moral dangers of town, these School parents very often revealed a difference of ultimate aspiration. The object of sending the child to the country is to provide it with a good moral background, not to make it into a rustic adult. As much as anything else, the country upbringing is to be a preparation for successful adult life *in town*. 'I want my children to remain in the country while young but to come to town when they have grown into responsible people.' 'Sons must be kept in the country at first, but should start coming to town at the age when a youth develops ambitions.' School parents preferred country-rearing mainly on pedagogic grounds, Red parents not only for pedagogic but for 'tribal' reasons: 'My children must stay in the country to learn all the things that belong to a real Red Xhosa.' 'They must learn country life and how to carry on the homestead as men.'

KIN-REARING AND FOSTER-REARING

A migrant whose children were in the country would usually describe them as being 'in the care of my father' (or elder brother, etc.). The mother—if she is there—is not thought of as bringing them up alone, but with the help of the kin. If she should come away the kin will take over. The widespread use of kin in the country to discharge pro-parental functions is not merely a device recently invented to suit the migrant parents' distrust of town education. It happens also to fit in with some distinctive features of rural Xhosa tradition, in themselves apparently unconnected with labour migrancy.

We might speak of children being either predominantly parent-reared or predominantly kin-reared, according to the norms of a particular society. The second term of course implies not that the parents are excluded, but that they are only one element in a more inclusive set of kin who jointly provide nurture and training, and are jointly entitled to the child's obedience or services. It is well known that most indigenous African societies emphasize kin-rearing in one form or another. For instance, children do not sleep always in their own parents' hut, but often with a paternal grandmother or some other relative; food may be given by a co-wife; deputies can be counted on where the parent is dead, absent or incapacitated; and stress is laid on the respect the child owes to all the senior kin around it. (Recent studies of the urban British working class have indicated that kin-rearing may also be more prominent in Western industrial societies than used to be supposed.) These familiar patterns occur among the Xhosa too; and it has also been seen how strongly the traditional Xhosa emphasize the duty of 'people' in general—as well as the parents—to discipline any child or youth. But this is not all. Among rural Xhosa some specific parental functions and attributes may be quite surrendered by the parents and transferred wholesale to other members of the kin: not (that is to say) merely in emergencies which call understudy roles into play, but as a matter of preference in normal life, with the 'real' parents still living alongside. That the 'real' parents should remain in charge whenever physically possible does not seem to be an unvarying assumption of the Xhosa. In the case of the Xhosa, therefore, one might say that foster-rearing as well as kin-rearing is institutionalized.

The functions which can be 'given away' to Xhosa foster-parents include custody, nurture, discipline, and verbal identification as father or mother. The commonest case is that of a child born into a three-generation extended family (the preferred pattern of conservative Xhosa). In this type of homestead group the senior woman will not uncommonly take over complete charge of her sons' children from weaning until adolescence. During this long period the grandchild 'is like a child of her own', sleeping in her hut, receiving food and daily care from her, and doing her errands as soon as it is old enough. It will call her (the actual grandmother) *mama*, 'mother', and will call her husband (the actual grandfather) *tata*, 'father'. These terms are used in address and reference too. The actual parents become *sisi* and *buti* (terms derived from

Afrikaans, now supplanting the Xhosa terms for 'elder sister' and 'elder brother' in many contexts). If the grandparents still have immature children of their own these are also classified as elder siblings.

The child is commonly handed over at an age when it is only beginning to speak; Xhosa say that this makes the 'role calling' come naturally. 'It learns to say *mama* and *tata* for the grandparents because this is what the other children of the same hut are saying.' The speech habit usually endures throughout life. An adult will say, 'X is the one whom I call *mama*, she is the one who brought me up'. The grandmother is definitely a foster-mother and not just a baby-minder. The transference of roles does not mean that the child is to deny its genealogical parentage, however. Special affection may be shown to the 'real' mother, who kept the child for the first year or two. On one occasion a child of about 3 years old was observed running after its actual mother with obvious recognition and affection; but what it called out to her was '*sisi umtshakazi, sisi umtshakazi!*' (term appropriate to the recently married wife of an elder brother).

Foster-rearing by grandparents is by no means the universal practice even of Red Xhosa. Whether or not it is followed in a given case may depend on many factors, e.g. on the age and health of the grandmother, or the number of children she and her daughters-in-law have on hand. But it is common enough to be regarded as one normal pattern. Many Xhosa say that it is what 'ought to' be done when the three generations remain in one homestead. The stereotyped explanation usually offered is a practical one: 'The older woman brings up the children, the younger woman gets on with the work in the fields.' Two other motives, however, may conceivably be involved in addition. First there is the question of shame or propriety. The child is removed from its parents at the time when the suckling taboo is lifted, i.e. when they can start to have sexual relations again. Secondly, there is the hierarchic interpretation of seniority which pervades Xhosa kinship and social structure. Age never absolves from continued deference to those still older, and particularly not in relation to one's own parents. The child's father and mother are still very much 'under' their own parents, the true heads of the homestead. This being so, they would be the less able to maintain the desired degree of autocratic dignity vis-à-vis their child. Xhosa sometimes say that 'a homestead can have only one mother and one father', implying that the head and his wife must be unchallenged at the apex of the pyramid of authority.

The other not uncommon case of foster-rearing involves sending a child away to a kinswoman in some other homestead 'because her own children are all grown up'. 'A woman does not like to be without a child in her house', particularly as children are a main source of domestic help. The term *mama* may be transferred to the foster mother. It is a matter of satisfaction to the woman when she can say, 'I am his *mama* now, he has forgotten about his old home'.

These institutions have been outlined in order to show that, what with kin-rearing and what with foster-rearing, niches can easily be found for children whose parents happen to be away in town. Little or no fear is felt that in the absence of its actual parents the child's upbringing will fail to be 'normal' or 'proper'. In fact many Xhosa might go to the other extreme and say that there would be something abnormal or improper in being brought up by the parents alone, such is the importance they attribute to the wider kin and the senior people generally in enforcing discipline and transmitting proper moral standards. The absence of this wider socializing agency in town is germane to the belief that no child can be brought up 'properly' there. If a choice has to be made, then, it may seem much more appropriate for children to stay among the kin and 'people' in the country—even without the parents—than in town with just the parents.

This is the orthodox view (of Red and conservative School people), not necessarily the universal view. But it was rare to find any migrant who would strongly maintain the opposite—that children must stay with their own parents, even if this means being permanently removed from the rest of their kin. Such an attitude is proper only for those (like the dispossessed farmworkers) who have lost the footing in the country and must perforce become town-rooted.

THE 'CHILDREN OF WOMEN'

Many Xhosa regard the child who grows up without male guardianship as something more than an anomaly—as an actual or potential social danger. In the common stereotype, 'children of women' are said to be uncontrolled and uncontrollable, and to have no moral sense. The excesses of tsotsis and other young delinquents in the East London locations are popularly associated with the high illegitimate birth-rate there, i.e. the stereotype of the tsotsi (as held by migrants especially) includes his having grown up under the care of a mother, who could neither discipline him herself nor tolerate his being disciplined by anyone else. 'The children of women never learn the difference between right and wrong. When you thrash the child of a woman, the mother instead of being grateful will rush out and start to scream at you. "This is my own child whom I bore in sorrow, you are treading him under like a piece of dirt!" '

Within the rural system the wider circle of kin can normally furnish a male guardian or guardians in the absence of a father. In the case of an 'illegitimate' child this will almost certainly be one of the male kin of the mother (in whose homestead the child is likely to be residing). The migrant unmarried mother who bears a child in town will in many cases still tend to regard her own kin in the country as its proper guardians.

Country Xhosa do not normally welcome a daughter back from town in a pregnant condition, and the children conceived out of wedlock in East London are generally born there. But the child—especially if it is a first child—will probably be received with a good grace after weaning. The pattern of foster-rearing which comes in so conveniently for the children of migrant sons and daughters-in-law is equally well adapted to the unmarried daughter's child. One might almost say that, if the daughter is still young and under parental control, she would feel she has no right to keep the child in town with her. The general feeling seems to be that such children belong to the family at home and are entitled to a place there. This is not to say that the kin at home make no reservations. The daughter's child is not exactly an object of pride; if she is young her 'fall' may be regarded as a family disgrace. In the country one often comes across the homestead-head who becomes evasive when questioned about the relationships between the rest of the household group. Of a particular child or children he will refuse to say anything more than that they are 'children of relatives', 'have their parents in town'.

With a woman who is already an *inkazana* or a multiple unmarried mother the position may be different. She is more independent of the family and therefore more likely to be held responsible for her own children. This, no doubt, is why so many migrants said that a first or second child will be welcomed at home, but that the mother cannot expect her parents to be so obliging about subsequent children. There may be a battle of wills in such cases in so far as the mother herself would prefer to be relieved of the burden of rearing the child in town.

The *ukushweshwa* type of sexual relation in town differs from the 'visiting' type in that it apparently offers the child a domestic upbringing with two parents instead of only one. But when the jural aspects are considered the differences appear a good deal slighter. Even in an *ukushweshwa* household the natural father's relation to the children may be marginal. Guardianship and authority are not his: they belong to the mother's male kin in the country.

The parallel question of a genitor's relation to his natural child in the rural Xhosa system has to be reviewed, as it makes the town situation more intelligible. In the country there are two approved ways open to a man who fathers a child on a woman to whom he is not married. The first is to marry her subsequently, which will give him full paternal rights over the premarital child. This is what he 'ought to' do if he and she are still both marriageable. But if not (e.g. if the woman is an *inkazana*), or if he refuses to be involved in marriage, the other approved way is to make peace with her kin by paying damages for seduction. This is normally five head of cattle. Payment leaves the child within the orbit of its mother's kin, and apparently belonging to their lineage and clan. But at the same time it serves to identify the genitor as the bearer of some fatherly obligations. It is he who 'ought to' provide the sacrificial animal for the child's ritual introduction to the ancestors (*ukubingelela*), and also in due course for the important occasion of initiation, in the case of a boy. The true identity of the genitor 'ought to' be revealed to the natural son at the time of initiation, if not before; some say also to a daughter on reaching marriageable age. Moreover, the genitor may choose to pay an additional beast 'for maintenance' (*isondlo*) in addition to the seduction damages, and by doing so he will acquire further attributes of paternity. A son for whom *isondlo* has been paid should take his genitor's clan name at initiation.

In the rural system, in cases where these standard procedures are used, the word 'illegitimate' seems rather inappropriate. The Red Xhosa—after all—do not merely condone, but institutionalize, childbearing by unmarriageable women. These procedures for regularizing the status of children born out of wedlock can be regarded as basically similar to those for children born in wedlock, i.e. an agreement between the mother's and the father's kin group, and a cattle transaction to mark the agreement. The main difference is that for the extra-marital child fewer cattle are required, and fewer rights pass to the father's kin.

The truly 'illegitimate' child, within the traditional system, is the one whose genitor defaults or deserts, failing to pay the seduction fee or otherwise honour the obligations of his position. Then there is nothing left for the child but to be affiliated exclusively to its mother's family. In the Red countryside this kind of illegitimacy is rare, for the kin groups exert pressure on each other and public opinion on both of them. But in town such pressures are often not felt at all. 'Seducing girls and then denying paternity' is accordingly one of the sins which migrants mention as typical of the anonymous and wicked world of town.

In the case of *ukushweshwa* the genitor, while hardly able to 'deny' paternity in the literal sense, need render no account to the woman's kin. Unless she happens to be from his home place (which is unlikely), no seduction fee and no *isondlo* will change hands to signalize his relation to the child. The removal of the partners from the orbit of their respective kin groups, and the absence of a bond of community between them, radically alter the balance. For the woman, the escape to sexual freedom has cut both ways: 'the people at home' cannot interfere but neither can they help. The genitor, taking no formal steps to establish his status, acquires neither rights nor obligations. All his rights and obligations remain connected with his legitimate family at home. This monopoly is a country wife's strongest weapon against the 'other woman' in town. Her children, and only hers, can continue the lineage, carry on the homestead, perpetuate the father's name and minister to his spirit after death.

RED MIGRANT FATHERS AND THEIR NATURAL CHILDREN

Red migrants themselves were always quick to point out that the *ukushweshwa* children, who might be sharing the household in town with them, were 'not really mine', while the unseen children miles away at the rural home 'are really mine'. The men even avoided the phrase 'my children' in casual conversation when speaking of the offspring in town. The formula would be 'my *ishweshwe*'s children', 'my *inkazana*'s children'. 'My own children, by my wife, are legally mine. My *ishweshwe*'s children are only mine in the sense that they are from my blood, that's all.' 'My *inkazana*'s children do not belong to me. They belong to her and to her parents.' From the point of view of a man's own kin in the country, his offspring by the *ishweshwe* in town practically do not exist. There is no social relation between these biological half-siblings. As one Red father put it, 'when I die these children here [i.e. by his *ishweshwe*] will never be of any help to my own children'. The same applies to all his kin. 'My own children know my sister as *dadebawo* [paternal aunt]. She is nothing to these children of my *ishweshwe*.'

The fact that the *ishweshwe*'s children are on the spot, while the legitimate children are far away, is seen as constituting a temptation which must be resisted—a temptation to become too much entangled with them. The natural children 'must not' seriously rival the legitimate ones, just as the *ishweshwe* 'must not' rival the real wife. It would be a grave wrong, not only against the legitimate wife and children themselves, but against all the kin and ancestors who sanctioned the lawful marriage. 'The *ishweshwe*'s children are not legally mine because there was no parents' consent to our relation.' How strongly the parents and ancestors, as supreme embodiments of morality, guard the home citadel against invasion, was seen in the comments of a man whose lawful wife is no longer alive. Her death has not made him feel any freer. 'Even since her death I cannot treat the *ishweshwe*'s children as if they were my own. For my late wife was the choice of my late parents. They [i.e. their spirits] may disapprove of what I do. The old people did not like the idea of having an *ishweshwe*. They felt it might cause a rift between man and wife.' Another married man made a similar point: 'My wife was the choice of my parents solely, though I love her myself too, as fortunately she is beautiful and pleasant. . . . My children by her are my real children because born of the wife who was chosen by my own parents, through an insight given to them by the ancestors. For the sake of the ancestors, although I love my *ishweshwe*'s children too, I

cannot do anything that would look as if I loved them more than my own.'
Most migrants suggested that it would be morally impossible to let the town-
born illegitimate children visit the *father's* homestead in the country, though
they are free to go to the mother's.

Ritual, financial and domestic arrangements made for the *ukushweshwa*
children reflected the same principle of non-involvement. The first ritual question
to arise is that of the *ukubingelela* sacrifice which introduces to the ancestors.
For a child born in wedlock this is normally performed by the father, or his
deputy, at the paternal kraal, in the presence of the agnatic kin. *Ukubingelela*
is not only a ritual for the ancestors but a standard *rite de passage*, needed by
every infant, whether son or daughter. This duality leads to some difficulties
in the case of an *ishweshwe's* children, who need the *rite de passage* like anyone
else, but have less standing with the ancestors. The usual solution is a compromise. A man will give his *ishweshwe's* children one *ukubingelela* between them,
and this not at home but in town, where any sacrifice *ipso facto* touches the
ancestors less than if done at home. One Red man of about 38 had two legitimate
children at home and two by his *ishweshwe* in town. He had made no sacrifice
yet for the *ishweshwe's* children, but said that he intended to do one *ukubingelela*
for them all, 'some day'. 'For any other sacrifice I would go home, of course,
as I did to *ukubingelela* my own children. But since my *ishweshwe* and her
children cannot go to my home, I shall do it for them here in town, as men in
my situation have always done.'

When it comes to providing for the children's marriage, there must be no
question of the father's taking away from the patrimony of 'his' children in
order to endow 'hers'. A typical response was: 'My wife's children are my
own responsibility. I will pay out marriage cattle for them and will be
responsible for their weddings. But I will never pay out any marriage cattle
for the children of my *ishweshwe*.' Similarly the *ishweshwe's* son can only request,
as a favour, help with initiation expenses, which is the birthright of any
legitimate son. One Red man of nearly 50, whose children by an *ishweshwe*
are beginning to grow up, said he 'thinks he may pay something towards'
their initiation. But of his three legitimate children he said: 'Of course I am
going to send them to circumcision and bear every expense connected with
their well-being.'

Marriage, circumcision, and the like are only occasional questions, while
day-to-day care and support are perpetual ones. Here too, the arrangements
reported and the sentiments expressed by Red migrants brought out the theme
of gift versus right, gratification versus obligation. A wife's children (it would be
explained) can demand support as a birthright, but those of an *ishweshwe*
can only 'request', as of grace and favour. And since money is the practical issue,
the giving and getting and the asking and demanding are phrased in monetary
terms: the crucial questions are about wages earned and handed over, about
expenditure on food, clothes, and medicines.

'I have got two children by my *ishweshwe* here in town', said one Red migrant;
'when they are hungry they know better than to complain to me, as my own
children at home complain'. Another contrasted his *ishweshwe's* children with
his two children by his late wife at home in the country, for whom he was
providing full maintenance including expenses at primary school. 'Those two
at home are my own burden, being my own children. It falls solely on my
shoulders to provide everything they need, up till the time they have their

own homesteads.' But as to his three children in town (by an *ishweshwe* with whom he has associated for nearly twenty years) he said: 'I only give them clothes when I feel like it, or when she pleads. Nor do I bear the whole cost of their food. My *ishweshwe* knows that they are not just my dependants but her own.' Recently the two children from home spent a week-end in town with their father, sleeping in the same room which he shares with his *ishweshwe*. 'She liked them all right, but I could see she had a watchful eye open to see how much money I would spend on them. I bought them everything they wanted. She now wants me to treat her own children in the same way. This I cannot do, because they are not the same as my own. My wife knew about the *ishweshwe* during her lifetime but she never worried, seeing that I always supported the family at home with my entire wages.'

While financial competition with an *ishweshwe* may assume some importance for the wife at home, there is always this concept of right versus mere favour to strengthen her morally. A migrant week-ender illustrated this ideology in explaining how he takes his children a present nearly every time he goes home. 'If I do not bring them something nice, such as sweets, pineapples or meat, my wife will ask me why. She grumbles a lot and complains loudly to every relative who comes near. She usually says: "I don't know what this man has done with all the money, I think he must have spent it for the *ishweshwe* he keeps in East London." When I hear this I just keep quiet, for sometimes she may be right—I may have been helping my *ishweshwe*.' In his own justification he added: 'I always buy more food for my own children, and take them to doctors whenever they are sick, which I would not do for the *ishweshwe's* children. I let those be mainly her own burden.'

In contrast to the usual warnings about the need to inspect an *ishweshwe's* monetary demands very closely, and the danger that she may divert money from the child's needs to her own, Red men often emphasized the virtue of 'believing' the demands of lawful wife for the lawful children. 'My wife at home lets me know every single need of our children there, such as poverty, accidents, illness. She knows she has only to tell me if they need clothes or blankets and I will buy these.' 'I often do not believe my *inkazana* here if she tells me that her two children by me are in want of something, but I always believe my wife.'

It seems that in Red men's insistence on not meeting all of the *ishweshwe's* requests there is more involved than the actual money itself. Of course the money is vital, and anything that diverts it from home and family is wrong; but even more important is the necessity of not seeming to be involved in a new jural relationship. The actual amount spent on the *ishweshwe's* children may matter less than the spirit of non-obligation in which it is offered. If a man were to undertake the financial maintenance of his natural children as a matter of duty, he would *ipso facto* be establishing a jural relation. He might appear like the genitor who establishes relationship by paying *isondlo*, or even like the pater who feeds a son in childhood and later claims his wages in return. The *ishweshwe* being one of those 'things of town' whose entanglements 'ought to' be avoided, any man who wants to keep up appearances must describe every contribution he makes to her children as being in the nature of a voluntary 'gift'. The formula indicates detachment and keeps her in her place, as a mere *inkazana*.

This interpretation is supported by the men's habit of speaking in terms of jural reciprocity. The wife's children must 'get more from me' because they will also have to 'give more to me'. The *ishweshwe's* children must receive more from, and give more to, their mother and her kin. 'My legitimate children when old enough to work will hand over their wages to me. But these children here [i.e. by his *ishweshwe*] will never give me money, from the day they start earning. In fact that is when quarrels will begin between me and their mother.' It is on the same grounds that this migrant will never (he said) contribute anything to their marriage payments: 'The parent who received a young man's wages is the only one who will ever pay marriage cattle for him.' Often a migrant explaining his close-fistedness towards his *ishweshwe's* children said that 'they will never become any help to me either'. 'The *inkazana* and her parents are the only people who will profit by them.'

Similar attitudes were reflected in domestic manners. Most *ukushweshwa* couples discourage the children from calling their natural father 'father'. 'I do not want these children to call me *tata* as though I were married to their mother. She is just an *ishweshwe*. . . . If they call me *tata* my people at home would consider that I am using the *ishweshwe* as a wife, and this would be very unfaithful to my real wife.' 'My *ishweshwe's* children, imitating their mother, address me as *buti mBongwe*, that is, of the *amaBongwe* clan. But they use their mother's clan name for themselves.' 'When my *ishweshwe's* children call me *tata* they are using the word just as they would use it to any man of about my age.' Indeed the actual relation may be concealed from the children entirely. 'My *inkazana's* children have never been told outright that I am their father. They take the mother's parents to be theirs.' 'My *ishweshwe's* children have visited her country home with her, but they know nothing of my country home, and just address me by my clan name.' In such cases the children are supposed to grow up regarding the natural father simply as a 'friend' of their mother's—a fiction which is, of course, more easily sustained if they can be sent away from the town household at an early age.

The fiction satisfies the sense of shame as well as the jural proprieties. That is, although *ukushweshwa* is nothing to be ashamed of among (Red) adults, a mother dislikes her own young children having to reflect about her sexual activities. It is a different matter to tell the child his true parentage privately after he has grown up.

Not being their 'real father', the man who fathers children by an *ishweshwe* cannot expect true filial affection from them. 'When I go home every week-end my children meet me half-way and appear very joyful. The *ishweshwe's* children have never run out to meet me like that. The *ishweshwe* does not like them to grow up thinking of me as a father.' 'Of course my own children show great joy when I arrive home however long I have been absent, for they have been taught by everyone that I am their father. But my *inkazana's* children never show any signs of joy, as I am taken to be simply a friend of their mother's.' The feelings are reciprocal. 'I love my wife's children more than my *ishweshwe's*. They are part and parcel of my family.' The other element in which the relation is notably deficient is the disciplinary one. Red men said that they could not thrash the children they fathered by their *ishweshwe* nor impose rules on them. 'If they do any wrong she prefers to thrash them herself. I suppose she thinks I will overdo it with her children as they are not really mine.' 'The mother wants them to abide by her own rulings rather than mine. If she possibly can, she wants to draw them nearer to her than to me.' 'They seem to fear their mother more than me. It is she who thrashes them. I have not much say in their training, as I have with my own children.'

It is recognized that some men sometimes compromise on the principle of the immutable inferiority of the illegitimate family. Particularly if a man has no legitimate children of his own, or if he is personally estranged from the family at home, he may wish to draw the *ishweshwe*'s children closer to himself, so as to enjoy at least the emotional and authoritarian privileges of fatherhood. But the Red code leaves no doubt that this is morally wrong. Sometimes a migrant's evident affection for an illegitimate child was attributed to the effects of witchcraft. There are said to be several pernicious medicines which an unscrupulous *ishweshwe* will use to fasten the father's affections on to her own child 'because she wants the man to stay with her for ever'. The medicine will be particularly effective if mixed with the child's tears (collected in a teaspoon when he happens to cry) before being secretly introduced into the father's food. This may be compared with the belief discussed in chapter 9, that witches seek to keep men in town, spirits to draw them back to the country.

The practical logic of the situation is that just as the man is not legally bound to his *ishweshwe*'s children, these children are not legally bound to him. Behind all his calculations must be the perpetual thought that anything he expends on them—whether in the form of money, time or moral training— may all too easily turn out to have been 'wasted'. 'Their mother can marry any man she likes and they would then be regarded as his. This may happen even after I have wasted my strength trying to treat them like my own children.' 'However much I might love my *inkazana's* children she could decide to reject me at any time and go away with them for ever.'

It is from the mother's point of view that the conflicts may appear more serious. To the mother the child may be equally important as asset and as liability. The child is an obvious liability in so far as it costs money for maintenance, diminishes earning power and sexual freedom, and perhaps causes recrimination from kin at home. But from a long-term point of view the mother seems usually to consider it an important asset. Red migrant fathers, when explaining why they would not like to introduce their extra-marital children into their home kraals, did not merely emphasize the wrong it would be in the eyes of their own kin; they also emphasized the wrong it would be in the eyes of the mother. 'Those are the *ishweshwe*'s own children. She is the one who has a right to take them to her country home, whenever she likes. She will not want them to go to my [the father's] kraal.' 'My *ishweshwe* is quite afraid lest one day the children should leave her alone, and go to my home, and try to adopt my clan name instead of hers.' 'The children of an *ishweshwe* are all she has.'

The eventual prize is the right to the allegiance of the children in one's old age. 'The *ishweshwe* wants to keep her children to look after her when she is old.' Thus even from the economic point of view immediate arguments have to be weighed against long-term ones. It is true that if the *ishweshwe* can persuade a man to 'treat her children like a real father', in terms of money, she will have things financially easier for the time being, but in proportion she may have jeopardized her moral claim to the children's earnings one day. By currently bearing the burden herself she takes out some insurance for her future.

PATRIARCHAL AND 'MATRIFOCAL' TENDENCIES

These *ukushweshwa* households, and the 'visiting' households mentioned in the previous chapter, invite comparison with the 'matrifocal' families reported for Negroes in the New World. In East London, where sexual liaisons are so commonplace and the natural fathers so firmly repudiate real responsibility, one might well have expected the development of families which are 'matrifocal, in one or another sense. ('Matrifocal' seems a term capable of being used rather ambiguously, e.g. its referent may be primarily the jural system (children not being effectively affiliated to their father's kin) or primarily only domestic relations (predominance of mother and maternal kin in child-rearing, etc.). Both senses would apply here.) It has been shown how the migrant Xhosa sidestep this tendency by causing many of the children to be absorbed into patriarchally defined groups, though on the mother's not the father's side.

R. T. Smith has pointed out that in the so-called common law marriages of Negroes in British Guiana the husband contributes little to the family which could not equally well be contributed by the mother.[2] The father is of little significance in either economic or social senses. This is equally true of the Xhosa male (in both the *ukushweshwa* and the 'visiting' types of union) and it makes him an equally marginal figure. But it must always be remembered that these unions, however prominent in town, are secondary in the context of the Xhosa migrants' social system as a whole. Many and perhaps most of the men who live under *ukushweshwa* in town, or beget children by 'visiting', are also legally married to wives in the country. In this other setting they enjoy full patriarchal privileges. And even if the man has no legitimate family, the fact remains that *ukushweshwa* (or 'visiting') is not socially a substitute for marriage. Most Xhosa men still aspire to 'proper' marriage as the first choice; the man left with only an *ishweshwe* or an *inkazana* 'has missed his chances in life'. From the woman's point of view, too, it is more respectable to be a wife, or even a daughter whose children are accepted into the patriarchal family at home, than an unattached mother whose children stay permanently in town as 'children of women'.

Thus the patriarchal family system of the migrant Xhosa remains intact alongside the matrifocal system, one being associated with the country and the other with the town. The matrifocal families are essentially more possible in the urban than in the peasant setting. In the peasant setting the male is an economically necessary member of the family. Even if routine agricultural tasks are largely left to Xhosa women, men remain responsible for livestock and for some heavy incidents of the agricultural cycle. Secondly, the peasant family needs a nucleus of property (homestead, fields, cattle), as its basis for subsistence; the male head has importance there as the property-owner and channel for transmitting inheritance. Thirdly, the male head is necessary in the country to transmit social status, since lineage and clan are still so important there. All this falls away in town, where wages are earned and spent from day to day, and achieved 'class' status counts for more than ascribed descent status.

In so far as the country retains the stronger moral pull, so does the patriarchal set of institutions. For the Xhosa unmarried mother, to send the children away is to reclaim them for rustic and for patriarchal values at one and the same time.

[2] Smith, Raymond T.: *The Negro Family in British Guiana*.

PART FIVE

SUMMARY AND CONCLUSIONS

18

Network, Culture and Change

IN COLLABORATION WITH IONA MAYER

RECAPITULATION: COMPULSION AND CHOICE

The country-bred Xhosa who migrates to East London must, as is obvious, learn another mode of living in order to accommodate himself to this very different environment; we have seen that the new mode may or may not be an urbanized one. It may involve cultural urbanization (learning a preference for urban ways and institutions) and/or structural urbanization (striking permanent roots in town), which in present conditions do not necessarily go hand in hand. But it may involve neither; some kinds of migrants, particularly Red men, have been found to stay for long years in town ('stabilization') without doing either. If some migrants become genuinely urbanized, then, there are many who resist urbanization, continuing to look on themselves as countrymen in temporary or perhaps permanent exile; and many others whose response is ambiguous, and their ultimate fate uncertain.

All the migrants have to act within a limiting framework of compulsion. There is the economic compulsion of having to earn in town in order to supplement the living that can be made in the country. There is the administrative compulsion of influx control, which forces migrants to stay in town for long periods but also prevents them from easily making permanent homes there. There is the occupational compulsion: they have to be employed while they are in town (on pain of being expelled), but also have to confine themselves to strictly limited kinds of employment. Nevertheless, it was suggested in chapter 1 that life in town demands more numerous acts of choice from the migrant than life in the country. Not only is there more variety in town, but distance from home increases freedom. Choice has its sphere in the private and leisure lives of the migrants, including their domestic, religious, and recreational activities. By examining choices made in these fields (it has seemed) one can go some way towards distinguishing the migrant who is becoming urbanized from the one who is not; or at least the one whose strong desire for urbanization is now being officially frustrated, from the one who had not intended to become urbanized in any case.

The principle that the town life demands more acts of choice than the country life could be said to operate on both levels of analysis, the 'structural' and the 'cultural'. Structurally speaking, i.e. when considering the question of social ties, we have suggested that the migrant's original relations in the country are mainly ascribed to him, but that the town-located part of his network has to be constructed through his own acts of choice. Culturally, i.e. when considering the question of institutions, habits, and values, it appeared that the individual is left little choice how to act while he is in his rural community, but that the urban system is marked by greater institutional diversification—availability of several alternative answers to a given cultural question—which allows and even compels him to build up his own personal synthesis when in town. Thus (remembering always that we are concerned with personal, spare-time activities) from both viewpoints the contrast between migrants' town opportunities and their country opportunities has seemed to be a contrast between the optional and the inescapable, the alternative and the given; the over-all contrast is between organization on the one hand, and structure on the other.

THE RED LIMITATION OF CHOICE

It has been shown (chapter 5) that the conservative Red migrant's choices in the matter of forming or maintaining his social network are generally guided by three principles: (1) to keep the country relations in good repair, (2) to avoid new ties, especially with non-Red people in town, (3) to show solidarity with the rest of his 'home people' in town. It is from among these home people in town that he chooses his initial host, his room-mates (chapter 5), his regular drinking companions, and his leisure-time associates generally (chapter 6). It is they who are expected to help him in emergency, to arbitrate in his quarrels and to guide him along the paths of right conduct (chapter 7). These are men related to him by old personal ties, often existing since boyhood. He may have grown up alongside them, or 'played sticks' with them, or been initiated with them, or attended the same Red weekly entertainments in the country. Hence it was said (chapter 7) that the Red migrant relies on 'stretching' his network (geographically) rather than on 'enlarging' it by working in new acquaintances. He uses the same individuals for his town purposes as for his country purposes, whenever possible.

The School migrant's choice of associates, it has been seen (in chapters 13–14), is not necessarily or usually guided by these principles. The School migrant does not emphasize the paramountcy of home ties as such. He need not be drawn home by his dependants, for he has moral liberty to take them into town with him. He does not avoid making new friends in town. He does not cling to his home people there. He tends to build up a new section of network in town, which has no inherent connexion with his old network in the country.

It has seemed fair to say that these different patterns result from different choices, or moral drives, as much as from external pressures. True, the School migrant is better qualified to make new friends in town, because of his wider range of cultural aptitudes. The Red migrant is handicapped in that the smarter and more educated people in the town locations evidently do not want a 'raw' tribesman as their associate; often enough the church people do not seem to want him much either (chapter 12). If he tries to mingle with them he may meet with rebuffs or insults. Associating with home people is easier and more convenient for him. But one cannot regard this as the sole explanation.

Possibilities exist for crossing the barriers if one tries hard enough, as some Red migrants have found (chapters 11–12).

In the cultural frame of reference, the question was seen as that of choosing between the alternative institutions, habits or standards, which are encountered in the urban locations: the alternative recreational and religious practices, the alternative personal habits and style of life. In this context, just as in the matter of network formation, it has seemed to be equally true that conservative Red migrants when in town refuse to explore their local powers of choice. Such a man seems to allow himself little alternative to Red-style drinking, or Red-style singing and dancing, or pagan ritual. We have seen (chapter 6) how, through long years of residence in town, he will hardly avail himself of the many urban amusements, but will prefer to spend his evenings shut up in a room where he and his friends can drink in Red fashion and 'talk about home'. He will spend little on new clothes or amenities; he may still sleep on the floor, as Red people do in the country (chapter 8). He will cling to pagan religious practices (chapter 9) and refuse to be drawn into Christian church activities (chapter 12); he will remain uneducated or semi-educated, or will learn to read and write solely for practical purposes (chapter 11); he will not aspire to higher education, to white-collar jobs, to 'civilization' generally. Twenty or more years in town need not affect this pattern fundamentally (chapter 7).

Here too it seems clear that 'will not' is involved together with 'cannot'. Illiteracy and other Red rustic attributes are initial handicaps to changing the style of life in town, but they are not insuperable ones. A Red migrant who is really determined to civilize himself can find ways and means in town: the Bhengu Church perhaps, the dance hall, or the night school. The outstanding fact is that according to Red ideas he 'ought not' to want to. From childhood he has been taught to despise ukurumsha, the learning of town ways, and to regard it as a sign of moral failure only second to ukutshipha, absconding.

This conservative ideal, which has been noticed as typical of the Red Xhosa, in country and town alike, works in two ways. First there is the negative aspect: Red people are hostile on principle to most non-Red institutions, and therefore avoid most of the available associations, churches, amusements, and urban-style amenities, and also such innovations as having married women come to earn money in town. We have seen how deep this suspicion of non-Red ways goes in the country, where the institutions and practices of the School people are deliberately avoided by their Red neighbours (chapter 2). The Red Xhosa have elevated abstention into a moral duty. Secondly there is the positive aspect. A 'good' Red man must remain committed to Red institutions or habits for the very reason that they are Red. He must value the ways of the ancestors, 'who like people to go on living in the way they themselves used to live'. Conservatism, i.e. continuance in specifically Red ways, is equated with tribal loyalty. 'I want to go on looking what I am, a proper Red man' (chapter 2). Of course there are many institutions of the traditional Red way of life which cannot well be transplanted to town, but the migrants do their best. For their leisure activities in town they devise such imitations or near-substitutes as the iseti and the mbutho, the so-called intlombe of town (chapter 6), or the curtailed ancestor sacrifices performed there at some personal risk (chapter 9).

As a combined result of these negative and these positive tendencies, the Red men in town are found still practising (as to leisure activities) undiversified institutions. They are mostly still confined within the institutional limits of their home rural culture; mostly doing the same kinds of things as each other, and similar things to their friends at home in the country. Hence culturally speaking they appear more homogeneous than either the School migrants (whose morality is less restrictive) or the born East Londoners. It is one aspect of this that (by other people's reckoning) they do not appear to be diffused through the class structure, but rather to be lumped together in a particular stratum, at the bottom (chapter 4).

REMAINING WITHIN THE HOME SYSTEM

It was said that the Red migrant to East London seems to refuse to explore the powers of choice allowed to him by the new social environment—the East London locations, with their absence of unitary social structure or culture. To put it in a somewhat different way, what such a man apparently chooses is to continue to act as if his network were still ascribed to him. The ascriptions he assumes are those of the home rural community. To live with a brother or an age-mate from home, to drink with these and other *amakhaya*, to keep within the home circle for all possible purposes, is to obey the structural rules of the home community, which assign these men to each other as the proper companions for periods of exile. Similarly in the cultural frame of reference: he chooses still to follow the ways prescribed for him before in the institutionally undiversified home culture.

The School migrant, not using *amakhaya* as his preferred associates in town, is largely freed from the structure of his home community. It is not necessarily the frame of reference within which he still feels himself to be acting *while in town*. If he picks up new friends in town, the common frame of reference within which he and they interact is presumably something belonging to the town; perhaps a church or some other association, perhaps a class, or a set, or a clique. Nor are his habits, when in town, necessarily limited to what the home culture prescribed.

The suggestion is, then, that the general relegation of Red migrants to the bottom of the class ladder in town does not *only* reflect their inability to rise by reason of lack of skill, but is also due to their persistence in acting out parts according to the expectations of the home peasant society instead of the expectations of local (non-Red) society. For example, we have seen (chapter 8) that Red migrants can often do as well as or better than School migrants in economic terms. Admittedly they are excluded from the few highest-ranking occupations, but within the limits of the unskilled or semi-skilled work which is the lot of the great majority of all migrants, the Red man does not seem to be seriously handicapped. He may stay longer in a job, and be better thought of by the employer, than a colleague who is not Red. Not a few Red men attain positions which are enviable by location standards (foremen, drivers, house-owners). But the Red success man, as long as he remains incapsulated, refuses to play the part according to local non-Red expectations. Those would require him to spend more on consumer goods as his income rises, and visibly to improve his standard of living. Instead he acts his part according to rural Red ideas, which call for something quite different—a careful hoarding and investment with the direct or indirect object of benefiting the family and homestead in the country.

Generally speaking, rich or poor, the Red migrant himself remains comparatively insensitive to the urban sanction of snobbish disapproval, because he is not measuring himself or his achievements by local urban standards. He is doing well according to his own lights if he makes use of the years in town to 'protect' his peasant homestead economically (chapter 5), and so to acquire hope of a dignified old age in the country.

Can one account for this 'unnecessary' persistence in acting as if still within the confines of another structure? We know that from the first moment the moral pressures are strong. The Red migrant is taught that he 'ought to' prefer his own *amakhaya* to any other possible associates in town. He ought to remain under their eyes, for by so doing he will also remain in sight of his people at home, and of the supreme moral guardians—the spirits of the ancestors, on whom all well-being depends. In fact one who tries to evade the *amakhaya* in town is also (it is felt) trying to evade the voice of morality or conscience, for this is represented by parents, ancestors, and 'people' (chapter 9).[1] Similarly in the matter of making new friends in town: the Red migrant is taught that he 'ought to' abstain, that 'getting mixed up with other people' can only lead to demoralization and trouble, unless indeed they are culturally similar Red people who will not interfere with the basic loyalty to the home. But the question remains how these principles can continue in operation for so long after the migrant leaves home. To understand this, it may help to consider the 'close-knit' nature of the typical Red migrant's network.[2]

Migrant life in a teeming city offers, as life in the country does not, the opportunity to build up a network of the 'loose-knit' type, in which there are few relationships between the component members. Networks in the Xhosa country community are necessarily rather 'close-knit', i.e. most of those whom ego knows also know each other. The Red migrant's choices result in his continuing to have a network of the close-knit type. His regular spare-time associates in town are necessarily known to each other as well as to him, for the fact which recommends each of them to him (i.e. coming from the same home-place) also recommends each of them to all the others. The 'group' nature of the typical Red leisure activities in town, e.g. the *iseti*, the *mbutho*, the 'case-hearing' of the *amakhaya*, illustrates this high degree of network-connectedness; so does the Red migrant's reluctance to claim any one individual as his 'best' friend (chapter 6). (It was shown that both these features have parallels in Red rural society.) It is not a matter of 'A being one friend to B, and C being another friend to B', but rather of 'A and B and C all being friends together'. But this 'close-knit' tendency does not only characterize the town-located part of a Red migrant's network: it also characterizes his entire network considered as a whole —country-located plus town-located—for the *amakhaya* in town are necessarily known to the people at home as well.

The influence of absent parents and seniors can persist precisely because, in the direct relations between *amakhaya* in town, indirect relations are implied too. These consist in the consciousness that each man still has kin or friends in the same community at home. Thus indirect or third-party sanctions emanating from home do much to regulate the men's interactions while they are in town. The preference for leaving wives and children in the country, the emphasis on

---

[1] This aspect of the ancestor cult is stressed by M. Fortes in a different context: '. . . the individual has no choice. Submission to his ancestors is symbolic of his encapsulation in a social order which permits of no voluntary alteration of his status and social capacity.' *Oedipus and Job in West African religion*, p. 67.

[2] This usage of the terms 'loose-knit' and 'close-knit' follows Bott: *Family and Social Network*.

frequent visits home and on retiring as soon as possible, help to keep this pressure up. A man is aware that what he does in town will be known in the country, and he knows how it will be judged. If he offends one of his *amakhaya*, the people at home—as well as the home-people in town—can be expected to invoke sanctions against him. It is obvious that this system helps to keep the horizons narrower than one would prima facie have expected for people moving into the great world of town.

Since these Red men who have relations in town are related within another frame of reference at the same time, they can regard themselves as a kind of extension of the home community into the town setting—a still-incorporated section of it, not excised, merely displaced for the present. Each Red migrant when dealing with his associates in town can feel that he is still operating within the social structure of his home community.

NETWORK, CULTURE AND CHANGE

It can be said that in using two frames of reference (namely social ties and cultural habits) to demonstrate one Red tendency (namely the refusal to depart from previous ascriptions) we have only been looking at two dimensions of the same reality. However, it may be useful to try to formulate more explicitly the connexion between Red network patterns and Red institutions, and School network patterns and School institutions.

The School migrant is far less likely to maintain a close-knit network. Even if he builds up a circle of friends in town who mostly know each other (as, for instance, by moving within the confines of a particular church congregation), these need not be known to his people at home. The move to town, it has appeared (chapter 13), usually creates for the School migrant a 'discontinuous' network pattern, the second network section not being connected with the first except through the link of ego himself. Nor need his second network section, located in town, in itself be close-knit like his first. If he happens to avail himself freely of associational opportunities in town—as many School migrants do—there may be every reason for it to appear loose-knit. Suppose he not only belongs to the Ethiopian Church but plays rugby and joins the Vigilance Association, he is making use of three specialized agencies, none of which necessarily overlaps with the others in terms of personnel. His associates need not associate with each other.

The contrast suggests that the close-knit form of the network is dependent upon, or at least encouraged by, the absence of institutional diversification. A similar point has been made by Bott, who remarks that network-connectedness is discouraged in urban environments, because separate agencies take charge of separate aspects of life there. For present purposes, however, we are not concerned with formal and functionally specific relations of the kind enumerated by Bott (relations with the employer, school, hospital, etc.), but only with the migrant's personal friends and associates. Even on this level, it has appeared that the activities of the Red people are less diversified, just as their networks are less often loose-knit. Where the institutions of a particular set of people remain undiversified, individuals cannot diverge by reason of their different choices. In this way each circle of Red migrants, by all subscribing to the one inclusive set of institutions and standards in their domestic and private lives, can be said to have bought for themselves a general all-round compatibility, i.e. the ability to co-act through the whole range of institutions which they recognize. A and B and C, and the rest of them, who were co-actors in stick-fights and *iintlombe* at home, were at that time equally well qualified to co-act in ritual, work parties, and other activities. Having come to town, and refusing to subscribe to non-Red alternative institutions, they find themselves all still qualified to act with each other for all private purposes—their *iseti*, their *mbutho*, their rituals, their case-hearing, their reception to the tribal chief, their week-end journeys home. These are essentially multiplex relations, therefore.

By contrast, where people recognize a high proportion of optional or alternative (non-compulsory) institutions, the conditions which automatically make for close-knit networks and multiplex relations are lacking. This applies to the School migrants. Although the School rural community appears to offer little more institutional diversity than the Red rural community, its limits are set more by poverty of resources than by disapproval in principle. For a migrant from an 'undiversified' School community, movement into the more varied society of the East London locations straight away means a demand to choose between the various available alternatives there, which his culture recognizes as all equally proper(e.g. which church, or none?; which recreations, or none?). In making such choices A diverges from B in one respect, from C in another. Only if two School individuals happen to build up the same synthesis of preferred habits will they find themselves remaining compatible for all purposes of their private lives. More likely each man needs, for his different purposes, different individual friends or sets of friends, whose roles in relation to himself become specific and distinct, perhaps even antipathetic (as in the case of church friends versus drinking friends). Thus in the case of the School migrant the allotment of roles or functions to the various associates is much less combinative, the close-knit type of network much less practicable.

In the close-knit Red network, consistent influences must be felt always, wherever one happens to be for the time being. There is no growing-point for change.

But when one departs from the close-knit pattern of network (as most School migrants do), the possibility of experiencing alternately a number of inconsistent cultural influences or pressures is admitted. There is, it is true, no reason in principle why a network of the loose-knit type might not happen to consist of culturally similar individuals, all exercising compatible moral and cultural pressures. This might happen in the case of the 'free-lance' Reds discussed in the next section. But a loose-knit network offers no such *guarantee*. A migrant with a loose-knit network in town may start to apply, when with his club-mates, standards of conduct or etiquette which differ from the standards taught by his church associates, or his girl-friend; more probably still, any or all of these may differ from standards expected at home in the country. We have noticed the significant case of the School migrant who cannot bear his drinking-friends to recognize him if he happens to meet them when in the company of his church friends. This is the loose-knit principle carried to extreme: not merely an absence of relations between the component members (with their different standards) but a deliberate policy of preventing such relations. It can be done in town; it could not be done in the face-to-face rural community.

The discontinuity of the School network (as between the town section as a whole and the country section as a whole) has a similar effect. A man can easily begin to practise 'town ways' for the benefit of his friends in East London, yet shed them for the benefit of his more orthodox-minded friends at home, because there is no active relation between these two sets of people.

It is true that the loose-knit condition which admits inconsistent pressures (and therefore the possibility of change), will also make inconsistencies endurable. The personality need not suffer too much as a battle-ground for the conflicting standards of different friends; the battle can be indefinitely evaded, in a sense, by simply adjusting to the standards of the company one happens to be in for the time being. Thus the tempo of change need not be forced, or the rural ways may be resumed when 'at home', despite the new cultural lessons learnt. A sharper conflict seems to be the lot of (for instance) the Red convert to Bhenguism, whose network is discontinuous without being loose-knit on either side; i.e. it consists of two incongruent sections, each in itself of the close-knit and morally demanding type. In such cases there may be a stronger temptation to resolve the personal conflict quickly by repudiating the ties on one side or the other. (Chapter 12.)

TRIBAL LOYALTY AND THE RED NETWORK

There is a further point to be noticed in the case of the Red network pattern: the relation between local and Red Xhosa (or 'tribal') loyalties. The warning to the Red migrants against making new friends, it was observed, refers particularly to School and town-born friends. New friendships with other *Red* people may be tolerated (chapter 6), e.g. sharing off-duty breaks with a Red workmate, or living with a Red concubine, irrespective of the home place of origin. Such excursions can evidently be tolerated because the workmate and the concubine, being Red, are not likely to come between a man and his own *amakhaya*. Either they serve as auxiliaries to the home circle (as when the Red concubine supplies the beer for the man's *iseti* of home people [chapter 6]) or at least they refrain from intruding on it (as when the 'decent' *ishweshwe* defers to the wife [chapter 16]).

It was also seen that besides the type of 'incapsulating' network *par excellence* (where nearly all the intimate associates are *amakhaya*), there exists an alternative form for the Red man who has not been able to remain within any particular group of *amakhaya*. He may choose to become what one might call a free-lance Red: he is content to make friends with other men in town regardless of their home origin, provided only that they are all Red country people of some kind or another. These free-lances are often former farm servants (chapter 10), or dispossessed peasants whose rural connexions have all broken down. Independent Red women are found following a similar pattern (chapter 15). They thus go on belonging to the Red section as such, though not to any particular Red community outside town.

The patterns of Red migrants' networks in town, then, reflect two distinct loyalties, which are combined in the case of incapsulation proper, while in the alternative type one has persisted longer than the other. One is the specific community loyalty, the other the general Red-section loyalty. Both are carried over from the country. Community loyalty in the country begins with the rural location (witness the organized stick-fights between Red youths of near-by locations, which are a regular feature of country life), though it may have a wider referent—the location cluster or the district—according to context. Some of it, carried over into the town setting, helps to bind together (say) the

Tshabo men, or the Middledrift men, or the Kentani men. If the home district is sufficiently near to East London, regular home-visiting helps to maintain the local patriotism; if it is further afield, the organization of the *amakhaya* in town itself assumes greater importance (chapter 5).

The second of the two loyalties, to what they see as the 'true Xhosa' section, produces the sectional exclusiveness of Reds as Reds—their preference for mingling with each other and not with non-Reds—which we have seen to be a marked feature in Xhosa rural society (chapter 2). The Red people feel that they themselves constitute an in-group, that all others belong to an out-group, that relations which transcend this boundary may have to be endured but should never be sought. The kind of avoidance-pattern which results in the country is repeated in town: Red people fight shy of personal intimacies with non-Red people (chapters 2–4). The sense of patriotic opposition to White people (chapters 2, 3) has been extended to cover those 'renegade' Xhosa (i.e. School and town people) who are held to have aligned themselves with the White man.

In town as in the country these two loyalties, the local and 'tribal', are interwoven. They maintain and reinforce each other. The Red Xhosa as a whole expect one to remain loyal to one's home people; the home people expect one to remain loyal to the Red section. These expectations cannot be enforced on the genuinely unwilling. They are backed by a kind of sanction which, however, retains its dreadful force only so long as ego himself continues to feel morally bound to the group. It is the sanction of excommunication—the power of the powerless. Anyone who fails in loyalty is felt to have invited his own excommunication. 'He does not want us, so we do not want him.' The *amakhaya*, the parents and the ancestor-spirits are entitled to wash their hands of the man who cuts himself off from home, or who joins the non-Red outgroup (chapter 7). This kind of sanction has meaning only in the context of the circular or close-knit type of relation.

As has been stressed, all the migrants, Red and School alike, are faced by the same kind of external situation—the transition from the relatively undiversified institutions of the country to the wide variety of town. It is the question of their *willingness* to branch out into alternatives, when given the opportunity, that makes the critical difference: in other words, Red morality is involved. This morality is not only conservative in tendency (as one would expect in association with an ancestor cult): it must also be called markedly conformist and totalitarian, for it tends to evaluate a great many actions (regardless of their intrinsic importance or unimportance) by the one unvarying test, the test of congruence with 'real Xhosa' loyalties and tradition. This is the morality which condemns one for apparent trivialities like wearing a tie or going to a cinema, and obviously it must circumscribe both a migrant's participation in urban institutions and his ability to enjoy new relations.

The Red Xhosa are not the only category we have noticed in East London who combine exclusiveness with marked moral conformism. Some churches, particularly the Bhengu Church, do the same. The Bhenguist is taught that moral value attaches to such personal details as cleanliness, tidiness, non-smoking and non-drinking. To this extent he too finds it difficult or risky to mingle sociably with outsiders; he too is thrown back into something very like incapsulation. He finds general compatibility with members of his own sect and little compatibility with outsiders.

CONCLUSION

The social organization of School migrants in town seems to reflect a willingness to move in various directions—they take advantage of their liberty. But that of Red migrants seems to reflect a wish to remain bound by the structure from which their migration could have liberated them. Their way of organizing themselves amounts to voluntarily rebuilding something as like the home system as possible.

This power of certain systems to recreate themselves in a greatly changed environment—a power which might be termed conservative dynamism—has been observed also in some of the notable studies of American ethnic groups. In the present work, instead of the rich comparative material of (say) Yankee City,[3] we have had to limit ourselves to comparing two groups only—groups of the same linguistic and ethnic background, at a similar distance from their homes of origin. On the basis of the present material it could at least be said that the organizational features which we have noticed among the migrants on each side seem to be related by more than chance association: they seem to form two regular syndromes. The Red syndrome, which has been termed incapsulation, has as one feature a 'tribal' type of moral conformism, stressing the superiority of the original undiversified institutions; such institutions make for multiplex relations and the close-knit type of network; and this again makes for consistent moral pressure and conservatism. The processes are two-way or circular ones. It is by refusing to branch out into new habits that Red migrants retain a basis for close-knit networks; while it is by keeping the networks close-knit that they inhibit cultural branching-out.

In the other syndrome, more characteristic of School migrants, we find a culture which has been more tolerant in principle of the engagement in diversified institutions; accordingly, a tendency towards the single-strand type of relation and the loose-knit type of network. Again this produces two-way or circular effects. Cultural specialization makes for looser-knit networks, while the looseness of the network allows for cultural specialization. The School culture, with its institutional diversification, thus carries within itself its own dynamic of change in the migrant situation.

We could represent the two alternatives diagrammatically:

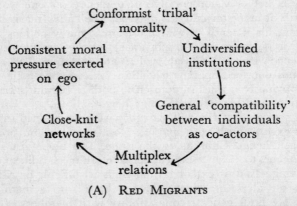

(A) RED MIGRANTS

[3] Warner, W. Lloyd, and Srole, L.: *The Social Systems of American ethnic groups*, 1945.

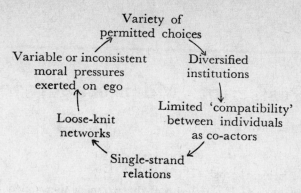

(B) SCHOOL MIGRANTS

There seem to be no overriding reasons in the East London situation itself why one syndrome should occur rather than the other. On the one hand, Xhosa migrants in East London have excellent opportunities for remaining incapsulated within their old social systems if they wish. They are mostly not too far away from their homes of origin; they are officially discouraged from tearing up roots there; and they come to town in such numbers that material for building up the community-in-exile is readily available. On the other hand the opportunities for becoming assimilated and incorporated into the urban society are likewise excellent. The migrants are ethnically and linguistically at one with the people they meet in the East London locations; there are no insuperable barriers to prevent them from attaining prestige or high class-standing there—rewards which are offered to those who become urbanized, not to those who resist. Seeing that all these situational factors apply equally to Red and School migrants, one can seek explanation only in the Red–School cultural difference itself.

One of the most relevant features of the Red culture, evidently, is the emphasis on group activities and group judgement, and the evaluation of group friendships as more important than person-to-person friendships. Another is the 'tribal' attitude of the Red people (of which their conformist morality is an aspect). If we can define tribalism as a group's belief that a unique and exclusive relation must exist between itself and its institutions, the Red Xhosa are more tribal, and the School Xhosa less so. The School Xhosa long ago agreed that certain institutions of another group or groups—notably Christianity and formal education—were to be shared by themselves; the Red Xhosa refused. Thus, in the long run, the different potentialities for urbanization shown by these two categories of Xhosa today can be said to have a basis in the different reactions of an earlier generation to a particular conquest situation over a hundred years ago. We have discussed some reasons why these differences have remained significant in vastly changed circumstances.

19

Postscript: Mdantsane 1970

MOVE TO THE 'HOMELANDS'

Ten years after this book was written, the prospect mentioned in chapter 3 (page 45) has come to pass. The old East London locations are being pulled down. The Xhosa labour force is being progressively rehoused in Mdantsane, a 'homeland' township, where the workers are to have settled homes, along with their wives and families.

The book has been specially concerned with the perpetuation among migrants of the sharp Red/School opposition, and the conservative Red migrants' technique of incapsulating themselves in small close-knit networks of *amakhaya* (home people) while in town. This postscript gives some of the grounds for thinking that neither phenomenon can continue unchanged in Mdantsane—owing to its very different ecological and administrative framework—but that nevertheless the people will remain socially and morally attached to their country homes.

The book has depicted Red people in the slums of East London, beset by administrative restrictions and battling with poverty, remaining proudly attached to their tribal ways and values. The intervening ten years have been (in the words of the South African Minister of Finance) 'the most fantastic decade' —the one in which the country's economic growth was faster than that of any other country in the Western world. As in other countries, 'growth' has actually meant a widening gap between rich and poor. Thus for the African section of the population profit and loss were not as happily balanced as for most whites, although many did achieve higher incomes and better standards of living.

To sustain the rapid growth of the 1960's, great numbers of Africans were needed to man South African factories. The resulting flow of black workers to urban areas led to the whites being progressively outnumbered there. Government policies were designed to halt and eventually reverse this 'worsening' demographic trend. Negatively, whatever permanent rights of residence black people still had in urban areas (see page 56 ff.) were curtailed, and the new acquisition of such rights virtually stopped. Positively, the Government forged ahead with its plans for 'Bantu homelands', and for 'Border industries'. The object of these is to have industries located in 'white' areas close to the borders of Bantu 'homelands', so that black people can live in the homelands and still go out day by day to work for white employers, as they have done hitherto from the urban locations of the 'white' cities. The hope is that the ratio of white to black in the 'white areas' can thus be improved without withdrawing labour from industry; and that black people will also enjoy fuller rights within their 'homelands' than they did in the towns, including the right of a man to have his

family living with him permanently. In more concrete terms, this new phase
of Government policy means that large numbers of often reluctant black people
are being removed to the 'homelands', where new towns, villages, and settlements are being erected by the Government to receive them.

In the case of East London the operation constitutes a massive slum clearance;
it also provides a showpiece for the border industry policy. A huge new all-
black town, Mdantsane, has arisen out of nothing on the veld some twelve
miles from the city centre. (About early plans for the new 'satellite town', see
page 45.) Administratively it does not belong with the city but with the Ciskeian
Territorial Authority, the second homeland for the Xhosa, which was officially
inaugurated in 1968. The new town is administered by officials of the Department of Bantu Administration and Development, with headquarters in Pretoria.
Some 60,000 Africans have been removed from the old East London locations
which this book described, and rehoused in Mdantsane, along with smaller
numbers from other 'white' towns and farms. The Duncan Village shack area,
where the Red people congregated, has been almost completely demolished
already. The whole of the East London location area is being set aside for
Coloured and Indian occupation.

While the political and administrative framework of Mdantsane is largely
peculiar to South Africa, nevertheless much of what it offers and what it
imposes, as a place to live, can be paralleled from slum clearance and rehousing
schemes in other countries, e.g. in Nigeria (see P. Marris, *Family and Social
Change in an African City: A Study of Rehousing in Lagos*, Routledge and Kegan
Paul, 1961) and also in Britain. The prize is to be able to rent (or in some
circumstances buy) a decent new house, with a garden of one's own, in clean
and pleasant surroundings, with amenities like proper water and electricity
supply and indoor sanitation. The price is a long and expensive daily journey
to work, but beyond this (as we shall see) a suburban syndrome of loneliness
and boredom: a life with 'nothing to do' and 'nowhere to go' outside working
hours; the isolation of the family from its friends and relatives, and the absence
of anything like an organic neighbourhood or community life. It is all in
marked contrast to the teeming life of the shacks on the one hand, and the old-
established community life of the rural reserves on the other.

THE PRICE OF REHOUSING

The way of life which Mdantsane implies is something totally new in the
people's experience. They used to be either migrants or townspeople—now they
are to be commuters. The family home used to be either in the tribal countryside
or in the city—now it is to be in a dormitory suburb, more or less. The process
of urbanization has presented itself in a new guise, and both Red and School
people have had to readjust accordingly.

Mdantsane consists almost entirely of detached four-roomed houses, each
intended to be occupied by a worker with his dependants (wife, unmarried
children, aged parents, etc.). The occupants can take in lodgers too, but this
requires special permits. New houses are going up at the rate of between thirty
and forty a week, and are being filled straight away. They are let at sub-economic
rentals of (at present) about R6 per month; they can also be purchased over
forty years. The authorities estimate that the whole population transfer will be
completed by about 1976. Mdantsane (it is envisaged) will then hold upwards
of 200,000 people. According to the 1970 census it already has 71,000, as against

60,500 remaining in the Duncan Village location. But the authorities admit that the real figures for Mdantsane are probably thirty per cent higher.

Compared with the shacks of Duncan Village, Mdantsane is hygienic and spacious. The town has been ambitiously designed by a special planning unit in Pretoria. The streets are skilfully laid out along the contours of the hilly site instead of in the familiar monotonous grids of straight roads and rectangular blocks. The main streets are tarred and wide. Each house stands on a largish plot of garden. From almost any point one may see two or three of the twenty-six schools which have been built so far, mainly on hilltops. The administrative offices of the six zones of the town (each with 1,900 to 2,000 houses) are prominently placed also, usually next to small shopping centres. Central space has been left for an ambitious town centre, with positions assigned to hotels, cinemas, social and recreation halls, shops, crèches, parks, a sports stadium, etc. None of these exist so far, but work is in progress on a community hall, on buildings for supermarkets and banks, a post office and an hotel.

All the houses are of a uniform pattern. They have four rooms and are built of concrete blocks, with cement floors, asbestos roofs and no ceilings. Those built more recently have indoor flush sanitation. Outside, the houses are colour washed in different pastel colours. Many occupiers have planted trees, flowers and vegetables in their gardens. The houses meet with approval. The only major grouse is about the cement floors; the more affluent cover them with lino or floor tiles, and also provide ceilings themselves. 'Here I have four rooms which belong to me. The house is airy and light, compared to the stinking shacks we lived in at Duncan Village. I have my lavatory. Altogether it is a pleasant place to live in.' 'It is like four houses in one. I have got a garden and everything to myself.' The privacy is valued. 'There are no houses here attached to mine as in the shacks where one would not sleep because of noises made by people next door. In Duncan Village there were many families living under one roof—all types of people with different thoughts. Some were drunkards, some naturally noisy, some had no respect for anybody else, others were beggars who would pester people day and night, some were of simple mind.' 'In Mdantsane I can lock all the doors and nobody disturbs me and my family at night.' The new surroundings are cleaner too: 'We are no longer crowded and all on top of one another. The nearby gutters are not full of rotten food and human droppings.'

Those with decent incomes may well enjoy the blessings of peace and privacy, and perhaps a certain protection against the demands of needy relatives or homepeople. But the majority can barely live within their income. To them, indoor sanitation and gardens may seem luxuries they cannot really afford. Their immediate experience of Mdantsane is one of economic and social deprivation. As seems to have happened with rehousing elsewhere, the transplantation of a community has led to increased travelling expenses, longer journeys to work, and the disruption of established social ties.

The cost of the fares to East London is a universal complaint.[1] The people maintain that they were told they would have little or no additional expense for transport, as fares would be subsidized by the Government or the employers. They feel that these are broken promises. The expense of travel hits people in many ways. It restricts their social life and prevents them from attending

[1] 11c to 22c single, 80c to R1.10 for a weekly ticket, about ten per cent of a breadwinner's salary.

entertainments; above all it cuts off opportunities to seek work in person, which hits women specially hard. The services of the impersonal labour office are not a proper substitute. 'Nowadays I am sent to a madam by the labour office and when I get there she will say she has engaged somebody already. I am left to pay the return fare for nothing.' Besides, many people believe that employers are reluctant to employ anyone from Mdantsane because they don't want to be asked to contribute to fares; or because through no fault of his own the worker is often late at work.

Mdantsane is not a protected labour market in the same sense as Duncan Village was. There seems to be a great deal of unemployment. There are numerous visitors who cannot obtain work in East London through the labour bureau, nor can the many 'illegal' residents: one has to produce a document proving one's legality first. However, it should be added that there are good prospects of an imminent speed-up in the industrial development of East London and more particularly in the 'Border area' known as Berlin Flats, on the other side of Mdantsane. This could make a great difference.

So far the unemployment problem increases the urge to make a little money by some humble entrepreneurial activity. Much as in Duncan Village, favourite forms are hawking meat, vegetables, etc. or selling home-brewed beer. Some people sell at 'private' street markets (*ikhowu*), others have 'private' shops (*isiroxo*) in their houses. Sub-letting to as many lodgers as possible is another source of income. But all these are illegal, and it is much commented on that the police, instead of preventing robberies or 'quelling serious fighting', busy themselves 'arresting people who sell things for a living'. This appears the more frustrating as there are still very few licensed shops. 'We had been given to believe that there would be many shops, run exactly like those in town, with no radius demarcation, and that many licences were to be issued for shops, dairies, cafés, etc. But our applications for licences are turned down.' It is not widely realized that licences are being granted, but only to people who already held them in East London; a fair number of these will soon open shop in Mdantsane.

The gap is widening in Mdantsane between those who have reasonably satisfactory steady employment in East London, and those who are living below the breadline, casually employed or out of work. One hears many comments to the effect that 'Here the people are really without money', 'We are starving here.'

Travelling to work does not only cost money; it also costs time and energy. The journey to work from Duncan Village was short and cheap. Many could easily do it on foot. Now it is about twelve miles by rail or road. Adding on the distance from home to station and from station to work, over thirty miles may have to be travelled every working day. And the time that this requires cannot be measured by the miles alone. Rush hour bus queues are hundreds of yards long. To the annoyance of the administration the expensively provided railways are not fully used, for the simple reason that the stations are thirty to sixty minutes' walk away from parts of the township, and hardly any feeder buses are provided. Many workers now need nearly two hours for the one-way trip from home to work. Three or four hours' travelling every weekday leave little time or strength for social life or leisure activities.

Little has been done to help the people to repair the torn social fabric. There seem to be the best intentions in Pretoria that social amenities will be provided in due course. But by the end of 1970, seven years after the first batch of people were transferred, realization seems a long way off. The inadequacy of the bus services isolates people from one another. Because of the hilly contours, winding roads and spacious layout, distances are very much greater than they were in the closely packed Duncan Village. Visiting relatives or friends becomes a problem when it may involve a four-mile walk each way. The social isolation is aggravated by the complete absence of public or private telephones and the still very rudimentary nature of postal services.

All this matters the more because there is so little else to do during spare time. Duncan Village bordered on the business centre of East London. Town people and School people with urban tastes appreciated the easy access to the city, with its wide range of shops for buying or window shopping—a kind of vicarious participation in the shiny complex world of the whites. One could also visit public places like the East London Zoo with its attractive grounds, or the Museum. And then Duncan Village had its own recreational amenities: notably the sports stadium (where football matches attracted great crowds), the community halls, and a cinema. In Mdantsane there are as yet none of these. A special trip into East London or Duncan Village at the week-end, to see a good football or boxing match for example, is too expensive for many people. There are many comments about the heavy, lonely boredom that descends on Mdantsane during week-ends.

In effect, neighbourhood drinking has emerged as the principal form of recreation. In theory this should be quite to the liking of Red people, since they always preferred it on principle to Western-style urban entertainments. But as we shall see, in practice the residential patterns of Mdantsane have undermined the basis of the old-style Red drinking groups.

Boredom, poverty and alcohol encourage thuggery and violence. The rule of the Tsotsi element after nightfall is generally felt to be more frightening than it ever was in Duncan Village (see page 74). Even vigorous men rarely dare to venture out at night.

African clergy, teachers and other potential leaders of the community view the situation with apprehension and frustration. Since the move to Mdantsane was a move to the 'homelands', they expected it to mean not only improved housing, but fuller civic status for Africans, with more say in the running of their affairs. 'We were given to believe that it was to be a wonderful model township for our freedom.' Addresses given by officials to facilitate the move seem to have encouraged such notions. 'We were made to expect a paradise of a homeland in the urbanized form.' Many had thought 'that all offices would be staffed by Africans.' They were disillusioned when it turned out that the figures of authority on the spot, i.e. the manager and four out of five section superintendents, are whites who in turn are responsible to other whites. Little delegation of authority to blacks is so far in evidence. 'We have Europeans even as foremen on road work.'

In fact the people feel they have, if anything, less influence on administration than they had in Duncan Village. There the elected members of the Joint Location Advisory Council have served as an official channel through which views or wishes of the people may sometimes reach the ear of authority. Nothing of the kind exists in Mdantsane. Attempts made in 1969 to establish a liaison committee proved abortive, as elements unacceptable to the authorities came to the fore in the elections. At present an African information officer in the employ of the Department of Information has been given the task of trying to create channels of communication through a system of ward committees. But so far they cannot do anything significant towards creating, in the hygienic but cheerless new environment, the atmosphere of a live community.

The Red way of life has been specially affected. The privately owned shacks in which Red people congregated in Duncan Village were disgraceful eyesores, but they allowed and in fact encouraged the group life which the detached houses of Mdantsane discourage. Most Reds feel their style of life threatened and in part already destroyed by the new environment. It is true that in one aspect, Mdantsane today looks much 'redder' than the old East London locations did ten years ago: namely that one can see a great number of obviously Red women, 'dressed for town' in their long print dresses and big fancifully arranged turbans. In the words of an old man from Chalumna—echoed by many visitors and residents—'in all my life I have never seen the Red women and children being so numerous in town'. These women (as we shall see) are mainly long-term visitors, though some are permanent residents. Compared with the regulations for Duncan Village, those for Mdantsane positively encourage husband and wife to stay in town together. But this is difficult to reconcile with continued Redness. (See page 308 ff.)

INCAPSULATION AND URBAN ECOLOGY

One single part of the Duncan Village shack area is still standing (August 1970). Here the social life of Red migrants has continued with remarkably little change from what has been described in this book. So also in Mdantsane for some 'lucky' Red men—those who find themselves still living so close to amakhaya that they can continue the incapsulated way of life. For the majority of Reds, however, the move has made this impossible. They envy the others and refer nostalgically to what they call 'our Red way of living in groups, as it used to be in Duncan Village'.

This section considers some of the reasons for the change: namely the geographical dispersion of amakhaya groups, the poor communication with friends at a distance, the growing reliance on clansmen as a second best, and the pressures to establish neighbourly relations regardless of what the neighbours' cultural background may be. All these factors are directly connected with the ecology and administrative framework of the new township.

In the shacks of Duncan Village (as we saw), a young man would share a room with one or more other men, and these carefully chosen intimates would generally be his amakhaya. Moreover the lodging would be chosen for its nearness to other amakhaya: in the same house perhaps, or one not too far away. There was an element of choice because rooms were rented from Xhosa houseowners, who were often themselves Reds. In this way neighbourhood clusters of amakhaya were formed within the generally Red areas. The men could visit each other regularly after working hours for company and entertainment. 'It was easy for us to see each other daily.' But the transfer to Mdantsane has 'scattered the people', and the housing there has also proved unsuitable for the 'group-life' of the amakhaya.

There is no specially Red area in Mdantsane. People have to take the houses that are allocated to them by the authorities, and the allocation takes no account of subculture or social class. It was widely believed beforehand that it would do so. 'Doctors, nurses and business people were to be in a separate area, where they would be given sites on which to build their houses. The proper School people would live by themselves, and so would the Reds. It was said that this classification would prevent friction between the classes. The Reds would not be irritated by revival meetings and church services, and the School people would not be troubled by the sacrifices and drinking parties of the Reds next door. The better class of people would have better houses and pay higher rents.' But this seems to have been a case of wishful thinking. All that has materialized in practice, is that some plots have been made available for private building, suitable for a 'higher class', and some business men have availed themselves of the opportunity. Everywhere else, 'the people are all mixed up'.

Old-established neighbourhood units were likewise broken and scattered in the course of transfer. Here and there a few houses in one street may be occupied by people who came from the same section of the shack area (e.g. Ghomorra or Moriva); and sometimes former inhabitants of the same shack dwelling now occupy neighbouring houses. But with few exceptions the overall effect (as the people see it) is that 'We are all divided'. 'The people I stayed with live quite far from me now.' 'Mdantsane is a place where a cow misses its calf. Those who love each other miss each other greatly.' (See Marris, 1961, for the same phenomenon in a rehousing scheme in Lagos.)

In the scattering of old neighbourhood units, old *amakhaya* clusters were inevitably broken up too. 'The way we lived with our *amakhaya* in Duncan Village will be forgotten in practice, and will only remain in our hearts and wishes. It is the distances which divide us now.'

It may be that the residential pattern will partly unscramble itself in the course of time. The Area Superintendents are not unsympathetic to people who want to swop houses because they do not like the kind of neighbours they have, and at least one of them believes that this will result in the 'better classes' gradually sorting themselves out from the Reds. However, the process can only be very slow. Swopping requires the agreement of two parties and, besides, Reds will seldom have the know-how to initiate it, or the money wherewith to bribe the other party if need be. It does not look as if *amakhaya* neighbourhood clusters can ever be reconstituted in this way.

The possibility of re-forming them is limited also by the uniform pattern of detached family houses. Marris criticizes a rehousing scheme in Lagos for having discounted 'the communal family life which flourished in the old courtyards . . . for the sake of a very English concern with privacy' (op. cit., page 128). Many more Africans in East London than in Lagos (it seems) appreciate self-contained houses, but the Reds specifically preferred the 'communal pattern of living', and would probably have settled into Mdantsane more easily if a different kind of housing had been provided for them, perhaps on the lines that Marris suggests (op. cit., page 128 f.).

We have seen how largely the Red way of life in East London depended on the particular conditions of the shack housing (see page 185). It was here that conservative Red migrants stayed for preference, in spite of the crowding and squalor. When the council houses in Duncan Village and Extension were built, the School people transferred into them as fast as they could, whereas the Red people 'were very pleased to remain. It suited our way of living, in groups rather than in families'. The few Red families who did live in Council houses appeared rather isolated and out of place, and soon tended to adopt School ways.

No house tenant in Mdantsane can bring so many lodgers together as did the shack owners. These had often as many as fifteen 'rooms' around one yard, with two, three, or more people lodging in each. 'In the shacks one paraffin or pressure stove would cook for a group of eight or more men from one home place, but not here.' The Mdantsane house has no more than four rooms; it is specifically intended for family occupation, and the occupier can only get permits for a few lodgers at best. Even allowing for illegal lodgers, there are rarely more than twelve people under one roof in Mdantsane. The legal maximum is seven adults.

Perhaps because house-tenancies are officially allotted only to people with resident families, and because Red people so far remain the least willing to bring their families permanently into town, there seem to be relatively more Red than School people wanting single lodgings, and relatively fewer Red 'landlords' to supply them. At any rate, Red landlords let exclusively to Red lodgers, who are generally their own kin and/or *amakhaya*, while the 'surplus' Red lodgers are reduced (as they would not have been in Duncan Village) to staying with School people, generally of humble or ex-Red background themselves. Many of these lodgers are bound to be 'illegal'. Single men — a term officially used to include men whose families are in the country — are supposed to go into the so-called single quarters, which are highly unpopular.

MIXED 'ISETI'

Very important for the group life of incapsulated Red men in Duncan Village was the *iseti* of regular drinking companions (see chapter 6). The scattering of *amakhaya* has had a marked effect on the composition of these drinking groups.

There is certainly not less drinking in Mdantsane than there was in Duncan Village. In fact there is probably more, because there is so little else to do. School people in particular complain that whereas in Duncan Village they would have attended a show at the week-end, or watched a game, 'here we just sit and drink'. (I was told on good authority that when the two bottle-stores in Mdantsane were opened, liquor sales for East London as a whole dropped by 30 per cent.) But School people in any case think of drinking mainly as a week-end pastime, whereas Red people like to drink with their friends every day. *Amakhaya*, generally speaking, now live too far from each other for daily drinking together to seem practicable. Even if there were buses, the fare would be a deterrent. Besides, the men feel that the long journey to and from work has seriously contracted their leisure time and they are reluctant to face another long journey to the *iseti*. 'Mdantsane is so far from our places of employment that one is donkey tired by the time one gets home.' 'In the country I wouldn't think twice about walking half an hour to get to a beer drink, but here there is so little time.' Above all, it is not safe to walk the streets alone at night, especially if one is not quite sober. 'Those who come from farther away usually drink their beer in a great hurry, to be on their heels before dusk, as they are afraid of thugs on the way home.' 'At first we had two men in our *iseti* who used to walk an hour each way, to and from our drinks. But they were both attacked, and now they have left us and joined an *iseti* nearer where they live. Only on Saturdays and Sundays do our *amakhaya* sometimes manage to come together.'

The *iseti* pattern is also affected by the greater difficulty of procuring home-brewed beer in Mdantsane. Brewing has to be done out of doors; fires are necessary, and large drums. Illegal brewing – and all brewing for sale is illegal – could be carried on with less fear of detection in the warren of shacks and narrow alleys than it can among the free-standing four-square houses in Mdantsane.

People are under the impression that the police in Mdantsane 'spend too much of their time raiding the brewers, spilling the beer and even arresting them'; and that 'the real reason is to encourage the drinking of "Jabulani" (beer made from a powdered base), which makes a profit for the Government'. (They may know that in theory 'the profits are to benefit the African people', but they say that 'this is unbelievable since these moneys are never handled by Africans'.) It is also said that the police are specially hard on illegal brewing in the houses with indoor sanitation; and that there have been warnings that drunkards would cause disease to spread through these houses by fouling the indoor latrines. To have one's wife or *shweshwe* brew beer, then, means the risk of being fined or paying a bribe to the police; while venturing out after dark to drink with old friends means risking life and limb. Most Reds prefer the former.

However, most Red men in Mdantsane still manage to belong to something they call their *iseti*, and the *iseti* still serve many of the old functions. It is worth considering how these groups are composed in the new surroundings.

Iseti are self-recruiting groups for the purposes of relaxation, and ideally they should consist of people who feel completely at ease with each other. Red people in Duncan Village assumed that this is best guaranteed among those who have grown up from childhood in the same home place, with or without kinship links in addition. Thus the Red man's drinking partners were so to speak 'ascribed' (they were to be the men who came from the same home as he and who lived near him in the shacks), whereas School people 'chose' their drinking partners, and did not necessarily require any other kind of link than that of personal friendship (see page 222). In Mdantsane the Red people, too, have to choose their drinking partners, thanks to the geographical break-up of the old *amakhaya* clusters. Sometimes they, like School people, admit to drinking with 'friends' – simply people whom they have got to know since coming to Mdantsane. But much more often they allege some kind of 'ascribed' link in addition. Often this is clanship. A man says he joined this *iseti* to be with another who has the same clan name (*isiduko*) as himself, or the same as his wife, or mother, and so on. This reflects both a preferred choice and a preferred way of validating choices. No doubt the friendship (not the clanship) may be the pragmatic 'reason why' the men started drinking together; but the clan-ship provides the required theory of friendship.

Among such 'reasons' cited by members of Red *iseti* are: tracing a kinship link by descent or marriage; coming from a nearby place in the country; being or having been work-mates in East London; belonging to the same association in town (e.g. burial society); having been neighbours or members of one *iseti* in Duncan Village. Neighbourhood in Mdantsane itself is seldom cited, and then usually only by women members or hangers-on. It seems a general rule in Mdantsane that those who become intimate through neighbourhood as such are mainly women. (See Parkin, 1969, page 65, for a similar situation in Kampala.)

Two examples may be given, of an 'old style' and a 'new style' *iseti* in Mdantsane. The first might just as well have come from Duncan Village: four of its members are *amakhaya*, and the other two are Red young men of similar outlook. In the second example none of the members are proper *amakhaya* and they are not even all Red. No member is included for a single axiomatic 'reason' (as with *amakhaya*), but for a number of reasons, none of which would be decisive by itself, e.g. being a clansman and also an acquaintance from work. The 'role summation' (Nadel) of multiplex relations is still manifest, but it is multiplexity of a new, more urban kind. (About the old kind of multiplex relations see page 292; on the significance of multi-stranded or multiplex relations see Mitchell, 1969, page 22 f., and Kapferer, 1969, page 213 f.)

1. Ndevu's *iseti*. Ndevu is a Red man in his 30's, with no school education, earning about R9 a week at the East London abattoir. His country home is in King William's Town district; he has left his wife and several children there, and is lodging in Mdantsane. He drinks every evening at a house about ten minutes' walk away, with two young Red men who lodge there and whose women friends do the brewing. One of these young men is from the Transkei, the other from East London District; Ndevu used to know one of them at work when they still lived in Duncan Village, though he did not drink with them then. The other three members of the *iseti* are all *amakhaya* of Ndevu. One is his younger brother, who lives twenty minutes' walk away; another is lodging together with the brother; and the third is a kinsman too (maternal cousin's son). These men count themselves 'lucky' to be living close enough for daily drinking. They say that twenty minutes' walk is more than one can normally risk in Mdantsane, but that it is all right in this case as two men walk it together.

2. Mema's *iseti*. Mema is a Red man of about 50 with Sub-standard B education. He earns R9.50 a week as a labourer. He is tenant of a house in Mdantsane and has his wife and three children with him. He also has three lodgers (two senior boys, one man), all Red and all from his own home place, Mtyolo in the King William's Town district. He is apologetic about having his wife in town, saying that she only came to escape from witches at home. Mema's house is the meeting place and his wife does the brewing. The *iseti* 'regulars', who come to drink every night, are a Red man, a partly Red woman and a School woman. The man (living fifteen minutes away) comes from a rural location not far from Mema's, and is also of the same clan, Amagotyeni. He and Mema belonged to the same *iseti* in Duncan Village. The first woman is a next-door neighbour; she looks School but is of Red background. She belonged to the same burial society as Mema and the other members – it 'was very strong when we first came to Mdantsane' but is now defunct. The other woman is typically School, and comes from Alice in the Ciskei. He only met her in Mdantsane, through the burial society. She is of the same clan too. At weekends Mema's *iseti* are joined by two more men. One is Mema's workmate, who lives about a mile away. 'We just became friendly at work.' The other comes from the same rural location as the workmate (Kwelera in East London district) and also worked in the same place for a few months. Mema refers to him as 'brother-in-law', but only because he is married to a clanswoman of his.

In the absence of *amakhaya* or kinship links the idea of clan links is sometimes tsretched to the utmost as a legitimation of *iseti* membership. Thus one young man, who has his wife with him in Mdantsane, said that he drinks with 'four 'regulars': (1) a man 'of my wife's clan', (2) a woman 'of my own clan [Qoco]; she belonged to my *iseti* already in Duncan Village', (3) a woman 'married to a Qoco', and (4) a man 'who is in love with a Qoco woman'.

In some cases the new-style *iseti*, with mixed membership, have taken over some of the insurance functions that were described for the *iseti* of *amakhaya* in Duncan Village. They may contribute money in emergencies. When Mthembu lost his third child within five months, and his wife and another child were seriously ill, his *iseti* collected something over R6. It was contributed towards the child's burial, though some members argued that it would be better used for sending the wife to a white doctor, or a diviner, as she might well be carrying the disease which killed the children—she looked thin enough to have *iphepha* ('the paper', lung disease 'which causes one to cough as if a paper were flapping in one's throat'). Ndamambi, from the Transkei, lost his job and was endorsed out. He stayed on illegally in Mdantsane for a long time, trying to find someone who would help him with his documents, but all his supposed helpers played him false and 'robbed him of his bribe money', so that he was left penniless. His *iseti* collected R7—enough for his fare to the Transkei, plus some provisions and tobacco. The money was handed over with speeches, and women members of the *iseti* wept when Ndamambi replied expressing his sorrow at leaving.

But there are other sorts of crises where people feel that only *amakhaya* or kin can help. And then they seek out such people regardless of where they live in Mdantsane, or whether they belong in the same drinking set. This is one of the ways in which the total network has become so to speak wider and looser, and the moral bonds between individuals less intense. The daily companions and the advisers and helpers in calamity are no longer necessarily the same individuals. These crises are particularly the ones which are going to concern family and elders at home in the country.

A young Red man of 27, who drinks regularly in a set composed of his fellow clansmen and neighbours, says he would not turn to any of them in case of death of a relative, pregnancy of a girl or difficulty with his wife. He would go to a slightly older man whom he knows from his home place in King William's Town district—'we grew up together'—and to his own younger brother, who lives in a different unit of Mdantsane. A Red man of about 32, whose predominantly Red *iseti* consists of workmates, shebeen friends and *inkazana*, says that in the event of a death he would call two *amakhaya* of his, who are also of his clan (Amatshawe), and who are still living in Duncan Village, as well as a third fellow-clansman (not an *umkhaya*) who lives in Mdantsane. In cases of minor trouble with his wife he would approach 'the Amatshawe clanspeople nearer here', or neighbours 'like Masiko who is a clever man', but really serious domestic problems 'I would refer directly to my home'.

THE CHANGING SIGNIFICANCE OF CLANSMEN, NEIGHBOURS AND KIN

Clanspeople, irrespective of their home origin, have acquired an increased significance in Mdantsane networks in the role of 'fictitious kin' (see Pons, 1969, page 119). In routine jural and ritual matters, fellow clansmen are called in as understudies for kin or lineage members even without being *amakhaya*, much more readily than was the case in Duncan Village. This is more a practical adjustment than an ideological innovation. Both Red and

School have always claimed that fellow clansmen 'are like brothers', but a Red man who needed the co-operation of such people in town could usually find them within his *amakhaya* circle, just as in the country he could find them within his home community. In Mdantsane (men say), 'if we cannot reach *amakhaya*, we can try to solve the matter first with other men of the *isiduko* (clan), before we decide to refer it home'. This is notably the case in connexion with the ancestor cult. 'People of the *isiduko*, even if not *amakhaya*, will gather here like people of the family when the diviner tells you to sacrifice because of your illness.' A middle-aged Red man of the Miya clan organized *isichinene* (a free beer drink 'for the ancestors', usually preceding a sacrifice) in thanks for the recovery of his brother who had been on sick leave for seven weeks. Only one *umkhaya* and no kin were present. Eight of the nineteen guests were Miya people from various parts of the Ciskei and Transkei, the rest were neighbours in Mdantsane.

Similarly in jural matters: 'People of your *isiduko*, wherever they come from, may play the parts of brothers and sisters, even parents, when you are in a foreign place.' They can act as understudies in cases of pregnancies of girls for example. 'Migijima called me recently for this purpose. He is of my clan [Radebe] but comes from Alice. He calls me for all occasions which require senior men of the family.' 'Mabulu's girl got pregnant, so I and another man of our clan went to claim the damages. Neither of us is from Mabulu's home.' Fellow clansmen are also appealed to when a man needs a lodging and cannot find a kinsman or an *umkhaya* to take him in. In this connexion people labour to find clan links through marriage, or sister's marriage, etc., or even through girl friends or *amankazana*: 'They will search for relatives of the same clan name.' Staying with clanspeople is claimed to be like staying with *amakhaya* or kin, in that 'there are hardly any fights, only petty quarrels'. 'Money is better saved there, as the senior looks at you with a parental eye, and stops you being extravagant.'

The dispersion of *amakhaya* (then) is the background to the people's insistence that 'here in Mdantsane it is necessary to know as many people of your clan as possible'. But even the clansmen usually have to be sought for. 'We don't know each other here as we did in Duncan Village. I remember when a man of the Amagiqwa clan held a sacrifice there, the yard was packed out with Amagiqwa. That is impossible here.' To find the fellow clansmen one approaches one or two older men who are known to have many acquaintances. 'If I needed the help of Qoqo people [speaker's clansmen] I would consult my father's brother. He would know whom to call, being an elderly man.' 'When my child died,' says an unmarried mother, 'I consulted my father's brother here. He collected many people of our clan in Mdantsane and they buried my child.'

Neighbours form another significant section of the Mdantsane Red man's network. Dependence on neighbours has increased, as contact with the *amakhaya* has become more difficult. 'Mdantsane has taught us the lesson of loving one's neighbours more than oneself.' 'Here the neighbour is very important because nearly everyone's relatives are very far; so neighbours become helpers and advisers.'

Dependence on the neighbours is greatest in case of attack or any other emergency that calls for speedy help. 'There was not as much robbery in Duncan Village as there is here. This has caused neighbours to be more combined, and to be always ready to help each other.' 'They protect each other like relatives.' In this respect the economically better-off and the poor find themselves under the same necessity. Besides, there is much isolation and loneliness in the detached houses. In the shacks people lived so close together that they deliberately distanced themselves from neighbours: 'they lived in great numbers under one roof, therefore did not take much note of those next door' (see page 79). Here they are glad to get together – especially the women. Neighbourly relations even develop between Red and School. 'Most school people talk to the Reds now in Mdantsane, when they happen to be close neighbours.' The old avoidance patterns are increasingly ignored. They sometimes help each other in financial emergencies, or where someone has been taken seriously ill, 'if no relative can be reached'. 'A church person in Duncan Village would always try to go and live among other church people. Here it is a matter of "must", not of choice, where you live. A very proud person is forced to dismount his high horse. Of course there are still some bad ones, like the Bhengu people, who hate their non-Christian neighbours because they are not saved.'

In the event of a death, Red and School neighbours alike are expected to come and console the bereaved. In the rare case of a Red initiation taking place in Mdantsane, all neighbours are invited to the festivities, 'even the school people'. In short, Reds have come to allot to neighbours in Mdantsane a role much like that of the neighbour in the country (see page 21), whereas in Duncan Village they had little to do with them unless they were also *amakhaya*.

Some neighbours even become friends and confidants, to be consulted in crisis situations which by custom would be family or lineage matters. 'I would call Baqo. He is my close neighbour, and we are very friendly. He is not related and he is School. I did not know him before I moved here. I know nobody of the Amantlane clan here, and those of my family are very far.'

But people also remain well aware that neighbours' help is not axiomatic like that of relatives or *amakhaya*. It is something to be achieved by nursing the relationship. 'A neighbour is not obliged to help, not even in an emergency.' 'Even a good neighbour will only come to your help in real emergencies like a case of death, or fighting. Otherwise he only comes when there is feasting, to collect a lion's share.' Also, neighbours have their dangerous side. 'He may pick a quarrel with you and kill you.' Ill will in a neighbour is especially feared, because 'everybody is bound to violate the many laws and regulations sometimes'. 'One can easily lose one's house because of the neighbours. Unlike in Duncan Village all houses belong to the Government. If the neighbour informs the officials that you have lodgers without permits, your house could be taken away from you.' 'If they report you for brewing you would be in trouble. They could always say that the brewing or the lodgers were disturbing them.'

Ideally the kin remain the ultimate source of help and advice. Many Reds manage to maintain contact in Mdantsane with a variety of affines and cognates beyond the immediate family. 'Here relatives are still as connected as in Duncan Village although they cannot visit each other as they did there, where people were near each other.' 'Relatives are bound to give help, without expectation of any return.' 'Relatives will defend one, and one is safe with them.' 'Quarrels between relatives never lead to physical harm. A relative is stopped by nature which forbids him to raise his hand against someone who is part of the same ancestor as himself.' 'A relative's home is your home. You can demand food, even take food when nobody is at home; you will not be regarded as a thief.' 'A relative will help in the garden, with cooking or washing, for no remuneration. They help you with money and food. A neighbour, even if you are very friendly, is never like that.' But even the kinship relations are felt to be changing — the gap between the ideal and the reality is felt to be widening. The Mdantsane environment is blamed for this, particularly the poverty and the flood of visitors from the country. 'Here in Mdantsane the new thing is the many visits of relatives from home. They come for health reasons, or to seek casual jobs; others come for help in financial matters or advice in domestic affairs. Whatever the reason, they have to be cared for, and this may be hard on their hosts.' In Duncan Village Red people were proud that they were not like town people, 'who often lend a deaf ear to their poor relations'. But in Mdantsane some feel that 'people here often have so many of their family from the country staying with them that they can't help other relatives as they used to'. 'The little most people have is just enough to provide for their wife and children here or in the country.'

STRUCTURAL URBANIZATION AND LEGAL UNCERTAINTIES

A major aspect of the incapsulation syndrome in Duncan Village was the paramountcy of home ties, i.e. the fundamental moral imperative to keep country relations in good repair and to leave wife and children at the country home, resisting any temptation to strike permanent roots in town. This was discussed above as resistance to 'structural urbanization' (see page 283 f.).

Red people still rate the rural ties as paramount, but their reasons have become distinctly less ideological and more pragmatic. Ten years ago the School people were the pragmatists: they were morally free to cut loose from their country homes, and if in practice many preferred to remain 'doubly rooted' it was because influx control made them feel insecure in town (see pages 203 f.). Today many Reds seem to be reaching the same position, to the extent that they would be willing to consider striking roots in Mdantsane, if there were a material advantage. What deters them is the sense of insecurity.

Those who were not born in Duncan Village or had not yet qualified under Section 10 (and this means a great proportion of the Reds in particular) see no future for themselves in Mdantsane, once their working life is over. People are deeply apprehensive that unless they have a rural home they may end up 'nobody quite knows where'. It is true that because Mdantsane is a 'homeland' town, tenants (as distinct from lodgers) cannot be endorsed out for being out of work. But a tenant's certificate of occupancy (of a house) can be withdrawn, *inter alia* for no longer having his family living with him, or for ceasing to be in the opinion of the Manager a 'fit and proper person'. Unlike 'endorsing out', a certificate of occupancy cannot be withdrawn without a hearing before the Magistrate (Chapter 2 Sec. 23(2) of 293 of 1962); but the people do not seem greatly struck by the difference.

If the Government intends to encourage structural urbanization in the homeland towns, it would first have to provide genuine legal security, which is not yet the case in Mdantsane. But even this would not be enough. The hard fact is that to an economically marginal, rent-paying population the prospect of unemployment, illness and old age in town must remain extremely daunting. To become dependants of their children in old age is to most Reds still an unhappy prospect. Poverty and absence of urban property rights, for all but a few, make it seem natural to cherish one's rights to house and land in the rural community.

De facto, the insecurity decreed by law is compounded by uncertainties of interpretation. The administrative status of Mdantsane is ambiguous. It is a township in the homelands, but also the dormitory for the East London labour force, and the place for the resettlement of the lawful inhabitants of Duncan Village. Thus even the crucial question of whether a man legally belongs in the town or in the country is often less clear than in the days of Duncan Village.

According to the law the grant of a certificate of occupancy of a house in a township in Bantu areas is conditional on the grantee renouncing his rights to residential and arable land in the rural reserves (Section 7 of R 293 of 1962). It is the official view that 'a Bantu cannot expect to have two properties'. When the transfers from Duncan Village to Mdantsane started, people were asked to sign these renunciations of their rural land rights. This created something like panic. 'It caused many people to evade the transfer. When the officials noticed this, they relaxed their harsh attitude.' A partial solution, often adopted, is to renounce rural land rights in favour of one's own eldest son.

AMBIGUITIES IN THE POSITION OF WOMEN

The legal and administrative position is most confusing with regard to wives and children. Whereas the law strongly discourages their presence in urban areas, it favours it for homeland towns. It provides that wives, children and other dependent relatives may be included in the certificate of occupancy or lodger's permit of the head of the family. But in the case of Mdantsane these permissive regulations are being interpreted restrictively. Wives and children who were not legal residents of Duncan Village are being deemed illegal here too, the reasoning being that after all Mdantsane has been created first and foremost to receive the lawful population of Duncan Village.

And yet there are, conspicuous and known to everyone, large numbers of wives staying in Mdantsane semi-permanently who are not being 'hunted' by the municipal police as they would have been in Duncan Village. They manage to stay on as 'visitors'. The law clearly stipulates that visitors are allowed thirty days in a township in Bantu areas (compared with 72 hours in a 'white' urban area) before they must regularize their stay by obtaining a lodger's permit (para. 19 of Regulations for the Administration and Control of Townships in Bantu Areas, R 293 of 1962). The onus of proof that someone has exceeded the thirty-day limit is on the authorities, and proof is extremely difficult to get. Thus while the Mdantsane authorities will not normally include in husbands' permits any wives who had not previously qualified in Duncan Village, in practice it is almost impossible to get rid of them.

Many inhabitants have been quick to understand and manipulate the legal uncertainties. In connexion with the transfer to Mdantsane (they say) 'we were told that if we admit that our wives and children are in the country then no house can be allocated to us. So to bluff the eyes of the authorities we sent for our families and claimed that they had always been with us.' Many of the men have since sent their wives back to the country, which could mean losing their house in Mdantsane if they were found out (Section 23 I. of R 293 of 1962). But those who did not manage to have their wives included in their documents are apprehensive too, because of uncertainty about what the authorities might do next. It is foreseen that if or when administrative measures were to be taken against 'illegal' wives 'they would vanish within a week. Most of the Red people are very scared of being arrested'.

Given this element of choice (for the time being) in deciding where the wife shall be, the men seem mostly ambivalent. On the one hand many wish their wives would not come to Mdantsane so often or stay so long. The notion that husband and wife should be together has still no overriding value for the Red man. They are as convinced as ever that town is not a good place for either wives or children, and they also regard the wife's presence in the country as indispensable for maintaining the home there. They complain about the subterfuges which women use to persuade their husbands to allow them to come to stay in Mdantsane. 'They malinger and deceive us by pretending to be seriously sick. They even teach their children to pretend to be ailing. They try to convince us about dreams they had about their enemies, and that they cannot go on staying alone in the country where they will be targets of witches.' Their real motive, the men say, is that they like the easier life in town. 'In town they can just sit down, eat, drink and do nothing.' Other men (though not above witchcraft beliefs themselves) suggest that, even if the young children really are sick, the reason is malnutrition, and not witchcraft at the country home.

On the other hand, 1970 has been the climax to a period of exceptionally severe drought in the Eastern Cape, the worst on record according to the Press. This has caused many men to call their wives into town (or not to send them back if they came uncalled), rather than go to the country themselves. The drought means there is no work for the men to do in the country; also 'they like to hide their eyes from the sickening conditions of their stock'. There are few 'pleasures' to attract them in such a season; few sacrifices, or rituals with their attendant beer drinks. 'The people are half starved, and their bodies and clothes filthy for lack of water.' There are also Red men who have changed their minds (whether or not as a result of their wives' manoeuvring) about the proper place for a woman. Some claim that nowadays the wife may be a greater economic asset in town than in the country. 'We are shamefully underpaid and it is a help if the wife comes and runs a little private business to increase the income a bit.' But practically all these minor entrepreneurial attempts are illegal, as we saw; casual employment is much harder to find from Mdantsane than it was from Duncan Village, and regular jobs are not available to women who do not have documents to prove lawful residence.

There can be little doubt that many Red wives would like to stay in Mdantsane for a long time, perhaps for good. (About women's inclinations to strike roots in town, see page 244.) Some come there in good faith believing that the house their husband is renting from the authorities is his property, as so many shacks in Duncan Village had been the property of Red men or women. 'I have many times heard men boasting at beer drinks in the country that they have two kraals now, one in Mdantsane and the other at home. The women take a pride in their husband's new house and feel they have a right to go and stay there.' But even when they discover the real position, they continue to like the houses, so much more spacious than the cramped rooms their husbands had in Duncan Village. Children too 'find it a great pleasure' to stay as long as possible and are reluctant to return to the country.

While wives' chances in the administrative lottery have improved for the

time being, those of *amashweshwe* (see chapter 16) have worsened. In the
shacks *ukushweshwa* was the private concern of the three parties involved,
husband, wife and *shweshwe*. Married and single men and women were equally
entitled to lodge in the shacks, and in the maze of rooms and lanes it was
difficult to ascertain who was sharing a room with whom. But in Mdantsane
'men are scared to stay with a *shweshwe*', because if they are reported they risk
not only a fine, but being deprived of their house. And the probability of being
reported by the wife or a relative or friend of hers, or by some unsympathetic
neighbour, is high in Mdantsane, because of the practical impossibility of
disguising the *shweshwe's* presence in a free-standing house.

Given the greater administrative tolerance of wives on the one hand, and
the people's ambivalence on the other, it is unpredictable whether many of the
visiting wives will become *de facto* residents of Mdantsane. In cases where
there are strong practical reasons in favour (e.g. impoverishment at the country
home), no doubt the men will feel freer than in Duncan Village to take the
plunge, because the voice of the *amakhaya* is not so clearly heard in Mdantsane.
However, very few men have so far risked any arrangement that would weaken
their hold on the country home. The women have brought only small children,
leaving the bigger ones at home. The fathers are apologetic even about the
small children. 'It is human nature for mothers to think that their small
children will be neglected if they leave them behind.' And of course there is
always the possibility of official policy changing so that the wives will have no
choice after all.

Ten years ago a wife's *permanent* presence in town could be construed as a
decisive step towards structural urbanization. That is not so today. Hardly
any man is now prepared to endanger his rights in the country for any consideration at all. The people are extremely suspicious of the regulations which
seem to tempt them to bring their wives into town, at the cost of signing away
their right in the country, but without giving them proper security in town
either. Not even the younger men, who can still look foward to many working
years in town, seem to feel confident about long-term possibilities there. At
any rate, 'homeland' or no, all the Red men in Mdantsane apparently make
careful arrangements with 'brothers', mothers, mothers-in-law, etc., to take
care of their interests in the country, as a practical necessity; and School
people are no less concerned than Reds.

The wife's presence in Mdantsane need not indicate that the couple have
become double-rooted (see page 224). Sometimes she has come there specifically
for the sake of the rural home. 'My mother and my wife have come to town to
brew beer for sale. They do this to help us in collecting money for our new
house in the country, which is almost finished.' 'My wife and daughter visited
me because I sent them word to come and fetch corrugated iron which I have
bought for our home.' And some Red men say that the reason they have to
call their wives into town at week-ends, although they (the men) would rather
have visited the country home is that too many town houses have been 'ransacked by thugs' when empty during week-ends.

THE EROSION OF RED CONFIDENCE

The Red way of life belongs to the country. It could be carried on in Duncan
Village, in a modified form, because the Red migrants there kept in close
touch with their Red home communities in the country, while also shielding

themselves by incapsulation from the cultural influences of non-Red people in town. We now have to consider the cultural effects on the migrants of changes at both ends (country and town).

Some of the Red rural areas in the East London hinterland look as Red as ever today. But others, notably in the King William's Town district (always a 'mixed' district), have changed visibly in the past ten years. Here the obviously Red homesteads have become fewer; some Red pockets have been absorbed; and even in the parts that are still predominantly Red the Red way of life has lost some of its savour.

Perhaps it is less remarkable that Red ways have lost ground in these areas than that they have kept kept going so strongly in others. There have been at least three major developments in the past decade which seem inimical to old-style Red rural community life.

First, there is the unparalleled industrial development of South Africa as a whole. The reserves, however isolated, have found themselves part of an expanding economy. There are more consumer goods to test the self-denying ordinance of the Reds, and more people are experimenting with items of shop clothing, domestic utensils and furniture.

Secondly, rural schools have multiplied since the take-over of Bantu education by the Department of Bantu Development and Administration, and they are much more acceptable to Red parents than the mission schools used to be. Today in most country areas there are few Red children who have not passed at least Standard 2 (four years at school). Twelve years ago, a Red rural elder was heard proclaiming: 'Give school education to all our children and there will be no Red people left in one generation' (page 28). He may have been right about the trend though probably underestimating the time it would take. It is not necessarily the school as such that works against Redness (though many teachers openly indoctrinate children against Red ways and values) but the fact that children from Red and School homes meet and mingle there. The Red ones soon get used to moving with ease in either milieu. A girl will be seen in complete Red costume on one occasion, and in good-looking shop clothes on another. When asked which they prefer they say 'both'. They are as happy with their Red families as with their School friends. They are the rural prototype of the so-called 'Bat' (*ilulwane*) (page 24), the double-natured person who is 'School among School people and Red among Reds'. 'They take everything that is best: the concerts from their School companions and the *intlombe* from their Red friends.'

The third heavy blow to Red ways has been the implementation of the rural betterment schemes, involving fencing off arable from grazing lands and concentrating the homesteads into compact villages. Betterment villages have become almost universal in the King William's Town district during the 1960's; even the most conservative locations, who swore to resist to the end, had to accept them. Today 'in the new reserves houses are arranged almost as in the townships. In some places one finds streets and even numbers on the walls of houses'. 'We can no longer build several separate huts, because the space allowed to us is too restricted. So we start to build houses of many rooms and shapes like the school people.' Besides there is restriction on the number of stock, and as cattle become fewer, so do sacrifices. 'Our stock and our arable lands are limited and we have too many taxes to pay.'

Yet Red life does go on, and the Red rural community, whether modernized or not, still has its attraction for Red town dwellers. Contact with the country home still 'keeps them proud of their worth'. The older Red men and women in Mdantsane like to speak of the pleasant time they have had at ceremonies 'at home' or the sacrifices they have performed or hope to perform there. The younger still go to attend *intlombes* over the week-end, if their country homes are within reach; these entertainments continue to flourish (see page 15). Thus, although the scattering of *amakhaya* in town means that ego's total rural-plus-urban networks cannot be close-knit and 'continuous' any more, his network does still have a rural section, and he does keep this section in good repair.

The old Red self-confidence in the superiority of their own ways, however, is no longer as deep and universal. It has begun to waver as they have begun to feel apprehensions about their economic prospects. According to a formula that is heard on all sides, 'One must have education to obtain good jobs nowadays.' A man summed it up bitterly, 'The (whole) country today is for the Europeans, there is no pleasant life for us anywhere.' Another said, 'As a nation we are now moving very fast towards *imphalalo*' (being spilt like water).

Red migrants have always emphasized that they come to town 'for the money', but also, that they handle money more successfully than School or town people; they invest it in worth-while things at the country home, instead of 'wasting' it in town (see chapter 8). Today, what with drought, overcrowding and rising prices, the country home needs money more sorely than ever just to keep going. It has become almost impossible to build up the good herd of cattle which always figured in the Red dream. Simultaneously the Red migrant finds himself at a new disadvantage as regards opportunities for earning in town. The rapid growth of the South African economy during the 1960's has made a much wider range of occupations available to Africans (in spite of all the restrictions of job reservation). The better-paid jobs are not for the illiterate or poorly educated. Where formerly Red men might become drivers or 'boss boys', today a fairly good knowledge of English or Afrikaans will be expected in such posts. An illiterate Red woman, refused an office cleaner's job, remarked bitterly that 'it is the first time I heard that reading and writing are necessary for sweeping floors, emptying rubbish and polishing windows'.

Red people have pride, and hate the idea of sinking into helpless poverty or not being able to cope. The only positive course they can see is to have their children educated. That is why so many are pessimistic about the future of their way of life. A young man ventured that 'those of my age are going to be the last generation to live in the Xhosa way'. And a woman said that she 'cannot see any more good in the Red life these days, unless we just want to go on as a disappointed group'.

INCORPORATION IN THE URBAN SYSTEM

We have already seen how the networks of Red people tend to open up in consequence of the move to Mdantsane: how only the 'lucky' ones can still confine their intimate relations to their own home people, or even to Red people. It was mentioned for instance that some Red men now regularly drink in a mixed Red and School *iseti*. Such associations may be termed either a cause or an effect of increasing acculturation.

Since the School and town people normally rate themselves superior to the Reds in the urban status system, open undisguised Reds still rarely make School friends, unless in one of two circumstances: either the School party is socially handicapped (e.g. is a lonely newcomer, or down and out, or a deserted wife, etc.) or the Red party is an exceptional personality and has a rather wide-ranging social network. Nonzwakazi is a young woman with Standard 7 education, a member of the Anglican church, with two young children to maintain. She is separated from her husband and has not been able to find employment. She has made friends with a slightly younger Red woman of her own clan, who lives close by. They go together to collect firewood for sale. She speaks with great warmth of her Red friend, 'I do not know what would have happened without her'. Michael is a Red man in his 40's, with a wife in the country and an *inkazana* in Mdantsane. The *inkazana* brews for his *iseti*. Four of its members are School. At first the School members only came to buy drinks, but Michael's strong personality drew them and now they are his firm friends. Michael has also become intimate with a School neighbour, a young man in his 30's, and has long chats with him. In addition Michael is the founder and moving spirit of what he calls the Hunting Club. It has ten members, of mixed rural origin, including three School men. At week-ends they go hunting with their dogs for small game (duikers, hares, dassies, etc.) in what they call the Mdantsane Forest. They usually bring home enough for a hearty meal, which they prepare and eat together.

A commoner pattern in mixed association, however, is that the Red partner adapts to the School one, playing down his Redness, which in the end ceases to be noticeable. In fact it is commonly said in Mdantsane that 'the Red people who stay here become difficult to spot after a few years'. 'Many Reds here get to like clothes and furniture, perhaps because they are so much more mixed up with School people than they were in Duncan Village.' This is most true of the young generation. The Red people over 40 or so have usually got their friends already, and feel no urge to venture out into new directions, so they do not mind remaining recognized as Red. The women flaunt their turbans, and the men, although they have to dress 'presentably' for work, still show their identity by their woollen caps and so forth, as they did in Duncan Village too (page 26).

As regards the younger generation of Reds the same is happening in Mdantsane (on a much larger scale) as happened in the sub-economic housing area of Duncan Village for those few who moved there from the shacks (see page 185). They are starting to see themselves through the eyes of their School neighbours, and to internalize their criticisms, being no longer protected by an approving circle of like-minded *amakhaya*. Here as there, 'this kind of house whispers to you that it needs more furniture'. 'The younger people in Mdantsane have become shy of being called *amaqaba*. They think its real implication is that they know nothing.' 'They dislike being mocked at as *imikhaka* [literally, those who wear ivory armlets], meaning those who are ignorant and old-fashioned.'

Without the *amakhaya* as a support, it no longer makes much sense to pretend to oneself or others that one really belongs in a different social system – a rural and tribal system, as against the urban one – and that one is therefore indifferent to the judgments of the local town people. The Bhengu followers, like the Red people, have come in for a lot of mockery, but they have been able to stand it because they are sheltered within the close-knit exclusive circle of their brethren in faith (see Mayer, 1971). If an isolated individual, without such a shelter, insists on his own otherness, he will only make himself feel excluded rather than exclusive.

Those young Red people who have been to school in the country do not find it difficult to adjust to School company in Mdantsane. It is harder of course for the 'raw', illiterate or semi-literate types. There are many jokes about the mistakes such people make when they try to use English words and phrases, or about their excessive delight when they find a School girl who is willing to be their girl friend. Youths of this type can often only find their foothold in the urban society via the *ipotsoyi* — 'hobo dances' held in shebeens or in private houses — which self-respecting young people avoid because of the violence and vulgarity. Some get stuck at that level. But many graduate to the company of a 'better class of people', helped by the fact that today there are so many half-Reds or ex-Reds in those circles too.

The other ready-made way into urban society is via the sects and churches. Some of the sects seem to attract the younger people of raw Red type through the prominence they give to music and emotionalism. 'There is this *Igqaza* [a healing sect], which has its members trained to sing as if they were mad. They are very active and this appeals to the young people.'

Ten years ago Reds who threw in their lot with a church were mostly people from farms who had little to lose (see chapter 12). It seems as if more young people from the reserves are also experimenting with church member-ship. It is easier today to take the initial step because of the slackened control of the *amakhaya*; and the penalties are less severe, because it no longer involves 'excommunication' by one's *amakhaya* and a clean break with one's former network (see pages 200 ff.). Some said openly that they have joined for social reasons; 'for improving ourselves, and to be more respectable. Church members are esteemed by the public'.

The older generation of Reds have become notably more tolerant of such tendencies in the young — probably another symptom of increasing self-doubt. For themselves, as long as life goes reasonably well, they still mock at the sects, and 'resist the Christian religion' as stubbornly as ever. 'My father pokes fun at the sects. He says there is always a clever man who is the leader and is assisted by simple men who do his work for him, and never discover that the leader is using them to get more money and more women; it is these he is really after.' But crises may shake their confidence. 'When they have lost their health or are in hopeless difficulties, some become quite gullible over religion.' And in Mdantsane many people are in great trouble.

Women are specially attracted by the healing churches. 'Women are the first to change. This is because women are always sick. They always need some-one to heal them, and so they listen to Christian healers. When they get better they have great faith in these churches.' Women mostly join the 'low class' sects like Postile, Gqaza, Zionist groups, etc. 'These churches appeal to them because they do not despise the traditional life at all.' Bhengu's Church is not making converts to the extent it did in the 50's (see chapter 12).

BLURRING OF THE RED–SCHOOL OPPOSITION

One can also frequently encounter in Mdantsane Red men and women, most of them youngish, who are neither religious converts nor expressly aspiring to become School people, but who deviate in various ways from proper Red manners and views. They have broken away from the old conformist totalitarian Red morality (Mayer, 1971), and are aware perhaps that the Red life style is becoming anachronistic, but they do not feel apologetic either about their Red mannerisms among School people, or about their half-heartedness among Reds. Indeed, 'partly School and partly Red' people are a well-known feature of the Mdantsane scene. In East London they were mostly a second-generation phenomenon (see Pauw, 1962, p. 42, on 'semi-Reds'), and hardly to be found among migrants proper.

Some of these half-and-half people in Mdantsane, when questioned, will cheerfully insist that they are 'amaqaba really', though their appearance and life style may show few or none of the diacritical signs of Redness. Others claim to be 'School really', but are still openly displaying signs of Red background. That these intermediate types have become so much commoner is significant evidence that the opposition of the two sub-cultures is losing its sharpness. It also points to a widening gap between 'actual characteristics' and Red/School 'self-classification'. (On the correspondence between self-classification and actual characteristics see A. A. Dubb, 1966.) Many come from homes in the country where Red and School are mixed. For others it is an urban adaptation and the degree of 'Redness' they maintain is influenced by the strength of the Red element at their home.

Another newly important category is that commonly spoken of as 'bats' (ilulwane) or as 'which-side-which-side' (Umgaphigaphi). Bats, 'neither bird nor animal', are of two worlds in the sense of being prepared to switch to the norms of either system, according to the situation and the relationship involved. They include especially younger Reds who have had a fair amount of schooling and are therefore already adept at moving in two worlds before they come to town. Some of the older Reds suspect them of insincerity. 'When he goes to his family in the country he attends sacrifices and tries to convince everybody that he prefers the Red way of life and has adopted School ways only because he works in town. Yet in town he pretends to his School friends that he is joining the Red lot only for the fun of it.' 'They are mostly on the clever and eloquent side.' However, most people in Mdantsane accept them as a fact of present-day life. 'The saying of the bats is that all people are the same. There is no Red and no School. Our ancestors were all red.' It is widely conceded that they have a point there.

There are some (not yet many) children of Red parents who have been brought up and gone to school in town, whether in Duncan Village or Mdantsane. Unlike the typical rural 'bats' they overwhelmingly prefer the School or urban way of life and see their future in terms of it. There seems to be no prospect whatever for a second generation of town-living Reds in Mdantsane. (The same applied in Duncan Village: see Pauw, 1962, especially pages 17 f.) Everybody seems to see this as inevitable. 'At home I wear my blankets,' says a middle-aged, typically Red man. 'My daughter too used to be completely Red, although since she started working in East London she looks like a School woman. Her children attend school here in Mdantsane. They know no country life at all. They will never be Red again. When I die they will stop attending Red peoples' affairs. I and their mother are still their stumbling blocks.' Natalie, an elderly Red woman, intends to retire to the country. But 'my son wears suits worth a good number of sheep and goats. He says I will stay there alone. He grew up here and attended school. He has never used a stick for fighting, but knows how to use his long pocket knife'. Thus in town-settled families of Red background one constantly notices a cultural gap between the generations. Thembakhazi is about 34; she has two children by a man who was to marry her but who disappeared when *thelekwa*'d by her brother (pressed for lobola). She dresses like a School woman, but her mother with whom she is staying is completely Red. The mother's bedroom and the dining-room are furnished in the typical way of Reds in town, with few and 'home-made' pieces. The daughter's room is 'smart' with a new wardrobe and matching dressing-table; the beds have good mattresses and bedspreads.

The entertainments and sports which can be sampled at school or on visits to Duncan Village, or now and again in Mdantsane itself, are a major factor in committing the young to the town, exactly as the Red youth activities keep many youngsters in the country within the Red fold. 'I will never be Red, because I am interested in many School things like shows, dances and sports' (boy of 17). The Red parents are in a dilemma: 'What social occasions are our children going to have here if we try to keep them strictly Red? There would be nothing for them, and they would envy the others who go to their dance sessions.'

RED PARENTS AND SCHOOL CHILDREN

Some parents do try to keep children Red. 'They are fast turning School, but are forced by the iron will of their parents and other kin to support the Red people's ways.' 'My brother working in Cape Town does not care for these traditional things. My Red parents frequently criticize him and he answers back strongly about their remoteness from modern ideas, and their remaining attached to a fading way of life.' A girl of 15 who attends school in Mdantsane says that when she has done anything wrong her parents 'usually say it is because I am educated, that I behave badly like the children of the *amagqoboka*. My father often says he will marry me to a Red *umfana*, but I do not like that for I will never be Red again. They think we will all be Red again when we go back to the country, but we will not. We are used to the life of School children.' More often parents are resigned to their children's choice. If Red parents in the country attach great importance to the school education of their children, those in Mdantsane are even more emphatic about its necessity. Some go further: 'I like my children to be School. In Mdantsane, it is neither possible nor necessary to be Red.'

From what one sees and hears, relations between Red parents and their renegade children are on the whole remarkably warm and successful. If anything the children are even more understanding than the parents. 'I do not blame my parents for being Red. If we had not come to town we would also be Red, as are my equals in Igoda. I love my parents and they love us. They do not prohibit us from attending concerts, as they say those are our *intlombes*.' 'I do not see any difference between my mother and School women of her age,' says another girl of 16. 'She is kinder-hearted than many Christians. I will never part from her because she is Red. I respect her greatly.' And a boy of 17 (Standard 3) says that he 'respects' his parents and 'whenever they instruct me to do anything, I willingly do it. The little education I have, I have through them. They do not nag me for being School'. I spoke to an intelligent handsome youth in the presence of his completely Red mother. Shyly but firmly he explained that he was only interested in School things, and would never feel at home at the social functions of young Red people. His mother was silent, but told me later what a good son he is, that he is always respectful and a great help to her.

One testimony to the good understanding between Red parents and children is that the parents manage to transmit much of the moral content of the ancestor religion. These boys and girls who so emphatically insisted that they could never be Red seemed to have scarcely a doubt that 'the spirits can protect me in trouble'. The parents' religious teaching seems to prevail over the Christian religious instruction given in school. 'We can see them in our dreams. . . . Even here in this house our dead are amongst us. At a sacrifice they collect together.' 'Yes, I believe so, because my parents and other old people always say that, if one despises the dead people, one will have misfortune, and may even die because of their anger.' 'Old people have brains, they would not waste their last beast for a sacrifice and their last money on beer, just for nothing.'

CONCLUSIONS

This postscript has been concerned with social changes which, like layers of clouds, seem to be moving along at different speeds on different levels. On one level we have noted some ways in which Red Xhosa culture and values, even in the country, are being affected by national economic growth: The ever-greater necessity of school education for earning money, the spread of consumer goods (with consequent pressure on the old self-denying morality), the re-shaping of rural communities through betterment schemes. This cloud (it seems) is moving along at a steady but moderate speed. On the second level, we have noted some specific effects of the new 'homeland' laws and policies represented by Mdantsane, particularly the changed network patterns entailed in changed residence rights. The speed of this movement is much more dramatic, and the effect on individual lives much more disturbing. However, the two need to be seen in relation to each other. Red people who have already learnt to make concessions to 'the ways of the European' in the country, are more likely to recognize the opportunity as well as deprivation in the new Mdantsane life style, outside incapsulation. Such a person can face new choices because neither the 'will not' nor the 'cannot' applies with the same force as before (see page 285).

Incapsulation depended on the Red 'group life', which could flourish in the special conditions of the privately owned wood and iron shacks of Duncan Village. The suburban ecology of Mdantsane has largely destroyed the prerequisites for it. In consequence the social networks of many Red people have begun to approximate in form to those of School people, or for that matter to those of recently rural Africans in cities of other African countries (see Parkin, 1969; Pons, 1969). Fellow clansmen, friends, and neighbours (that is) have come to figure more prominently in them. And while the historical categories of Red and School are still very much in evidence, determining behaviour and serving as reference groups, one senses a weakening in the opposition, a weakening self-confidence in the Red section, and an increase of in-between types.

What is the effect on urbanization? The border industry policy, with its offer of respectable family housing in a 'homeland' township, seems paradoxically to have hardened the people's determination to hang on to whatever rural land rights they possess, as the only real security they can envisage. The Government (of course) intends the workers living in 'white' areas to retain this migrant mentality, and have their roots in the Bantustans, but the homeland towns are meant on the contrary to encourage complete urbanization and discourage the maintenance of rural ties. The fact that the people have so far shown little confidence in the new alternative reflects a combination of different insecurity feelings. There is the special insecurity of a group which is for ever being legislated for, and legislated about, without having a voice in the legislation—the feeling 'in the bones' that even in the new town a man will still find himself liable to be sent away, or moved about, or parted from his family, and so on, in the name of political or administrative planning. And then there is the insecurity of peasants confronting proletarianization. Security in a house in Mdantsane depends on being able to keep up with the rent, which depends on keeping in steady work, which is something that nobody can feel secure of, even in the short run, let alone in old age. Social security benefits for Africans are still minimal.

The old style of migrant life seemed to threaten Xhosa people with disruption of family ties; the homeland town seems to threaten loss of land. Two things are lost when family land is lost: security of a 'place to be', as of right, in one's old age, and personal status in a stable community. In the Western world, industrialization and urbanization are still the most widely recommended remedies for the poverty of underdeveloped countries, but as Mdantsane illustrates, the discomforts they entail through landlessness and proletarianization may rival those of the disease they are meant to cure.

METHODS OF FIELDWORK

The book has required fieldwork both in town and in the country. As was to be expected, the two main tasks which any anthropological field study has to face—making sure that data are valid, and making sure they are representative—appeared a good deal more difficult in town.

The rural fieldwork was carried out by classical methods. Tshabo, some 25 miles from East London, was the first community chosen for an intensive study. Practically all its adult able-bodied men work or have worked in East London. I lived in the heart of Tshabo (in a caravan) for five months during 1956. For three more months I directed a pair of Xhosa assistants after my return to teaching duties at Rhodes, 100 miles away. The normal methods of observation, interview, etc., could be freely used. Suspicion was marked at first, but in time the Tshabo community accepted us and our work with patience, and increasingly in a spirit of co-operation. Briefer excursions were made to other rural fields in the Ciskei, and checks were also provided by Mr. M. Wilkes who was then engaged on fieldwork in Khalana rural location not far away. In 1959, fieldwork was extended to the Transkei, three months being spent by me in Shixini (Willowvale district).

Urban fieldwork began in December 1956. As a White person I could not lawfully have lived in a town location, but the East London authorities allowed me to come and go freely provided that I slept in the White town each night.

Before launching out into the main fieldwork in town two pilot schemes were first applied there. One was meant to indicate how, if at all, the Red and School categories might be retaining their distinctive characteristics in the urban setting. A lengthy questionnaire was applied to 50 migrant informants, 25 being self-declared Red and 25 self-declared School people. It covered a wide range of subjects including kinship relations and attitudes, relations with neighbours and friends, economic circumstances, religious and magical beliefs and practices, activities outside working hours, race attitudes and attitudes to other kinds of Xhosa, intentions for one's own and one's children's future, knowledge of affairs outside the immediate environment. Nearly all the questions were open-ended and all respondents were encouraged to speak at length and to give concrete examples from their own and other people's experience. The work was slow going, in that each respondent required several hours of intensive interviewing to himself or herself (which usually had to be fitted into his off-duty hours and week-ends), not counting the time for writing up notes.

The second pilot scheme was applied to a larger sample (150) including representatives of all the categories we now considered significant—men, youths, women and girls, of the Red peasant, Red farm servant, School peasant and town-born sections, from the Ciskei and from the Transkei, low-paid and better-paid. The questionnaire designed as the base for the guided interviews, in this second instance, was somewhat shorter than the first, and was focused specifically on topics which seemed relevant to the problem of urbanization, in either the cultural or the structural sense. As before, lengthy answers and concrete case-histories were encouraged. Since this pilot scheme was meant mainly as a pointer to lines for further inquiry, the results were not quantified or tabulated.

The main fieldwork could now begin. In general the methods to be followed would not necessarily be the same as those appropriate when one is mapping out a total urban community or system, and having to establish most of the categories *pari passu*. Having started with an open mind as to whether such categories as Red and School remain significant in town, I was led by the two pilot surveys to think that they do remain significant, as long as one is focusing attention on migrants' private and off-duty activities. But it also became clear that in this particular area of interest the more rapid forms of survey and questionnaire techniques could not (or not yet) replace the close observation of individuals, the intensive interview, and the open-ended question. It was relevant that many of the topics being investigated were delicate ones, some being illegal by White definition, some immoral by Xhosa definition. Reader's experience had already shown that quick survey methods, so useful in other fields, produced wildly inconsistent results when applied to topics considered delicate in relation to an outsider, e.g. to marital and sexual partnerships.[1]

As to quantitative data, Reader's findings and also those of the companion economic studies[2] could be drawn on freely. Since my own broad object was to observe and record patterns which seemed to be accepted or institutionalized among each category of migrants in specific fields, I expected to use quantification myself only as a supplementary tool. Quantification starts to be indispensable where several or many alternative practices seem to be freely available to one social category of persons in one field of activity. This predicament, typical of really 'urban' populations (such as the town Xhosa studied by Pauw), was much less apparent in studying the leisure-time activities of Red migrants. It appeared more often among the School migrants.

Specific new questions were constantly being designed to deal with each topic of interest *ad hoc* as it emerged, to fill gaps in the picture, or to test hypotheses being formed. We made it a general rule to try out the new questions on new sets of informants, embedding them in a repetition of earlier questions, rather than go back to old informants. Valuable checks were obtained by this means and larger numbers were brought in. The number of new informants involved each time might be small or might range up to a hundred or so, depending on the nature and complexity of the question. For instance, the arguments which School married men use for leaving their wives in the country or for bringing their wives into town were investigated in a special sample of 80, over and above those who had already given their views in the two pilot surveys. But a narrow question such as 'Who provides the *bingelela* sacrifice for the child of an *ishweshwe*?' could be satisfactorily settled by recourse to nine or ten new informants, once we had amassed sufficient background knowledge of the *ukushweshwa* institution. Naturally, the numbers interviewed on a specific point would partly depend on how many significant divergencies appeared in the first sets of answers.

This phase of the work continued from the middle of 1957 till the end of 1958. Another spell of fieldwork in December 1958–January 1959 served *inter alia* for observation of the 'beating of boys' outbreak and its aftermath.

[1] Cf. Reader: *The Black Man's Portion*, Appendix on Method.
[2] Houghton, D. H. (ed.): *Economic Development in a Plural Society*.

The book was now completed in first draft, but investigations went on through the first half of 1959 for filling in gaps and tying up some loose ends.

Having full-time teaching duties at Rhodes during term time, I could spend a maximum of four months each year in East London itself (the long vacations plus the July vacations) apart from an extra period of two months' study leave which was granted to me for the purpose in May and June 1957. However, work went on when I was not on the spot, by means of proxy interviewing, carried out by Xhosa assistants on detailed instructions from me. This method has obvious hazards, but by taking stringent precautions we made it a reliable and eventually a fruitful one. Each time I defined a sample beforehand by stipulating how many informants of which categories and in which particular situations had to be interviewed, and carefully formulated the questions which were to be put to them, drawing up a detailed plan for a guided interview. The assistants remained in touch with me by twice-weekly letters or telephone. By keeping questions largely open-ended, by encouraging concrete case-histories, and additional 'free' material, we were not only avoiding falsely stereotyped answers but continually widening our field of knowledge. A number of assistants were trained for the work at various times. Two in particular deserve mention—Mr. S. C. Mvalo and Mr. Enos Xotyeni. To their intelligence, unfailing interest and scientific integrity much is owed.

Proxy interviewing had another reason. Though I encountered much personal friendliness in the East London locations I was also conscious of a denser barrier than the one experienced in Tshabo or other country places. The fact has to be faced that in a present-day South African town the role of a White newcomer closely questioning Black informants about their private affairs can never be a grateful one, and that he may risk being given incomplete or misleading information because of his colour. There were many times when it worked better to have a Xhosa assistant ask questions than to ask them myself

RED AND SCHOOL HOMESTEADS IN THE BANTU AREAS OF THE EAST LONDON AND KING WILLIAM'S TOWN DISTRICTS

Figures collected and supplied (1958–9) by the headmen of the respective locations at the instance of the Bantu Commissioners (at my request). The map at the end of the book is based on these figures.

(NOTE: Spelling in brackets are those in current use by the Department of Bantu Administration and Development. They are also used on the map at the end of the book.)

1. EAST LONDON DISTRICT

Name of location	No. of Red homesteads	%	No. of School homesteads	%	Total homesteads
Released Area No. 33	853	90·3	91	9·7	944
Released Area No. 36*	366	93·3	26	6·7	392
Released Area No. 35	17	80·9	4	19·1	21
Dongwe	237	92·6	19	7·4	256
Farm 309	21	60·0	14	40·0	35
Kwelegha (Kwelera)	412	78·1	115	21·9	527
Mabaleni	117	92·1	10	7·9	127
Mncotsho No. 5	212	87·9	29	12·1	241
Mncotsho No. 30	198	69·2	88	30·8	286
Mntlabati	140	80·0	35	20·0	175
Mooiplaats (Mooiplaas)	394	82·5	83	17·5	477
Newlands	427	74·8	144	25·2	571
Tshabo	782	88·2	105	11·8	887
Total	4,176	84·6	763	15·4	4,939

* Transferred to East London District for administrative purposes in 1957. Not shown on map; adjoins Mooiplaats.

2. KING WILLIAM'S TOWN DISTRICT

Name of location	No. of Red homesteads	%	No. of School homesteads	%	Total homesteads
Anders Mission	56	48·7	59	51·3	115
Bhalasi (Balasi)	34	30·4	78	69·6	112
Bulembu	96	58·9	67	41·1	163
Dikidikana	—	—	65	100·0	65
Donnington	68	42·0	94	58·0	162
Dube	208	83·5	41	16·5	249
Ezeleni (Zeleni)	75	41·2	107	58·8	182
Godidi	54	88·5	7	11·5	61
Gqodi	55	68·7	25	31·3	80
Gwaba	53	96·4	2	3·6	55
Released Area No. 28	7	12·5	49	87·5	56
Jafta/Kwelerana	42	21·3	155	78·7	197
Joseph Williams	—	—	129	100·0	129
Khalana (Kalana)	111	96·5	4	3·5	115
Kolele	—	—	115	100·0	115
Kwalini	19	35·2	35	64·8	54
Kwelerana	55	27·9	142	72·1	197
Mabhongo (Mabongo)	99	76·7	30	23·3	129
Mabhongo (Mabongo)	208	87·4	30	12·6	238
Macibi	196	77·2	58	22·8	254
Mamata	75	57·3	56	42·7	131
Masele	138	54·8	114	45·2	252

Name of location	No. of Red homesteads	%	No. of School homesteads	%	Total homesteads
Masingatha (Masingata)	—	—	130	100·0	130
Matebese	74	62·7	44	37·3	118
Mdizeni	33	26·0	94	74·0	127
Menziwa	93	93·9	6	6·1	99
Mlakalaka (Malakalaka)	—	—	81	100·0	81
Mngqesha	—	—	57	100·0	57
Mthathi (Mtati)	94	81·0	22	19·0	116
Mthathi Siwani (Mtati Siwani)	217	45·5	260	54·5	477
Mthwaku (Mtwaku)	39	52·0	36	48·0	75
Mtombe	76	71·7	30	28·3	106
Mtyholo (Mtyolo)	122	52·8	109	47·2	231
Mxaxo	72	63·2	42	36·8	114
Mzantsi	87	81·3	20	18·7	107
Ndubungela	96	78·0	27	22·0	123
Ngcamageni (Ncamgeni)	53	93·0	4	7·0	57
Ngqokweni	9	22·5	31	77·5	40
Ngxwalane	42	34·4	80	65·6	122
Noncampa	9	10·1	80	89·9	89
Nonibe	42	27·8	109	72·2	151
Ntsikizini	66	62·3	40	37·7	106
Nxwashu	54	46·2	63	53·8	117
Nyatyora	53	65·4	28	34·6	81
Peelton	200	26·3	560	73·7	760
Phunzana (Punzana)	296	89·2	36	10·8	332
Pirie	4	1·6	251	98·4	255
Qaga	112	57·1	84	42·9	196
Qawukeni	114	75·0	38	25·0	152
Qhugqwala (Qugwala)	341	25·4	1,001	74·6	1,342
Qongqotha (Qongqota)	65	53·7	56	46·3	121
Rayi (Rhayi)	—	—	81	100·0	81
Released Area No. 27	27	36·0	48	64·0	75
Released Area No. 32	91	54·8	75	45·2	166
Sheshegu	65	65·7	34	34·3	99
Sikhobeni (Sikobeni)	33	43·4	43	56·6	76
Tolofiyeni	56	45·9	66	54·1	122
Tshatshu (Jan Tshatshus)	232	25·1	693	74·9	925
Thwecu (Twecu)	65	57·5	48	42·5	113
Tyhusha (Tyusha)	95	50·0	95	50·0	190
Tshoxa	5	7·9	58	92·1	63
Tyutyu	56	64·4	31	35·6	87
Upper Ezeleni (Izeleni)	—	—	119	100·0	119
Xengxe	140	85·9	23	14·1	163
Zalara	168	87·0	25	13·0	193
Total	5,145	44·9	6,320	55·1	11,405

BIBLIOGRAPHY OF WORKS REFERRED TO IN THE TEXT

B

Balandier, G. *Sociologie des Brazzavilles Noires*. Paris, 1955.
Balandier, G. 'Urbanisation in West and Central Africa', in *Social Implications of Industrialisation and Urbanisation in Africa South of the Sahara*. UNESCO, 1956. p. 495 ff.
Banton, M. *West African City*. O.U.P., 1957.
Barnes, J. A. 'Class and Committee in a Norwegian Island Parish', *Human Relations*, vol. 7, no. 1, 1954.
Bott, E. *Family and Social Network*. Tavistock Publications, London, 1957.
Brownlee, C. *Reminiscences of Kaffir Life and History*. Lovedale, 1896.

D

Dubb, A. A. 'Red and School: A Quantitative Approach', *Africa*, vol. 36, pp. 292–302, 1966.
Du Toit, A. E. 'The Cape Frontier 1847–1866', *Archives Year Book for South African History*. 17th Year, 1954, vol. 1.

E

Eiselen, W. W. M. 'Harmonious Multi-Community Development', *Optima*, March 1959.
Eisenstadt, S. N. *The Absorption of Immigrants*. Routledge & Kegan Paul, 1954.
Epstein, A. L. *Politics in an Urban African Community*. Manchester University Press, 1958.

F

Firth, R. *Elements of Social Organisation*. Watts, 1951.
Firth, R. 'Some Principles of Social Organisation', *J. of R. Anthr. Inst.*, vol. 85, Parts I and II.
Forde, Daryll, 'Introduction' in *Social Implications of Industrialisation and Urbanisation in Africa South of the Sahara*. UNESCO, 1956.
Fortes, M. 'Culture Contact as a Dynamic Process', in *Methods of Study of Culture Contact in Africa*. O.U.P., 1938, p. 60 ff.
Fortes, M. *Oedipus and Job in West African religion*. Cambridge U.P., 1959.
Fourie, L. & Lumsden, G. 'Employment and Wages': Chapter 7 in Houghton, D. H. (Ed.): *Economic Development in a Plural Society*. O.U.P., 1960.

G

Gluckman, M. 'Foreword' in Watson: *Tribal Cohesion in a Money Economy*.
Gluckman, M. *Analysis of a Social Situation in modern Zululand*. (Rhodes-Livingstone Papers No. 28.) Manchester University Press, 1958.
Gluckman, M. 'Tribalism in modern British Central Africa', in *Cahiers d'Etudes africaines*, 1960, pp. 55 ff.

H

Hammond-Tooke, W. D. *The Tribes of Mount Frere District*. Union of South Africa, Department of Native Affairs, Ethnological Publication, 1955.
Hammond-Tooke, W. D. *The Tribes of Willowvale District*. Ibid., 1956.
Hammond-Tooke, W. D. *The Tribes of Umtata District*. Ibid., 1957.
Hammond-Tooke, W. D. *The Tribes of the King William's Town District*. Ibid., 1958.
Hellmann, E. *Rooiyard: a sociological study of an urban slum yard*. (Rhodes-Livingstone Papers No. 13.) O.U.P., 1948.
Hellmann, E. 'The development of social groupings among Urban Africans in the Union of South Africa', in *Social Implications of Industrialisation and Urbanisation in Africa South of the Sahara*. UNESCO, 1956. p. 724 ff.
Houghton, D. H. (ed.) *Economic Development in a Plural Society*, O.U.P., 1960.
Houghton, D. H. & Walton, E. M. *The Economy of a Native Reserve (Keiskammahoek Rural Survey*, vol. II). Shuter and Shooter, 1952.
Hunter, M. *Reaction to Conquest*. O.U.P., 1936.

K

Kapferer, B. 'Norms and the Manipulation of Relationships in a Work Context', in J. Clyde Mitchell (ed.): *Social Network in Urban Situations*. Manchester University Press, 1969.

L

Laubscher, B. J. F. *Sex, Custom and Psychopathology*. Routledge, 1937.
Little, K. L. (ed.). 'Urbanism in West Africa', in *The Sociological Review*, New Series, vol. 7, No. 1, July 1959.

M

Marris, P. *Family and Social Change in an African City.* Routledge and Kegan Paul, London, 1961.

Mayer, P. *Witches.* Inaugural lecture, Rhodes University, Grahamstown, South Africa, 1954.

Mayer, P. 'Migrancy and the Study of Africans in Town', *American Anthropologist*, vol. 64, pp. 576–92, 1962.

Mayer, P. 'Labour Migrancy and the Social Network', in J. F. Holleman *et al.* (eds.): *Problems of Transition.* Natal University Press, Pietermaritzburg, 1964.

Mayer, P. 'Religion and Social Change in an African Township', in Heribert Adam (ed.): *South Africa: Sociological Perspectives.* Oxford University Press, London, 1971.

McCulloch, M. 'Survey of recent and current field studies on the social effects of economic development in tropical Africa', in *Social Implications of Industrialisation and Urbanisation in Africa South of the Sahara.* UNESCO, 1956. p. 53 ff.

Mitchell, J. C. *African urbanisation in Ndola and Luanshya.* Rhodes-Livingstone Communication No. 6, 1954.

Mitchell, J. C. *The Kalela Dance.* (Rhodes-Livingstone Paper No. 27). Manchester University Press, 1956.

Mitchell, J. C. 'Urbanisation, detribalisation and stabilisation in Southern Africa', in *Social Implications of Industrialisation and Urbanisation in Africa South of the Sahara.* UNESCO 1956. p. 693 ff.

Mitchell, J. C. *Tribalism and the Plural Society.* Inaugural lecture, University College of Rhodesia and Nyasaland. O.U.P., 1960.

Mitchell, J. C., 'Theoretical Orientations in African Urban Studies', in *The Social Anthropology of Complex Societies*, ASA Monographs 4. Tavistock Publications, London, 1966.

Mitchell, J. C. (ed), *Social Networks in Urban Situations.* Manchester University Press, 1969.

Mitchell, J. C., and Epstein, A. L. 'Occupational Prestige and Social Status among Urban Africans in N. Rhodesia', in *Africa*, vol. 29, January 1958.

N

Nadel, S. F. 'The concept of Social Status', *International Social Science Bulletin*, vol. VIII, p. 413, 1956.

Nadel, S. F. *The Theory of Social Structure.* Cohen and West, London, 1957.

P

Parkins, D. *Neighbours and Nationals in an African City Ward.* Routledge and Kegan Paul, London, 1969.

Pauw, B. A. *The Second Generation.* Oxford University Press, Cape Town, 1963.

Pons, V. *Stanleyville.* Oxford University Press, London, 1969.

R

Reader, D. H. *The Black Man's Portion.* O.U.P., 1961.

Roberts, M. *Labour in the Farm Economy.* South African Institute of Race Relations, 1958.

Roux, E. *Time longer than Rope.* Gollancz, London, 1949.

S

Schapera, I. *Migrant Labour and Tribal Life.* O.U.P., 1947.

Schlosser, K. *Eingeborenenkirchen in Süd- und Südwestafrika.* W. G. Mühlau, Kiel, 1958.

Shaw, W. *The Story of my Mission in South Eastern Africa.* London, 1860.

Smith, R. T. *The Negro Family in British Guiana.* Routledge & Kegan Paul, 1956.

Southall, A. W. & Gutkind, P. C. W. *Townsmen in the Making.* Kampala, East African Institute of Social Research, 1957.

Stewart, G. R. *American Ways of Life.* Doubleday, 1954.

Sundkler, B. *Bantu Prophets in South Africa.* Lutterworth Press London, 1948.

V

Vilakazi, A. 'A Reserve from Within', *African Studies*, vol. 16, no. 2, 1957. p. 93 ff.

W

Warner, W. Lloyd, and Srole, L. *The social systems of American ethnic groups.* Yale U.P., 1945.

Watson, W. *Tribal Cohesion in a Money Economy.* Manchester University Press, 1958.

Wilson, G. & M. *The Analysis of Social Change*, 1954.

Wilson, Kaplan, Maki and Walton. *Social Structure (Keiskammahoek Rural Survey*, vol. III). Shuter and Shooter, 1952.

Wilson, M. & Elton Mills, M. E. *Land Tenure (Keiskammahoek Rural Survey*, vol. IV). Shuter and Shooter, 1952.

INDEX

not incorporating new *chapter 19*

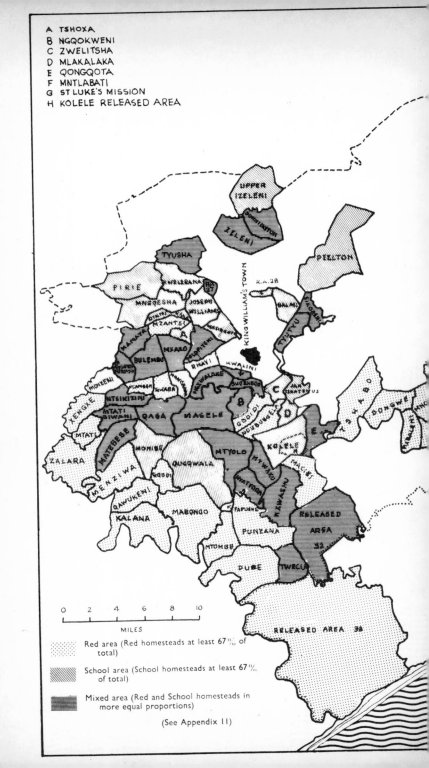

A TSHOXA
B NGQOKWENI
C ZWELITSHA
D MLAKALAKA
E QONGQOTA
F MNTLABATI
G ST LUKE'S MISSION
H KOLELE RELEASED AREA

0 2 4 6 8 10
MILES

Red area (Red homesteads at least 67%, of total)

School area (School homesteads at least 67%, of total)

Mixed area (Red and School homesteads in more equal proportions)

(See Appendix II)